The Professional Wordsworth

The Professional

Law, Labor & the

Mark Schoenfield

Wordsworth

Poet's Contract

The University of Georgia Press *Athens and London*

Athens, Georgia 30602

Set in Janson by Books International, Inc.
Printed and bound by Thomson-Shore, Inc.
The paper in this book meets the guidelines for permanence and durability of the Committee on Production Guidelines for Book Longevity of the Council on Library Resources.

Printed in the United States of America

00 99 98 97 96 c 5 4 3 2 1

Library of Congress Cataloging in Publication Data

Schoenfield, Mark L.
The professional Wordsworth : law, labor, and the poet's contract / Mark Schoenfield.
p. cm.
Includes bibliographical references and index.
ISBN 0-8203-1791-8 (alk. paper)
1. Wordsworth, William, 1770–1850—Knowledge—Law. 2. Law and literature—Great Britain—History—19th century. 3. Literature and society—England—History—19th century. 4. Wordsworth, William, 1770–1850—Authorship. 5. Law—Great Britain—History—19th century. 6. Poetry—Authorship—History—19th century. 7. Law in literature. I. Title.
PR5892.L3S36 1996
821'.7—dc20 95-4679

British Library Cataloging in Publication Data available

The mislayer of a mere-stone [property marker] is to blame.
But it is the unjust judge that is the capital remover of
landmarks, when he defineth amiss of lands and property.
—Francis Bacon, "Of Judicature"

For Steve Fisher, Jack Gifford, and Harvey Goldstein, teachers

I say, if a man upon trial were stained with blood instead of
ink,—if he were covered over with crimes of which human
nature would start at the naming, the means against him would
not be the less disgraceful. . . . —Thomas Erskine, in defense of
Thomas Paine, 1792

CONTENTS

ACKNOWLEDGMENTS

It is with great pleasure that I thank some of the numerous people—colleagues, friends, lawyers, family, and intersections between these categories—who took an interest in this project. Theresa Kelley, Kurt Heinzelman, and Andrew Cooper all offered useful suggestions on an earlier version of chapter 2, while Max Schulz, Harvey Goldstein, and Ronald Garet carefully read through an early draft of the whole.

At Vanderbilt, I have found wonderful colleagues, who have been inspirational and eager to discuss the wide range of problems—from eighteenth-century painting to the history of rights theory to the rhetoric of professionalization both within and outside the academy—that provide the backdrop to my more focused questions of Wordsworth and law: Cecelia Tichi, Margaret Doody, Vereen Bell, Jaya Mehta, Michael Kreyling, Mark Jarman, and Mark Wollaeger. Paul Elledge and Laurence Lerner made substantial and spirited suggestions, and Jay Clayton's astute eye has influenced every chapter, including, perhaps most important, one no longer here; his surgical abilities have made the operation a success, and saved the patient along the way. Valerie Traub has been throughout an emotional and intellectual presence. These friends have helped me to see not just what I was claiming but why it was worth arguing.

I turn now to what is becoming something of a subgenre in Romanticist acknowledgments, the hopeless effort to express sufficient gratitude for Peter Manning, whose encouragement, subtle reading, and astute conversation have been an ideal model of teaching, a continual lesson in scholarship, and an immeasurable aid to this study; it would be impossible to list the ways in which he has made this work, and this career, possible. Beside Peter—in many significant ways—I wish to place Clare Simmons, whose knowledge of nineteenth-century historiography and history is surpassed only by her willingness to share it, and whose keen wit is surpassed only by her still keener ability to find what is best in any text, institution, or person.

Misty Anderson, Nina Barrett, Bart Selden, Sandra Ross, Charlie Booth, Harley Kornblum, Rosaria Champagne, Janet Kornblum, Margaret Russett, and especially my colleague Teresa Goddu (whose office is the gothic mirror of my own) have all intervened at crucial moments with advice, discussion, general good cheer, and their own versions of sanity.

I thank the University Research Council of Vanderbilt University, guided by Dean Russell Hamilton, for two grants toward the completion of this project, and an equally valuable dissertation fellowship from the Graduate School at the University of Southern California, headed by Bill Spitzer, which made the first draft possible. I would also like to express my gratitude to the many terrific people at the University of Georgia Press, including Karen Orchard, Kristine Blakeslee, and the anonymous readers, who saw this through. Carolyn Levinson and Lisa Cullum were foremost among the helpful team that brought the page proofs in.

Finally, I would like to thank, as metonymies for many others, four families—Hiestands and Schoenfields; Rogaways and Freundels—who have offered the support that makes surviving possible. Especially, Sarah for always being there since before the *Knight's Tale*, and Josh, Michael, and Diana for coming into my life before I realized how much I needed them.

ABBREVIATIONS AND SHORT TITLES

The following short forms are used for citation.

Borderers	William Wordsworth, *The Borderers*, edited by Robert Osborn (Ithaca, N.Y.: Cornell University Press, 1982). The play itself is cited as *A Tragedy* for the 1797–99 version and as *The Borderers* for the 1842 published version.
Butler and Green	William Wordsworth and Samuel Taylor Coleridge, *Lyrical Ballads and Other Poems: 1797–1800*, edited by James Butler and Karen Green (Ithaca, N.Y.: Cornell University Press, 1992).
DC MS 15	William Wordsworth, Dove Cottage Manuscript 15. Opening of the First Part [of the 1799 *Prelude*], reproduced and transcribed in William Wordsworth, *The Prelude, 1798–1799*, edited by Stephen Parrish (Ithaca, N.Y.: Cornell University Press, 1977).
DNB	*Dictionary of National Biography.*
ER	*English Reports.*
Excursion	William Wordsworth, *The Excursion*, vol. 5 in *The Poetical Works of William Wordsworth*, edited by E. de Selincourt and H. Darbishire, 5 vols. (Oxford: Clarendon, 1940–49). Poetry is cited by book and line number; prose by page number.

Hill	Bridget Hill, *Women, Work, and Sexual Politics in Eighteenth-Century England* (London: Basil Blackwell, 1989).
Holden	James Milnes Holden, *The History of Negotiable Instruments in English Law* (London: University of London Press, 1955).
Holdsworth	Holdsworth, William, *A History of English Law*, 17 vols. (London: Methuen, 1938). Citations are by volume and page.
Journals	Dorothy Wordsworth, *Journals of Dorothy Wordsworth*, edited by E. de Selincourt, 2 vols. (New York: Macmillan, 1941).
Lamb	Charles Lamb, *The Portable Charles Lamb*, edited by J. M. Brown (New York: Penguin, 1949).
LEY	*Letters of William and Dorothy Wordsworth: The Early Years*, vol. 1, edited by E. de Selincourt, rev. ed. Chester L. Shaver (Oxford: Clarendon, 1967).
LLY	*Letters of William and Dorothy Wordsworth: The Later Years*, edited by E. de Selincourt, rev. ed. Alan Hill, IV parts, vols. 4–7 (Oxford: Clarendon, 1978–88). Cited by part and page number.
LMY	*Letters of William and Dorothy Wordsworth: The Middle Years*, edited by E. de Selincourt, rev. ed. Mary Moorman and Alan Hill, II parts, vols. 2–3 (Oxford: Clarendon, 1969–70). Cited by part and page number.
Lyrical Ballads	William Wordsworth and Samuel Taylor Coleridge, *Lyrical Ballads with a Few Other Poems*, edited by R. L. Brett and A. R. Jones. (London: Methuen, 1963). All poems cited by title and line number from this edition except where otherwise noted. Prose

matter, including excerpts from the Fenwick notes, from this edition cited by page number.

Moorman I	Mary Moorman, *William Wordsworth, A Biography: The Early Years, 1770–1803* (Oxford: Clarendon, 1957).
Moorman II	Mary Moorman, *William Wordsworth, A Biography: The Later Years: 1803–1850* (Oxford: Clarendon, 1965).
OED	*Oxford English Dictionary.*
Prelude	William Wordsworth, *The Prelude: A Parallel Text,* edited by J. C. Maxwell (New Haven, Conn.: Yale University Press, 1971). Unless otherwise noted, citations are to the 1805 version of the poem.
Prose	William Wordsworth, *Prose Works of William Wordsworth,* edited by J. B. Owen and J. W. Smyser, 3 vols. (Oxford: Clarendon, 1974).
Reflections	Edmund Burke, *Reflections on the Revolution in France and on the Proceedings in Certain Societies in London Relative to that Event* (1790), edited by Conor Cruise O'Brien (New York: Penguin, 1982).
Spectator	Joseph Addison and Richard Steele, *The Spectator* (1709–1714), edited by Donald Bond, 4 vols. (Oxford: Clarendon, 1965). Cited by original number, followed by volume and page of this edition.
Teeven	Kevin Teeven, *A History of the Anglo-American Common Law of Contract* (New York: Greenwood, 1990).
Wealth of Nations	Adam Smith, *An Inquiry into the Nature and Causes of the Wealth of Nations* (1776), edited by Edwin Cannan (Chicago: University of Chicago Press, 1976).

A note on contemporary reviews: Although I have cited most reviews from the original runs of the magazines, most are available in facsimile versions from Donald Reiman, ed., *The Romantics Reviewed: Contemporary Reviews of British Romantic Writers.* I have not included reviews in my bibliography but have provided volume and date within the text. Legal cases have been cited from the *English Reports* or *Howell's State Trials,* and are listed in works cited by the name of the case.

The Professional Wordsworth

INTRODUCTION

Law and Literature

> [A Conveyancer, a lawyer specializing in property transfers] happened to see the Volumes lying on Montagu's mantelpiece and to glance his eye upon this Very Poem of the Daffodils; "aye," says he, "a fine morsel this for the Reviewers."
> —William Wordsworth to Francis Wrangham, 4 November 1807

LAW and literature have been systematically connected throughout history. The adjective *kritikos*, in ancient Greek, signified at once critic and judge. This etymological link underscores the Athenian practice of selecting by lot from the same citizenry the critics who awarded the prizes at the dramatic festivals and the judges who issued the verdicts in the law courts. The regulation of the Athenian festivals, which required wealthy patrons to support productions, reinforced the social structure that provided the values of justice and democracy. The criteria of probability, internal consistency, and rhetorical propriety applied both in the Theater of Dionysus and the nearby court of the Areopagus.

Fifth-century Athenian plays achieved thematic depth within the context of a society contemplating its legal institutions through literary productions. The only surviving trilogy, Aeschylus' *Oresteia*, details a mythic transformation from a system of justice rooted in revenge to one built upon law. To the extent that the play concerns the origins of trial by jury in Athens, signaled by the presence of the Areopagus near the theater and the site of Orestes' mythic trial, the staging of the final action is telling. After Orestes' acquittal, the formal division between actors, chorus, and audience dissolves into the procession toward the Areopagus (see Fagles, "The Serpent and the Eagle" 86). A vision of communal unity enacted within the play mirrors the experience of participation in the theater, and serves to mitigate a specific political crisis: the contemporary legal event relevant to the audience/judges was not the formation of the Areopagus, as an ahistorical reading of the play might suggest, but Periclean reforms that reduced the Areopagus' vast judicial power to jurisdiction only for murder trials and sacred property. The play asserts the importance of these activities left to the Areopagus by offering an argument of original intent, while still celebrating judicial progress. As such, the play constituted an active intervention in Athenian law.

Looking to a different period—England in the decades following the French Revolution—I propose that recognizing the dialogue between the literary and legal institutions illuminates both the disciplinary boundaries we have inherited (which are radically different from those operative in ancient Athens) and the specific negotiations of those boundaries by particular romantic writers. From Leigh Hunt, whose imprisonment was acknowledged in a sonnet by Keats, to Sir Walter Scott, who pursued a highly successful legal career; from Lord Byron, whose only speech in the House of Lords concerned a criminal matter, to the Poet Laureate Robert Southey, who sought an injunction to suppress the piracy of his early radical play *Wat Tyler*, the writers of the romantic period wrote about, and in the shadow of, the law. The romantic writers encountered the law both as a crucial site of ideological production, as William Blake's *Book of Urizen* and William Godwin's *Caleb Williams* suggest, and as a substantial force in the management of their more individual affairs; Percy Bysshe Shelley lost custody of his children in a case in which his *Queen Mab* was offered as evidence for his unfitness as a father.

William Wordsworth was the most methodically professional of the major romantics, and his career was shaped by his sustained encounter with legal discourse and legal professionalism as encoded both in the reviews and in the wider social debates in which Wordsworth participated. Ventriloquizing with some irony the Scottish outlaw Rob Roy, William Wordsworth expressed an exasperation many of his fellow writers must have felt:

> Said generous Rob, "What need of Books?
> "Burn all the Statutes and their shelves:
> "They stir us up against our kind;
>   "And worse, against ourselves.

"We have a passion, make a law,
"Too false to guide us or controul!
"And for the law itself we fight
"In bitterness of soul."
("Rob Roy's Grave" 21–28)

"Very dull," Francis Jeffrey writes of this poem in his review of *Poems, in Two Volumes*, which ends with the hope that Wordsworth's "open violation of the established laws of poetry, will operate as a wholesome warning" to other poetic rebels and thereby be "the means of restoring to that antient and venerable code [of aesthetic law] its due honor and authority" (*Edinburgh Review* 11 [Oct. 1807]: 231). The strategic way in which Jeffrey—editor of the *Edinburgh*, a lawyer, and a future Lord of Sessions—aligns Wordsworth with Rob Roy, and offers law as the universal metaphor for judgment, typifies the argument between Wordsworth and his reviewers, each playing upon the other's presuppositions and self-representations. My project, then, explores Wordsworth's contribution to the historical debates on contract, property, labor, and professionalism, and seeks to understand how his sense of the social possibilities of his poetry confronted a legal discourse that was crucially interested in the cultural representations literature could achieve—whether in concert with or in opposition to legal representations.

Law and literature, like other social institutions, create, embody, and replicate values. The representational force of these institutions is crucial to constructing the concepts that render experience experiential. As Martha Minow puts it in *Making All the Difference*, "Law 'is part of a distinctive manner of imagining the real,' says Clifford Geertz. Legal decisions engrave upon our culture the stories we tell to and about ourselves, the meanings that constitute the traditions we invent, the dialogue through which we remake the normative endowment that shapes current understandings," (389, footnote omitted)."[1] Crucial to Minow's analysis is the question of how such stories are generated: Who are their speakers and their interpreters? Who is asked to enact or stage them? How do these narratives function as interpretations, enablers, and limitations for other stories that might be told? In what ways is legal speech distinctive, self-perpetuating, dependent upon other discourses?[2]

In *Economy and Society*, Max Weber has argued that the normative function of law arises sociologically at the moment in which individual and collective action is "oriented to legal duties recognized 'for their own sakes' as 'binding' by a group of men."[3] In this moment, Weber contends, law emerges as a distinctive formation that could organize itself around the need for its own preservation as an independent political body. Weber delineates two consequences of this institutionalization. First, "as a result of technological and economic developments, the legal ignorance of laymen will increase" so that it becomes increasingly "a specialists' domain"; and second, the notion will spread throughout society that "the law is a rational technical apparatus which is continually transformable in the light of expediential considerations and devoid of all sacredness of content" (*Economy and Society* 895). This continuous transformability, in turn, suggests the capacity of legal institutions to claim the authority for adjudication across increasingly diverse fields. The tendency toward formalization, however, is a function of various and historically specific causes.[4] The meaning of a legal construct—say, a contract—is dependent upon other social discourses that speak to agreement, social cohesion, and so on. Although today, in Anglo-American societies, it seems foundational that courts should arbitrate significant private financial agreements, that assumption developed slowly, haphazardly, and at times reluctantly.

Because no institution operates unconditioned by other social factors, the persuasiveness of literary and legal representations fluctuates through history as they compete with other institutions, the church, the military, and medicine, as well as with each other.[5] Neither law nor literature achieves hegemony for several reasons. First, both require other discourses as the object of their interpretations, and second, both contemporary legal and literary institutions developed from diverse and competing prior institutions whose traces endure in, for example, the divisions between law and equity and between fiction and nonfiction (see Lennard Davis, *Factual Fictions* chaps. 3 and 5). Third, the effectiveness of the law depends upon the normalizing functions not only of its own discourse but also of other discourses.[6]

Although twentieth-century Anglo-American law may seem more estranged from literature than was the law of ancient Greece, these discourses remain significantly linked, and not only in the direction of the courtroom serving as a favorite fictional location for both novels and screen media. In its 1990 opinion abolishing criminal conversation, a civil action to recover monetary damages against the seducer of one's wife, the Supreme

Court of Tennessee quoted a stanza from Byron's *Don Juan* to clarify the legal notion of the *femme couvert;* at one level, this was a judge or a clerk being clever, but it demonstrates assumptions about the durability of literature to document human nature.[7] In *The Alchemy of Race and Rights* (1991), Patricia Williams analyzes an exam from a criminal law course that uses an "updated version of Shakespeare's *Othello.*" The "model answer" requires recognizing that "a rough untutored Moor might understandably be deceived by the wiles of a more sophisticated European." Confronted by the racist attitudes embedded in this rationale, the professor said it was not he who had "dreamed up the facts but Shakespeare," as if reinscribing a play as an exam question and model answer preserved a Shakespearean core beyond ethical reproach (Williams, *Alchemy* 80–81). Further, the model answer too easily accepts and reproduces a particular interpretation that is actually disputed in the play; here, a canonical understanding prescribes the range of interpretations, stripping the play of historical complexities in order to claim transhistorical value. Such moments exemplify the use of literature as a repository for verities of human nature independent of context. At its furthest extreme, the canon becomes a mechanism for translating works of contested meaning—*Othello* and *Don Juan*—into aphorisms and truisms. By corollary, restoring the polemical context to works of literature and charting the institutional terrain on which such contests of meaning are fought forms an important critical task.

But beyond such specific instances, literature continues to provide cultural capital for arguments in other institutions. The Chief Justice of the Seventh Circuit Appellate Court, Richard Posner, offers as his critical methodology in *Problems of Jurisprudence* W. B. Yeats's admonition, "Cast a cold eye / On life, on death," while in a previous work he argued that "Romanticism is the annihilation of the boundaries between individuals" (*Law and Literature: A Misunderstood Relation* 151). The assumption is that the boundaries, by which Posner means those boundaries of property and self maintained by law, are fundamentally coherent, but continuously threatened by the "'Romantic' temperament," which is "one of humankind's fundamental moods" (140). Posner is then able to stage a struggle between the potential oppression implicit in Romanticism and the "enabling" or "liberating" powers of law (152). This position, part of his larger project to argue for the utility of an economic approach to law, continues the argument between Wordsworth and Francis Jeffrey.

Like Jeffrey, Posner generalizes from the law a notion of "form" which immediately implicates language. He claims, "Form facilitates; it does not just constrain. (The best example is the rules of language; they are the precondition, rather than the impediment, to communication.) The attack on form . . . is a worrisome characteristic of Romantic and neoromantic thought" (*Law and Literature* 152–53). Jeffrey was equally worried, insisting in the first issue of the *Edinburgh Review* that "we cannot discharge our inquistitorial office conscientiously" without some general remarks on the "*sect* of poets" who have "broken loose from the bondage of ancient authority, and re-asserted the independence of genius" (1 [Oct. 1802]: 63). Wordsworth's contention, by contrast, is not that his poetry eschews form but that his poetic form coheres through something other than legal formalism and the accompanying system of aesthetic and social manners—it coheres in a different type of experience that would generate a different set of aesthetic and social manners, as he wrote to Coleridge, not "transitory manners reflecting the wearisome unintelligible obliquities of city-life, but manners connected with the permanent objects of nature and partaking of the simplicity of those objects" (LEY 255). Two emblems of the transitory manners of the city that Wordsworth offers in the *Prelude* are

> the brawls of lawyers in their courts
> Before the ermined judge, or that great stage
> Where senators, tongue-favoured Men, perform,
> Admired and envied.
>
> (VII 520–23)

Even though this is a book of literary scholarship directed to romanticists and not written for legal scholars, I believe that a dialogue between the two institutions is vital. Romanticists do well to remember that we teach future lawyers, future jurists, and future litigants.[8] The relationship between teacher and student is articulated through a series of contracts, legal duties, and prohibitions, and the formal features of our classrooms affect their pedagogical content. At the same time, the values that literature encodes and replays are not bracketed off in our classrooms but part of the social fabric by which "law" itself remains an intelligible category besides other abstractions such as justice, honor, and agreement.

Focused primarily on the *Lyrical Ballads* and *The Excursion*, this study uses the contested category of property to situate the arguments between

Wordsworth and his reviewers, between, in a wider sense, literature and law. The first chapter grounds the study in biographical information. The personal psyche exists, in Alan Liu's words, only "as it is shaped by a collective history" and the "family belongs at the head of the list of prior social institutions against which the self defines itself" (*Wordsworth: The Sense of History* 302–3). I would add that collective history exists through class-specific mechanisms of collection (common-law institutes, archives, heirlooms). The child and sibling of lawyers, Wordsworth encountered the law in a variety of ways. His early family life was shaped by the monumental lawsuit fought with his father's employer, and his career involved continual negotiations over contracts and copyrights. More signigicant, however, his position is typical of the *professional* poet who found himself competing with other professional producers of ideology for the ability to shape the marketplace of ideas. Although the church, architecture, medicine, and other sciences were significant in this heteroglossic competition, the law held a special power with regard to literature by virtue of the number of lawyers who were also reviewers, and because of its investment in the discourses of agreement and boundary, shaped within the law in the more rigid structures of contract and property, respectively. Fashioning his labor both as a mirror of and in opposition to the lawyer's, Wordsworth developed what would become a dominant notion of poetic professional labor.

Chapter 2 provides a practical demonstration that the recognition of the interrelation of law, labor, and literature will illuminate specific poems of Wordsworth. Expanding on work by David Simpson and Marjorie Levinson, I read the contractual moments of Wordsworth's "Michael," composed during a period of considerable readjustment of contract law, and suggest Wordsworth's ability to negotiate, at the same time as criticize, this developing discourse. This chapter pulls out of sequence the final poem of the *Lyrical Ballads* to suggest the career trajectory that the subsequent chapters trace, because it points to the limits of his critique, namely his inability to evade the figure of a middle-class reader who already refracts his individuality through his legal rights.

The eighteenth century, the focus of the third chapter, saw the rise of the professional writer, whose livelihood came from publishing and who was consequently committed to certain ideological positions. Antonio Gramsci has insisted that "every 'essential' social group which emerges into history out of the preceding economic structure" has found preexisting intellectual categories that appeared to "represent a historical continuity uninterrupted even by the most complicated and radical changes in political and social forms" (*An Antonio Gramsci Reader: Selected Writings, 1916–1935* 302). Both Addison and Hume consider law and aesthetic theory because of the conditions in which their texts were produced.[9] To explore Wordsworth's early ideas about literary professionalism, I turn to a series of early letters in which he contemplated the publication of a monthly miscellany and demonstrated his awareness that the interaction of law and economy had serious implications for the career of a poet.

Chapter 4 opens a three-chapter sequence on the *Lyrical Ballads*. In Francis Jeffrey's campaign against Wordsworth's poetry, the terms of literary criticism were drawn from jurisprudence, not merely because it offered convenient metaphors but because the interpretive practices of the two discourses had similar social consequences: both portrayed a market subject to precise economic regulation while justifying that regulation as an expression of "natural" sentiments and historical development. The first edition of the *Lyrical Ballads* exploits the concept of an unmediated exchange of labor between the writer and the reader as a mode of social commentary. Specifically, "Goody Blake and Harry Gill" and the responses of the reviewers to the volume demonstrate that this social investment was formulated through legal concepts. Chapter 5 analyzes Wordsworth's influential manifesto of poetic regulation, the Preface of 1800, as both a defense (in the legal sense) and a contract (in the economic sense). In chapter 6, extended readings of many of the poems of the *Lyrical Ballads* show how they employ legal and economic metaphors and structures and touch on ancillary issues, such as labor, criminality, and feudalism.

Chapters 7 and 8 explore the poem Wordsworth and his generation considered his most important, *The Excursion*, by revealing through the dialogue of its production and reviewers' responses Wordsworth's conception of poetic jurisprudence, arguing his understanding of property as the intersection of imaginative acts and material reality, and examining the relation of the Wanderer and the young poet as enacting the idealized evolution of the economic market.

ONE

The Poet and Professional Patriarchy

"The Magistracy shows the Man"
That searching test thy public course has stood—
—"To the Earl of Lonsdale," 1833

Common History

Many of his strongest, most insightful critics have argued that William Wordsworth displaced, replaced, denied, evaded, avoided, and voided history, or History. Other (and sometimes the same) strong critics have demonstrated Wordsworth's obsessive attention to historical moments, local detail, and his own position within such sweeping events as the French Revolution and industrialization.[1] Such claims are contradictory only to the extent that "history" is reified into actualities that transcend their various narrative forms. I propose that Wordsworth himself recognized histories, like poems, and History, like Poetry, as products in professional marketplaces that competed for consumers, that offered to those consumers images of their proper behavior, and that shaped their reading habits.[2] One of the most pervasive formal assumptions about "history" during Wordsworth's time was that it was related to the development of English common law. Equally important, history and the law were subject to similar (although not identical) pressures of institutionalization and professionalization. Legal thinkers, indeed lawyers, were among the foremost historians, and history was seen as decisively shaped by the growth of common law.

The English historiography dominant in Wordsworth's England had developed within the intellectual and institutional debate over the status of common law. Hayden White has voiced the "suspicion" that "fully realized 'history' has to do with the topics of law, legality, legitimacy, or, more generally, *authority*" ("The Value of Narrativity in the Representation of Reality," 17). J. G. A. Pocock proposes that Renaissance historians "were more or less consciously engaged in returning facts to their historical context and interpreting them there, and . . . this was bound to present complex problems for historical reflexion. . . . With the lawyers this was peculiarly the case, because the data they were assigning to a past context were simultaneously the principles on which present society was endeavouring to govern itself" (*The Ancient Constitution and the Feudal Law* 8). In the mid-eighteenth century, William Temple, lamenting the pitiable state of English histories and especially the lack of a "good national historian," did cite a few historians as "acceptable fragmentary historical writers": "More, Francis Bacon, Herbert, Haywood, Camden, and Plydore" (James Johnson, *The Formation of English Neo-Classical Thought* 39).

Temple's emphasis in this list on legal thinkers, in both common and civil courts, complements the developing eighteenth-century historiographic justification that history serves as judicious precedent; as Peter Whalley wrote in his 1746 *Essay on the Manner of Writing History*, "the *Statesman* travels in the Field of History, to enrich himself with Maxims of *Prudence*, and civil *Policy*" (Johnson, *Formation* 38).[3] David Hume composed his most lucrative work, *The History of Great Britain*, while the Keeper of the Advocates' Library for the Scottish Bar. Adam Smith's 1766 *Lectures on Jurisprudence* interpolate a history of English government from the Roman Conquest to the Revolution under the heading of "Public Jurisprudence" (401–23) as a means of highlighting, legitimating, and expanding current legal practices regarding economic markets.[4] William Blackstone, whose career and writing embodied eighteenth-century rationalism and who understood such rationalism as refined through the continuity of natural, scientific, and public law, was, according to Jeremy Bentham, "first of all institutional writers [who] taught Jurisprudence to speak the language of the Scholar and the Gentleman: put a polish upon that rugged science" ("A Fragment on Government" 413). In doing so, Blackstone helped expand a market for legal tracts which had invariable recourse to history for both example and justification; in turn, what constituted the historical was determined by legal, as well as social, significance. Bentham's own attacks on Blackstone's *Commentaries on the Laws of England* (the concluding chapter of which is "an historical review of the most remarkable changes and alterations" of the law [*Commentaries* 4: 400]) focused on both Blackstone's theories and representations of history, while his own schemes for legal transformation were justified by an alternative history.

Among political philosophers, the effort to correlate the aesthetic and the legal received frequent reformulation through recourse to history and precedent. Edmund Burke argued that "public affections, combined with manners, are required sometimes as supplements, sometimes as correctives, always as aids to law. . . . There ought to be a system of manners in every nation which a well-formed mind would be disposed to relish. To make us love our country, our country ought to be lovely" (*Reflections on the Revolution in France* 172). Terry Eagleton, who quotes this passage in *The Ideology of the Aesthetic*, observes that "what knits society together for Burke, as with Hume, is the aesthetic phenomenon of mimesis, which is a matter more of custom than of law" (53). But because common law is the contemporary embodiment of custom, especially those customs of possession and property which Burke insists secure social stability, the law serves as a locus of historical investigation which reveals, or enacts, custom's harmonizing function.

The late eighteenth century also witnessed an explosion in specifically artistic histories. In 1776, the first two English histories of music were published; Walpole produced the first history of English art in 1780 and the next year saw Johnson's *Lives of the Poets* and Warton's *History of English Poetry* (Lawrence Lipking, *The Ordering of the Arts* 6). As Lipking's study shows, these were not the first texts that dealt with the arts, but were the first that tried to give them precise order and completeness consonant with the Blackstonean project of ordering the common law in his *Commentaries*.[5] These were works at once regulatory and professional, as Lipking's description of Hawkins's *History of Music* suggests: "The prose style draws upon the weighty jargon of courts and contracts, and the tone can only be described as magisterial. But most of all, law furnishes a pattern for Hawkins' view of history" (*Ordering* 249, note omitted).[6] Lipking is right to insist that the pattern that law provides has as much to do with worldview as with rhetorical strategy. History is not simply the temporal category in which law takes place but a perceptual frame that legal institutions condition.

Although explicable in a variety of ways, the number of lawyers producing historical works in the first half of the nineteenth century is suggestive of the legal investment in controlling articulation of the past. Sharon Turner, John Murray's lawyer, published the first volume of *History of the Anglo-Saxons* in 1799; the barrister Walter Scott published *Original Memoirs Written during the Great Civil War* (1806) the year after writing the first scraps of *Waverley;* Francis Palgrave, called to the bar four years before the publication of *History of Normandy and of England* (1831), argued that the Norman invasion "preserved the most vital institutions of the ancient English state," a view critical to maintaining the English authority of common law.[7] Additionally, the many lawyers who wrote and edited both the *Edinburgh* and *Quarterly* reviews struggled to secure the meanings of specific historical events—the English and French revolutions foremost among them—as part of their political strategies.[8] Their invocation of precedent and other legal concepts was not incidental to their historical projects, but organized what they regarded as historical. To describe the French Revolution was, as even its earliest chroniclers recognized, to articulate a theory of English property law; similarly, no discussion of English class structure could proceed without an understanding of the criminal and civil laws that organized English labor markets. At the same time, the legal theorizing that might structure a review of a Benthamite tract on justice could serve as a powerful metaphoric device in the discussion of a new work on optics or in the review of a poem.

Like law, literature, economics, and religion, history as a discursive organization comprises only a component of the historical field, a field which, at other times or from other perspectives, might more aptly be identified as the religious, economic, legal, or literary field. Its shape, consequently, is a product of various institutional interventions—whether directly, as in Whig and Tory historians' defense of common law; less directly, with art historians using legal order as a structuring principle; or secondarily, as with Scott's reconstructions of law in his historical novels. As Scott's weaving of legal, familial, and legendary precedent in the *Waverley* novels suggests, History itself, for the romantic age, had a more particular referent than uninterpreted "facts"; it was connected to the development of the

English legal system with its procedures of precedent and constitution.[9] Within this legal-historical dialogue, Wordsworth experienced his own personal history, the history of his age, and that of his profession.

The Attorney's Son

After reading the second edition of the *Lyrical Ballads*, Anne Taylor wrote to Wordsworth, praising his poems and inquiring about the growth of the poet's mind. He responded with a single paragraph, which James Chandler has suggested might be labeled "a *biographia geographia* rather than an account of the events that shaped his opinions" (*Wordsworth's Second Nature* 7). Wordsworth apologizes to Taylor for providing "little which will throw any light on my writings" (LEY 327, 9 April 1801), and as Chandler has shown,[10] the omitted events would have been more revealing (at least for scholarship interested in Wordsworth's historical contexts[11]).

The last sentences of the paragraph, however, provide a starting point for an investigation into Wordsworth's concern with legal and economic institutions: "At present I am permanently fixed in my native country. I have taken a house in the Vale of *Grasmere*, (a very beautiful spot of which almost every body has heard,) and I live with my Sister, meaning, if my health will permit me, to devote my life to literature. It may be proper to add that my Father was by profession an Attorney, and that he and my Mother both died when I was a Boy." (LEY 327). Exactly as he consecrates himself to literature, having achieved an end of his wanderings by acquiring ("taking") Dove Cottage, he invokes the profession of his father.[12] This point, its counterpoint of the father's death, and the propriety of the disclosure ("It may be proper to add . . .") legitimate the poet as a landholder occupying his patrimony (generalized as "native country") and as a professional writer who will reinscribe the value of his possession in his work.[13] Given F. W. Bateson's remark that in "the whole of Wordsworth's poetical work," there are only two allusions "of any kind to his father" (*Wordsworth: A Re-interpretation* 50–51),[14] the intrusion of his father's profession at the end of this scant biography suggests its importance to Wordsworth's sense of poetic professionalism. As Laura Claridge, citing Bateson, observes, "From the beginning of his career, Wordsworth writes a poetry grounded as deeply in the lawful space culturally occupied by the paternal as in the mythic, maternal, pre-oedipal sublime" (*Romantic Potency* 35).

As an attorney managing an estate in the Lake District into the 1780s, the poet's father John Wordsworth (1741–83) operated at the margins between nature and real property and between the individualized and common ownership that figure in the letter to Anne Taylor, in *Lyrical Ballads*, and throughout Wordsworth's career. His son's concern (desire, worry) for property (a portion of which were the poems Wordsworth named his "store") arises within a general social debate with legal and critical discourses that were themselves engaged in defining property.[15] Such definition was simultaneously linguistic—what the word denoted; economic—what could be bought or sold; and material—what could be held in hand, or heart, or deed. Further, property signified a control over not only land but also human beings, and consequently, John Wordsworth's managerial duties included directing the voting of tenants, manipulating rents, and driving out workers.[16] Perhaps most relevant to the equivocal tension between ownership and occupancy in Wordsworth's poetry are the complex legal maneuvers to deprive the Duke of Portland of lands his family had quietly occupied in adverse possession for more than sixty years (Brian Bonsall, *Sir James Lowther . . . 1754–75* 83–85, 121–22); in the resulting litigation, John Wordsworth prepared "the evidence from Cumberland for Sir James" (Joanne Dann, "Some Notes on the . . . Families" 81).

In the letter to Taylor, John Wordsworth's relation to the Lonsdale estate and property is reduced to the generic term of "Attorney," and then nullified by his death. William Wordsworth himself occupies, but without disrupting, the "Vale of *Grasmere*," a phrase both "poetical" (Johnson denotes *vale* as a "poetical word") and characteristic of the tourist guides that have allowed "almost every body" to know about Grasmere.[17] For Wordsworth, the management of his poetry as a property and as the center of a cottage industry provided an answer to his father's inability to manage James Lowther's estate to insure his own family's cohesion, or even survival. But the decision to become a poet constituted a revision of earlier professional plans, on which most of the family was willing to stake the bulk of their small patrimony. In July 1787, Dorothy recounts that John (who became a sailor) would need "very little" and would "wish Wm to have the rest for his education, as he has a wish to be a Lawyer if his health will permit."

Dorothy herself had "little doubt of" her brother's success, which would insure her own security and his financial viability (LEY 4–5).[18] The financial and filial responsibility was not eliminated by Wordsworth's turn from the law to literature, but reorganized.

In an allusion to his father unnoticed by Bateson, Wordsworth describes the path of the Derwent in the famous passage of Book One of the *Prelude* beginning "Was it for this. . . ." After the Derwent leaves the mountains, in the 1805 version, "to the towers / Of Cockermouth that beauteous river came, / Behind my father's house he passed, close by, / Along the margin of our terrace walk" (I 286–89). Here, the father's house constitutes a stable, identifiable location,[19] but the doubly possessive phrase "my father's house" might be complicated with the recognition that John Wordsworth had no house; he neither owned nor rented, but lived at the pleasure of Lord Lonsdale. The one other occurrence of the phrase in Wordsworth's poetry is in "The Sparrow's Nest," a poem that comments implicitly on the fragility of the house by pairing it against the "Sparrow's dwelling," a "home and sheltered bed" that Emmeline (Dorothy) approaches "Dreading, tho' wishing to be near it" (6–12).[20] The complex undertones that invoking his father entailed for Wordsworth are further suggested in the revision of the lines quoted above for the 1850 *Prelude:*

> [The Derwent] received
> On his smooth breast the shadow of those towers
> That yet survive, a shattered monument
> Of feudal sway, the bright blue river passed
> Along the margin of our terrace walk.
>
> (I 282–86)

Like "Ozymandias," perhaps here echoed, these lines produce an image of broken power. The ruin of Cockermouth castle is a palimpsest replacement of the father's house; its strength is only a shadow. While the literal referent for the tower is a castle ruined before John Wordsworth's birth, in juxtaposition to the earlier version, the lines suggest the broken power of Lord Lonsdale and of Wordsworth's own father. At the same time, the erasure of the father generalizes the feudal implications of his father's professional activities and provides a space in which Wordsworth may escape from the looming fate that prompted the question of "Was it for this . . .," namely whether Wordsworth the poet would "Unprofitably travel[ ] towards the grave, / Like a false steward (I 269–70).[21] Though clearly John Wordsworth was not a false steward to Lowther, from William Wordsworth's perspective, he may well have seemed one to his family and to nature. Mary Moorman points out that inquiries "after his death revealed that there had never been any agreement between the baronet and his agent as to payments or reimbursements" (Moorman I 7–8), thus leaving his children financially vulnerable; Lowther was ruthless in exploiting natural resources for economic and political gain, and John Wordsworth aided this project.

While this analysis could insert into Wordsworth's bland biographical sketch a personal anxiety about his audience, financial success, and the presence of his absent, professional father, Wordsworth's own procedures of generalization allow me to locate that anxiety also within the wider social context, specifically the patriarchical role of legal discourse in the structure of what Jon Klancher has termed the "social text," that is, the cultural frames through which individuals read their own existence (*The Making of the English Reading Audiences, 1790–1832* chap. 2). This metatext both conditions and is conditioned by the institutions that generate the discourses available to writers and readers. As M. M. Bakhtin puts the point: "Language is not a neutral medium that passes freely and easily into the private property of the speaker's intentions; it is populated—overpopulated—with the intentions of others. Expropriating it, forcing it to submit to one's own intentions and accents, is a difficult and complicated process" (*The Dialogic Imagination* 294).[22] Language, it follows, is not merely the property of particular institutions, and the struggle to determine institutional powers and boundaries is necessarily part of the history and criticism of particular poetic works. Through Klancher's observation, we glimpse why Wordsworth thought it proper to mention that his father had been an attorney; it was both an honest assessment of his professional heritage and an assertion of professional pedigree.

If, as Paul Fry suggests ("The Diligence of Desire" 162), the internal structure of romantic poetry is an epistemological critique of the historical, then the legal inflection of history demands critical attention to legal allusion in poetry. The study of Wordsworth in the context of the law that surrounded him not only adds another dimension to the efforts at positioning Wordsworth's work within its historical circumstances but restores to that work a more specific articulation of its polemical character.

The Barrister's Brother

Drawing primarily on the *Lyrical Ballads* and *The Excursion*, this study connects William Wordsworth's sense of himself as a professional poet and his concerns with English law and jurisprudence. Many biographical facts justify such a study. In 1798, his eldest brother Richard requested that William return the two volumes of Blackstone's *Commentaries* concerned with civil law (LEY 674); Blackstone's importance lies not only in his systemization of law but in his popularization of it, and its methods of analysis, for polite and political society.[23] Whether or not he read the volumes of Blackstone, Wordsworth, the child and sibling of attorneys, had various avenues for learning about the law, including prominent trials reported in the papers (several involving writers) and the "master pamphlets" (*Prelude* IX 96) debating the status of the British Constitution as a question inseparable from the French Revolution and domestic industrialization. Wordsworth's *Ecclesiastical Sonnets* (1822, rev. 1827), tracing the history of the English church, explicitly discuss a series of legal crises; Clare Simmons has shown in "Prejudged by Foes" how his treatment of William Laud, Archbishop of Canterbury, anticipates the lawyer and historian Macaulay's use of Laud to attack Henry Hallam's *Constitutional History of England.*

Wordsworth's family was involved in several legal disputes, including complex litigation regarding a debt that "overshadowed the youth of the Wordsworths, giving to their lives an atmosphere of uncertainty and frustration" (Moorman I: 169). When John Wordsworth died in 1783, his employer James Lowther owed him, according to Richard Wordsworth's calculations, about 4,600 pounds. After expending about a thousand pounds of money and labor, the Wordsworth family gained a positive judgment, but the matter, referred to arbitration to determine the compensation, was never settled (Moorman I: 196). The final resolution of that debt worked itself out partly as an intrafamily struggle between two professionals, Richard the lawyer and William the poet. When James Lowther died and his heir printed "an advertisement in the *Cumberland Paquet* inviting all those with claims against the late earl to send in their statements" (Moorman I: 559), a vigorous debate erupted between William and Richard regarding how to approach the delicate matter. William proposed to "draw up a memorial immediately" and to use his literary skills to detail "the utter destitution of my Sister on account of the affair" (LEY 361, 10 June 1802). He urged his brother Richard to "try what an appeal to Lord Lowther's Honour and Conscientiousness may produce" (Moorman I: 559). He clearly worried that Richard would favor a more legalistic approach, demanding payment of principal and interest and threatening legal action since the "statute of limitations d[id] not bar" the Wordsworths' claim (LEY 369, 24 June 1802). William reminded Richard of their past failures[24] and Richard's response to what amounted to an attack on his profession was apparently strident, since Wordsworth's next letter chides him for his tone: "Many parts of [your letter] are totally deficient in that respect with which *Man ought to deal with Man, and Brother with Brother*. You seem to speak to me as if you were speaking to a Child" (LEY 371, 3 July 1802, my italics).[25] Richard apparently rejected William's advice and planned to proceed on the basis of his own legal expertise, a course with which Wordsworth strongly disagreed:

> We see what Lawyers and Attornies have done in it already; and depend upon it if you proceed according to the letter in this track we are ruined. Though the affair must be bottomed no doubt upon a right in Law, that right will be lost to us, and we shall draw no advantage from it whatsoever, if we do not constantly bear in mind that our hopes of success (both in the conduct and in the final settlement) must depend entirely upon our combining with this right certain principles of natural justice, and considering the affair as an affair *betwixt man and man*. (LEY 372, my italics)

The repetition of the image of a man facing a man relates the intrafamily struggle with the external effort to recover the debt. In both cases, natural justice—the sense of propriety in communication between brothers and the sense of honor between men—will prove ultimately effective, and it cannot be achieved by lawyers, but rather by writers who preserve the face-to-face character of conversation in their letters. Richard had counseled patience, and Wordsworth had termed that advice "a sort of mechanic rule [that 'hackney men of business'] lay down, easy to adhere to; and thus they cheaply purchase to themselves the applause of being methodical, circumspect, and temperate men" (LEY 372). Richard's response was conciliatory; he promised to avoid litigation and to proceed "as expeditiously as circumstances would permit" (Moorman I: 561). The series of letters displays offers and counteroffers, which reconcile not only the two brothers but the two forms of discourse. Wordsworth retracted his idea of a memorial, and Richard, in his correspondence with Lonsdale's agents, kept all reference to possible litigation suitably veiled under the guise of a gentlemanly appeal. He uses the rhetorical device of *occupatio*, a favorite of both litigators and romantic poets, to conjure precisely the memorial that Wordsworth had proposed: "Your Lordship may easier conceive than I describe, the hardships and uneasiness we have suffered from the suspence of nearly twenty years" (LEY 689, 3 February 1803).

By 1803, without litigation, an agreement was reached for about £8,000, roughly £2,000 less than the value of the debt Richard had estimated, but as he himself acknowledged, at law, at least £2,000 would have been struck down. Wordsworth responded by noting the effectiveness of Richard's strategy and pointing out his own contribution; musing on why Mr. Graham, Lowther's lawyer, might find the arrangement acceptable, Wordsworth wrote: "It is evident he does not consider the case merely as a man of business; that is, he does not merely look at what we could recover in a court of Law, else he would be for making still larger deductions from the Bill as sent in. It is clear that he looks at the case with the feelings also of a just man, attending to the claim which we have in moral equity . . . it becomes us to shew to him and Lord Lowther that we have a proper sense of their handsome conduct" (LEY 382, 23 February 1803).

To view the case with the "feelings . . . of a just man" corresponds to the social role Wordsworth had proposed for the poet in the Preface to the *Lyrical Ballads*, and upon which he would insist for his entire career. Indeed, he positions Graham much as he positioned himself in the previous paragraph of the letter; having said that if Richard is satisfied, he and Dorothy will be, he decides "however [to] add a few words for your consideration, I not speaking as a man of business but with the plain understanding of a common person" (LEY 382). Again, such plain understanding is the distinguishing characteristic of the poet who sees into "the life of things" ("Tintern Abbey" 50).[26]

Throughout this correspondence with Richard, Wordsworth claims an understanding of the law's operation across classes. He acknowledges and appropriates its power, and also limits it. Wordsworth's position is typical of the professional poet during the English romantic period, because that position is shaped by circumstances which include the rise of the professional lawyer and the naturalization of the theory of rights.[27] This naturalization was partly a matter of rhetoric; but it also involved profound shifts in the understanding of property, the right that Blackstone and Burke understood to secure all others. Changes in contract law, litigation procedures, labor and wage regulation, and criminal prosecution all contributed to the practical enactment of the new understanding of property. Further, the poets of the period were not passive victims of such forces, but actively engaged in polemics regarding property and justice.[28]

Maturing in the English intellectual turmoil surrounding the French Revolution, those poets commonly regarded as romantic (and their critics) again and again circled the concept of property. Byron expresses an aristocratic notion by his giving away the copyrights to his early poems and by his satires on the clutter of law in *Don Juan:*

> Dying intestate, Juan was sole heir
> To a chancery suit and messuages and lands,
> Which with a long minority and care,
> Promised to turn out well in proper hands.
> (I 37, 1–4)

The dangling participle enacts the confused inheritance, as Juan grammatically occupies his father's position, which in the social world eludes him for the rest of the poem.[29] For whom the legal actions will "turn out well" is left hanging. "Long minority" suggests Juan and the subsequent lines suggest his mother, Donna Inez, but the lawyers are perhaps better candidates. In any event, Juan is first displaced from his lands by law, or more precisely, legal procedure, before beginning his legendary journeys.

Articulating a Godwinian radicalism, Shelley attacks paper currency as enslaving in the same poem that ridicules Lord Chancellor Eldon, *The Mask of Anarchy:*

> Next came Fraud, and he had on,
> Like Eldon, an ermine gown;

His big tears, for he wept well,
Turned to mill-stones as they fell

. . . .

"Paper coin—that forgery
Of the title deeds, which ye
Hold to something of the worth
Of the inheritance of Earth."
(14–17, 180–83)

Fraud and Eldon are maintained by legal pomp (the ermine gown) rather than by political justice, and a similar fraud occurs when paper replaces the coin it claims to signify. In both poems, social relations—father/son; worker/master; man/earth—are inscribed through the legal status of property. That legal status, further, is situated within texts, the writs of a chancery suit and title deeds, and within a visible economy predicated on legal intervention. The satirical force of each passage relies on the recognition that the signifiers of property—the title deeds and chancery suit—have acquired reality and value equal to the land and labor they signify within the economy, just as Fraud/Eldon's tears become stone. This satiric reification mimics the ongoing expansion of property to include any item capable of being possessed, contracted, sold, or legally protected. *The Masque of Anarchy*, written in response to the massacre in St. Peter's Field, Manchester, in 1819, implicitly suggested that human labor and lives were now regarded within that rubric.

In his business dealings, Byron evoked the laws of property where necessary and avoided them in favor of a more noble morality when affordable. An 1820 letter to Jean Antoine Galignani, who wished to publish Byron's complete works in France, demonstrates these tendencies. Byron responded to the request with graciousness: "I have no right to dispose of the property of Mr. Murray.—The copyright of the poems is his—and—although I might *legally* (it seems) sanction a re-publication in *France*—I could not do so *honestly*, without his permission" (*'What Comes Uppermost'* 57). Byron does not own the French right to the poems—except legally. But honesty is a higher, or more poetic, standard than legality, even if the terms of honesty are "copyright," "property," and "interest," all inescapable juridical echoes. Byron obsessively assures Galignani that he has no personal interest in the "business," and, "as far as mere feelings go," he would like Galignani to republish "because you seem to do so 'con amore.'"[30] But "mere feelings," even here articulated as an exchange, rarely constitute an operative term.

Writing in *The Statesman's Manual* in 1816, Coleridge described sweeping effects of the French Revolution. The "almost geometrical abstractions of the physiocratic politicians and economists" took such hold that "in the remotest villages," "public roads were crowded with armed enthusiasts disputing on the unalienable sovereignty of the people, the imprescriptible laws of the pure reason, and the universal constitution, which as rising out of the nature and rights of man as man, all nations alike were under the obligation of adopting" (21–22). For Wordsworth, of course, the French Revolution became, in part, a private crisis, but in expressing and shaping it, he also returns to the public discourse of the law. He articulates the loss of faith in Godwinian rationalism as a public trial:

> Thus I fared,
> Dragging all passions, notions, shapes of faith,
> Like culprits to the bar; suspiciously
> Calling the mind to establish in plain day
> Her titles and honours.
>
> (*Prelude* X 889–93)

His mind is turned against itself and lacks the foundation for judgment. The metaphor of the bar, with the verb *calling* positioning the mind simultaneously as lawyer being admitted and witness summoned, forces judgment as if passions and faith could be arraigned, when they are, as Hume recognized, the basis of judgment. Wordsworth describes the consequent contortions of his mind:

> now believing,
> Now disbelieving; endlessly perplexed
> With impulse, motive, right and wrong, the ground
> Of moral obligation, what the rule
> And what the sanction; till demanding *proof*,
> And seeking it in every thing, I lost
> All feeling of conviction, and, in fine,
> Sick, wearied out with contrarities,
> Yielded up moral questions in despair.
>
> (X 893–901)

Believing and disbelieving, the terms of faith, cannot adjudicate faith, and the consequence is that the goal of his internal court—certainty—prevents the establishment of any viable procedure. It seemed, at the time, that rules had to be derived independently of institutions, since the "advocates themselves / of ancient Institutions" including "custom and written law," had brought "disgrace upon their very names" (X 850–53). The result, however, of the effort to transcend a historical reality by mind alone was groundlessness; the transcendence was an illusion, as the necessity of resorting to legal metaphor demonstrates. In denying passions, conviction was also lost.

Wordsworth's first solution was a retreat from the social world into a realm of pure reason, mathematics:

> And for my future studies, as the sole
> Employment of the inquiring faculty
> Turned towards mathematics, and their clear
> And solid evidence—Ah! then it was
> That thou, most precious Friend! about this time
> First known to me, didst lend a living help
> To regulate my Soul, and then it was . . .
>
> (X 902–8)

Form without content (the "clear and solid evidence" of mathematics) replaces contents devoid of form, but, as both the quotation by Coleridge above and Wordsworth's own constant monetary calculations in his letters to Richard suggest, mathematics functioned as a rhetorical ground for jurisprudence and economics. Wordsworth's retreat is immediately contested by the appearance of Coleridge, who offers another method to "regulate the Soul." James Chandler has observed that this crisis marks a shift from Godwinian reason to Burkean custom (*Second Nature* 55–56). Such a shift does not erase the former, but incorporates both within a synthetic discourse. Pure reason is enabling, but not sufficient, just as historical "facts" are material but, without poetic interpretation, unavailable and unstructured. Although Wordsworth does not specify what is meant by "a living help," if one puts any weight on the economic charge of "living," then the movement is toward his collaboration with Coleridge on the *Lyrical Ballads*, which established Wordsworth as a poet within the literary market. Other valences of "living" invoke Coleridge's insistence on the poem that

Wordsworth always maintained would "live," that "philosophical poem, containing views of Man, Nature and Society; and to be titled, The Recluse" (*Excursion* 2). In the *Prelude*, the regulation acts indirectly, by opening Wordsworth to Dorothy and consequently to himself as poet:

> and then it was
> That the belovèd Woman in whose sight
> Those days were passed, now speaking in a voice
> Of sudden admonition—
> . . . .
> Maintained for me a saving intercourse
> With my true self
> . . . .
> She, in the midst of all, preserved me still
> A Poet, made me seek beneath that name
> My office upon earth, and nowhere else.
> (X 908–21)[31]

The regulation of Wordsworth's soul empowers Dorothy to admonish him, or to allow her judgment to bring his mind into harmony with itself. This harmony, in turn, produces a Poet from the chaos, although the production is figured as a preservation—the true soul existed through the Godwinian critique and the recoil from it, but was hidden. Godwin's effort to lift a veil of mystery from legal institutions was inadequate because it shifted that veil over what it sought to liberate, the individual's reason, which, without passion and moral foundation, could be nothing more than the historical reproduction of institutional ideologies.

The *Prelude* was preparation for *The Excursion* since, if it could establish Wordsworth as a poet to himself and thus locate him within a textual tradition (another term for a professional institution), he could offer a critique that did not end in the confusions of "demanding *proof*" where none is to be had. Wordsworth is not offering a panegyric to English law, but subsuming that discourse in such a way as to articulate both its strengths and weaknesses, and to position poetic discourse as its equal partner in rational and social thought. The justification for this equality could be derived from eighteenth-century aesthetic and political theory, which viewed society including the desiring individual as a series of correspondences, proportions, and symmetries, that, like concentric orbits, maintained one another through mutual attractions; as Hume put it: "The same love of order and uniformity, which arrranges the books in a library, and the chairs in a parlour, contributes to the formation of society . . . by modifying the general rule concerning the stability of possession. As property forms a relation betwixt a person and an object, 'tis natural to found it on some preceeding relation" (quoted in Eagleton, *The Ideology of the Aesthetic* 51).

Wordsworth's own articulations of such correspondences did not stand outside the system of possession, but were enmeshed within it through both his professional practices and thematic concerns. If the harmonious vision proposed in the *Prelude* book X seems finally to tame law into one system of regulation among many, the aesthetic difficulties in achieving this balance can be suggested by a brief look at *The Borderers.* Thomas McFarland characterizes the play as "a heap of cultural and personal debris," scraps of exactly what the "prophetic" Wordsworth needed to get beyond (*William Wordsworth: Intensity and Achievement* 139), but I wish to suggest that the debris—inflected with legal resonance—is not transcended in such passages as the *Prelude* book X, but rather arranged and harmonized.

The Borderers: Legal Debris

Robert Osborn has noted that the early version of *The Borderers*, called simply *A Tragedy*, was composed in 1796–99 at the "threshold of the 'great decade'" (*Borderers* ix) and published after much revision in 1842, when Wordsworth had accumulated such cultural capital that various editions of his complete works rested beside Milton and Shakespeare in middle-class homes (Klancher, *Reading Audiences* 150). The play borders the Wordsworthian career and demonstrates that, for Wordsworth, to move beyond the social world required a recursive turn toward engagement with that world and its institutions.[32] The allusive range of the play's "cultural debris" is impressive, and yet curiously centered. The play picks up Shakespearean echoes and their contemporary resonances in the debate on the French Revolution (Burke, Godwin, Paine, and Wollstonecraft all allude to *Macbeth* in their descriptions of the revolution); it rehearses eighteenth-century debates on the relations among reason, passion, and superstition (*A Tragedy* III iv 25–28); as Theresa Kelley has demonstrated, it exploits the social associations of its announced geographic location in the "Penrith-Stainmore region" (*Wordsworth's Revisionary Aesthetics* 73). Despite their disparity, all of these references encode (or, perhaps, take for granted) legal disputes, and in particular, disputes raising the issue of jurisdiction with regard to property. *Macbeth*, of course, resolves in a wager of battle, the stakes of which are Scotland itself. The ascendence of "reason" in the eighteenth century was partly through the application of a scientific method to jurisprudence; Mortimer, in a redemptive moment from which Rivers will seduce him, boasts that he will "go forth a teacher":

> And you shall see how deeply I will reason
> Of laws, of qualities and substances,
> Of actions, and their ends and differences.
> (*A Tragedy*, III ii 79–82)

The sense of "law" as a structure of reason (in the quotation) and as a social construct (in the play's context) is a typical eighteenth-century usage, visible in Blackstone, Hume, and Robert Chambers. Early in the play, a beggar inadvertently expresses the dilemma of living in a Border territory with respect to legal enforcement. In his speech, geography becomes legal demography:

> That good old Lady
> Has left a power of riches, and I say it,
> If there's a lawyer in the land, the rogue
> Shall give me half.
> (*A Tragedy* I iii 115–18)

Blackstone had acknowledged that there was no natural law supporting the concept of inheritance, but justified it on the basis of the need to prevent continual disputes with each death. Here, however, the beggar recognizes that the disputes are not dissolved but merely civilized, and brought into the purview of the court. The violence may be muted, but it still exists. Within the play, the irony is that there is not a lawyer left in the Border land. Rivers, the antihero of the play, articulates a negative relation between property and jurisdiction:

> Happy are we
> Who live in these disputed tracts that own

No law but what each man makes for himself.
Here justice has indeed a field of triumph!
(*A Tragedy* II i 51–54; 1842, *The Borderers* 594–97)[33]

These lines resist containment; they apply equally well to a monarch who claims ownership of the laws (in England, the crown retained copyright of the laws) and to a national assembly executing its former leaders.[34] On the one hand, the obverse of Rivers's comment is Burke's notion that property alone can stabilize government and give law effective enforcement. On the Godwinian hand, by contrast, is the recognition that property itself, as a subject of dispute, provides the grounds for criminality.[35] If these are the conundrums Wordsworth must struggle to get beyond—and critics of every political persuasion have recognized similarities between Rivers and Wordsworth—then we should note that Mortimer proposes to expiate his guilt by moving beyond property as "a wanderer on earth, / A shadowy thing" (V iii 265–66). And yet, in his final speech, he remains subject to his own law, now made visible to him through his blinding pain in its full relation to divine justice:

I will wander on
Living by mere intensity of thought,
A thing by pain and thought compelled to live,
Yet loathing life, till heaven in mercy strike me
With blank forgetfulness—that I may die.
(*A Tragedy* V iii 271–75)

The play, perhaps, does not get beyond its cultural debris, but becomes "a tragic parable of the terrible self-contradictions into which our sense of justice falls when 'we do not feel/For man as man'" (John Turner, *Wordsworth: Play and Politics, A Study of Poetry* 84). But that cultural debris, with its legal inflections, signals that to "feel / For man as man" (*A Tragedy* II iii 171–72; omitted in 1842) is a complex social activity, never free from the heteroglossic pressures Bakhtin identifies.

If, as Mary Jacobus asserts, the play is Wordsworth's "most sustained and eccentric study of guilt" (*Tradition and Experiment in Wordsworth's* Lyrical Ballads *(1798)* 24), then it must also be about the law(s) configuring guilt. In the same volume in which *The Borderers* made its first appearance, Wordsworth published *Sonnets upon the Punishment of Death*, a fourteen-poem sequence that argues in favor of retaining a penalty of death for some crimes. These poems explicitly translate the Wordsworthian concept of duty, initially borrowed from legal discourse, back into that discourse, modified by a career until it is a thing of fear and trembling, rather than a method of legitimating state power:

> Yes, though He well may tremble at the sound
> Of his own voice, who from the judgment-seat
> Sends the pale Convict to his last retreat
> In death; though Listeners shudder all around,
> They know the dread requital's source profound;
> Nor is, they feel, its wisdom obsolete—
> (Would that it were!)
>
> (XIII 1–7)

This convict, like Rivers/Oswald, is a type for the Wordsworthian outcasts that populate his poetry, and he may signify that the notion of an outcast in early nineteenth-century England cannot be historically articulated without reference to English law. The recognition of the convict's humanness, even in the moment of insisting on the Law's discipline, reminds us that in Wordsworth's experience, human law policed the borders of human identity, just as it parceled the common land into private ownership through enclosure. In the midst of an argument that today may seem caustically reactionary, he insists upon trembling and shuddering that position Law as the sign not of human accomplishment but of human limitations; these bodily gestures, figure and prophecy of the dying twitches of the condemned man, are visceral readings of a prophetic text of human mortality.

They disclose, for example, one social horizon at the edge of "A narrow girdle of rough stones and crags," one of the "Poems on the Naming of Places" in the *Lyrical Ballads.* In it, a poem in which the scene is a series of borders (the "narrow girdle" 1, the "margin of the lake" 52, the "new-discovered coast" of the final metaphor 85), the poet is walking with friends and spots a man fishing who, they conjecture in "one and the same voice," must be "idle" (later revised to "Improvident and reckless") to "lose a day / Of the mid harvest" (55–58). As they approach, they discover that he is too frail to work in the harvest, and their judgment becomes inward "admonishment" (76) in a reverse shudder in which their chatty happiness is stilled to "serious musings and self-reproach" (70). The reproach is not only directed inward but, as Kenneth MacLean noticed in *The Agrarian Age: A Background for Wordsworth* (22–23), is also projected into a public debate. At the poem's beginning, the companions "Play'd with our time" (11); the phrase, expressing both leisure and possession, allows Wordsworth to ventriloquize an aristocratic attitude, the obverse of which was the cliché that, as Sir Frederic Eden put it, "the miseries of the labouring poor" arise primarily "from their own improvidence and unthriftiness" (*Annals*, 1797; quoted in MacLean, *Agrarian Age* 22). In this poem, the projection of that attitude determines how the frail man is seen, until the illusion collapses in the face of close observation, the collective certainty of the friends preventing them from recognizing labor itself. My point, however, is that the private admonishment that follows is staged through an awareness of the wider debate—a debate of multiple forums, not the least of which were the law courts, Parliament, and the political journals. Although in "A narrow girdle" the judgment is rash, and in the "Punishment of Death" it is an act of duty, both poems construct judgment not as a transcendent category but as an action historically conditioned by the economics of English culture. "A narrow girdle," by its critique of judgment, reassesses the relationship between idleness and work. The idle poet's judgment is transformed into the labor of memorializing that repays the debt of the "delight[ ]" on which he "feed[s]" his "fancies" (46) on the output of the working "Reapers" (43).[36]

In his lifelong project of discovering a poetic identity, Wordsworth recognized, embraced, obscured, appropriated, applauded, and queried the role of law in society, partly out of social consciousness and partly because, as a dominant form of discourse, law was an inextricable part of the linguistic matrix available to the romantic poet. At the same time, theorists of property, jurisprudence, and economics appropriated a rhetoric of aesthetics to justify their positions; in particular, the Longinean categories of the sublime and the beautiful, as rearticulated by Burke, provided terms to discuss issues as seemingly diverse as the effects of enclosure on cattle-grazing and the proper role of the judge's instructions to a jury. By the circulation of terms through professional domains, a dialogue between law and literature ensued. William Wordsworth's role in that dialogue receives a particular inflection by virtue of his desire to be a *professional* poet, one who would control his own copyrights and marshal his words into a symbolic capital.

The challenge of that project can be seen in Byron's resistance to its formulation: "Did you read [Hunt's] skimble-skamble about [Wordsworth] being at the head of his own *profession*, in the *eyes* of *those* who followed it? I thought that Poetry was an *art*, or an *attribute*, and not a *profession*" (*Byron's Letters and Journals* 6:47; to Moore, 1818). An art or an artibute was come by naturally, by virtue of taste and class. A profession was a matter of training, and if it was free from an older patronage system, it smacked of pandering to a client. Where Byron would claim to dash off stanzas as a matter of compulsion, Wordsworth would painstakingly revise, repackage, and republish.[37] The possibility of managing a poetic career as Wordsworth did was relatively new, because it depended upon both a set of legal and material conditions that arose with eighteenth-century commerce and a reading public willing to accept such a self-representation.

One particular statement from the 1802 Preface to the *Lyrical Ballads* suggests how Wordsworth struggled to locate the professional poet as the producer of a particular discourse, the very particularity of which was its permeability with all other discourses and its (apparent) refusal of any mediation other than the need to provide pleasure: "The Poet writes under one restriction only, namely, that of the necessity of giving immediate pleasure to a human Being possessed of that information which may be expected from him, not as a lawyer, a physician, a mariner, an astronomer or a natural philosopher, but as a Man. Except this one restriction, there is no object standing between the Poet and the image of things; between this, and the Biographer and Historian there are a thousand" (*Lyrical Ballads* 257–58).

A Poet, a Man, the image of things. But whether as reader or writer, one encounters a text in a more specific position than these abstractions. If the Wordsworthian career was projected toward a transcendence of particularity, it depended upon particular discourses by which to establish its difference. From this quotation, one might suggest that placing Wordsworth's writing against any of these professions would be useful, and I suspect as much. For this book, I consider the domain of the first, the lawyer's legal discourse, and in the next chapter I turn to "Michael" as a case study of a narrative poem that, though located entirely away from any legal scene, is packed with legal interventions and resonances.

TWO

Law, Labor, and the Shepherd's Household: "Michael"

THE final poem of the 1800 *Lyrical Ballads*, "Michael," presents an overlay of obligations and promises: the explicitly legal contracts of the surety Michael signs and of the mortgage he overcomes; the marriage of Isabel and Michael and their subsequent negotiation about their son Luke's fate; the covenant between Michael and his son for dividing their labor between shepherding and commercial trade; and the letter of agreement from their kinsman to take Luke into business. Shadowing these are both the covenant forged by the sacrifice of Isaac and its New Testament analogue.[1] Similarly relevant is the contractual relationship between poet and reader established through the Preface and earlier poems (see chapters 5 and 6), a relationship that mediates the losses and gains entailed by the shift from an older system of local monopolistic exchange to the new economics of contract and negotiable instruments.[2] These speech acts, or their mere mention or recollection, comprise what Karl Kroeber has economically named "the paucity of notable incidents" and has contrasted to "the wealth of unimpressive detail" (*Romantic Narrative Art* 82).[3]

In a letter to Thomas Poole, Wordsworth claimed that in "Michael" he had "attempted to give a picture of a man, . . . agitated by two of the most powerful affections of the human heart; the parental affection, and the love of property, *landed* property, including the feelings of inheritance, home, and personal and family independence" (LEY 322, 9 April 1801). These impulses, complementary in the myth of inheritance that both Wordsworth and Michael had received, signified the internal continuity of family and its political analogue, the peaceful succession from generation to generation.

Three of the terms that articulate the love of "*landed* property" imply a parental relationship: inheritance, home, and family independence. The introduction of the various contracts in "Michael" disrupts the correspondence of the two feelings and recasts them as antagonists.[4]

Although the contractual arrangements in the poem can be loosely organized in a chronological matrix, in 1800 the older forms of covenant were not obsolete nor were the newer, "classical" forms of contract installed without opposition.[5] The legal expansion of contracts displaces alternative social mechanisms of adjudication, including church sanctions, local shame customs, and familial morality. J. Douglas Canfield has proposed the "word as bond" as a "master trope" of English literature from the early modern period until the 1690s. With the demise of feudalism, he suggests, the bond is appropriated and marginalized by a developing legalistic bourgeoisie (*Word as Bond in English Literature from the Middle Ages to the Restoration* 314). Trust is adjudicated not by a promise having been made, but by the courts' enforcement, or implicit threat to enforce, the promise. "Michael," as a tragedy about a shepherd caught within that transformation, reminds us that no language is transparent and that no medium of exchange operates without shaping the site and selves of the exchange.

Peter Manning (*Reading Romantics* 50) has noted a disjunction between the causes Wordsworth cites in his letter to Charles James Fox for the recent "rapid decay of the domestic affections among the lower orders of society"—that is, the "spreading of manufactures," "heavy taxes upon postage," "workhouses, Houses of Industry, and the invention of Soup-shops &c. &c. superadded to the encreasing disproportion between the price of labour and that of the necessaries of life" (LEY 313, 14 January 1801)—and the events that cause Michael's actual collapse. I would suggest, however, the precision of Wordsworth's connection at two levels. First, the drop in the value of labor may prevent Michael from restructuring the debt of the surety and paying it off as he did the mortgage; as Michael puts it, in justifying sending Luke into an expanding urban economy, "Where every one is poor / What can be gain'd?" (264–65). Although we do not know what remedies besides selling the land and sending off Luke he considers, he does think for at least two days before announcing his plan to Isabel (237). Second, the surety is attached to the causes Wordsworth mentions by the legal and legislative discourses and decisions, and their attendant ideologies of individualism and social engineering, which authorized an array of social reorganization. Although seeming to act as an individual, Michael's decisions are, ultimately, part of a wider network of policy, in which contract law plays a substantial role.

Blackstone, as late as 1766, allotted little space to contracts in his *Commentaries*. They are treated in a fraction of a chapter, "Of Title by Gift, Grant, and Contract," in a series of chapters on entitlement.[6] He defines "contract" succinctly: "'an agreement, upon sufficient consideration, to do or not to do a particular thing.' From which definition there arise three points to be contemplated in all contracts; 1. The *agreement:* 2. The *consideration*: and 3. The *thing* to be done or omitted, or the different species of contract" (2: 442). Blackstone devotes most of his discussion to the principle of consideration, the notion that a contract was enforceable only if some fair value—work performed, money given—validated the agreement. In a society where traditional wages and prices prevail, the doctrine of consideration restricts the possibility of contract. If a servant performs work, the existence of a contract does not require the master to pay; the work itself does. At the same time, work itself was construed as a duty the community could enforce which preceded any particular engagement. Blackstone emphasizes labor not as a contractual agreement but as a description of social standing by discussing it not under the heading of "Contracts" but within the sequence of personal relationships including "husband and wife" and "parent and child." W. R. Cornish and G. De N. Clark note that he "gave somewhat anachronistic prominence" to the Statute of Artificers, which directed the justices at session to set wages and established the requirements of apprenticeship "far longer than was needed to teach the [necessary] skills," and empowered them to compel "labour to get in the harvest" (*Law and Society in England* 294, 290).

In contrast to servant-master relations, which Blackstone does not discuss under the topic of contract, the exchanges of merchants were economically regulated by the availability of negotiable instruments, usually regarded as specialty contracts or bills of exchange. This division of legal forms both mirrored and enforced the division of English economy into local and national markets. With the breakdown of local monopolies and the influx of foreign trade, the traditional view of contracts that Blackstone espoused became a hindrance to enterprise.

Even as Blackstone wrote, the notion of "free" contract was undermining the principle of consideration, and his slight treatment of contracts is polemical on this point. Anticipated by Adam Smith's *Lectures on Jurisprudence*, Lord Chancellor Mansfield sought to "remove the doctrine of consideration from the law of contract or, at any rate, to reduce it to a shadowy and harmless fiction" (Holden 133). He attempted to replace consideration, as the validating moment of the contract, with the signature on a written contract. A critical case in this development was *Pillans v. Mierop*, which came before Mansfield in 1765. Pillans, a Dutch merchant, promised White, an Irish merchant, to accept a bill for £800 on condition that White would provide a London creditor as guarantor;[7] White provided Van Mierop. Pillans honored White's draft and then wrote to Van Mierop asking them to accept bills amounting to £800 drawn against Van Mierop on the credit of White. Van Mierop agreed in writing to this proposal. Before the bills were drawn, however, White went bankrupt and Van Mierop instructed Pillans not to draw them as they would not be honored. Pillans, acting on the authority of the written agreement with Van Mierop, drew the bills, which were dishonored by Van Mierop. Pillans brought suit, and the jury found for Van Mierop on the principle that Pillans had provided no adequate consideration for the contract. Pillans appealed and a panel of four judges, led by Lord Mansfield, unanimously set aside the verdict.

Mansfield presented two primary arguments, both opposing the doctrine of consideration. First, "the ancient notion about the want of consideration was for the sake of evidence only: for when it is reduced into writing, as in covenants, specialties, bonds, etc., there was no objection to the want of consideration. And the Statute of Frauds proceeded upon the same principle" (quoted in Teeven 134; see also S. J. Stoljar, *A History of Contract at Common Law* 102–4). This argument, unsupported by a cited authority ("The Statute of Frauds did not do this," Teeven 131), is not historically accurate, but elides the distinction between mercantile and other sorts of transactions. It reverses the priority of the written instrument, the contract, and the physical action, the consideration.[8] Where Blackstone maintains that the written agreement clarifies what is implicit in the consideration, Mansfield argues that the consideration merely provides evidence of an agreement, and that the written contract was sufficient evidence for its own enforcement.[9] A contract alters from a description of an agreement (a public recognition of a physical act) to an instrument that performed the agreement. This change contributed to the vast economic reforms that topple Michael, but it also shifted the form of public empowerment from orality to writing. Consequently, the contracts in the poem become a series of interpretive problems, moments when text, performance, and representation become confused, a problem even more pronounced since Michael's relation to both nature and community is marked by orality.

Wordsworth's own position on consideration recognized the usefulness of both the Blackstonean and Mansfieldian positions. Writing to his brother Richard in May 1797, he transcribed verbatim a "promissory note" signed by Charles Douglas and Basil Montagu for £220. He tells his brother: "I suppose in a court of justice this note would have no other effect but that of exposing me to a prosecution for usury, as I could shew no valuable consideration for this note but the 200£ lent at such a time" (LEY 183). After detailing a complicated flow of money, some well documented, some of a more "handshake" variety ("Montague had 300£ of mine in a sort of an irregularly secured annuity for which I have received ten percent"), he suggests, with a parenthetical joke that probably irritated Richard, that he can "trust to the honour of each [Douglas and Montagu] (if there can be any honour amongst usurers) for the payment of the additional interest" (LEY 184). At law, the older sense of consideration is in play; but, "at friendship," the signatures are sufficient. In this letter, Wordsworth demonstrates, or at least ventriloquizes, the legal understanding that Michael lacks. [10]

Before narrating the contracts that intrude on Michael's life, Wordsworth first establishes the rhythm of that life as one rooted in orality and labor. The lines on Michael's understanding of the winds contains one of the few similes in the poem:

> he had learn'd the meaning of all winds,
> Of blasts of every tone, and oft-times
> When others heeded not, He heard the South
> Make subterraneous music, like the noise
> Of Bagpipers on distant Highland hills.
>
> (48–52)

The winds resemble languages in which the blasts are words with various intonations. Michael's ability to read effects in sounds, however, is jeopardized in the metaphor that explains it. The interposition of nearly two complete lines between "all winds" and the end-stopped "South" allows the latter, a metonym for "South Wind," to suggest the direction of London and the industrial cities. The comparison to Bagpipers, who are from the North, perhaps indicates the depth of Michael's skills; he can read one wind disguised as another. Since "Michael" occurs in the decades after the Jacobite uprising of 1745, the bagpipes connote disruption. They are, it is true, metaphorical, but so are the ("subterraneous") winds of economics that undermine his land and that he cannot interpret.

Hearing winds that portend a storm, Michael says to himself:

> ["]The winds are now devising work for me![”]
> And truly at all times the storm, that drives
> The Traveller to a shelter, summon'd him
> Up to the mountains.
>
> (55–58)

The contrast to the Traveller is a contrast to the reader already placed as a visitor off the public way ("If from the public way you turn your steps . . ." 1). At first, to the reader/Traveller, Michael's exclamation may seem disgruntled. The winds, however, provide the means for him to be more himself, since his "Household" was "as a proverb in the vale / For endless industry" (95–97). The economics of wage labor, in which work is proportional to pay and presumably determined by the "free bargain" of supply and demand, does not seem to apply for Michael. His efforts respond to a nature that summons, a term of obedience from legal discourse and an intimation at the legal troubles to follow; Michael will be "*summon'd* to discharge the forfeiture" (226, my italics). Wordsworth anticipates a misreading of these lines on Michael's labor and corrects it in the first sentence of the next verse paragraph:

> And grossly that man errs, who should suppose
> That the green Valleys, and the Streams and Rocks
> Were things indifferent to the Shepherd's thoughts.
>
> (62–64)

A remark by Karl Kroeber suggests my understanding of these lines: "When we say that *Michael* is pure story we mean that it has no plot" (*Romantic Narrative Art* 81). The view presented of Michael's shepherding resembles Victor Shklovsky's view of narrative to which Kroeber alludes, but I suggest that a reader's sense of a "pure story" has to do with Michael's continual integration of disruptive plot elements into his self-story. The work of shepherding and the continuities are derived from disruptions that, like the winds, "others heeded not." In the continual mediation of nature as provider and nature as harm, the shepherd announces his value. But the subterraneous "plot" of the contracts cannot be integrated, and so, following the lead of Michael's strange silence, at the end, we are asked to overlook them in order to achieve a closure in the midst of "great changes" (487). In narrative, from the convergence of the will to achieve closure and the blocks to that closure, the plot emerges. The conversion of a story "ungarnish'd with events" (19) into "Michael" is the poetic equivalent to Michael's shepherding, of ceaseless integration, but achieved within the very economy of contract that destroys Michael.

In the next lines, Wordsworth explicitly connects shepherding with book making within an economic frame:

> ["Fields" and "hills"] which had impress'd
> So many incidents upon his mind
> Of hardship, skill or courage, joy or fear;
> Which like a book preserv'd the memory
> Of the dumb animals, whom he had sav'd,
> Had fed or shelter'd, linking to such acts,
> So grateful in themselves, the certainty
> Of honorable gains; these fields, these hills
> Which were his living Being, even more
> Than his own Blood—what could they less?
> (67–76)

Michael's mind, with incidents and their corresponding emotions impressed into it, and the fields and hills, described as a book of memory, join Michael to his land under the imagery of book manufacturing. This articulation refuses the key boundaries of contractual property, in which property gains value from its severability, and by which the individual can act in his own discrete personhood and body. Michael is his land as much as he is his body; such a position—by no means necessarily metaphorical—depends upon precisely the sort of economic entailments that Mansfield vigorously resisted through the restructuring of contract law.

If Michael's mind is like a book, then the fields and hills are less authors than (im)printers. In the process of printing, Michael functions as an author "linking" significance and, perhaps, giving a quasi-voice to "dumb animals," just as Wordsworth will invest Michael's silence with meaning. He writes his own being through a double composition; and similarly, the value of the incidents is double—in themselves and as the procurer of "honorable gains," a term itself doubling into gains in honor and gains that are honorable. In the interplay of remembered acts of kindness and their honorable economic gain, Michael's "Being" is written, seemingly fully integrated with the hills. David Simpson remarks that "Wordsworth's interest in shepherding as an ideal occupation is also to be connected with its intermediate status between the nomadic and the fixed, and thus the two stages of civil society as countless eighteenth-century writers described it" (*Wordsworth's Historical Imagination* 47). This intermediary status between nomadic and fixed is resisted/rejected by Michael in the desperate effort to transform the sheep-fold into a rock of covenant (and at the end of his life, he ceases his wanderings and merely sits at the unfinished structure). The "two stages of civil society" that Simpson notes mirror, and often encode, another division equally obsessive in countless eighteenth-century tracts, from Addison's *Spectator* to Powell's *Essay on Contracts and Agreements:* the "advance" from orality to writing. The failure of Michael's gesture to signify allows Wordsworth himself to enact the transformation from oral (a tale he heard) to written (the poem we read), and so reenact within literature the legal empowerment that is the object of his social critique both in the poem and, by implication, in the letter to Fox. In the collapse of Michael's "living Being" (75)—through the intercession of the new contractual economy—a written story of the sheep-fold emerges. The series of disruptions that structure this emergence are the various contracts to which I now turn.

SOON AFTER THE APPARENT UNITY of Michael and his land is established, inscripted through the metaphor of book making, the poem alludes to the first "contract": "He had not passed his days in singleness. / He had a Wife, a comely Matron" (80–81). Like most of the events of this narrative, the marriage is revealed late, and the redundancy of these two lines suggests that the first eliminates an expectation of the reader, based on the seeming fullness of the life already described. The structure of the poem is the increasing revelation of dependencies which mean and affect more than Michael can understand and contain. The description of Michael's relation to Isabel hardly seems contractual, though perhaps the traces of an external imposition remain both in the possessive "had" and in the overdetermined sexual status ("Wife" and "Matron" are supplemented by "Woman" two lines later, and her name is introduced only 150 lines later when Michael speaks it).

Although marriage had long been a legal category, "until 1753 the Church of England ceremony had to compete with a variety of rites which, if done correctly, made marriages just as securely" (John Gillis, *For Better, For Worse* 7).[11] Devised by the Lord Chancellor, Hardwicke's "Act for the better preventing of Clandestine Marriages" proscribed a range of marriage rituals and established a government monopoly on their forms (which, however, was only imperfectly implemented).[12] Although Michael's marriage cannot be dated as certainly before 1753, a reader in 1800 could recognize the state's imposition of meaning on that marriage, which may well have been, in the tradition of many rural communities, a "clandestine" form validated by public, not legal, scrutiny. The "Clipping Tree," (179) with its pun on "clepen" (to "name"; the word appears in the same line) could constitute the site of such a communal moment.

In William Shakespeare's *The Winter's Tale*, during a sheepshearing such as would take place at the Clipping Tree, Florizel and Perdita argue their ability to bind themselves in marriage. Perdita maintains "Your resolution cannot hold when 'tis / Opposed, as it must be, by th' power of the king," and Florizel counters with a metaphoric transformation of the sheepshearing festival into nuptials (IV iv 37–51). The resolution of *The Winter's Tale* relies on reintegrating severed communities and reassuring feudal lineage.

Such marital integration, at the beginning of "Michael," appears seamlessly connected to the familial "life of eager industry" through the image of the "antique" lamp. Allowing the family to work into the night, the light from the lamp:

> was famous in its neighbourhood,
> And was a public Symbol of the life,
> The thrifty Pair had liv'd. For, as it chanc'd,

Their Cottage on a plot of rising ground
Stood single, with large prospect North and South,
High into Easedale, up to Dunmail-Raise,
And Westward to the village near the Lake;
And from this constant light so regular
And so far seen, the House itself by all
Who dwelt within the limits of the vale,
Both old and young, was nam'd The Evening Star.
(136–46)

This description shifts in several directions. As Marjorie Levinson argues, "the narrator's emphasis on the locals' interpretation of Michael's lamp (they name the cottage 'The Evening Star') suggests that the value inherent in the object produced or maintained for private use can become available to the community as well" (*Wordsworth's Great Period Poems* 65). This remark requires slight amendment (at least out of its full context). The lamp's value is not "inherent," but continually reproduced by its deployment. As "the Housewife" nightly hangs the lamp, she affirms the knitting together of her family as her own labor, one based on the structural possibility afforded by "our antient uncouth country style" (113) of architecture that provides the room for the "aged utensil" (117). The manufactured light of the Lamp becomes valuable in its symbolic transformation into a natural light and the regularity of Michael's family allows the community to rename his existence in naturalistic terms, the "Evening Star."[13] The accidental nature of their visibility ("as it chanc'd") does not discredit it, but preserves a natural, rather than economic, basis.[14] The communal reiteration of the family's unity—the "Household" is proverbial for industry, the "house itself" is the "Evening Star"—renders irrelevant a legal marriage bond. The triple depiction, however, of the boundaries of Grasmere vale, first by direction (140), then by named landmarks (141–42), and finally by the geographic feature of the "limits of the vale" (145), maps the Evening Star into different concepts of property and reinforces the localness of the communal notion of the "Evening Star" as necessarily tentative within the national economy. What might seem redundant can also serve as an overdetermined resistance to the "great changes" that are "wrought / In all the neighbourhood" after Isabel's death (487–88). In the narration of the cottage's name, the agents of naming— "all / Who dwelt within the limits of the vale, / Both old and young"—are explicit and expansive; the phrase "old and young" suggests that, in the act of this naming, the generations are bonded together just as they are in the labor Michael and Luke share: "in us," the father reminds the son, "the old and young / Have play'd together" (364–65). When the phrase "was nam'd The Evening Star" recurs in the final, desolate verse paragraph, agency is erased. Only the poet, not the community, is left to grant the name; the economy and law of labor have changed.

The meaning of the status of the marriage fluctuates with the concepts of labor and with the economy in which it is viewed. The restructuring of marriage in the eighteenth century has been implicated in the shifts that are denoted as the industrial revolution. As E. J. Hobsbawm has noted, "the chief form of expanding industrial production" in the 1780s was not to construct factories but to extend "the so-called domestic or putting-out system" (*Age of Revolution* 36). In the first volume of his *Commentaries*, Blackstone denoted marriage as a contract, and outlined the grounds by which a marriage agreement is valid, the legal possibilities of divorce, and the relative rights between spouses. Only in a brief digression suggesting the utility of a system that allows easy access to marriage does he offer a rationale for marriage, one negatively posed: "Restraints upon marriage, especially among the lower class, are evidently detrimental to the public, by hindering the encrease of people; and to religion and morality, by encouraging licentiousness and debauchery among the single of both sexes" (1: 426).

Unlike Blackstone, who was suspicious about the consequences of economic expansion that Mansfield's revisions of contract law were designed to facilitate, the author of *The Laws Respecting Women* (Anon., 1777) opens his discussion of marriage with an aggressively economic rationale: "Indeed marriage seems to have been at first instituted as necessary to the very being of human society: for without the distinction of families there can be no encouragement to industry, nor any foundation for the care in acquiring riches" (23). The speculation that the desire for economic accumulation is originary to human society, and vested in it through the institution of marriage, superimposes onto marriage the contemporary rationale for the Mansfieldian view of contracts. This view of contracts is a key component to the restructuring of labor for industrialization because it aided the development of the wage markets that replaced more traditional labor regulation such as the Statute of Artifices. Arthur Young was confirming a truism in asserting: "It is employment that creates population: marriages are early and numerous in proportion to the amount of employment (quoted in David Levine, *Family Formation in an Age of Nascent Capitalism* 11–12). Levine has argued that "insofar as earnings, not property, became the prerequisite for family formation and marriage, a family economy emerged" (120).[15] This new economy employed a rhetoric of partnership; and an important corollary to the introduction of commercial language into the marital contract was the inculcation into the domestic sphere of an ideology of individualism as understood within the classical liberal economy:

> If the stock of our bliss is in strangers' hands rested
> The fund ill secured oft in bankruptcy ends,
> But the heart is given bills which are never protested
> When drawn on the firm of *Wife Children and Friends.*

This poem was used by a Wolverhampton salesman to his intended (cited by Catherine Hall, "Strains in the 'Firm of Wife, Children and Friends'?" 117); it suggests both his own personal ambition and the role he envisions for his family. Clearly, Michael and Isabel's marriage is not equivalent to this "firm," yet the difference may be less than it first appears. The family unit is precisely what Michael draws upon when he opts for sending Luke to London, and despite her reservations, Isabel never protests. Moreover, their marriage is structured through their labor, which becomes directed toward preventing their estate from falling into a "Stranger's hand" as it does after Isabel's death ("Michael" 484). In the reading of Isabel's labor which follows, I suggest that possible meanings of her labor are restructured within the ongoing debate about marriage as an economic institution, one dependent on viewing the components of marriage as contractually joined. Although Michael and Isabel may not recognize that such meaning can be imposed upon their marriage, the traces of this imposition can be seen in Isabel's investment in a national economy.

Despite the self-sufficiency of the household, which critics including Marjorie Levinson and Susan Eilenberg have remarked, Isabel is given the task to "Make ready Luke's best garments, of the best / *Buy* for him more" (289–90, my italics).[16] In part, the repetition of "best" suggests the confusion of Michael's values under economic stress. However, the purchasing plan also indicates his use of Isabel to mediate within a competitive marketplace, in which Luke (if things went well) would become both product and producer, just as—in the story Isabel remembers—Richard Bateman does. Additionally, the ready cash to buy expensive clothing suggests that the Evening Star exists beyond the subsistence levels that the poem elsewhere implies.

As Levinson (among others) has suggested, on first glance, Michael's household seems an emblem of both subsistence and self-sufficiency. At one level, then, the buying of Luke's additional "best clothes" may signal a deeper venture into dependency, but it also suggests that this first step has always already been made. What has been bought for Sunday clothes may become traveling garments. To be an emblem, or a proverb, for industry is not to be industry, but only to be its representation within specific fields of discourse. Eilenberg suggests that when the surety is revealed, "suppressed writing begins to disturb what is written over it" (*Strange Power of Speech* 95, note omitted). Her remark points to the extent to which the surety exposes previous investments in economies that define their labor differently, not as industry but as investment. I would further suggest that this suppression (in its more general form of Michael's connection to a national economy) is constantly exposed by the nature of Isabel's labor.

Although presumably an exaggeration, the narrator claims that "if one wheel [which Isabel spins] had rest, / It was because the other was at work" (86–87). Levinson points out that Michael's labor is unspecialized (*Great Period Poems* 73), but to this can be contrasted Isabel's specialized labor ("her own peculiar work" 128) divided between the two wheels. The tasks of the garden and dairy, typically female work like that of child raising (Hill 30),[17] are delegated to Michael (and Luke). If, with one wheel, as Levinson says, "Michael's wife spins the wool from the sheep that Michael tends" (*Great Period Poems* 63), then with the other wheel, she spins flax, not a product of Michael's shepherding. Rather, it is part of another complex industrial network, one in which she was probably making thread on consignment which would then, at other domestic sites, be transformed into linen, from there perhaps to become clothing (of the sort Isabel is told to purchase to set Luke on his way) or stationery.[18] As Bridget Hill points out in *Women, Work, and Sexual Politics*, the introduction of "Hargreave's

Spinning Jenny, patented in 1770" briefly "enabled women spinners to earn much higher prices" until it was "harnessed to water power" (Hill 63), and so the distribution of labor in Michael's household might maximize at least certain productive capacities. Although it is as a household that Michael's family becomes proverbial for industry, the men and Isabel use the light from the lamp differently:

> There by the light of this old lamp they sate,
> Father and Son, while late into the night
> The House-wife plied her own peculiar work.
> (126–28)

Her endless labor like her wheels, is bifurcated between a commitment to the Evening Star as insular and to its relation within community and nation. If she attempts to dissuade both Michael and then Luke from the scheme of Luke's leaving, she is also the one who shows around the letter that authorizes his departure to the community. In part, Isabel's greater connection to the community (remembering Bateman's story; showing the letter, shopping) was part of the fabric of traditional divisions of labor; "Almost always the preparation for, and attendance at, the local market was the women's work" (Hill 30).[19] But it also laid the foundation for the breach in that communal connection by creating markets that allowed for more industrial forms of production. By the time "Michael" was published, the wages of flax spinners in the north had collapsed (Ivy Pinchbeck, *Women Workers and the Industrial Revolution, 1750–1850* 146) and the transformation of the structure of labor was another of the "great changes" of the neighborhood.

I have discussed the least contractual relation in the poem at such length to demonstrate the way in which the meaning of a contract is only as stable as the discourses in which it takes place. The law, with the Hardwicke Act and subsequent litigation, had a vested interest in stabilizing the marriage contract, while it simultaneously pressured the communal circumstances that had once made nonlegal marriages workable. Clearly, this discussion of the legal/economic grounds of Isabel and Michael's marriage and of Isabel's labor ventures into territory which neither Wordsworth in his letter to Fox nor subsequent critics have charted. I suggest, however, by examining what the poem both makes visible[20] and compels us to overlook, that we learn about the discourses that Wordsworth sought to master, and about the stories he wished to unmoor from certain historical trajectories and relocate in his own "history / Homely and rude" (34–35).

After the description of Luke's childhood, the narrative introduces the first explicit contract with lines that Wordsworth told his printer should begin on a new page in the volume (Butler and Green 260):

> While this good household were thus living on
> From day to day, to Michael's ear there came
> Distressful tidings. Long before the time
> Of which I speak, the Shepherd had been bound
> In surety for his Brother's Son, a man
> Of an industrious life and ample means,
> But unforeseen misfortunes suddenly
> Had press'd upon him, and old Michael now
> Was summon'd to discharge the forfeiture,
> A grievous penalty, but little less
> Than half his substance.
> (217–27 from Butler and Green 260)

Like the belated introduction of Isabel, the surety is announced out of temporal sequence, a subterraneous eruption. The passage reverses the "good tidings of great joy" heard by shepherds on the eve of the new law (Luke 2:10) into "distressful tidings." The colloquialism of the first sentence—Michael *hears*, as if in the old legal tradition, what would have been a written communication—indicates that he encounters the problem as he did the winds. Unlike the winds that must arrive to do harm, the contract operates from afar, via the public way. Explicit about the lamp, and explicit about that explicitness, Wordsworth is vague about the surety, substituting details about Michael's nephew irrelevant to an assessment of the bond's legality.

Would a "grievous penalty" be enforceable in the absence of great harm? Possibly; R. P. Arden, in *Eaton v. Lyon* (1798), insisted that a forfeiture would be enforced only in the case of actual damages equivalent to the forfeiture, not as a penalty. Against this position, the possibility of enforcement because of willful negligence was maintained, but the nephew's "unforeseen circumstances" suggest a defense in keeping with the trend from the seventeenth century to void forfeitures.[21] Whether Michael was legally obligated to pay the forfeiture, even if bound to the surety (itself a complex legal matter), is not a given in 1800. Wordsworth does not suppress these points so much as take them for granted. Michael raises no question about executing the penalty; he understands his word as binding, but not in Mansfield's sense of "free" contract. He is bound by familial ties. As with his marriage, however, the full meaning of his bond to his nephew is articulated through external institutional forces, and their connection does not withstand the financial stress of the "unforeseen misfortunes." Distrust wells within Michael:

> I have liv'd to be *a fool at last*
> To my own family. *An evil Man*
> That was, and made an evil choice, if he
> Were false to us.
>
> (245–48, my italics)[22]

In this speech, Michael's identity is disassociated as his family ties unbind. "An evil Man" resonates at first with ambiguous reference, since it is in parallel with "a fool at last" and since Michael made the "choice." Momentarily checked by Michael's forgiveness, the dissociation quickly reappears as Michael seeks a solution marked by oral representation:

> 'Twere better *to be dumb* than *to talk* thus.
> When I began, my purpose was *to speak*
> Of remedies and of a chearful hope.
> Our Luke shall leave us, Isabel.
>
> (251–54, my italics)

Michael proposes to bind Luke to a kinsman who, as was the nephew for whom he signed the surety, is a "prosperous man, / Thriving in trade" (259–60). The analogy between land and Luke indicates that he duplicates his error of binding the land by binding Luke in similar circumstances; his attempt to cure his ill replicates it. When Michael explains his plan to Isabel, he exposes the contradictions of his economic position:

> Our Luke shall leave us, Isabel; the land
> Shall not go from us, and it shall be free,
> He shall possess it, free as the wind
> That passes over it.
>
> (254–57)

The emotional pitch catches the rapid confusions of Michael's thought, but these confusions are paradoxes the poem maintains. Land is free only when it is owned by its proper owner. Further, the freedom of the wind acts as a kind of entailment, a summons to the hills, a device for labor. Is it Luke or the land that is free as the wind? The dramatic answer is neither; Michael is mistaken; he hears and speaks what must be read and written.

The parable of Richard Bateman, the best possible scenario of middle-class development once Luke is sent away, is a sequence of economic and material transformations. The movement out of the country was not reversible, at least in the myth of economic growth which Wordsworth presents in Isabel's mind:

> [Richard Bateman] was a parish-boy—at the church-door
> They made a gathering for him, shillings, pence,
> And halfpennies, wherewith the Neighbours bought
> A Basket, which they fill'd with Pedlar's wares,
> And with this basket on his arm, the Lad
> Went up to London, found a Master there,
> Who out of many chose the trusty Boy
> To go and overlook his merchandise
> Beyond the seas, where he grew wond'rous rich,
> And left estates and monies to the poor,
> And at his birth-place built a Chapel, floor'd
> With Marble, which he sent from foreign lands.
>
> (269–80)

This story, rendered in one continuous sentence, is not a vision of wickedness but an appraisal of the costs of changes that do perform some good. The basket filled with "Pedlar's wares" is the local version of the merchant, and the boy's transformation into a mercantilist is sanctioned by the community. The enumeration of the small coins that make up the "gathering" and the Neighbours' control over their expenditure demonstrate the power of the community. The Neighbours convert the money into wares given to Bateman in trust, a parallel to the "Master" who chooses Bateman to "overlook his merchandise." But in Bateman's transformation, as with the death of the Cumberland Beggar, an element that drew the community together disappears.

The charitable "gathering" is an investment by the community against the expense of keeping Bateman on the parish rolls, and, in leaving "estates and monies to the poor," Bateman demonstrates the return on an investment of charity impossible with only parish rates. Qualifying these benefits, however, are two points, one hard economics, the other hard poetry. First, while Bateman became rich, he was chosen as one "out of many," and if his industry was instrumental, Michael's troubles show the insufficiency of that quality. The fate of the many William Hogarth, Jonathan Swift, and Tobias Smollett recorded (as, perhaps, did Wordsworth in "Poor Susan"[23]). Second, there is the image of the "Chapel, floor'd / With marble" (one of only two lines in the poem which is unbalanced by the combination of a caesura just before the final beat and an enjambment). Bateman erects an alternative site to the church, the door of which was the locus of community charity. The memorializing of the spot of his "birthplace" is intended primarily as an expression of gratitude, but it also shifts the meaning of the village by marking it as "Richard Bateman's birthplace"; as if to enforce the irony of this, Bateman is the only character outside Michael's nuclear family who is named in the poem. The inadvertent trespass is comically inappropriate, a point emphasized by the contrast to the rough stones of the sheep-fold, as well as by Bateman's ability to build from afar through the agency of his wealth, in contrast to Michael lifting stone by stone the materials for the sheep-fold. The emphasis of the foreignness of the stones plays on the fashionable rage in London for imports, but translates it, in the local community, into a kind of invasion.

By placing this story in Isabel's mind, Wordsworth suggests that these economic dynamics are experienced imperfectly in the mythologizing of community life.[24] Isabel's response to Bateman's story is uncertain. Peter Manning suggests that "Isabel decides to give her consent to Michael's plan because of the memory of Richard Bateman" (*Reading Romantics* 42), but the text is ambiguous:

> These thoughts, and many others of like sort,
> Pass'd quickly thro' the mind of Isabel,
> And her face brighten'd.
>
> (281–83)

She says nothing, and her face may brighten because of these thoughts or to fortify Michael against them. Michael does not consult Isabel but presents a "scheme" already decided. Her role is to "make ready Luke's best garments." Wordsworth creates a sense of consent between Michael and Isabel, an illusion aided by the ideology of agreement governing middle-class marriages, and internalized by Isabel who concentrates on Michael's loss, not her own. When she finally "gave consent," the issue is when, not if, Luke will leave, and the result focuses on her husband: "and Michael was at ease" (331).

Once the decision to send Luke off is made, Michael's household becomes a torrent of preparation, strictly necessary, yet strangely beside the point. The family awaits a letter to give the frenetic activity meaning. Even before Luke has left, the value of labor has shifted its locus. Isabel senses this shift when she warns Luke that "if thou leave thy Father he will die," but, with Luke's "jocund" response, she enters the household delusion: they sit "*Like* happy people round a Christmas fire" and "the house *appear'd* / As cheerful as a grove in Spring" (308–9, 313–16, my italics). The letter, when it arrives, is carefully drafted:

> The expected letter from their Kinsman came,
> With kind assurances that he would do
> His utmost for the welfare of the Boy,
> To which requests were added that forthwith
> He might be sent to him.
>
> (317–21)

As in Wordsworth's own letters, the kinsman slides between the diction of familial affection and vocabulary of business. A split between these heteroglossic realms, however, is maintained by the grammar. The active voice of the assurance "he would do / His utmost" contrasts to the "requests," which "were added" as though by another hand, and which ask that Luke "might be sent," again submerging the agent, Michael, in a passive voice.[25] Through this structuring, Michael's original entreaty to the kinsman is converted into the kinsman's request (or command) to Michael. This reciprocation can be read two ways: first, the kinsman is kindly recognizing the value Michael offers in sending Luke; second, the kinsman is an unconscious agent of "the dissolute city" (452). Wordsworth does not offer a choice between these readings, and the argument between them reflects unresolved historical circumstances. Was a contract the result of a mutual agreement or was it coercive and a replication of the same power structure that produced the forfeiture? The time frame implied by "forthwith" (the only spondee in the lines) glimpses this tension, since it both connotes eagerness and, in the contractual realm of offer-and-acceptance, limits the offer's duration because the kinsman can now make profitable use of Luke (by contrast, the winds summon Michael to work "at all times" 56).

Christopher Salvesen has noted that Wordsworth "deliberately sets his tale" in "natural time," a time that emerges in slow-paced continuity (*The Landscape of Memory* 147–49).[26] Against this temporality is the time of business, the "forthwith" of the kinsman and Michael's desire that Luke leave as quickly as possible despite Isabel's objection of "things / Which, if at such short notice he should go, / Would surely be forgotten" (328–30). Though she means material items left behind, these lines reverberate with more significance as Luke forgets natural time in his immersion in a city in which, Wordsworth wrote, his own "time passed in a strange manner; sometimes whirled about by the vortex of its *strenua inertia*, and sometimes thrown by the eddy into a corner of the stream" (LEY 49, 17 June 1791). By insisting on a time frame, the kinsman lays bare the contractual nature of the proposed apprenticeship (to use that term loosely), but the enthusiasm with which Isabel receives the news—she "Went forth to shew [the letter] to the neighbours round"—obscures the point.

MANNING HAS POINTED OUT that the "stark scene" of Michael at the unfinished sheep-fold after Luke must flee England "draws its power from its wordlessness" (*Reading Romantics* 46). This effect is achieved at the site of the two most significant contracts, the written agreement between reader and writer established early in the poem on the writer's ability to make the sheep-fold visible, and the spoken covenant between Michael and Luke (figured more generally as between "old and young" 354) to make the sheep-fold both real and symbolic. Michael tries to assure continual labor through a contract alien to his life; it is borrowed from his kinsmen and from Richard Bateman. The poet, by contrast, presents a document, the poem, the reading of which continually duplicates labor. In Mansfield's term, Michael's contract is founded only on a signature, not backed by his labor, because his labor is already entirely spoken for, entirely proverbial. For the poet, by contrast, his signature—the distinctness of the poet's hand—and consideration cohere; his signature constitutes his work, just as Wordsworth authored (authorized) by his signature a series of letters written by Coleridge about the *Lyrical Ballads.*

When Michael resolves to send Luke off, he does so with a capitalistic expectation of return, as Levinson has argued. He has violated his own code, and attempts to mitigate damages by overwriting his activity with a covenant between himself and his son. First, he acknowledges the instability of his code in its inability to link his "Forefathers" and his child:

> I wish'd that thou should'st live the life they live.
> But 'tis a long time to look back, my son,
> And see so little gain from sixty years.
>
> (381–83)

His use of the past tense, "wish'd," suggests that he has revised (if only subconsciously) his expectation that Luke "quickly will repair this loss, and then / May come again" (262–63) to the life of the Evening Star. At this moment, Michael recognizes the necessity of "gain" in order to stay even in an expanding economy; his glance backward changes the meaning of what is seen. This paradox, underscored by the doubling of "a long time" with "sixty years,"[27] marks the impossibility of his situation. To establish a covenant of labor with his son, Michael tries to transform his physical strength into a transcendent strength, a power to bind. In the terms of the Preface of the *Lyrical Ballads,* he tries to alter the real language of his daily work into the slippery discourse of legal promises;[28] his failure is foregone from the opening, in which the poet contracts to regain that real language in the midst of the public way. In keeping with the structure of the poem, in which past events such as the marriage and the surety erupt into the present, the sheep-fold is introduced as a preexisting idea:

> Near the tumultuous brook of Green-head Gill,
> In that deep Valley, Michael had design'd
> To build a Sheep-fold, and, *before he heard*
> *The tidings of his melancholy loss,*
> For this same purpose he had gathered up
> A heap of stones.
>
> (332–37, my italics)

The project is already in place, and Michael tries to adjust its significance by an agreement with Luke. At law, the preexisting duty of the sheep-fold precluded its acting as the considerable basis for a contract. Ironically, the courts would hold Michael's contract as void unless they invoked legal fictions that, as with Wordsworth's insistence on the newness of the retold story, allowed past work to become present through the way in which it was newly talked about (Stoljar, *Common Law* 59–60). The analogy to the poet altering the reader's encounter with the stones is underscored by the similarity of the opening line of this verse paragraph (332) to both the poem's second and final lines.[29] The crucial difference rests on the poet's success hewn from Michael's failure.

Michael speaks, interrupted only by Luke's sobbing and silence, for nearly ninety lines. His language associates him with Abraham, upon whose covenant with God the patriarchical nation of Israel rests:

> My Son,
> To-morrow thou wilt leave me; with full heart
> I look upon thee, for thou art the same
> That wert a promise to me ere thy birth,
> And all thy life hast been my daily joy.
> (341–45)

Luke's value to Michael is doubled, both in himself as a "daily joy," and in the fulfillment of and as "a promise." This promise exists without explanation, another eruption of the past, possibly Michael's revision since it reflects the projected future that Michael imagines when Luke's labor will both operate in the city and resonate in the country.

To constitute a coherent past for this projection, Michael reviews for Luke first "our two histories" (347) and then the story of his relation to the land. The lands were "burden'd," legally mortgaged and Michael freed them through his labor which he understands as exerting a mastery: the land "looks as if it never could endure / Another Master" (389–90). The continuity of the "tumultuous brook," through the land and through the poem, warns the reader that Michael is wrong in one sense; finally, the land has no master and is, as Michael says of Luke, "a gift" eventually returned. In other terms, in the "precapitalistic" world of common and entailed lands, nature and property describe the same domain, because neither exists, that is, "stands out" apart from the other ("to exist" derives from the Latin *existere*, to stand out). But, once property becomes a commodity produced within the sign-network of legal discourse, it becomes a symbol of a nature that, though it seems to exist before property, is produced only by that property. Michael's anxiety about his land arises because he has, literally, bought into the property system in reclaiming his lands and reassigning them via the surety. Michael's "history" is one of continual labor to reclaim his land, a labor that both concedes and resists the outside structures of property.

Having emphasized to Luke the importance of the past, Michael expresses the terms of their covenant:

> This was a work for us, and now, my Son,
> It is a work for me. But, lay one Stone—
> Here, lay it for me, Luke, with thine own hands.
> I for this purpose brought thee to this place.
> (395–98)

As Mansfield hoped for contracts in general, Michael here tries to make his covenant good based on its formal structure. The insistence on Luke's "own hands" becomes a call for self-sacrifice, echoing Abraham's taking "the fire in his hand" and "stretch[ing] forth his hand . . . to slay his son" (Genesis 22:6,9). The biblical story affirms the promise between God and Abraham, translated and doubled into God's promise to Isaac: "In blessing I will bless thee. . . . And in thy seed shall all nations of the earth be blessed" (Genesis 22:17–18). The authoritative speech act of God is both promise and fulfillment of promise, not *making* but presence, a distinction Wordsworth insisted upon: "In fact, there is nothing in the course of the religious education adopted in this country, and in the use made by us of the Holy Scriptures, that appears to me so injurious as perpetually talking about *making* by God." Human speech acts are making, and lack divine sovereign strength; they harken, juridically, to previous speech acts, just as "Michael" derives from earlier versions. The exchange between Michael and Luke, now founded on their own labor, is alienated from God and remakes their relationship. Once, Michael asserts, "thou hast been bound to me / Only by links of love" (411–12), which implies that a new bond now exists, but—too close to acknowledging the flaws of his plan—he retrenches with words that again mean too much: "But I forget / My purposes" (413–14).

Michael's language in this speech twists with uncertainty, and ends with an inadvertent negation of the covenant:

> When thou return'st, thou in this place wilt see
> A work which is not here, a covenant
> '*Twill* be between us— . . .
>
> (423–25)

In this view, Luke's placing of the cornerstone does not create the covenant; rather, Luke's act is like the signature on a contract without consideration. Only the labor of the completed sheep-fold constitutes a covenant and brings it into existence. At the denouement of his address, Michael falls upon the older form of contract in which only labor, not its promise or sign, constructs a contract. Michael would not recognize the shift in his language: he intends "this Sheep-fold," marked only by its cornerstone, to be sufficient "anchor" and "shield" for Luke. The poet, however, hints at the shift in describing the normalization of Michael's work after Luke has left:

> The Shepherd went about his daily work
> With confident and cheerful thoughts; and now
> Sometimes when he could find a leisure hour
> He to that valley took his way, and there
> Wrought at the Sheep-fold.
>
> (447–51)

What once was always present must now be found. What was to be "work" has become "leisure," and moreover, that binary distinction becomes meaningful; Michael is invested in the national economy, and the dissolution of "endless industry" marks that investment. The silent Luke is incapable of a sufficient speech act in the laying of the cornerstone and Michael feels his doom:

> but whatever fate
> Befall thee, I shall love thee to the last
> And bear thy memory with me to the grave.
>
> (425–27)

Luke's effort to obey and seal the covenant crystallizes Michael's feelings. When the cornerstone is laid, "The Old Man's grief broke from him, to his heart / He pressed his Son, he kissed him and wept" (431–32).

Michael "pressed" his son, as nature had "impressed" him, but here the full weakness of Michael's oral system is clear: no contract results, no book is made.

This private scene, developed slowly with its contradictions foregrounded, is immediately contrasted with Luke's public scene, which regroups these contradictions into near invisibility:

> when he had reach d
> The public Way, he put on a bold face;
> And all the Neighbours as he pass'd their doors
> Came forth, with wishes and with farewell pray'rs
> That follow'd him 'till he was out of sight.
>
> (435–39)

The gifts are verbal, not the wares which sped Bateman on his way. In practical terms, this shift arises because Michael and Isabel could outfit Luke without help, but the contrast suggests that, within the nascent capitalistic economy located on the public way rather than at the church door, discourse constitutes an act of giving. But the "pray'rs" can only follow him within sight of the speakers. The local words do not yet travel well; that strength awaits the poet.

Early in the poem, Wordsworth has directed the reader's wandering to a "place [where] a story appertains" (18). To recall the precise meanings of "appertain," the story belongs to the place, either by "right" or "by nature of appointment" (Samuel Johnson). Wordsworth imagines that the reader might walk past the unfinished sheep-fold without noticing it, and to prevent this trespass, he offers the story that makes the sheep-fold visible. To an actual reader who never goes up Green-head Gill, the story replaces the sheep-fold, and the poem itself works the transformation of the stones into the sheep-fold.

The second verse paragraph modulates between two justifications for the poem, the edification of the reader and the immortality of the poet, not in himself or in his writing but in other poets. The contract between the writer and the imagined reader is guaranteed by the consideration of the sheep-fold; for the actual reader, the guarantee is the written form of the poem, and the history of its transformation. The story

> Is not unfit, I deem, for the fire-side,
> Or for the summer shade. It was the first,

The earliest of those tales that spake to me
Of Shepherds.

(20–23)

The poet does not invent the story but repeats it, and suggests a reader can retell it at the fireplace.[30] But the poet also asserts the suitability of the story, and offers as evidence the effect it had on him when "yet a Boy":

Careless of books, yet having felt the power
Of Nature, by the gentle agency
Of natural objects led me on to feel
For passions that were not my own.

(28–31)

These lines replay the "first mild touch of sympathy" that the Old Cumberland Beggar evokes, "A thing more precious . . . [than] books / . . . can do" ("Old Cumberland Beggar" 106, 104–5). In "Michael," however, the source of sympathy is more dispersed, or, from another perspective, more unifying, since it is the arrangement of the land, the shepherds, and the tale that makes the effect. None of these is originary and each enters the narrator's consciousness in relation to the others: the shepherds are loved "not verily / For their own sakes, but for the fields and hills" ("Michael" 25–26); these lands exist as "occupation and abode," that is, already interpreted by rules of property (27). The poet's initiation into this life through the tale is a poetic version of a traditional contract; the tale constitutes an agreement between the Shepherds and the poet with respect to the land, nothing more than the expression of the natural relations already present. This vision, however, is a mystification in that the poem itself is dedicated to naturalizing the transfer of the poem from the oral shepherds to the writing poet. But Wordsworth had another version of how he came by the tale available to him, at least imaginatively, and the stress in articulating this transfer for Wordsworth can be seen in lines from *Ballad Michael*, an unpublished precursor:

Two shepherds we have, the two wits of the dale
Renown'd for song, satire, epistle and tale—

. . . .

To this sheepfold they went and a doggerel strain
They carved on a stone in the wall to explain
The cause of old Michael's decay.

> But all their suggestion and taunts to repeat,
> . . . .
> My pen it would sadly distress.
> (7–15, Butler and Green 319)

Here, the shepherds are already too empowered, capable of poetic genres and of writing in a way that would make the sheep-fold's intelligibility not depend on the narrator/Wordsworth. It is not the poet as "Man," but as metonymized by his "pen" (reduced to his labor), that would be distressed in being revealed. In "Michael," Wordsworth justifies his telling of the tale at two levels, both focused on their reproducibility:

> Therefore, although it be a history
> Homely and rude, I will relate the same
> For the delight of a few natural hearts,
> And with yet fonder feeling, for the sake
> Of youthful Poets, who among these Hills
> Will be my second self when I am gone.
> (34–39)

Both "Therefore" and "For" indicate justifications, one of which slides into the other. First, the tale is told because of its effect on the poet; second, it is told for the effect it will have on "a few natural hearts," and on "youthful Poets." But these youthful poets become the narrator's second self, and so the two explanations become, if not identical, variations on one another. The replacement of Dorothy as Wordsworth's second self at the end of the 1798 *Lyrical Ballads* ("Tintern Abbey") by "youthful poets" corresponds to the more public profile of the second edition. The perspective of the tale being transferred from shepherd to shepherd has modulated through the poet's own youth to the transfer from poet to poet. This shift is not entire—the "natural hearts" do matter—nor is it disingenuous—Wordsworth is aware of his copyright which radically alters the configuration of the transfer.

The shift from shepherd to poet as the source of value replays the historical change from traditional contracts that reflected social values to written, empowered instruments that could determine those values. The doubling of value, which, in the case of contract, was the reinforcement of an original (mythic) social contract that strengthened the national economy, has its insufficient precursor in Michael's continual doublings. Besides the examples of doubling already discussed, Michael doubles the land he owns through long toil, and it is this gain, not the entire land, that the surety threatens; the forfeiture is "little less / than half his substance" and when Michael inherited, "not more / Than half my inheritance was mine" (226, 385–86; the line breaks enforce the grammatical mirroring). But, for Michael, the doubled land is the whole land, both increased and unified, and its division would be disastrous. So, having doubled in spoken language at the sheep-fold/covenant what he had first doubled in labor, Michael sends Luke to the city.

In sixteen lines, the good reports of Luke degenerate into his escape from "ignominy and shame" by "seek[ing] a hiding-place beyond the seas" (456). Wordsworth avoids portraying the degradation of the city, and Luke's offense is, like his words throughout the poem, rendered vaguely, as is his kinsman's failure, within the older forms of obligation that motivate Michael, to take proper care of Michael's child. By focusing on Michael, Wordsworth centers the reader's sympathy there, and thus allows a reading in which, as Geoffrey Hartman puts it, "The poet is Michael's true heir" (*Wordsworth's Poetry* 266). Kurt Heinzelman concurs with Hartman's appraisal, but I would modify it more along the lines of Susan Eilenberg's assessment of "Michael" as "a work of usurpation" (*Strange Power* 97).

The case for associating Wordsworth with Luke is reinforced by the *Ballad Michael* (Butler and Green 598–601), which offers yet another way in which the poet may have come by the tale. In the fragment, as a correction for the false "pastoral ballad" that is "sung far & near," the speaker proposes to relate what Michael told him while they sat "by the ~~edge~~/side of his sheepfold." The manuscript (DC MS 15, 94^{r}) then breaks off and picks up with what becomes the core moment of "Michael," when Michael is telling his son that the sheep-fold can be "Thy anchor and watchtower a bond between thee." After a page break, on 93^{v}, come the fragmentary words "He [?stopp'd] & beginning to weep/He we[?t] [?lik] like [?an] infant & [?]." Although the ink on the manuscript suggests that the "He" here is Michael speaking to his son, it may also be Micheal speaking *about* his son and *to* the narrator who stands where once Luke did. Neither speech nor speech act can be completed. This palimpsestic association, however, reveals equally the extent to which the poet, in standing in for Luke, usurps him and figures even Luke as a potential usurper: when Michael suggests that the land could not bear any other "Master," he makes no exception for Luke, whom, both Michael and Isabel hint, he will outlive. Significantly, in reworking the frame of the tale, Wordsworth writes out any direct contact between his narrating voice and Michael, suggesting that such contact would undermine the transition of power that the poem enacts.

Finally Michael has no signifiable heir. Like Bateman, Wordsworth is uneasily aligned with the stranger who comes into possession of the "Evening Star" by strictly legal means. The Oak remains a reminder of Michael but is compromised as a symbol within the *Lyrical Ballads* by "The Oak and the Broom," which retells the homily of an unbending tree that breaks in the storm while a flexible broom survives. The "real" pastoral tradition that created Michaels has given rise to a new pastoral tradition of the poet whose speech constitutes a covenant by virtue of its labor. Rhetorically, Wordsworth reconciles the fissure in contracts by making his speech performative, and thus the contract and the consideration validating it become one act; yet even this rhetoric depends for its effect on its reiteration.

Michael's inability to join his speech and his action ultimately exclude him from his community and his own labor. The son fails in the city and his father, living through that failure, leaves the unfinished monument of the sheep-fold, and the estate, as Michael feared, goes into "a stranger's hand" (241, 485); this hand, twice invoked, holds what Luke's symbolic hand gesture (signature) cannot do. Michael goes to the sheep-fold and renders it in his melancholy complete ("by the Sheep-fold, sometimes was he seen" 467). But it is, for all others, incomplete—and that incompleteness is a violation of the covenant exactly reciprocal to Luke's:

> 'tis believ'd by all
> That many and many a day he thither went,
> And never lifted up a single stone.
>
> (473–75)

Michael's reality is absorbed into the community's perception of him; this inverts the earlier view, in which Michael's household, by virtue of its regular light, guided the community. The stranger is from afar, indifferent to the cottage which is destroyed; "the ploughshare has been through the ground / On which it stood" (486–87). The ploughshare, that into which all swords were to be beaten, has become an instrument of violence against land, and against the community, as Wordsworth reminds the reader of the communal function of the cottage by recalling its name, "The Evening Star" (485) in the line previous to describing its destruction.

Yet, the stranger is already figured, first in the estranged nephew and second in the remade Richard Bateman, and more obliquely, perhaps in the capitalistic "agent" (Hill 25) who distributed Isabel's flaxen thread. The disjunction between the right of property earned through work and that of ownership by legal contract (the surety is the emblem) lies at the heart of this tragedy, a tragedy to Michael, to his community, and to the reader to the extent that we have invested ourselves in the poem. It is also a victory of storytelling, and of the reciprocal labor of reader and writer, because the poet, like the reader, turns from the "public" and professional way, in order, like the tourists about whom Wordsworth felt so ambivalent, to return again to it with the *publication* of the *Lyrical Ballads*. Wordsworth wrote to Poole: "This Poem has, I know, drawn tears from the eyes of more than one . . .; and moreover, persons who never wept, in reading verse, before. This is a favourable augury for me" (LEY 322). The victory is in the experience of the tragedy, and if, ultimately, legalistic binds are what the final image of the poem overcomes, what is crucial as an augury for Wordsworth is his discovery of a way to overcome those bonds by constructing new, powerful ones, bonds wrought from sympathies that readers have never before possessed. Unlike Michael's contract or Luke's silent, unknowing resistance, Wordsworth's speech act may yet do. These new bonds, however, are constructed by rewriting the old ones.

THREE

Marketing the Professions: Addison, Hume, Wordsworth

In "Michael," the shepherd discovers himself overwhelmed by (and overinvested in) an economy, metonymized as "unforeseen misfortune," that had remained largely invisible to him. This invisibility is posed in a reciprocal relation to the mistakes and blindnesses of middle-class readers to whom the poem is addressed. Once they have turned their steps "from the public way" (probably improved by public funding), readers are confronted with a series of interpretive problems. First, because the "pastoral Mountains front you, face to face," the reader "will suppose that with an upright path / Your feet must struggle" (3–5); next, there is "one object [the sheep-fold itself] which you might pass by, / Might see and notice not" (15–16); and as the poem develops, the narrator continues to correct presuppositions assumed to be held by the reader. If Michael cannot negotiate the "City," the term for the economic center of London, neither can the middle-class reader negotiate the hills alone. Wordsworth proposes to act as a guide, by furnishing a story that will render the "object" intelligible; in exchange, the reader agrees to be figured as a "you" (1, 3, 5, 15) distinct from the "Public way" and, by the logic of pronoun reference, constituted in a binary with the author. Rather than meeting the "pastoral Mountains . . . face to face," the reader is asked to imagine the reading of the poem itself as a face-to-face exchange.

The poem seems to endorse the eighteenth-century truism recorded by Burke in 1796: "Men are not tied to one another by papers and seals. They are led to associate by resemblances, by conformities, by sympathies" ("First Letter on a Regicide Peace" 247). Yet the inscripting of the tale of Michael projects it into the world of papers and seals, and, similarly, the proponents of resemblences, conformities, and sympathies throughout the eighteenth century from Addison to Burke proposed these natural connections in order to reinforce social and economic contracts, both literal and metaphorical. Jerome Christensen has articulated this tension in terms of Cicero's importance to Hume as a model who must be exceeded. The "orator's centrality must be [i.e., seemed to Hume] a literal fact" while "the modern man of letters is, on the contrary, situated in the midst of a people whose very dispersion makes the actual fact of a center only a metaphor. If he is central, it is not because he resides in a territorial, institutional, or political center but because of his symbolic role and symbolizing practice" (*Practicing Enlightenment* 126).

The paradox within "Michael," in which the poet re*tells* through writing the shepherd's oral tale, is that poetry is afforded the particular status within the world of letters of being immune from the transformational and reifying power writing had exerted over orality. As Mary Jacobus has observed, "where Hannah More wished to edify the semi-literate, Wordsworth was asking his literate readers to think about their own code" (*Tradition* 239). Moreover, Wordsworth wished to rearticulate that code, or, in Richard Bourke's amendation, "the dominant code of political culture as [Wordsworth] perceived it" (*Romantic Discourse and Political Modernity* 128), to preserve for the poet a representational power which was not proscribed by the very fact of writing.

But, as an early reader of my asessment of "Michael" asked, if Michael cannot complete the sheep-fold because he is paralyzed by a conflicted awareness of his bad faith, then just what saves the reader's imaginative act of completion from the bad faith of nostalgia? Further, what is *our* relation to the legal-economic developments that have destroyed Michael and his family? These are crucial questions, precisely because they reveal that the foundation of Wordsworth's contract is no more than its ceaseless reassertion of its own validity; and this depends upon the reiterate structure of middle-class literacy. In keeping with the emerging ideology of individualism, the reader as a "you" constructs individuality from the exchange with the writer (while suspending investment in the "public way"); but this "you" is possible only as a collective being, one bound within the system of economics that allows for middle-class readers. The power of the poem's nostalgia is in rendering momentarily invisible the reader's own world and his reliance on legal identity, in order to address the reader, as Wordsworth put it in the 1802 Preface, "not as a lawyer, a physician, a mariner, an astronomer or a natural philosopher, but as a Man" (*Lyrical Ballads* 258).

Wordsworth is here working within an eighteenth-century strategy of mystification, in which, as Bourke puts it, the "'polite arts' are located outside the mechanisms of social causation" (*Modernity* 1): "The 'gradual sequestration of the aesthetic realm'. . . became possible in the context of the establishment of commercial relations as a dominant concern for political inquiry: 'culture' in the eighteenth century—in Addison, in Hume, in Smith—was taken to demonstrate the autonomy of taste in relation to social and economic expansion" (*Modernity* 151, note omitted). This process, however, was enmeshed within a reciprocal project which Terry Eagleton describes with reference to Adam Smith's *Theory of Moral Sentiments:* "The whole of social life is aestheticized. . . . A sound political regime is one in which subjects conduct themselves gracefully—where . . . the law is no longer external to individuals but is lived out, with fine cavalier insouciance, as the very principle of their free identities" (*Ideology* 37).

In these two mutually constitutive programs—divorcing the aesthetic realm from the political, and aestheticizing the social world—the role of the professional writer is secured, and it is this legacy that Wordsworth exploits in his own poetic development. Therefore, in order to understand the professional Wordsworth's self-fashioning as a poet, I want to turn to three precursors: Addison's Spectator, David Hume, and finally, a younger Wordsworth who, not certain of his career as a professional poet, considered forming a journal to intervene in the turbulent political world of the mid-1790s. For all these figures, self-fashioning required representing themselves with respect both to the marketplace and to the legal discourse by which the marketplace was structured; it depended, at the same time, upon disarticulating this connection through the construction of a domain of "natural" behaviors, sentiments, and sympathies, which could, in turn, be redeployed within both legal and economic institutions but would not be recognized as produced by those institutions.

Addison, Hume, and the Economics of Letters

> I thought I might say to him, "Good Charon, I have been correcting my works for a new edition. Allow me a little time, that I may see how the Public receives the alterations." But Charon would answer, "When you have seen the effect of these, you will be for making other alterations. There will be no end of such excuses; so, honest friend, please step into the boat."—David Hume, on his death bed, as quoted by Adam Smith

In *The Great Transformation: The Political and Economic Origins of Our Time*, Karl Polanyi has insisted that the development of the late eighteenth-century English economy required three ideological transformations by which human effort, land, and money each became commodities that could be subjected to the operations of the market. In its final form, the factual existence of these markets is demarcated by scarcity elsewhere (produced, for example, by competitive wage markets); and the fictional character of commodification is obscured since it is experienced in the lived alienation of worker, owner, and financier. This commodification, however, had initially to be achieved despite the natures (as understood in mercantilism) of these three "elements of industry" as things categorically *not* produced for sale: "Labor is only another name for a human activity which goes with life itself . . . ; land is only another name for nature, which is not produced by man; actual money, finally, is merely a token of purchasing power which, as a rule, is not produced at all." The creation of fictional commodities, "therefore, supplies a vital organizing principle in regard to the whole of society" (*Transformation* 72–73).

Edmund Burke offers a polemic defense of commodified labor in his "Thoughts and Details on Scarcity." He accepts an economy marked by a troublesome relation of property and labor, intensified by the famine and war that occasioned these "Thoughts" addressed to Pitt in 1795. He asserts, "Labour is . . . a commodity, and as such, an article of trade. If I am right in this notion, then labour must be subject to all the laws and principles of trade. . . . When any commodity is carried to market, it is not the necessity of the vender, but the necessity of the purchaser that raises the price" ("Thoughts and Details on Scarcity" 126). The Malthusian premise, and consequence, of this analysis is that "to provide for us in our necessities is not in the power of Government" (120). The strategic use of "us" universalizes the commodified status of the laborer's body, and at the same time insists on the individual's responsibility in choosing what commodity—body, turnips, scribblings—to bring to market. Characteristically, the laborer is at a disadvantage in an exchange because, unlike mercantile commodities, such work cannot be stored for later deployment or operate apart from the laborer's physical self. Professionals, however, by transforming their knowledge (figured as the quintessence of their labor) into words, books, writs, prescriptions, and other written forms, commodify their own work, and can, in Jerome Christensen's formulation of the exiled writer, "hope to amass disparate reputations into the symbolic capital of universal fame" (*Practicing Enlightenment* 85). Professionals participated in the fictional commodification of their own intellectual labor to gain a privileged position vis-à-vis both the common laborer and an aristocracy still powerful but hearing voices prophesying destruction.[1]

Modern professions, Magali Sarfatti Larson contends in *The Rise of Professionalism: A Sociological Analysis*, "are a typical product of the 'great transformation.' They emerge, thus, as the age-old foundations of status are being destroyed by the twin processes of urbanization and industrialization. . . . [T]he increasingly complex social division of labor opens new roles at the top of the ladder" (76). The professions were both a "typical product" and a typical producer of the transformation. The career of the professional provided, as Larson notes, "a pattern of organization of the self" (229), but this pattern was itself the work performed, and hence produced, by the professional. The self, considered as a product, required institutional mechanisms for maintaining itself distinct from the individual body; the materials necessary for textual circulation allowed the incorporation of writers into Authors and, on the consuming side, the transformation of people into a Public hungry for pamphlets, legal reports, sermons, and other encoded professional selves. Second, professions were (and are) characterized by speech, which is at once the description of their labor and the labor itself.[2] When an observer in 1680 noted that "it has now come to a Civil War, not with the sword, but law" (quoted in Michael Landon, *The Triumph of the Lawyers* 101), he was confirming the power legal speech had acquired. This was the power the eighteenth-century professional writers sought to replicate.

The proliferation of English professionals in the eighteenth century did not involve the creation of new occupations.[3] Lawyers, doctors, and writers are found far into English antiquity; and through such groupings as the Inns of Court and theater companies limited by royal charter, fragments of these professions were organized into social and economic structures.[4] By a modern profession, then, I mean the reorganization of previously recognized occupations through specific strategies that made the knowledge of the professional appear as a commodity both necessary to the nation's well-being and as real (thing-like) as a piece of cloth or a loaf of bread, and as subject to harvests of scarcity and plenty. This procedure depended upon another economic transformation, namely that in becoming a commodity, an object becomes abstracted and ceases to function as a thing. Thus, cloth, bread, writing, and bodies could, with properly engineered representation, meet on the same abstract field of exchange value; such transformability corresponds to the development of advertisement as a powerful print medium. Marcus Wood has detailed the enormous development of advertisement in the first half of the eighteenth century and has noted its influence across a range of discourses: "Mainstream political and literary authors including Defoe, Swift, Addison, Pope, the Fieldings, Dr. Johnson, Wilkes, and Junius analysed and experimented with advertising in a variety of contexts" (*Radical Satire and Print Culture* 19–20).

Professionalism required both the development of a specialized language, and, conversely, the naturalization of that language as the necessary form to perform the function of the profession. Adam Smith, commenting on the commercial dimension of the law, asserts that European nations

> regulate, upon most occasions, the payments of the attornies and clerks of court, according to the number of pages they had occasion to write; the court, however, requiring each page should contain so many lines, and each line so many words. In order to increase their payment, the attornies and clerks have contrived to multiply words beyond all necessity, to the corruption of the law language of, I believe, every court of justice in Europe. A like temptation might perhaps occasion a like corruption in the form of law proceedings. (*Wealth of Nations* 242–43)

For most professionals, word production was, arguably, secondary to the announced tasks of curing a patient or winning a law suit, although for doctor and lawyer, payment was rarely contingent on results. For the professional writer, however, the production of words was both the means and end of the activity. The professional writer hovers between being worker and owner, in that producing an object for sale like a worker does means simultaneously producing a property, a copyright, possession of which is unaltered by sales of the written object. The distinctions between work and text, book and copyright, represent the critical and legal institutionalization of the peculiar status of professional writers: the value of ownership is not in the possession but in the dispersion of property. To put it in the terms of market economics, the subsistence production of a writer was simultaneously a surplus production because, since the labor of the writer was a commodity fictionalized by the writing, the writing, as a commodity, continued to duplicate the labor through its dispersal.

The *Spectator*

For Joseph Addison, the great popularizer of John Locke's philosophy, the three great professions were "Divinity, Law and Physick" (*Spectator* No. 21, 1: 88); by the operation of the *Spectator*, he adds another, that of the Writer. Throughout the *Spectator*, other professions provide both models and subject matter, but always subsumed into what might be called the metaprofession of word production.

In the opening issue, the first episode concerning the Spectator is truncated in a Shandyesque way that anticipates his career: "There runs a Story in the Family, that when my Mother was gone with Child of me about three Months, she dreamt that she was brought to Bed of a Judge: Whether this might proceed from a Law-Suit which was then depending [i.e., pending] in the Family, or my Father's being a Justice of the Peace, I cannot determine; for I am not so vain as to think it presaged any Dignity that I should arrive at in my future Life, though that was the Interpretation which the Neighborhood put upon it" (*Spectator* No. 1, 1: 2). The fairytale beginning, exploiting the slipperiness between story and history, wavers between a pseudobiography and a small myth. No claim for truth is made, except the fact of the story's being told ("There runs a story . . ."), a claim validated by its appearance in *The Spectator*. The communal interpretation of the Spectator's birth awaits its fulfillment in his literary birth within the larger serial community of subscribers and readers. The doubling of the father as party to a suit and Justice of the Peace locates him as object and as interpreter of law, and points the Spectator toward a professional career (a mark of "Dignity"), likely in the law. The narrative, however, never reveals a career, but paints a man capable of infinite circulation and observation. He is chameleon in aspect: "I have been taken for a Merchant upon the *Exchange* for above these ten Years, and sometimes pass for a *Jew* in the Assembly of Stock-Jobbers at *Jonathan's*" (No. 1, 1: 4). Although an observer, he fits in, reproducing without disrupting the economic and social sites of human interaction.

The Spectator's silent absorption into his surroundings allows the empirical gathering of information that results in the *Spectator*, yet the *Spec-*

tator itself, as the vehicle of his speaking, is associated with the polite society of his club, the site where that data is interpreted and transformed into maxims: "Where-ever I see a Cluster of People I always mix with them, though I never open my Lips but at my own Club" (1: 4). While his public silence becomes the occasion for written communication (1: 4–5), his polite "speech" reconstructs other linguistic productions as similar to collected data, rather than as equivalent to his own utterances. The first issue ends by announcing that "tho' our Club meets only on *Tuesdays* and *Thursdays*, we have appointed a Committee to sit every Night, for the Inspection of all such Papers as may contribute to the Advancement of the Publick Weal" (1: 4).

The metaphor of "sitting" situates the Committee as judges taking writs under consideration, and the aesthetic standards are aligned with the social goal of advancing the "Public Weal." The exchange between contributors and Spectator becomes a hierarchy of letters grafted onto a legalistic social structure. As the Club expands its meeting times, the Spectator shifts terms from "Club" to "Society"; "Spectator, No. 2" opens, "The first of our Society is a Gentleman of *Worcestershire*" (1: 7). Like Chaucer opening his "General Prologue" with the Knight, Addison puts the Baronet, Sir Roger de Coverley, first; but where Chaucer moves next to the Knight's son, the Spectator places a "Batchelor, who is a Member of the *Inner-Temple*" as the "Gentleman next in Esteem and Authority among us" (1: 9). This gesture does not replace family order with social rank, but recognizes that they no longer coincide. The right of inheritance has given place to the legal structure that authorizes inheritance and Addison constructs a mild joke that plays on this slippage; the lawyer has "chosen his Place of Residence rather to obey the Directions of an old humoursom Father, than in Pursuit of his own Inclinations. He was placed there to study the Laws of the Land, and is the most learned of any of the House in those of the stage" (1: 9). If patriarchy seems to suffer in the small satire, legal authority is given wider scope in its generalized form: laws structure both court and stage, and, if the Batchelor seems a poor law student, he is an "excellent Critick." A "Merchant" having "natural unaffected Eloquence" and the doubly punning name of "Freeport" is next (1: 10). This is not the Chaucerian hierarchy, which orders and encompasses the entire world through a structure of resemblances; membership proper ends with an aristocrat, the gallant

"Will. Honeycomb" (1: 12), and adds "a Clergyman, a very Philosophick Man," who, since he seldom visits, cannot be certainly "account[ed] . . . one of our Company" (1: 13); he is "among Divines what a Chamber-Counsellor is among Lawyers" (1: 13). Professions, linked through analogy, are located at both the center and margins of a society framed by aristocrats.

The Spectator's noncareer is precisely the career of the eighteenth-century man of letters, and the text insists on the literal aspect of a man composed of letters.[5] The Spectator, still in the introductory number, comments that he has "given the Reader just so much of my History and Character, as to let him see I am not altogether unqualified for the Business I have undertaken" (1: 5). He reserves "other Particulars" of his life to create a coherence in the subsequent numbers, and he hopes finally "to Print my self out, if possible, before I Die" (1: 5). To Print himself out is the experiment, and on its results hangs the question of whether writing can adequately represent the society in which it functions. The "self" in this formulation is fully amenable to Print, or rather, fully expendable as Print. For the Spectator, a corporate production, this formulation is a tautology; unembodied, he exists only so far as he is projected into his periodical.

David Hume

David Hume presents an interesting comparison to the Spectator. In his philosophical work, Hume posited repetition as the fundamental structure of knowledge; from it, he derives scientific causation, social organization, and individual experience. Moreover, as Jerome Christensen has demonstrated, the structures of repetition characterize the Humean literary career as itself a repetition of the Spectator's periodicity. Like the Spectator's, Hume's existence, as he represented it, was thoroughly positional: "For my part, when I enter most intimately into what I call *myself*, I always stumble on some particular perception or other, of heat or cold, light or shade, love or hatred, pleasure or pain. I never can catch *myself* at any time without a perception, and never can observe any thing but the perception" (*A Treatise of Human Nature* 252).

His final public act of iteration is the pseudoliterary, pseudolegal documentation of his life, a short biography that, by the provisions of his will, was to appear at the beginning of all editions of his work. Titled "My Own

Life," the document both "owns" the life, claiming its possession, and disperses it across his other literary productions: "It may be thought an instance of vanity that I pretend at all to write my life; but this Narrative shall contain little more than the History of my Writings; as, indeed, almost all my life has been spent in literary pursuits and occupations" (in *The History of England* 1: xxvii). To "write my life" is to achieve, or at least to assert the achievement of, the Spectator's task of printing himself out; it is to profess and professionalize by repetition the self that cannot be perceived.

Early in "My Own Life," Hume notes: "My studious disposition, my sobriety, and my industry, gave my family a notion that law was a proper profession for me; but I found an unsurmountable aversion to every thing but the pursuits of philosophy and general learning" (xxvii). Like the Batchelor of Addison's club, he slides from the narrow world of law to the wider but equally regulatory and linguistic realm of polite letters: the Batchelor "better understood" the writings of "*Aristotle* and *Longinus* . . . than *Littleton* or *Cooke*," while when Hume's family "fancied [he] was poring upon Voet and Vinnius, Cicero and Virgil were the authors which I was secretly devouring" (xxvii). That both figures must fight presumptions about their interest in law suggests its crucial importance as a differential by which the new man of letters can be recognized. At the same time, both Addison's Spectator and Hume's autobiographical voice construct a tradition through the appropriation that disciplinary boundaries allow, as Hume's decision to pair Cicero, an active jurist, with Virgil and against Vinnius suggests.

Hume's self-representation embodies Jerome Christensen's description of the man of letters who projects his "body of writing in a symbolic practice, a career, that exploited, facilitated, and epitomized the operations of the commercial society which it persuasively represented" (*Practicing Enlightenment* 4). The economic dimensions of such careers were contingent on a continual engagement with concepts of law. In this sense, Addison was a crucial precursor for Hume, and William Wordsworth, publishing his *Lyrical Ballads* at the end of the eighteenth century, an important follower.

Professions aim to represent to a society its own structure as acceptable, even desirable, and as dependent for stability on the profession that puts forward the representation.[6] Antonio Gramsci viewed the role of the intellectual as handmaiden to a social class: "Every social class, coming into existence on the original basis of an essential function in the world of economic production, creates with itself, organically, one or more groups of intellectuals who give it homogeneity and consciousness of its function not only in the economic field but in the social and political field as well" ("The Formation of Intellectuals" 118).[7] This formulation accepts a necessary material priority of the empowered class over the intellectual, because, for Gramsci, discourses such as law always assumed the role of legitimizing the discontinuities of power into a social continuum. But the "essential function" of a social class itself is an interpretive act. While professional classes provided legitimacy through constructions such as property, mental illness, and aesthetics, they also provided the means for shifts in power by creating the very lacks that could be filled by new "essential functions."[8] Certain eighteenth-century figures such as political economists fill the ancillary ideological role for a rising property class by arguing for the value of a market economy per se.

Adam Smith, an admirer of David Hume's *Treatise of Human Nature*, lectured on law and ethics as Chair of Logic at Glasgow University before producing *The Wealth of Nations* (1776), the fifth book of which makes an extended argument for the legislation and regulation of a *laissez-faire* marketplace.[9] When ideologists such as Smith used a principle of self-interest to liberate the new property class from tradition, that same principle allowed their own works to circulate within the markets they were defining and to construct their own intellectual labor as an economic force. In this manner, individual professions accumulate capital not only within the market but as the outlines of the market. Their class interests are poised between those of the property owner and of the laborer.

The development of the market depended on the development of lack as a constitutive element of the market, and thus demanded that individuals seek, rather than adequate subsistence, considered (if not unchecked) gain. Hume grasped the literary possibilities of such a market; he realized that lack could be construed as the difference between the actual and the desired, and could be articulated as a presence within the human psyche and within society: "As man of letters, it is Hume's office to create that lack in others and in himself. It is the singularity of the Enlightenment man of letters that his lack of anything in particular is the condition of his art of the general, of his ability to *form* by affiliation a class that could reasonably hope to dominate not by virtue of a God-given right or a historically sanctioned prerogative but by means of a refined and refining prose" (Christensen, *Practicing Enlightenment* 4). This refined prose, however, had to be deployed through notions of right and prerogative, through an allegiance to the king who was the basis of copyright law, and through an expressed loyalty to the wealthy merchant class who could physically produce and circulate that prose. In essence, the exchange of prose for currency had to be articulated in the prose as an exchange of presences. When contrasted with the materiality of traditional barter exchange, the exchange of money and print switched one symbol for another, both denoting lack; money was the sign of materials sold, print the mark of an absent (often anonymous) author.

Traditionally, money was invoked to exchange with a stranger (Polanyi, *Transformation* 58), so the prose had also to readjust the symbolism of money, to resituate its transparency as something at the heart of all human exchange, not only of those marginal exchanges in surplus markets. How to discuss lack, while concealing its presence in the very discourse, was a problem Hume devoted his career to solving. The "process" of Hume's career constituted his solution to this problem; "the man of letters' practice was 'maintained at a continuous present by various devices of repetition'" (Christensen, *Practicing Enlightenment* 12, quoting Northrop Frye). The repetitions epitomized human behavior; the typical Hume essay presents a political point, demonstrates its truth, and then, as a demonstration not of truth but rather of continuity, provides historical examples of the same problem in other cultures, frequently the Roman and Athenian empires.

In 1752, the year he was appointed Keeper of the Advocates' Library in Edinburgh, Hume published a collection titled *Essays Moral, Political, and Literary, Part Two* as a supplement to a volume published in 1742. Despite the casual title, the fourteen essays of this volume (some previously published) sustain an argument for the inevitable stability of the market economy as mediated by the law. Entailed in the rhetoric of such an argument is, paradoxically, the conclusion that there is no need to make it; that is, the constitution is self-reliant and capable of transparent self-representation. Hume recognizes that this claim of self-reliance is fictitious, and he chooses the rhetorical stance of indifference, reminiscent of the Spectator's remote objectivity, to suggest inevitability. [10]

The first nine essays concern the development of commerce and address such topics as money,[11] taxes,[12] and the relation of the balance of trade to the balance of power in Europe. Hume constantly proposes equalities and correspondences: decrying public credit, he asks: "For why should the case be so different between the public and the individual, as to make us establish different maxims for both?" (*Essays Moral* 347). Although posed as an issue of economic practice, Hume's argument continually presses at correspondences.

He interrupts these economic reflections with an essay entitled "Of some Remarkable Customs" which he introduces with a seemingly clear thesis: "I shall observe three remarkable customs in three celebrated governments; and shall conclude from the whole, that all general maxims in politics ought to be established with great caution; and that irregular and extraordinary appearances are frequently discovered in the moral, as well as in the physical world" (*Essays Moral* 363). The three historical examples are from Athens, Rome, and England. The essay demonstrates, rather than its stated thesis, the regularity despite "extraordinary appearances" by which the constitution is identifiable. The Athenian government had an "indictment of illegality" which, according to Hume, provided that anyone proposing a law could be held legally liable for consequences detrimental to the state if the law were enacted. To demonstrate that "nothing was more commonly practiced," Hume provides three examples. In each case, however, the proposer of the law is acquitted—by a speech. Thus, that which appeared to infringe upon free speech provides a public forum for speech, including one "sublime piece of eloquence [by Demosthenes defending Ctesiphon for a law bestowing honors on Demosthenes], that has ever since been the admiration of mankind" (365). The law, Hume concludes, was deemed necessary in the Athenian democracy because all citizens voted with impunity and it was necessary "at least, to check their demagogues and counsellours." Hume portrays the Athenian democracy as a competitive marketplace of speech, and the liability is equivalent to legal checks on the English free-market economy, which ultimately strengthen the market and culture itself ("sublime eloquence").

As Christensen observes, Hume's ability to abstract particular arguments into general representations characterizes his productions. Boswell's Johnson would have agreed. Regarding Adam Smith, he observes that "a man who has never been engaged in trade himself may undoubtedly write well upon trade, and there is nothing that requires more to be illustrated by philosophy than trade does" (*Life of Johnson* 682–83). Johnson argues that traders in the market have too limited a perspective, where the philosopher may have "extensive views" (an echo to his own meditation on "The Vanity of Human Wishes"). In the same paragraph, Johnson comments that Blackstone "had not been much in practice when he published his *Commentaries.*" The general point is that the understanding of trade and law is derived from a vantage that allows abstraction.

Hume, arguing in "Of Civil Liberty" that a monarchy can be a "*government of Laws, not of Men,*" laments the current state of the polite arts, since they are linked to the commerce that would permit a monarchy of laws: "The elegance and propriety of style have been very much neglected among us. We have no dictionary of our language, and scarcely a tolerable grammar" (*Essays Moral* 85).[13] Johnson's *Dictionary* sought to fill this need. Alvin Kernan describes Johnson's contribution to the print industry: "The *Dictionary* was in the first place a practical handbook needed by the printing business to establish the authoritative spellings and, to only a slightly lesser degree, the fixed meanings which print, with its inbuilt tendency toward systematic regularity, required for its day-to-day operations of editing manuscripts and setting type with some consistency" (*Printing Technology, Letters & Samuel Johnson* 184). Further, Johnson's emphasis on certain aspects of dictionary making contributes to the regularization of the concept of the regular. His strategy, derived from personal history and economic context, inflects his vocabulary with legal discourse. His *Plan of an English Dictionary* distinguishes words based on status: "naturalized and incorporated" as against "aliens, . . . which are rather auxiliaries than subjects" (6). The rules governing orthography, pronunciation, syntax, and phraseology must be ordered, since, as Johnson says of etymology, it "now stands in our dictionaries a confused heap of words without dependence, and without relation" (14). He says that the rules of style, "like those of law, arise from precedents often repeated, collect the testimonies on both sides, and endeavor to discover and promulgate the decrees of custom, who has so long possessed, whether by right or by usurpation, the sovereignty of words" (25). At its most ambitious, the *Dictionary*, for which the *Plan* was an advertisement, turns the English heap of words into language by arraying them in fields of dependence and relation, and so continues the Humean project of systemization and abstraction.

For Wordsworth (for whom the term *system-maker* has remained in the critical discourse from his Preface to the *Lyrical Ballads*, through the contemporary reviews into the 1840s, and down to current New Historical work), the possibilities opened by the eighteenth century allowed him to conceive of his own poetic practice as representing, and producing, a wholeness which could be named the Poet. Such a being was a particular abstraction and systemization of the self (of "Man") that not only characterized human nature but enacted and reproduced it without the disruption of individual particularity. Wordsworth's presentation of the disciplinary development of poetry in his 1802 "Appendix on Poetic Diction" for *Lyrical Ballads* is able to produce the poet's commonness as the sign of his uniqueness: "It is indeed true that the language of the earliest Poets was felt to differ materially from ordinary language, because it was the language of extraordinary occasions; but it was really spoken by men." The distinctiveness of poetry was not in itself, but in the scene (occasion) of its presentation, events of community agreement and sanctification. The "early" addition of meter "separated the genuine language of Poetry still further from common life"; this separation empowered poetry to move its auditor "in a way in which he had not been accustomed to be moved in real life." Rather than commemorating an extraordinary occasion, poetry produced one; its content *as poetry*, like law for Weber, moved from being substantive to formal, and this tendency continued until the poet regularly introduced "adulterated phraseology into his compositions" until "this language was received as a natural language; and, at length, by the influence of books upon men, did to a certain degree really become so" (Butler and Green 762).

It is, Wordsworth contends, thinking of the eighteenth century, this disciplinary history that accounts for poetry's current condition as "thrusting out of sight the plain humanities of nature by a motley masquerade of tricks, quaintnesses, heiroglyphics, and engimas" (762). The disdain for specialized language may seem to imply that Wordsworth would oppose the professionalization of poetry along the lines of the law, but this is only partly true. Because poetry's artificiality has become its "natural" language, Wordsworth's efforts to recover in his poetry a "real language of men" that will, he assumes, seem strange to his readers constitutes a reprofessionalization by which "the plain humanities of nature" can again be made visible, but necessarily through the mediated experience of Wordsworth.

The Economics of Literary Philanthropy

Like David Hume before him, William Wordsworth sought to represent the market economy in a way that facilitated the financial and ideological success of his writing. The markets he encountered, however, were not isolated, but already marked by legal and ideological inscription. This condition, though not new, emerged into public visibility during the reaction to the French Revolution, which featured acrimonious debates about public credit, trade deficits, and national security. In the exchange between Burke and Paine, the attitudes taken on these issues became moral signs of personal and national integrity.[14] As commodified labor became the subject of increasing discussion,[15] legal interventions became more expansive and pervasive (see Polanyi's rehearsal of the antecedents to the Speenhamland Acts, *Transformation* 86–95). Wordsworth's task was neither to applaud nor to condemn these changes, but to suggest that poetic experience could mitigate dangers without squelching gains, and, more significantly, could question the grounds of such evaluations from a perspective not hopelessly compromised.

Like Addison's Spectator, an emblem of the circulating writer and the polite professional, Wordsworth ruled out the professions of law and clergy before turning to writing: "What is to become of me I know not; I cannot bow down my mind to take orders, and as for the law I have neither strength of mind purse or constitution, to engage in that pursuit" (LEY 112, 17 February 1794). In this letter to William Mathews, Wordsworth's lament resembles one Mathews had put forward a few years earlier, and Wordsworth's reply then responds well to his present quandary: "The field of Letters is very extensive, and it is astonishing if we cannot find some little corner, which with a little tillage will produce us enough for the necessities, nay even the comforts, of life" (LEY 76, 19 May 1792). Wordsworth's use of "Letters" implies a wide network of opportunity; he recognizes publishing, editing, journalism, and poetry as continuous,[16] and the modulation from the "necessities" to the "comforts" of life suggests the capitalistic management of a career in which literary status permits production beyond subsistence levels.

Mathews and Wordsworth had met at Cambridge, where "presumably," they "joined . . . in welcoming the events of 1789" (Nicholas Roe, *Wordsworth and Coleridge* 19–20). After leaving Cambridge, Mathews had been a teacher and in 1794 he was a resident of the Middle Temple and an experienced parliamentary reporter (LEY 48). His connections to law and education made him a good sounding board for Wordsworth, and their correspondence demonstrates Wordsworth's awareness of the public situation of writers. In the midst of the English reaction to the French Revolution, they planned a magazine for moral instruction and entertainment, which, though not realized, illuminates Wordsworth's emerging professionalism. The journal, tentatively titled *The Philanthropist, a Monthly Miscellany*, took up a theme of the "Friend to Man," that, already circulating in the moderate revolutionary discourses of the Girondins and of William Godwin, provided a trope to mediate (or create) a public self as the expression of a coherent private being. Nicholas Roe's analysis of these letters demonstrates their Godwinian strain, but this radicalism was even at its inception constrained within Wordsworth's ability to envision the project as economically viable. Wordsworth's attitudes in the letters construct a notion of literary professionalism that imagines exploiting the marketing potential of situating himself outside the dominant discourse. The remainder of this chapter examines Wordsworth's early ideas about literary persuasiveness in institutional contexts by delineating in terms of politics and audience the market he encountered in the 1790s; and by exploring in Wordsworth's letters to Mathews the relation of competing systems of value. In the final section, I discuss his recognition of the body as a contested site of legal and literary inscription to reassert more specifically Wordsworth's recognition of the connection between literary possibilities and legal power.

Controlling the Radical Market

Within a "field of Letters" self-conscious about the politics of audience, Wordsworth looked first to a republican magazine for his "little corner" of audience. William Galperin, borrowing terms from Charles Rzepka, accepts that Wordsworth was "constitutionally in need of an Other" both as audience and as reflection of his self but insists that in his "'professional' dispositions" Wordsworth "was able *as a poet* to satisfy that need immediately" in the imagining of his audience (*Revision and Authority in Wordsworth* 67). This "immediacy" is an illusion fostered by earlier modes of literary production in which the imaginative creation of the audience is sustained through the relatively unhampered dispersal of the text, as in the (self-represented) cases of the *Spectator* and David Hume. Writing as a potential poet and a potential radical in 1794, Wordsworth formulated a notion of audience against a complex background of the treason trials and suspension of *habeas corpus*, as well as a public debate regarding the true forms of justice and government. Imagining his audience in these terms was a crucial corollary to imagining his professional self as a social interventionist.

Thomas Erskine, in considering *The Causes and Consequences of the Present War with France*, locates the origin of the war as the "first Royal Proclamation against Seditious Writings on 21 May 1792":

> The proclamation had unquestionably for its object to spread the alarm against French principles; and to do it effectually, all principles were considered French by his Majesty's ministers which questioned the infallibility of their own government. . . . The spirit which became prevalent about this time, which bore down everything before it, and prepared the nation for war, was an absolute horror of everything connected with France. It confounded the casual intemperance of an enlarged and warm zeal for the freedom and happiness of mankind with a tendency to universal anarchy. (Quoted in Roe, *Wordsworth and Coleridge* 119)[17]

In Erskine's view, prohibiting debate blocked any rational resolution by sustaining a xenophobia that made the prohibition appear reasonable. The government, Erskine believed, was able to define "French principles" not by reference to France but by reifying as "English" its own principles and letting the contaminated term "French" denote all difference. Erskine's position resembled Godwin's arguments for open debate over libel laws: "From the collision of disagreeing accounts, justice and reason will be produced" (William Godwin, *Enquiry Concerning Political Justice* 598). Godwin reverses the juridical relation between the market of ideas and the courts. In the liberal formulation, the courts protect and judge the market;[18] in Godwin's position, the disclosure of truth by the collision of ideas provides the standards of justice. The current "injurious interference of political institutions" reserves judgment for easily corrupted courts, forces the anonymous appearance of publications, which makes assessing them more difficult, and provides an institutional excuse for insincerity (Godwin, *Political Justice* 599–600). Godwin's argument at the time and Erskine's retrospective analysis both suggest that the market of ideas shaped the ideas that circulated in it.

Wordsworth acknowledges this notion by lamenting the sameness of the current magazines, while denying them a genuine audience, as opposed to one manufactured by government subsidy and intervention: "Were we ignorant or wicked enough to be so employed [as producing a similar review], in our views of pecuniary advantage (from the public at least) we should be disappointed" (LEY 119, 23 May 1794). His parenthetical phrase implies that government patronage substitutes for a genuine public market in order to foster within the literary market the same illusions of representation to which the government pretends in the political realm. In refusing sameness, Wordsworth resists commodification by denying that all legally acquired money is of the same value regardless of its source. The exchange of free-market money from "the public" for a journal of reformist political possibilities would, by its contrast with the other magazines of ideological sameness, constitute an exchange of presence, not absence, because it would retain the character of face-to-face exchange.

But, because that face-to-face exchange was only rhetorical, entering the public discourse entailed producing a virtual self (the Spectator, the Rambler, the Friend) that risked re-representation, as the tradition of eighteenth-century parody showed. Consequently, one specific problem for Wordsworth was how to express a moderate republican view without being co-opted by, or shoved into, the violence of one side or the other. While in France, he had witnessed the moderate Girondins destroyed on those grounds.[19] They fell from power in October 1793 and twenty-one of them were brought to trial "not to discover whether the persons tried [were] guilty, but to justify their execution" and "advertise" their "overthrow." The trial, nonetheless, provided them a last forum, but this opportunity was forestalled by a resolution of the Convention that "after three days' hearing, the President of the court might closure the trial [that is, ask for a verdict], if the jury had declared that 'their conscience was sufficiently enlightened.'" On the sixth day of the trial, after three hours of deliberation by the jury, they were condemned. Their final symbolic speech act, a deliberate connection of their voices with the economy and legal system they had helped to forge, was throwing "*assignats* among the crowd, and cry[ing] *A nous, nos amis*"; the gesture of friendship was rejected as the crowd ripped up the notes and shouted "*Vive la république*" (J. M. Thompson, *The French Revolution* 370–72).[20] The Girondins had lost their audience, less through what they said than by how their words and symbols were appropriated, and Robespierre's reign of terror began.

While Wordsworth would not have understood the French trial only as a question of audience and economy, in the 1805 *Prelude* he recognized a continuity between speech and action, between commanding an audience and being driven to desperate acts. Moreover, he locates this realization at the start of the Terror, in a passage that moves from a legalistic register to contemplating outlaw activity and ends with a gesture at a transcendent historicity:

> I thought
> Of oppositions and of remedies:
> An insignificant stranger and obscure,
> Mean as I was, and little graced with power
> Of eloquence even in my native speech,
> And all unfit for tumult and intrigue,
> Yet would I willingly have taken up
> A service at this time for a cause so great,
> However dangerous. Inly I revolved
> How much the destiny of Man had still
> Hung upon single persons.
>
> (X 129–39)

The modesty is not false, but an appraisal of a poet who has not found his voice and who has not established in his own mind whether a modern poet could be one of those "single persons" on whom human destiny might hang.[21] The search for that voice could occur only within (or in concerted opposition to) the established institutions of language: the law, the church, the publishing industry.

Contemplating a journal in 1794 was a political act, one about which Dorothy assured their brother Richard that Wordsworth was "very cautious" and "well aware of the dangers of a contrary conduct" (LEY 121, 28 May 1794). The government's measures reflect not mindless oppression by a ruling class, but an accurate assessment of the periodical industry as a competing (if often allied) producer of value. Magazines circulated in a literary marketplace based on aristocratic values yet representing itself as a universalizing, and sometimes democratizing, force. Using the Edinburgh *Bee* as a model, Jon Klancher has shown that the "democratic 'exchange' of reading and writing depends on a hierarchical notion of the public, implying an intricate social chain of 'ranks,' 'gradations,' and 'degrees.' The social text of periodical writing thus joins two dissonant orders: inside the text, a communal, democratic exchange; outside the text, a hierarchically ranked world" (*Reading Audiences* 23). In the 1790s, any periodical would necessarily reinterpret the confrontation between aristocratic and universalizing impulses.

Maintaining an interchangeability between reader and writer, the equality the *Spectator* had represented as the "well-regulated Family" daily "serv[ing] up" the well-regulating periodical (*Spectator* No.10, 1:44), became a radical act, as E. P. Thompson's analysis of the London Corresponding Society (LCS) shows. The first leading rule of the Society, started in early 1792, was "that the number of our Members be unlimited," and the first task, assigned to Thomas Hardy, was the purchasing of paper "for the purpose of corresponding with like-minded groups in the country" (*The Making of the English Working Class* 19). These two gestures, one ideological and one material, merge into a reinterpretation of the ideas and materials that underpinned England's economic and legal structures. For the LCS, correspondence, in its complementary senses, authorized its potentially unlimited membership to represent itself in government; audience and political alignment were congruous. Within six months, two thousand "Tradesmen, Shopkeepers, and Mechanics" had joined, giving the required affirmation to this question: "Are you thoroughly persuaded that the welfare of these kingdoms require that every adult person, in possession of his reason, and not incapacitated by crimes, should have a vote for a Member of Parliament?" (quoted in Thompson, *Working Class*, 19). In reserving power for legal and medical institutions to disqualify persons from voting, the Society affirmed the social investment in law, but as secondary to the public right of representation.

For Hume, for Blackstone, and for his proponent Burke, order (and the disciplinary category of criminality) were possible only within a society governed by property relations, relations that universal suffrage would undercut by supplanting a system in which landowners controlled votes; Thomas Paine, the crucial ideologue for the LCS, observed that "one man in a hundred" can vote (*Rights of Man* 73).[22] Paine, who wished that "Mr. Burke possessed talents similar to the author of 'On the Wealth of Nations'" (*Rights* 75), did not propose to abolish property, but subsumed it into a social text at odds with Blackstone's constitutionalism. The controlling metaphors shifted in significance. Where property established rights for Blackstone, rights establish property for Paine. He draws implications for the nature of the judiciary: "A man, by natural right, has a right to judge in his own cause; and so far as the right of mind is concerned, he never surrenders it: But what availeth it him to judge, if he has not power to redress? He therefore deposits this right in the common stock of society, and takes the arm of society, of which he is a part, in preference and in addition to his own. Society *grants* him nothing. Every man is a proprietor in society and draws on the capital as a matter of right" (*Rights of Man* 68–69). The right of judgment, in this economically adumbrated model, is not reserved to the government, but attaches to any institution sufficiently transparent to maintain the will of individuals.[23] Where Burke had used the metaphor of a joint-stock company to explain the limits of individual rights, Paine reinterprets the financial metaphor to insist on those rights.[24] Each equates his own theory of rights to market economics in order to claim that the theory enables the marketplace. Not accidentally, each also claimed the skill, and right, of literary interpretation through a display of linguistic wit.

Continuing his attack against Burke in the preface of part two, Paine positions competing interpretations as questions both of debate and of institutional power: "'If,' says he [Burke], 'such writing [as part one of *Rights of Man*] shall be thought to deserve any other refutation than that of *criminal* justice.' Pardoning the pun, it must be *criminal* justice indeed that should condemn a work as a substitute for not being able to refute it" (*Rights* 155). Shifting the meaning of "criminal" from the domain of justice to a description of it, Paine subverts legal categories to emphasize that Burke does believe that legal condemnation is refutation, and so Paine seeks clemency among his readers.

Paine's pun was not pardoned by the law, and his trial is well regarded as a sustained, hostile interpretation of his work because his writing was an interpretation of the law; as the attorney general asked, "Can any thing add to his slander upon the constitution . . . more than that sweeping imputation upon the whole system of law that binds us together—namely, that it is null and void?" Arguing that law, as a coherent system, coheres the society, the attorney general deconstructs Paine's book, which made the same claim for itself, namely that its logical coherence mirrored and could produce a stronger social body politic. Here is the attorney general at work: "This is the gross artifice; and when you come to dissect the book in the careful manner that I have done, I believe you and every other reader will easily detect the artifice" (*Proceeding against Thomas Paine* 383).[25] In a telling hyperbole insinuating an infectious consumption, the attorney general observed that the book was "thrust into the hands of all persons . . . even children's sweetmeats were wrapped up with parts of this, and delivered into their hands, in the hope that they would read it" (*Proceeding against Thomas Paine*

381). In the rhetoric of such a submerged metaphor, legal interpretive strategies oppose other interpretive institutions. As Wordsworth detailed his plans for the *Philanthropist*, it was with the consciousness that his work must fit into this complex institutional debate, and, if it were to be useful, must transform the very terms of that debate.

Imagining/Managing Money and Geography

Wordsworth's letter of 23 May 1794 (LEY 118–120) to Mathews is the first about starting a journal.[26] He frames the subject with two difficulties of writing. It opens: "I am sorry I did not receive your's of the 11th till yesterday, as I certainly should have answered it sooner,"[27] and it ends with the postscript: "This pen and ink are so bad, I can scarce write with them at all." The implication is that Mathews's efforts to read the poor ink are matched by, and originate with, Wordsworth's problem of writing with it. The letter announces Wordsworth's confidence in overcoming both problems—circulation of the mails and the material impediments to producing words—not only in his personal correspondence, of which this letter provides an example, but also in professional dealings, into which future writing could transform the letter.

The structure of the letter makes the distinction between the personal and the professional murky.[28] In the first paragraph, an exordium of mutual admiration begins this process: "I assure you it would give me great pleasure to cultivate your friendship in person, but I really cannot on any account venture to London unless upon the certainty of a regular income" (LEY 118). Although this sentence is largely civility, its arrangement underscores a division which Wordsworth intends to contain within his writing. The play of the country image of "cultivate," surrounded by humanizing words such as "pleasure" and "friendship," against the economic metaphor of "venture" enforced by "account" and "income" suggests the differences between the local economy of the Lake District and the national economy of London. The next paragraph, however, notes that while London is expensive, Whitehaven is not free and he "must do something to maintain" himself "even in this country." Economic necessity creates between London and Whitehaven a continuum that can authorize other connections. Wordsworth uses this point as a transition into considering the "monthly miscellany from which some emolument might be drawn."

This discussion of money has a counterpart which ends the letter proper, creating a kind of inner and more elaborate frame than the one on the difficulties of writing. After a discussion of morality and audience, to which I will return shortly, Wordsworth discusses the publication of his poems, again from both personal and professional perspectives mediated by money: "I am at present *nearly quite* at leisure, so that with industry I think I can perform my share. I say *nearly* at leisure, for I am not *quite* so as I am correcting and considerably adding to those poems which I published in your absence [*An Evening Walk* and *Descriptive Sketches*]" (LEY 120, my italics). Wordsworth's rhetorical repetitions of "nearly" and "quite" create a sentence suggesting a leisure devoid of slothfulness and characterized by the same industriousness needed for the success of the venture Mathews and Wordsworth are considering.

The continual revision that Hume fancifully imagines might, except for Charon's rhetorical skills, stave off death's boatman, serves equally deep and deferring functions for Wordsworth. If the published poems are already under revision, a periodical, defined by its continual reissue, is constant revision. Placing the poems in relation to his audience ("in your absence") authorizes a typically Wordsworthian (and Humean) confession: "It was with great reluctance I huddled up those two works and sent them into the world in so imperfect a state. But as I had done nothing by which to distinguish myself at the university, I thought these little things might shew that I could do something" (LEY 120). Wordsworth moderates between terms of labor and repose. His "leisure" allows for "industry," and his having "done nothing" inspires publication to "shew I could do something." His poetic labor stems from both choice and necessity. Like the laborer, he must work; but, like the capitalist, he chooses his time to disburse his labor in the marketplace.[29] The public appearance within the literary marketplace reverberates back to, and corrects, the college days Mathews and Wordsworth shared.

The need for public validation, expressed here in a sophomoric tone, is ambivalent partly because it has two distinct, and often contradictory, measures—the profit of sales and the reviews: "They [the poems] have been treated with unmerited contempt by some of the periodical publications, and others have spoken in higher terms of them than they deserve. I have another poem written last summer ready for the press, though I certainly should not publish it unless I hoped to derive from it some pecuniary recompense" (LEY 120). The first sentence, chiasmic in structure, suspends the reviews on either side of the poem's actual merit—something Wordsworth discloses only as the negation of the reviewers' opinions. The force of the "should" of the second sentence seems double: first, the conditional sense that only if he can anticipate a profit *will* he publish, but second, a moral obligation to publish only what will be profitable. This position, that the market ought not to be burdened by unprofitable ventures that deplete its overall effectiveness, echoes Adam Smith, and justifies the increasing regulation of the market to keep it operating freely. The contradiction, for Wordsworth, as for Adam Smith, is only apparent; the market itself would, in due time, rid itself of unprofitable ventures, but such regulation (whether by law as Mansfield proposed or, as Wordsworth here suggests, by personal morality) enhances that market operation.

Wordsworth's attitude toward money, both in refusing to publish except for "some pecuniary recompense" and in hoping that "some emolument might be drawn" from the proposed miscellany, hangs between two eighteenth-century attitudes toward writing for money. Hume wrote to Strahan a "general rule" that "no good book was ever wrote for money" (*Letters of David Hume* 285); Boswell's Johnson declared that "no man but a blockhead ever wrote, except for money" (*Life*, 731). Presumably neither Hume nor Boswell's Johnson would have defended his position staunchly against the easily compiled counter-examples, but their comments reflect attitudes about the relationship between money and meaning that Wordsworth inherits.[30] He declares his intentions to make money by writing and simultaneously contextualizes that desire by insisting that the public good will accrue a value in proportion to his own profits.

Rhetorically evading the stumbling block of money, Wordsworth, in the core of the letter, sets out the aspects of professionalism concerned with the poet's self-figuration. Having recognized both his and Mathews's poverty, he suggests that "perhaps however this might be got over if we could be sure of the patronage of the public" (LEY 118). One might anticipate that he would next consider how to insure such patronage, but he does not. To be a poet already implies such patronage, and he immediately considers his location outside London: "I do not see that my being in the country would have any tendency to diminish the number or deduct from the value of my communications." In the subsequent letter of June 8, Wordsworth uses a geographic metaphor to confess his limitations regarding marketing, "the first or last province of the work," but in "every other" province, he can promise his "best exertion." Mathews, by contrast, is in London but so "much engaged" that Wordsworth suggests he may have "to free yourself [Mathews] from" other "occupations" (LEY 127). The metaphoric terrain of literary provinces maps onto English geography. Absence from London is removal from the alpha and omega of writing (marketing), but to be within the city risks everything in between.

Because Wordsworth intends a reciprocity with the London audience, it poses a threat from a professional perspective. In the terms of commodity and gift exchange (C. A. Gregory, *Gifts and Commodities* 48–49), what Wordsworth gives as a gift—the *Philanthropist*—London may treat as a commodity (not least because Wordsworth wishes and needs to be paid for it). The two issues of audience and the poet's location, seemingly disparate, are inseparable. He ends the paragraph with a question that clarifies their relationship: "What class of readers ought we to aim at procuring; in what do we, each of us, suppose ourselves the most able either to entertain or instruct?" (LEY 119). The problem of patronage has become one of aiming at a class of readers who exist not within a geography (London) so much as within a political category.

In the next paragraph, Wordsworth asserts, "I am of that odious class of men called democrats, and of that class I shall for ever continue." The distance from London gives Wordsworth a perspective that the irony of "odious" shades as privileged.[31] The poet's audience is, for Wordsworth, inevitably forged out of political convictions by the very act of circulating a periodical: "It will be impossible (and indeed it would render our publication worthless were we to attempt it,) not to inculcate principles of government and forms of social order of one kind or another . . . Beside essays on morals and politics I think I could communicate critical remarks upon poetry, &c, &c,. . . . But I should principally wish our attention to be fixed upon life and manners, and to make our publication a vehicle of sound and exalted Morality." Aesthetics are not so much secondary as necessarily implicated in political questions.[32]

Wordsworth seizes this position, a commonplace of the late eighteenth century, for his own by denying its moral possibilities to other publications: "All the periodical miscellanies that I am acquainted with, except one or two of the reviews, appear to be written to maintain the existence of prejudice and to disseminate error" (LEY 119). The notion of writing as a procedure of maintenance and dissemination is critical to Wordsworth's project. He insists, however, that his product, even as it circulates, will not become error, because of his own fixed position in the "class of democrats." In later years, he would seek the same control of meaning by "permanently fix[ing]" himself in Grasmere, as he told Anne Taylor.

Poetic Formation and the Body Legal

In a subsequent letter to Mathews (LEY 123–29, 8 June 1794), Wordsworth provides a more specific context for his remarks concerning the role of institutions such as "the reviews" as meaning-producing. He tempers his opposition to monarchy and aristocracy by the Burkean concerns for the practical structures—the economy, the courts, and so on—that he identifies collectively as "the nature of the grounds where the race [i.e., the modification of the British Constitution] is to be run." Wordsworth recognizes "two causes which appear to me to be accomplishing the subversion of this constitution; first, the infatuation profligacy and extravagance of men in power, and secondly, the changes of opinion respecting matters of Government which within these few years have rapidly taken place in the minds of speculative men." (LEY 124). The first clause is a packed series of three different problems all inhering in "men of power," while the second is a temporally laid-out sequence; this rhetorical difference reinforces Wordsworth's condemnation of "men in power" and his support for "speculative men" who operate in history. The journal, then, would become an empowering agent of speculation and, in this way, Wordsworth hopes not for revolution but for reform, accomplished by a shift in ideology: "There is a further duty incumbent upon every enlightened friend of mankind; . . . he should diffuse by every method a knowledge of those rules of political justice, from which the farther any government deviates the more effectually must it defeat the object for which government was ordained" (LEY 124).

The allusion to Godwin insists that knowledge itself is power, while "men in power" are deceived, enmeshed in self-contradiction. The image is a nation shrouded by its own inadequate constitution. How to lift the shroud? "Freedom of inquiry is all that I wish for; let nothing be deemed too sacred for investigation. . . . let the field be open and unencumbered, and truth must be victorious" (LEY 125). The dynamic Wordsworth here envisions is part of a larger movement within both the polite and radical press, in which, as Marcus Wood has demonstrated for the radical press, the freedom of the press itself became a metonymy for English freedom (see *Radical Satire* chaps. 2 and 3), even though the divisions within the popular press meant that a continual struggle for legitimacy was inevitable. Wordsworth's journal will argue for precisely the liberty that it will assert; it will not operate within the range determined by other journals but will restructure the mechanisms of journalism by its own example. Moreover, the victory of "truth" is not possible within a fully free marketplace, but only in one in which the laws of scarcity operate sufficiently that "truth" can vanquish its opponents by depriving them of readership, paper, or legal rights.

Further, when Wordsworth insists that philanthropists should enforce "general principles of the social order that are applicable to all places," Wordsworth is laying down the implicit regulation of the literary marketplace that it should not violate those "general principles," because it should not be bounded by specific place. Therefore, the preconditions for free expression must be preserved against attacks which "free expression" would seem to authorize, and so Wordworth adds a caveat: "I severely condemn all inflammatory addresses to the passions of men, even when it is intended to direct those passions to a good purpose. I know that the multitude walk in darkness." Like Godwin, Wordsworth insists on reason, "a lantern" in "each man's hand," rather than passion, "abortive flashes of lightning, or the coruscations of transitory meteors" (LEY 125). The tamed light, the predictable, the manufactured (reproduced in "Michael" as "the Evening Star") are enabling, while the unrestrained power of lightning frightens, provokes, and must be rejected. Both lantern and lightning are metaphors for powers of speech, and within the structure of the letter, provide a segue into practical matters: what should the miscellany be called and what should it contain? He offers the name "*The Philanthropist a monthly Miscellany*," instead of Mathews's suggestion which "seems too common to attract attention"; this title "includes everything that can instruct and amuse mankind." Its uniqueness is in its generality, and in this sense it harkens to its ancestor the *Spectator*.

As to the journal's contents, Wordsworth envisions a radical agenda marketed within the structure of a polite journal (such as the *Monthly Magazine*), rather than within the budgetary restraints that the radical press generally faced (and that Wordsworth and Mathews certainly would have, given their economic circumstances). Each issue, Wordsworth suggests, will begin with "the topic of general politics" that "illustrate[s] the tendency of particular doctrines of government"; move on to "essays upon morals and manners, and institutions whether social or political"; and then "essays partly for instruction and partly for amusement." These essays, such as "biographical papers" on men "distinguished for their exertions in the cause of liberty" are not to be randomly arranged but "should, as much as possible form a series exhibiting the advancement of the human mind in moral knowledge" (LEY 125–26). History has a structure of advancement that can be exploited by the arrangement of articles and furthered by circulation. Reiterating the "exertions" of thinkers such "as Turgot, as Milton, [Algernon] Sydney, Machiavel, Beccaria" constitutes progress, not mere repetition, because it establishes intellectual progress as a mode of history, and justifies the arrangement and the goal of the miscellany. An interior law, that of succession, to use Michel Foucault's phrases, relates the subject of the miscellany to its own structure.[33]

The last sections will have "essays of taste and criticism," as well as reviews of publications (LEY 126). The dialogue between journals and other publications replaces the letters by correspondents to the *Spectator*. In choosing to engage other publications by critique, Wordsworth simultaneously suggests dialogue and superiority. This approach reworks the eighteenth-century journal's mediation of communal exchange and hierarchical rank, but at the metalevel of the professional industry itself. The audience, outside the dialogue, partakes through economic consumption.

"Some poetry we should have" (LEY 126). The inversion, the brevity of the sentence, and the displacement of the moral imperative onto themselves heighten the importance of the poetry, but not within the hierarchical structure of the miscellany itself. Wordsworth does not say where poetry should appear, leaving it free to infiltrate at all levels;[34] it is at once politics and morality, instruction and amusement. Poetry moves independently through the hierarchy; or, to rephrase, it re-expresses the hierarchy to itself by containing that hierarchy within its own discourse. If the structure of the miscellany does offer a parallel to historical structure, then poetry is a liberated moment, necessarily freed from the very constraints it will engage. It is not so much beyond law as a lawmaker, or, more precisely, a trace of the totemic moment which, as Freud speculates, preceded law as an institution.[35] It is less beyond economy than the representor and precursor of economics. Within the field of literature, poetry gleans with impunity.

In the paragraph outlining the structure of the work, Wordsworth considers audience more specifically than in the previous letter: "As to our readers you think that we should endeavor to obtain as great a variety as possible, you cannot, however, be ignorant that amongst the partizans of this war, and of the suspension of the *habeas corpus* act amongst the mighty class of selfish alarmists we cannot obtain a single friend. We must then look for protection entirely amongst the dispassionate advocates of liberty and discussion" (LEY 126). Readers are friends, a word that echoes his earlier phrase, "enlightened friend of mankind," and they stand in a particular relation to "this war," the specifying pronoun referring at once to the war against France and the more general struggle against liberty, the central symbol of which was the suspension of *habeas corpus*.

Between his first and second letter to Mathews about the *Philanthropist*, Wordsworth had received a letter from Richard with this caution: "I hope you will be cautious in writing or expressing your political opinions. By the suspension of the Habeas Corpus Acts the Ministers have great powers" (LEY 121, 23 May 1794). The majority of this letter details a series of complicated and linked civil actions, especially the "enormously expensive" cause against Lord Lonsdale, the description of which echoes Richard's warning to William: "I have always avoided writing and speaking upon this subject, because His Lordship has so many Spies in every part of the country." The suspension of *habeas corpus* and spies are dangerous in the same way to the expression of ideas, whether a poet's political notions or a lawyer's thoughts on a law suit against a wealthy opponent.[36] Ideas can be seized and used against their owners and Richard, as a barrister, knew that the site of the danger was the law courts.

"*Habeas corpus*" ("you have the body") were the emphatic words that began a writ that required the government, or other confiner, to produce the prisoner's body before the court and demonstrate just cause for imprisonment; Blackstone was typical in considering it the "great writ of liberty" (*Commentaries* 3: 129). After receiving secret reports about the Corresponding Society, both houses passed 34 George III c. 54, suspending the right to apply for this relief. Like Hume's "Remarkable Custom" of impressment—an unconstitutional method of protecting the Constitution

(*Essays Moral* 380–82)—the state manipulated its constitution (body politic) to claim its rights over the body of the citizen. The immediate consequence was the arrest of Hardy, Horne Tooke, Thelwall, and ten others who were never tried after the principals were acquitted (Holdsworth 13: 162). The charge was high treason for their roles as leading members of the London Corresponding Society. Because the action was based on constructive treason, the trial turned on the question of whether, from the almost certainly seditious resolutions, treason could be constructed, or interpreted. It would not have been difficult to sense similarities to the trials of the Girondins, in which the president of the court had reasoned that "if the court were investigating a definite crime, I should not allow evidence as to opinions, but since the issue is a conspiracy against the state, it may be established by proof of association of the accused: and such proof can be obtained only from the identity of their opinions" (quoted in J. M. Thompson, *French Revolution* 370). The subordination of the body and the interpretation of a text had conjoined, not coincidentally but through the specific mechanisms of state power.

The juridical power of interpretation corresponded to the police power of arrest and, but for the interposition of the jury, to the penal powers of execution.[37] In the letter of 23 May, Wordsworth had already connected doctrine and punishment as something regulated by writing: "Here at the very threshold I *solemnly affirm* that in no writings of mine will I ever admit of any sentiment which can have the least tendency to induce my readers to suppose that the doctrines which are now enforced by banishment, imprisonment, &c, &c, are other than pregnant with every species of misery" (LEY 119, my italics).[38] The outset of Mathews and Wordsworth's project is an extralegal oath (possibly seditious, and solemn for that reason) to break a cycle in which doctrines otherwise detestable first gain social status when upheld by corporal punishment and then, through the accumulated tendencies embodied in "writings," become normalized into sentiment (internalized politics). At this point, the miseries—endlessly replicated like Errour's brood whom the Red Crosse Knight encounters at the threshold of his adventure in the *Faerie Queene*—are no longer dependent on the doctrines that produced them and are consequently reproduced by writers who "admit" the "least tendency" in that direction. To police his own writing, Wordsworth rejects the state's police powers. Writing before the outcome of the trials (Hardy was acquitted on Guy Fawkes Day, 5 November),

Wordsworth understands this political problem as one of audience. To support the suspension of *habeas corpus* is to read the body, the body politic, and writing in a certain way. Against such readers, who constitute a "mighty class" through their individual self-interest, Wordsworth conceives of his audience as "advocates." In this metaphoric structure, the poet/publisher is on trial, and his readers protect him from those who would destroy liberty.[39]

Wordsworth's understanding of what it means to be a poet and what it means to produce a journal begins engaged in questions of liberty, justice, and jurisprudence. Furthermore, this engagement arises not solely as an act of personal judgment but from the internal structures by which English society creates the marketplace in which journals flourish or fail. Wordsworth eventually decided against pursuing the publishing venture: "The more nearly we approached the time fixed for action, the more strongly was I persuaded that we should decline the field" (LEY 134–36, 7 November 1794). E. P. Thompson has suggested that "we have no reason to suppose that [Wordsworth] would have succeeded as a radical editor" ("Wordsworth's Crisis" 4), and Wordsworth may have come to that same conclusion, though in the letter, he is responding to Mathews's suggestion of abandoning the publication. He may also have determined that his professional identity as a poet was incompatible with the role of producing a journal. But it is worth glancing at the terms by which he backs out of the project.

His "distance from town" now would "be a great obstacle," not, as he earlier wrote, a "circumstance [that] would not be of much consequence." He still cannot leave Whitehaven because of Raisley Calvert, but he alters the reason—shifting the focus from his own body to Calvert's. Initially, Calvert's generosity required that he stay: "It would be using [Calvert] very ill to run the risque of destroying my usefulness by precipitating myself into distress and poverty at the time when he is so ready to support me" (LEY 127, 8 June 1794). Now, Calvert "has every symptom of a confirmed consumption of the lungs, and I cannot think of quitting him in his present debilitated state" (LEY 134–35). Wordsworth represented the situation fairly; Calvert died the following year. But rhetorically, in backing out of the project, Wordsworth refigures himself from professional to personal friend. He mentions his brother's prizes at Oxford (exaggerating a third prize into a second), and sets his discussion of his poetry in filial terms:

"my poetical bantlings," "children," "offspring" that are "christened." For Mathews's work, he deploys other images, those of labor: "service performed," "employment," "prospect." He had signed the June letter "your fellow labourer and friend," and the November one concludes, "Believe [me,] dear Mathews, your very affectionate friend" (LEY 136). He reinstates the divisions their *Philanthropist* was to have overcome.

Mathews was not deterred by Wordsworth's objections and formed the *Telegraph*, which started on 30 December 1794. Wordsworth wrote to Mathews from Penrith: "Your paper I have heard is out. I have learned nothing further of it than that it is democratical, and full of advertisements! . . . you would oblige me highly, very highly, by sending [a copy] down to me here, even if it were the day after its publication. I think also I might forward its circulation in this little place" (LEY 139, 7 January 1795). Wordsworth positions himself as the outsider, the audience equally curious about democracy and advertisements, and yet not purely a consuming audience since in "this little place" perhaps he can aid the journal's circulation. The excitement indicated by the exclamation point indicates his approval of Mathews's ability to conjoin "democratical" and "full of advertisements," for democracy, as Wordsworth and Paine both understood it, depended on functioning marketplaces of informed purchasers. The postscript to this letter revises Wordsworth's previously announced readiness to overcome material problems of writing. In the first letter broaching the *Philanthropist*, Wordsworth complained that the pen and ink were so bad he could "scarce write at all"; now he laments, "I fear you will be unable to decypher this scrawl. I must learn to write a better hand, before I can earn my bread by my pen" (LEY 139). Unprepared to write for a living, he must learn to manipulate the physical instruments of writing before he can make it his trade. This joke encourages Mathews to proceed alone; Wordsworth is content to be part of an appreciative audience, a word already associated in their correspondence with "friend." His own public expression occurred gradually with the sequential publication of the editions of the *Lyrical Ballads*, in which the poet emerges as distinct from the other tillers in the "field of letters."[40]

FOUR

Goody Blake and the Reviewers

There is a law severe of penury
Which bends the cottage boy to early thought
To thought whose premature necessity
Blocks out the forms of nature, preconsumes
The reason, famishes the heart, shuts up
The infant being in itself, and makes
Its very spring a season of decay.
—fragment, 1798 (Butler and Green 307–8)

THE publishing information announced on the title page of the first issue of the *Lyrical Ballads* implies that the volume integrates a provincial production into an urban economy:

BRISTOL:
Printed by Biggs and Cottle,
For T. N. Longman, Paternoster-Row, London
1798

The usual meaning of this information would be that Biggs and Cottle printed the edition and that Longman published it, that is, held the rights of occupation and distribution. As Wordsworth had suggested to Mathews regarding the *Philanthropist*, his distance from London is not a problem but a component of the peripatetic poetic composition suggested by the wandering poems that frame the volume, "The Ancyent Marinere" and "Tintern Abbey." In terms of actual book production, Bristol labor is transformed into London profits.

This reading of the title page, however, does not correspond with the publication history. In 1799, Cottle "went out of business and sold all his copyrights [including the *Lyrical Ballads*] in a package to Longman" (John Jordan, *Why the* Lyrical Ballads? 46),[1] so Longman did not own the rights in

1798. Why Longman appears on the title page is uncertain, but, considered as part of a fictional frame of the first issue, the gesture can be read as a manipulation of standard market practice.[2] The local publisher borrows the London name as an entry into the market.[3]

Wordsworth's role in these machinations is murky. Jordan observes that a letter of introduction Wordsworth planned to take to London (en route to Germany) perhaps "betokens an agreement [with Cottle]" to sound out Longman on taking over the *Lyrical Ballads* (*Why* 45); if so, it failed. Wordsworth wrote from Germany to a London correspondent that "I do not yet know what is to become of my poems, that is, who is their publisher. It was undecided when I came off, which prevented my sending you a copy, but you will see them advertized and so learn where you may get them" (LEY 232, 3 October 1798). Wordsworth equates the fate of the poems with their having a publisher. The publishing, then, is a validating moment, and self-maintaining since advertisement substitutes for the absent, and anonymous, author(s) by supplying the text.

Once Wordsworth regained the copyright for the volume, he never surrendered it. He granted Longman only limited publication rights for the second edition. The repurchase by the publisher of what had been returned *gratis* suggests that poetry, in gaining an audience, operated as capital that accrued value by the manipulation of its relative availability. The decision to name himself in the second edition exploits that capital by providing the means to invest it in his poetic identity. Wordsworth wrote to his brother, on 8 June 1800, about Longman's offer to print a second edition: "I am offered by Longman 80£. I think I shall accept the offer as if the books sell quickly I shall soon have the right of going to market with them again when their merit will be known, and if they do not sell tolerably, Longman will have given enough for them" (LEY 283). Wordsworth gets full value for the poems and retains them, increased in value for having been given away. Wordsworth's management of his copyrights involved not merely using legal authority to enforce his rights but suggesting that the world of social relations, which legal discourse inscribed within property relations, could be reinscribed within the poetic relation of reading and writing. To give away what remains yours in the giving is, in terms of how obligation accrues, as much gift exchange as market economics (Marcel Mauss, *The Gift* 8–12; Gregory, *Gifts* 62), or rather, a way of effecting a gift exchange within a market.

The notion of redeploying materials, as Jerome Christensen has demonstrated for David Hume, characterizes the man of letters' operation in the marketplace, and the publication history of the *Lyrical Ballads* confirms Wordsworth's abilities in such a procedure. In addition to the two accretive editions with their expanding prefaces, he disperses the poems in other volumes. The 1815 edition of Wordsworth's poems, for example, is titled *Poems by WILLIAM WORDSWORTH, including Lyrical Ballads, and the Miscellaneous Pieces of the Author, with Additional Poems, a new Preface and a Supplementary Essay.* The ballads are at once integrated and, because of the title, maintained as distinctive.[4] About half of the poems mentioned (and three of the four quoted) in the *Augustan Review's* favorable notice of this collection appeared first in the *Lyrical Ballads.* Only two other reviews appear in Donald Reiman's *Romantics Reviewed.* One is the attack in the *Monthly Review,* which had previously printed an extensive, lukewarm response to the *Lyrical Ballads.* About a third of the poems it considers are from the *Lyrical Ballads.* The second is in the *Quarterly,* which criticizes *Poems* along with *The White Doe of Rylstone;* from the *Poems,* it quotes only prose material, most extensively from the Preface to the *Lyrical Ballads.*[5]

Early Reviews

Marilyn Butler's contention that "[Francis] Jeffrey's persistent campaign had unfortunately made the *Ballads* notorious, and far more salient than Wordsworth's greater and safer later work" (*Romantics* 63) must be balanced with Wordsworth's own continual efforts to keep the *Lyrical Ballads* before the public. Throughout Wordsworth's career a struggle between critic and poet was fought over the *Lyrical Ballads.* Although this battle was concerned with aesthetics, in the contours of professionalization available to Wordsworth and his reviewers, the question of aesthetics was connected to legal and economic issues. To determine if a poem was *good* was to determine what (and whom) it was *good for.* While the "originality" of the ballads has been explored in formal terms (with critics noting both novelty and conventionality), I maintain that the rhetoric of originality enabled Wordsworth to address salient political topics, and that reviewers challenged this effort from their own political and professional biases.

Wordsworth struck the first blow in the Advertisement to the *Ballads.* His first gesture is to ground himself in a historical continuum by locating his poetry within a field of similar poems: "It is the honourable characteristic of Poetry that its materials are to be found in every subject which can interest the human mind. The evidence of this fact is to be sought, not in the writings of Critics, but in those of Poets themselves" (*Lyrical Ballads* 7). For Wordsworth, poetic discourse subsumed other discourses; for Hume, polite letters, and for Blackstone, jurisprudence had similar roles, and such words as "honorable characteristic" and "evidence" glance at these other linguistic registers. Recalling poetry's mobility in the projected *Philanthropist*, here, poetry maps onto the domain of human interest, a function determined by the empirical evidence of "Poets themselves."[6]

Kurt Heinzelman has observed that for Wordsworth "the labor of the man of science (such as the economist) produces 'facts,' but the poet's labor reproduces itself" (*The Economics of the Imagination* 203). In his 1802 addition to the Preface, Wordsworth provided a metaphor that could complicate this formulation: "[Poetry] is the impassioned expression which is in the countenance of all Science" (*Lyrical Ballads* 259). The reproduction of labor is a production of fact, a point highlighted by the claim in the Advertisement that "Goody Blake and Harry Gill," is "founded on a well-authenticated fact" (*Lyrical Ballads* 8). The story of "Goody Blake" is presented as poetic and scientific. Its factual status is a function of the formal transformation from a "well-authenticated fact" to a poetic fact that the reader (re)authenticates by linking a freakish event (Harry's hysterical coldness) to the "human mind" as both the object of that mind's "interest" and the subject of its psychological mechanisms. Focused on psychological refigurings of the world—in, for example, "The Mad Mother," "The Female Vagrant," "The Thorn," "We Are Seven," and the culminating "Tintern Abbey"—the ballads represent this psychological doubling as the genealogy of poetry. For Blackstone, jurisprudence was both the law of laws and a psychology of human behavior. As a rationale for why law is "an highly useful, I had almost said *essential*, part of liberal and polite education," Blackstone begins by "pointing out its [municipal law's] uses in all *considerable* situations of life" (*Commentaries* 1: 6; my italics). For Wordsworth, similarly, poetry is both the process of poetry and a model of the mind.[7] Defending his profession in 1802, Wordsworth asserts that the poet "*considers* man and nature as *essentially* adopted to each other, and the mind of man as naturally the mirror of the fairest and most interesting qualities of nature" (*Lyrical Ballads* 259, my italics). Both Blackstone and Wordsworth offer their professions as horizons in which human being appears to itself; and the coincidental echoes of their diction suggest that they draw on the shared register of professional language.

In the Advertisement, Wordsworth's claim relies not on a specific author (his anonymous self) but on a class, poets, defined against other producers of words, critics. Wordsworth positions poetic production as prior to a parasitic critical theorizing about limitations, precisely the charge Jeffrey will oppose in modeling his professional reviewer on the lawyer. Given the hostility toward the critics in the Advertisement, the largely favorable reviews are at first peculiar. These reviewers, however, were not professionals, and they could read themselves as outside the "critics" Wordsworth ridicules. Butler has commented that "if Wordsworth's contributions to the *Lyrical Ballads* had appeared a decade earlier . . ., they would hardly have attracted attention except, for their merits" (*Romantics* 61).[8] The same volume seven years later, however, would have faced a tougher professional critic, and, like the *Poems, in Two Volumes*, would likely have been roundly panned. The initial reviews invariably began with a consideration of the Advertisement, often quoting the majority of it.[9]

Only the two most favorable reviews, however, quote the opening paragraph, and only the *British Critic*'s writer, probably Wordsworth's friend Francis Wrangham, comments specifically on it: "We fully agree with the author, that the true notion of poetry must be sought among the poets, rather than the critics; and we will add that, unless a critic is a poet also, he will generally make but indifferent work in judging of the effusions of Genius" (*British Critic* 14 [October 1799]: 365). Wrangham's addition unravels the division upon which Wordsworth's "notion of poetry" depends, since if a critic can be a poet—not a practicing poet, but a poet by sensibility—then the Poet cannot dominate the literary marketplace. Wrangham himself was an amateur poet, an occasional critic, a translator, whose living came from the church (LEY 159, 317), and he seems inattentive to issues of the literary marketplace. While he attempts to bolster the poet, his own language turns against Wordsworth as Poet, and emphasizes the critic's role. In his next sentence, he observes: "In the collection of poems subjoined to this introduction, we do not often find expressions that we esteem too familiar, or deficient in dignity; on the contrary, we think that in general the author has succeeded in attaining that judicious degree of simplicity, which accommodates itself with ease even to the sublime" (*British Critic* 14: 365). The use of "subjoined" ("To add at the end, to add afterwards"—Johnson) relegates the poems as secondary to the critical introduction.[10] Second, while Wordsworth has described his effort as an experiment, implying a foray into new ground, Wrangham applauds him for rediscovering known territory, "that judicious degree of simplicity"; the word "judicious" emphasizes that the correct "degree" has already been adjudicated.

Similarly, to turn to one specific, in discussing "Goody Blake and Harry Gill," Wrangham comments on the claim of authenticity: "Yet it is a miracle; and modern miracles can seldom be admitted, without some degree of credulity, or a very uncommon weight of evidence" (367). No discussion ensues about what constitutes evidence, but the legalistic register suggests that the poem is inadmissable—eliding other purposes for which it might serve as evidence. Wrangham does not consciously argue against Wordsworth's presuppositions, but rather, in the *British Critic*, Wrangham's text appropriates Wordsworth's words on behalf of the periodical industry. His closing summary, adjudicating the morality of the volume, suggests this inadvertent impulse: "nor does there appear any offensive mixture of enmity to present institutions, except in one or two instances, which are so unobtrusive as hardly to deserve notice" (369). Offensiveness to "present institutions" is offered as an established aesthetic criterion, and the poem's violations of it are "unobtrusive" because the *British Critic* refuses to notice its obstruction, and directs its readers to do so also.

Charles Burney, in his review for the *Monthly Review*, is more aware of the implication of Wordsworth's position; like Wordsworth, he had contemplated a partnership for a journal in 1797, a "satiric anti-radical magazine (something like the *Anti-Jacobin*)" (Margaret Doody, *Frances Burney* 205). His review of Wordsworth reworks the material of the poet's Advertisement, repositioning aesthetic and political implications: "The author of these ingenious compositions presents the major part of them to the public as *experiments;* since they were written, as he informs us in the *advertisement* prefixed, 'chiefly with a view to ascertain how far the language of conversation in the middle and lower classes of society is adapted to the purposes of poetic pleasure'" (*Monthy Review* 29 [June 1799]: 202). His use of "presents" suggests that Wordsworth chooses a rhetorical stance to justify himself. Burney continues with qualified praise: "[although] we have been extremely entertained with the fancy, . . . of these pieces, we cannot regard them as poetry" (202). He responds as Wordsworth had anticipated that readers "accustomed to the gaudiness and inane phraseology of many modern writers" would; they would "be induced to wonder by what species of courtesy these attempts can be permitted to assume that title [of Poetry]" (Advertisement, *Lyrical Ballads* 7). From Burney's perspective, however, the reader will encounter the review first, and Wordsworth will have to defend himself.[11] The primacy of the critic is ensured by his co-option of the poet's prose. "Inane phraseology" becomes Wordsworth's characterization of Pope and Dryden, not their weak imitators, and Burney, secure in his eighteenth-century values, assumes that the readers will side with him.

Burney and Wordsworth, in review and advertisement respectively, slide from the "language of conversation" to an appeal to precedent. Wordsworth contends that "the more conversant the reader is with our elder writers, . . . the fewer complaints . . . will he have to make" (7–8). Burney, by contrast, argues that poetry has been subject to progress: "Would it not be degrading poetry, as well as the English language, to go back to the barbarous and uncouth numbers of Chaucer?" (203).[12] He accepts the "polished measures" of Dryden, Pope, and Gray as improvements, and as new standards. Both Wordsworth and Burney moot these arguments about "poetry" as mere semantic difference. Wordsworth presents his case thus: "It is desirable that such readers, for their own sakes, should not suffer the solitary word Poetry, a word of very disputed meaning, to stand in the way of their gratification" (7). The issue of whether the works are poetry should be suppressed for the reader's sake. The attitude suggests that the term *poetry* has become at once too technical and too obscure.

Burney reverses this position: "We will not, however, dispute any longer about names; the author shall style his rustic delineations of low-life, *poetry*, if he pleases" (202). The critic grants the poet the freedom to choose words; he can call it poetry, but only after Burney has identified its genus: "rustic delineations of low-life." Burney pursues this issue of word choice into the poems themselves: "When we confess that our author has had the art of pleasing and interesting . . . by his natural delineations of *human passions, human characters, and human incidents* [my italics], we must add that these effects were not produced by the *poetry:*—we have been as much affected by pictures of misery and unmerited distress, in *prose*" (203). Burney has silently quoted Wordsworth's three defining aspects of poetry (italicized in the quotation), and displaced them from the poet's domain to the realm of language more generally.[13] Burney contends that Wordsworth has performed no necessary labor in bringing these views of misery before the public, but has merely converted them into verse for his own gain. Wordsworth's position is, of course, the opposite: he has given voice to lives that lack voice, and so has cultivated agrarian language as a farmer cultivates a field.

In his comments on specific poems, Burney indicates that his attitude toward the eighteenth-century rise of science extends beyond poetry into economics, politics, and psychology. For the last, consider his discussion of "Anecdote for Fathers": "Of this the dialogue is ingenious and natural: but the object of the child's choice, and the inferences, are not quite obvious" (207). It is simplistic to say that Burney misreads the poem; he opposes its premises about the relation of external necessity and internal randomness and proffers instead, in Donald Reiman's phrase, "Augustan verities of his youth" (*Romantics Reviewed* pt. A, 2: 713). These verities, regarding correspondences, can be glimpsed in Burney's attack on harmonies in Renaissance music that "are founded upon *democratic* principles, which admit of no sovereignty" (*History of Music;* quoted in Lipking, *Ordering of the Arts* 307). Similarly, his critique of "The Last of the Flock" indicates a respect for Blackstonean jurisprudence, probably as filtered through Burke: "If the author be a wealthy man, he ought not to have suffered this poor peasant to part with *the last of the flock*. What but an Agrarian law can prevent poverty from visiting the door of the indolent, injudicious, extravagant, and, perhaps, vicious? and is it certain that rigid equality of property as well as of laws could remedy this evil? (*Monthy Review* 29: 207). It is not the equitable distribution of property but that of law (which entails an uneven distribution of property) that secures the health of the state. Law serves as infrastructure for social and economic interactions, and while it may be supplemented by charity, its function cannot be charitable.[14]

"Goody Blake and Harry Gill, A True Story"

The struggle between critic and poet for primacy reflects questions of textual ownership, and hence of (legal) property. Further, Wordsworth's poetry took up the themes of ownership in direct ways and "Goody Blake and Harry Gill, A True Story" provides an extended example. This ballad was the poem most often mentioned in the reviews of the *Lyrical Ballads*, and Wordsworth's own positioning of it indicates his sense of its importance. Of the poems composed after the conception of the *Ballads*, it appears first in the edition and leads the sequence of poems most fitted to the "experiment" described in the Advertisement. The *Analytic Review* reprinted it entirely as the conclusion to its favorable review (28 [December 1798]: 584–87). The unimpressed reviewer of the *New London Review* quoted eight lines describing Goody Blake (29–32, 45–48), and observed that "If such passages . . . find admirers, the writer is fortunate; for they never cost him any labour in the composition" (1 [January 1799]: 35). Such a charge strikes at the heart of Wordsworth's sense of self: if the poet performs no labor, he accumulates no property; if he is subject to fortune, he cannot regulate the marketplace. Noting that this economic criticism is applied to a description of the laboring Goody Blake and not the owning Harry Gill opens an argumentative dimension consistent with other reviews.

In the *Critical Review*, Robert Southey mused upon whether "Goody Blake and Harry Gill" was likely to "promote the popular superstition of witchcraft" (24 [October 1798]: 200). Southey slyly mistakes Wordsworth's characters for his audience, and deflects the political overtones of the poem, overtones that Charles Burney noted in the *Monthly Review:*

> Distress from poverty and want is admirably described, in the "*true story of Goody Blake and Harry Gill:*" but are we to imagine that Harry was bewitched by Goody Blake? The hardest heart must be softened into pity for the poor old woman;—and yet, if all the poor are to help themselves, and supply their wants from the possessions of their neighbours, what imaginary wants and real anarchy would it not create? Goody Blake should have been relieved out of the *two millions* annually allowed by the state to the poor of this country, not by the plunder of an individual. (29: 206–7)

Despite the ballad form and the history of authentication, Burney insists on its contemporary referent, and the government as the proper adjudicator of the problem. Further, his passive voice suggests that it is the poet who ought to have found the proper relief (just as, had he wealth, or "taste" in the aristocratic eighteenth-century sense, he would have aided the shepherd in "Last of the Flock"). Wordsworth's shift of the story from the location in his source—Warwickshire, a rapidly industrializing area in the 1790s—to the still rural Dorsetshire offered to the reviewers a political context of industrialization, which Burney refuses. Burney articulates the struggle between the wealthy and the poor in the conventional terms of "anarchy" rampant in critiques of the French Revolution.

This survey of reviews demonstrates that the poem brought to the fore issues of property, labor, and relief for contemporary readers. Wordsworth chooses to engage these questions within a displaced legal framework; the narrative is a crime, a trial, and a punishment, but rendered to criticize the legal structure that allows for such an *actual* occurrence. More specifically, Wordsworth overlays features of medieval law onto modern law to demonstrate the deficiency of the latter, and structures the trial as between two theories of property: the Burkean classical liberal theory to which Harry Gill consciously clings; and a more abstract, naturalized theory, the roots of which are at once in Godwinian utilitarianism and in the medieval (and possibly mythic [see Alan Macfarlane, *The Culture of Capitalism* 13–21]) common law that provided for common property. Goody Blake understands her defense as an appeal to God and could not articulate any theoretical ground. Rather, she feels it in her cold bones, as Harry Gill finally will; hers is, within the poem's rhetoric, genuinely common law.

This opposition is inscribed in a series of other oppositions, beginning with the two characters named in the title.[15] Harry Gill is "young" even in the first stanza where the narrative perspective is long after the incident at the hedge; the adjective is used twice more. First, "Young Harry was a lusty drover" (17). Since a drover drives sheep, he ought to have a congenial relation to a spinner (just as the old and young ought to have a mutually beneficial relationship in Wordsworth's sociology).[16] Johnson defines a "drover" as "one that fats oxen *for sale*, and drives them *to market*" (my italics); although the definition does not include sheep, that was a common usage *(OED)*. Johnson twice emphasizes the commodification that differentiates the drover from his predecessor (or threatened contemporary) the "shepherd" who, in "The Last of the Flock," loses his identity in taking his lamb (17) to market;[17] for that shepherd, his engagement in the market constitutes criminality, guilt, and shame: "To wicked deeds I was inclined, / And wicked fancies cross'd my mind, / And every man I chanced to see, / I thought he knew some ill of me" (71–74). Whether the "wicked deeds" are consequences of selling the sheep, or that action itself, remains ambiguous. The shepherd is unmanned in his projection of himself as the object of another's gaze. Harry Gill, by contrast, is subject to such scrutiny—also a projection—only after his "punishment"; until then, his is the empowered gaze. When Harry Gill awaits Goody Blake, the scene takes on a voyeuristic quality:

> —He hears a noise—he's all awake—
> Again?—on tip-toe down the hill
> He softly creeps—'Tis Goody Blake,
> She's at the hedge of Harry Gill.
> (77–80)

The stanza takes Harry Gill's perspective at first (echoing "a noise" with "awake" and "A[/]gain" to enforce a continual association between his sensory and internal experience). But the last line undercuts this: he sees Goody Blake, and experiences the hedge not as his own, but as "of Harry Gill." In his attitude toward Goody Blake, he is alienated from his property and his self. Immediately after Goody Blake's prayer/curse, Harry, again described as "young," is restored to himself to endure his punishment.

Goody Blake, in sharp contrast, is said to be old twice, and "auld" once;[18] her bones are twice referred to as old, and so is the hedge: "Could anything be more alluring / Than an old hedge to Goody Blake?" (59–60). Affinity gives Goody Blake a certain claim, especially if the hedge's oldness suggests that it predates young Harry Gill's possession of it. The contrast of poor and rich is more fluid. Five times Goody Blake or her possessions are labeled poor, and Harry Gill's wealth is constructed by the contrast; he has a superfluity of property, including the hedge and his warm fire, and his punishment underscores this excess by making all his coats useless. The final use of "poor" is Harry's own: "Poor Harry Gill is very cold" (124), he mutters to himself in a linguistic pun internalizing Goody Blake's "old" in his "c*old*." The allusion to Edgar's Poor Tom from Shakespeare's *King Lear* implies Harry's madness and his own responsibility for it, and to a reader who recalls what drove Edgar to his disguise, this links that madness to questions of property rights.[19] Unlike Michael, who needs land to raise his sheep, Harry Gill probably drives sheep owned by others across commons and easements; his own land is a superfluous capitalistic investment. He has gone too far beyond subsistence, while Goody Blake's subsistence poverty is underscored with a "telling" example: the three hours she stays up at night working "would not pay for [the] candlelight" by which she worked (27–28).

Despite these oppositions, and their alliance to either Goody Blake or Harry Gill, two terms, equally opposed, float between them—those of warmth and cold. Both Harry Gill and Goody Blake are susceptible to these sensations, but Goody Blake is dependent upon nature (the winds or "the long, warm, lightsome summer-day" [48]) whereas Harry Gill can produce his own heat and so does not recognize his dependence on it. He experiences his warmth as surplus; when in search of Goody Blake, "oft from his warm fire he'd go." The seemingly natural terms of *heat* and *cold*, then, become the grounds for adjudication between the two litigants.

The first stanza establishes Harry's ailment of chattering teeth which, given the context of speech acts (specifically prayer and poetry), suggests his worthlessness and plays it against his wealth, signified by his quantity of manufactured clothing. The inadequacy of this clothing, bought from afar, not locally, measures Harry's alienation from his community. He does not labor, but owns; Goody Blake, we learn later, is in the reverse circumstance; her constant labors of spinning cannot sustain her body temperature. The second stanza begins:

> In March, December, and in July,
> 'Tis all the same with Harry Gill
> The neighbours tell, and tell you truly,
> His teeth they chatter, chatter still.
>
> (9–12)

Harry does not experience nature's transitions, presented by their social names, the months. This punishment suits his cold inclinations and his lack of concern for those around him. The neighbors do not merely reinforce the truth of the story but fulfill a community obligation of speaking the truth. In the medieval period, a jury would be chosen from a community who knew the defendant or litigants, and it was their duty to discover the facts and to swear (Latin *jurare*, to swear) to their truth (Harold Potter, *An Historical Introduction to English Law and Its Institutions* 234). In the modern period, a juror was disqualified for having any knowledge of a case, and the rules of evidence arose. Under these modern rules, having "long suspected / This trespass" (65–66), Harry Gill sets out alone to catch Goody Blake in the act. He waits "Till she had filled her apron full" (84) to seize her. In sequence, "fiercely by the arm he took her," "by the arm he held her," and "fiercely by the arm he shook her" (89–91); the verbs condense a criminal proceeding of apprehension, detainment, and punishment. Two secondary meanings given in Johnson seem appropriate for the thrice repeated "arm" in the description of the arrest: first, the "bough of a tree," which again associates Goody Blake with the hedge and with nature, and second, "Power; might. In this sense is used the secular *arm* &c."[20] This meaning shadows Harry Gill's violence with his (in)judicious use of power. His presence as a landowner makes this moment constitute a parodic trial since he might well have been empowered as a justice of the peace. Goody Blake does not answer to him, but "pray'd / To God that is the judge of all" (95–96). The word "pray," while primarily religious, has a secondary legal sense: one prays relief from the court. Goody Blake has invoked her natural right of trial before God.

The image of the hedge, especially as a site of contention between rich and poor, would have focused the ongoing disputes about enclosures, the legality of which derived from notions of maximizing land use. Dorsetshire, where Wordsworth placed the story, was the location of the first Enclosure Act in 1604 (Michael Turner, *Enclosures in Britain, 1750–1830* 16). A hedge was a usual and cheap way of enclosing land and securing a property interest. Enclosures "have appropriately been called a revolution of the rich against the poor" (Polanyi, *Transformation* 35). If Polanyi's assessment has merit, then an alteration in the mechanisms of enclosure is of importance. The complaints against enclosures increased dramatically in the eighteenth century, but enclosures themselves had occurred in the middle ages. Much feudal land was acquired by enclosures in the name of defense, but gradually the method of enclosure shifted from one in which enclosures represented the immediate action of power to one in which Parliament and the courts granted the right of enclosure, and thus conveyed the power. Michael Turner's survey of counties shows that legal fees constituted the largest cost of enclosure; in Warwickshire, by the eighteenth century, "enclosures provided almost continuous employment for solicitors" (*Enclosures* 61).[21] The hedge, of neither defensive nor agricultural use, was a symbol of a legal determination made elsewhere. Consequently, Goody Blake's appeal to God becomes an act of civil disobedience, a challenge to contemporary legal procedures of enclosure.

A specific benefit alleged by the proponents of Enclosure Acts was the development of laborers entirely dependent upon wages. Thrown into the market economy, workers would be both more industrious and more moral. J. Clark argued for enclosures in 1794 in order to "put it as much as possible out of their power to live idle" (quoted in K. D. M. Snell, *Annals of the*

Labouring Poor 170). Similarly, the lack of external structure was assumed to cause a corresponding immorality; as one witness for the Select Committee on Enclosure (1844) reported: "I generally find them [people living in the neighborhood of unenclosed land] demoralized, they are generally of dissolute habits; many of them commit depredations, being out of sight of any person of authority" (quoted in Snell, *Annals* 171–72). Property bestows authority, and order is imposed through watching. Wordsworth emphasizes Goody Blake's unseen hard work, despite her poverty; by contrast, Harry Gill's leisure allows him to exercise the authority of watching. The implication is that the wage structure resulting from enclosure does not preclude idleness, but makes it a profitable pastime for the landowner, while the laborer's work does not avail to provide subsistence. The hedge is an emblem both of greed and of waste, and Goody Blake's action is unconscious political resistance.

If the legal procedure of enclosure bestows one property right on Harry Gill, the poet's moral argument confers a greater right on Goody Blake. In the fifth stanza, the narrator makes a first-person aside: "Two poor old dames, as I have known, / Will often live in one small cottage" (34–35). This knowledge of the actual distribution of living space asserts the authority of watching, but locates it within the local community. The only other first-person moment ends the poem: "Now think, ye farmers all, I pray, / Of Goody Blake and Harry Gill" (127–28). "Farmers" used generally encompasses both owners and laborers, and reusing the verb "pray" suggests that in thinking about this story, the farmers are being asked to judge it from the view not of legality but of a higher natural law, one provided simultaneously in God's judgment of Harry Gill and in the poet's rendering of the story into a plea. Southey's question of whether the poem promotes superstition can be re-expressed. An explanation of Harry Gill's chattering from David Hartley's associationist psychology would not prevent its being a punishment from God so much as express the mechanism of that punishment. Wordsworth prepares such a scene in the description of nature's occasional benevolence:

> Oh joy for her! when e'er in winter
> The winds at night had made a rout,
> And scatter'd many a lusty splinter,
> And many a rotten bough about.
>
> (49–52)

The adjective "lusty" recalls Harry Gill, suggesting his own splintered circumstance, separated from his neighbors. The wind (fulfilling Harry's feudal obligation as a landowner to provide for surrounding peasants) provides warmth by driving otherwise useless wood and reinforces Goody Blake's claim to relief.

The purpose of this analysis has not been to argue that emphasizing the legal aspects of this poem should overshadow other approaches but to suggest that, for Wordsworth, a consideration of "the primary laws of our nature" (1800 Preface, *Lyrical Ballads* 245) involves an interaction between those laws of association which Hartley outlined and those laws of jurisprudence which Blackstone categorized. Blackstone had suggested both continuity and analogy between these two kinds of law, and these relationships became explicable through the science of jurisprudence. Wordsworth, by contrast, embeds such explanatory power in poetry, implicitly in "Goody Blake," the center of which is a judicially efficacious speech act which acts either directly on the conscience of the guilty party or through the intercession of God. Within the rhetorical tradition of eighteenth-century aesthetics, Goody Blake's prayer could be viewed as efficacious poetry; to explain how "words influence the passions," Burke hoped to demonstrate (through particular reference to poetry) "by what powers they [words] were able to affect us often as strongly as the things they represent, and sometimes much more strongly" (*Sublime and Beautiful* 176–77); in this scenario, Harry Gill's reaction is just an extreme case of poetic effect. Curiously, despite Wordsworth's situating of the poem as a "well-authenticated fact" within the realm of psychological curiosity and Goody Blake's direct appeal to God, two of the reviewers, Southey and Burney, describe the event as witchcraft, which had been abolished in English law only under George II and still persisted sufficiently in the popular imagination that the misdemeanor of "persons pretending to use witchcraft" remained (Blackstone, *Commentaries* 4: 61). By referring to, or rather inventing, Goody Blake's witchcraft, the reviewers reinscribe her prayer within a criminal tradition, and register their uneasiness not only with her speech act but with Wordsworth's.[22] In his Preface to the second edition of *Lyrical Ballads*, Wordsworth would defend at length the transformational power of his poetry not as a violation of custom or law, but as the recuperation of the aesthetic roots of the former and a legitimate critique of the latter.

FIVE

The Contractual Basis for the *Lyrical Ballads*

> Without an appeal to laws and principles there can be no criticism. What passes under that name is, for the most part, little more than a string of random and extempore judgments, a mode of writing more cheap than any other, and utterly worthless.—Passage deleted in draft for the 1802 Preface, Butler and Green 765

In December 1799, Wordsworth wrote to Coleridge, "Take no pains to contradict the story that the L. B. are entirely yours" (LEY 281); he believed the rumor would aid sales since Coleridge's name was better known to the public than his own. In the 1800 edition, by contrast, Wordsworth inserted a "Note to the Ancient Mariner" that distinguishes the named Wordsworth as the proprietor of the *Lyrical Ballads* from Coleridge, who is figured as an unnamed apprentice in the shop.[1] Much had occurred in the interim: their trip to Germany, possibly the draft of "Essay on Morals,"[2] the gift of the copyright to the *Lyrical Ballads*, Wordsworth and Dorothy settling in Dove Cottage. This last, providing Wordsworth the role of householder, corresponds to the increased responsibility he takes for his poetry.[3] In a letter to Longman, Wordsworth implicitly makes this connection; after detailing the copyright agreement, Wordsworth explains his caution: "I mention this because, by some unaccountable mistake, Mr. Cottle sold the Copyright of the first volume when he had no more right so to do than to sell the house which I now inhabit" (LEY 310, 18 December 1800). The second volume circulated in a discourse "increasingly inflected with terms of commerce and business, accumulation and exchange"; in this phrase from *The Economics of the Imagination* (202) , Kurt Heinzelman aptly describes both the development of language in England over the last century and Wordsworth's own growing investment in monetary matters. The letter to Longman also suggests this connection by Wordsworth's "particular request that no Books be advertised at the end of the volumes" (LEY 310), at once acknowledging the advertising base of the market for his work and refusing to be a vehicle for other works. Wordsworth wishes his name to stand alone at the front of the volume, not as part of a frame of names marking the volume as a product of an industry (his volume, however, was advertised in Mary Robinson's *Lyrical Tales*).[4]

The poet's name and the Preface in the second edition of the *Lyrical Ballads* not only authorized the thirty-five new poems but altered those previously published. In reordering the first volume, Wordsworth announced a shift in emphasis, but one, he implied by both the content and placement of the Preface, that an able reader of the first edition could have deduced.[5] Such a revisionist illusion initiates Wordsworth's technique of rewriting history through restructuring poetry, a procedure at the problematic core of what Clifford Siskin has identified as the "historicity of romantic discourse."[6] Such a technique duplicates the revisionary aspects of common-law interpretation by which copyright emerges in the eighteenth century as having existed from time immemorial (before the mechanical means to copy).[7]

To sketch the full force of Wordsworth's rhetoric, the sum of employing his proper name as a juridical gesture, the legal strain of the Preface, as well as the organization of the poems, requires a digression into the contested relation of property and copyright that emerged in the simultaneous formation of a literary and a commercial market.[8] Copyright was not merely a troubling form of property but a form that troubled property at a delicate moment of legal expansion. Wordsworth's claims for a new type of poetry, for a new contract with his reader, and for a new formulation of "real language" depended on confusions in property law that arose in part because the state was creating new properties (and naming new contacts of human relation) and in part because natural-law theorists could not account for the alienability of property, the newly foregrounded aspect that enabled commerce and, hydra-like, engendered more incorporeal properties. Blackstone suggests something of this confusion: "Pleased as we are with the possession, we seem afraid to look back to the means by which it was acquired, as if fearful of some defect in our title. . . . We think it enough that our title is derived by the grant of the former proprietor; . . . not caring to reflect that (accurately and strictly speaking) there is no foundation in nature or in natural law, why a set of words upon parchment should convey the dominion of land" (*Commentaries* 2: 2). Though Blackstone seems to be discussing individual title, this passage serves as a preface to founding property as a principle; failure of title can occur either because the title within a system is inadequate or because the system—parchment conveying dominion—is faulty. The role of writing in the structure of property is instrumental, but without demonstrable basis. Ultimately Blackstone grafts this problem of property onto the relation between stable texts—the Bible and the laws of England, documents with royal copyrights protected in perpetuity—and transitory texts circulating under the protection of the copyright statute of 1709.[9]

To naturalize new modes of property that derived obviously from social structure, Blackstone invoked a traditional division between corporeal and incorporeal properties. He insisted that in the case of an incorporeal hereditament, the actual value resided in the corporeal object from which it derived (*Commentaries* 2: 20)—for example, rent income derived from the value of the land, and so belonged to the landowner (a concept fundamental to Anglo-American law but by no means universal). More generally, the civil powers to create properties derived from natural possession, that is, from historical occupancy effectively mystified. The concept of copyright vexed this formulation since the marketplace, through both selling practices and literary criticism, reversed the priority of corporeal and incorporeal. Blackstone had to use that priority, because the Bible—a text that, as God's logos, preceded any particular translation—was the announced foundation of civil property rights.[10] In other words, at the heart of the relation between corporeal and incorporeal is an inversion of the hierarchy, namely the necessity to circulate the laws through their authorizing texts. Further, this inversion implied another, namely that natural law relied on, rather than grounded, human law. The particular role of textuality in the theorizing of property, in turn, produced an anxious relation between the literary market and a legal discourse that represented itself as delineating a market without participating in it.[11]

In a *Treatise on the Law of Copyright* published in 1842, George Ticknor Curtis observes that copyright cannot be derived directly from natural law, because inscription itself marks man as removed from that state and as situated within an economy of commodification (2). In a gesture typical for the previous hundred years, Curtis acknowledges that the "state of nature" is a legal fiction that emerges from the given of property: "all the speculations of philosophers, from the time of Aristotle to the present age, have sprung from and again conducted to one fact—the existence of property" (*Copyright* 4). Property, Curtis goes on to say, consists of two uses, the right of possession and the right of alienation which, in exchange for other value, ends the right of possession. But, for copyright, a contradiction emerges in the relation of these two rights. Transferring the individual book does not end, but reinforces, ownership of the noncorporeal text; and these transfers determine the value of that text. Thus, copyright enacts the overall scheme of the market in which the circulation of property increases the total value of the market, and threatens to expose the law not as indifferently adjudicating the disputes within the marketplace but as actively pursuing particular configurations of economic exchange. Pointing to the wealth of the Lord Chancellors and the circulation of power as itself economic, Jeremy Bentham insisted that the court system, like the polite letters of Addison's *Spectator*, only mimicked rhetorical disinterest, a strategy that the interpretive procedures of literary practice threatened to unmask: "Judge and Co." form a "virtual partnership—the law partnership—with the judges as managing partners at the head of it" (quoted in M. I. Zagday, "Bentham on Civil Procedure" 74).

By creating statutory limits on copyright, the "Act for the Encouragement of Learning, by Vesting the Copies of Printed Books in the Authors or Purchasers of Such copies, during the Times therein mentioned" (8 Anne 19) attempted to stabilize the concept of text.[12] Blackstone maintains that at common law, copyright was perpetual even without any specific means of enforcement beyond the limits of 8 Anne 19. Revising *Millar v. Taylor*, 1769, the House of Lords, in *Donaldson v. Beckett*, 1774, declared that "the author's common-law right to the sole printing, publishing, and vending of his works, a right which he could assign in perpetuity, is taken away and supplanted by the Statute of Anne. The case did not hold that the author's rights at common law consisted *only* of the right of printing, publishing, and vending his works" (Lyman Ray Patterson, *Copyright in Histori-*

cal Perspective 174). This meant, in practice, that while a literary property was perpetual, only those in fact held by the crown—laws and translations of the Bible—were protected perpetually, and these provide the basis of property law.[13]

If the rules of copyright insure a privileged position to legal reproduction as perpetually in copyright, they also entailed privileging linguistic reproduction itself as the safeguard of the market.[14] I suggest, then, two impulses for the legal anxiety regarding the formation of the literary market. The first was recognition of the ideological potential to construct social relations by managing the literary market.[15] The second, however, was that the law of copyright concealed, and so potentially revealed, a contradiction at the heart of property, namely, that any construction of the concept of property necessarily entailed the preexistence of a property on which to base the conception.

Wordsworth's own grounding of his property interest in his poetry could not be articulated by a foundational strategy, but was argued through its constructed difference from other notions of property. For Wordsworth, the use of his name on the *Lyrical Ballads* not only asserted a legal property right but also was an effort to *take* responsibility; this taking was intended to shift the locus of responsibility from the legal horizon of copyright law to the moral force of poetic creation itself, but that transfer could only be represented through the repetitive procedures of the professional career within the auspices of copyright law.

Expostulations and Replies

Paul Magnuson, among other critics, has articulated aspects of the dialogue between Wordsworth and Coleridge, and of the extent to which it was played out through the publishing procedures of the two poets, especially through the manipulations of *The Rime of the Ancient Mariner*.[16] Charles Lamb's response to the second edition clarifies the professional stakes for which, in Eilenberg's phrase, "Wordsworth engineered the disgrace of *The Rime*" (*Strange Power* 9).

The first edition opens with an address to a supernatural storyteller:

> It is an ancyent Marinere,
> And he stoppeth one of three

"By thy long grey beard and thy glittering eye
"Now wherefore stoppest me?["]

(1–4)

In the second edition, this poem is retitled and buried (twenty-third of twenty-four) in the volume. The change from "Rime of the Ancyent Marinere" to "The Ancient Mariner. A Poet's Reverie" strips the Mariner of his role of poet by emphasizing the modern poet's imagination.

Writing to Wordsworth, Lamb objects to this shift: "What new idea is gained by this Title, but one subversive of all credit, which the tale should force upon us, of its truth?" (Lamb 90, 30 January 1801). Lamb contends that the change does not alter the poem's meaning, but clumsily intrudes the mechanism of that meaning. The consistency, in Wordsworth's view, of the change with the second edition can be seen in three other criticisms Lamb makes: first, "The Poet's Epitaph is disfigured, to my taste by the vulgar satire upon parsons and lawyers in the beginning"; second, "the instructions conveyed in ['The Old Cumberland Beggar'] are too direct and like a lecture: they don't slide into the mind of the reader, while he is imagining no such matter"; and third, he "wished the Critical preface had appeared in a separate treatise" (89–90). These objections aim at minimizing the professional profile of poetry. Wishing to be seized like the unsuspecting Wedding Guest, Lamb resists the Poet's acknowledgement of his own mediation, despite his realization that such mediation is the precondition of poetry.[17] To judge by Lamb's summary of Wordsworth's lost reply, the poet was not pleased by his friend's response. I suggest Wordsworth's peevishness ("four sweating pages," Lamb wrote; LEY 316) arose because Lamb, denying the success of the "experiment," echoed Wordsworth's own fear that the literary marketplace could sustain the professional poet only through his denial of professional status and his acquiescence to poetry's subordination within the economics of culture to legal and business discourses.[18]

A difference in attitudes toward the professional taleteller between Wordsworth and Lamb further clarifies Wordsworth's sense of professionalism as a visible, or legible, enterprise. In his "Note to the Ancient Mariner" appended to the poem, Wordsworth claims that the poem's first defect is "that the principal person has no distinct character, . . . in his profession of Mariner" (*Lyrical Ballads* 276–77); for Wordsworth, marks of travel and of storytelling should particularize the professional. Lamb objects to this demand for particularity: "I totally differ from your idea that the Marinere should have had a character and profession. This is a Beauty in Gulliver's Travels, where the mind is kept in a placid state of little wonderments; but the Ancient Marinere undergoes such Trials, as overwhelm and bury all individuality" (Lamb 90). For Wordsworth, trials would not bury the profession's individuality, but provide the means of its proof.[19] Lamb's letter, preserving the first edition's spelling of "Marinere," privileges Coleridge's poem as the initial flagbearer; Wordsworth's response was invested with professional anxieties.

Jerome McGann has suggested that the method of "The Ancient Mariner" layers historically distinct linguistic registers (including "textual layers of the most primitive, even pre-Christian, sort"; *The Beauty of Inflection* 153), which a reader decodes not by grasping the meaning of symbols but by locating historical differences.[20] If this contention is right, then Wordsworth's decision to substitute "Expostulation and Reply" also substitutes different theories of reading and history. As Coleridge presents it, the *Ballads* was collaborative in the writing—he does not recall who first proposed the scheme (*Biographia Literaria* 2: 5–6); in the reading, however, the poems were competitive. Would the reader's first encounter with an interpreter be William, whose discussion is with "[his] good friend Matthew" ("Expostulation" 15) and who can reuse words offered against him in the first stanza in his defense in the last; or would it be the wedding guest, held not so much against his will but by the control of his will, and who ends "stunn'd" and silent? Determining that the first of these moods will dominate—without erasing—the second is important to Wordsworth's project, set out in the Preface, of poetry as a mutual labor and contract between equals.

The echo in "Expostulation" to the "Ancyent Marinere" in the first edition becomes an anticipation in the second edition. Both "William" and the wedding guest sit on a stone, and, after the change of title for the "Ancient Mariner," both are placed in the dreamy space of a poet's reverie (William "dream[s his] time away" 4). Responding to the charge that he is ignoring his books, William replies: "The eye it cannot chuse but see, / We cannot bid the ear be still;" (17–18). The wedding guest, held in thrall by the Marinere's voice, "cannot chuse but hear" ("Rime" 22). While William has positioned himself to have only the one choice, the wedding guest confronts a violent interruption of his ordinary life.

When "Expostulation and Reply" opens the volume, the first line is an address to the named poet: "Why William, on that old grey stone . . ." (1). In the eighteenth poem of the anonymous first edition, "William" carried no referential force within a matrix of commonly named characters. Nothing indicates that "William" is a poet, rather than, say, an idle student.[21] In the first poem of the second edition, the reference is unavoidable, and the authority of the poet sanctions a "reply" consistent with the Preface. "William" rejects "the light bequeath'd, . . . the spirit breath'd / From dead men to their kind" (5–8), now a literary inheritance, in favor of "things for ever speaking" (26). The specificity of "Expostulation and Reply" as a dialogue does not allow "reading nature" to be generalized; it requires a distinctive literacy gained in a rural youth. This model relies on neither the appeal to reason as sufficient of itself nor a strict reliance on custom, to invoke reductive commonplaces of Godwinian and Burkean epistemology in 1800. Rather, the writers' minds imprinted by nature feed a communal mind:

> ["]there are powers,
> "Which of themselves our minds impress,
> "That we can feed this mind of ours,
> "In a wise passiveness.["]
>
> (21–24)

This formulation, emphasizing engaged passivity, suggests to me the similarity between Addison's Spectator and William (Wordsworth) as professional writer, although the Spectator operated primarily in the realms of commerce and William in that of nature.

As James Chandler has observed, William's reply to Matthew's challenge is oblique, even nonresponsive (*Second Nature* 151). He locates himself at a center point that becomes a locus of distribution for his own works. "[M]id all this mighty sum / Of things forever speaking" he will remain "Conversing as I may" ("Expostulation" 25–30). His continual translation of natural speech to poetic writing preserves a transcendent illusion that such writing is a form of speech, and not, as "The Tables Turned" puts it, part of the "dull and endless strife" (9) that books encapsulate. If, as Chandler suggests, William does not refute Matthew, then Matthew's harangue may be seen as the discourse, loaded with the legal rights theory of moral philosophy, from which the reply constructs its own difference. The writings of human beings, disjointed because of the constraints of literary production (a writer cannot forever speak, but must shuffle creations off to press) are pitted against the endless production of nature's voice, which may have its human figura in endless circulation. This debate is less argued than enacted.

At the center of "Expostulation and Reply"—the division between the two speakers—resides not knowledge (a "sadder but wiser" state) but mystery; this central stanza is the only one in the narrator's voice:

> One morning thus, by Esthwaite lake,
> When Life was sweet I knew not why
> To me my good friend Matthew spake,
> And thus I made reply"
>
> (13–16)

Aligning himself with Nature, William (Wordsworth) carves a position for himself that is subsumed by neither the Burkean nor Godwinian sides of the current literary strife. The poet does not investigate the sweetness of life, but transmits it as the enabling center of the debate it presumes to transcend; other authors, by implication, "murder to dissect" ("The Tables Turned" 28; a probably unintentional, though apt, echo of the attorney general who "dissected" Paine's work in order to prosecute).

In the context of "Expostulation and Reply," two other poems that stage debate are of interest, "Anecdote for Fathers" and "We Are Seven." Appellate Judge Richard Posner, with some exasperation, comments that "Romantic literature is forever lamenting the loss of the child's sense of boundless potential" (*Law and Literature* 144); though he discusses only "Ode: Intimations of Immortality," his totalizing language invites considering "Anecdote for Fathers" and "We Are Seven" under the same rubric. Posner suggests that "aging and experience gradually rub off" a child's "sense of vitality" and "of infinite horizons" (145). These two poems can serve to remind that "aging" and "experience" are abstractions, and that they must be lived through within concrete social bonds, the effects of which are not inevitable, but contingent. John Thelwall, for example, was not finally cured of his enthusiasm until specific legal and political mechinations properly aged him, and even Simon Lee's seemingly archtypal oldness carries its history of the social changes of the fall of the "hall of Ivor" ("Simon Lee" 22) and enclosure.

"Anecdote for Fathers" not only shows how the art of lying is taught but locates such an art as a perversion of objective language. When a demand for sophisticated language (i.e., the cross-examination "Why? Edward, tell me why?" [48]) is inflicted on a more original emotion, the result must be untruth and its linguistic equivalent, unreal language. The answer of the boy, as he spots the weathercock, demonstrates that his language works through the associations of objects but also that such a method risks perversion.[22]

The poem implicitly rejects the common theory of property by prior possession (which relies on a Lockean assumption that originary labor established a right of occupancy). The narrator's first assertion of possession, "I have a boy of five years old" (1), is reiterated without conscious recognition by his habit of holding the child by the arm (30, 34), recalling Goody Blake and, perhaps, the Ancient Mariner. Every reference to Edward in the first eleven stanzas is either explicitly possessive ("my boy" 17, 45), implicitly possessive by the use of a diminutive adjective ("little Edward" 37), or both ("my little boy" 25, "my little Edward" 38). At the moment of the lie, the references become impersonal ("The boy" 53), and in the final stanza, the child remains independent but increased in value ("Oh dearest, dearest boy"), while the father claims as his own that which is his only rightful possession ("my heart" 57). But in this new form, the father names the lack the poet can fill:

> Oh dearest, dearest boy! my heart
> For better lore would seldom yearn,
> Could I but teach the hundredth part
> Of what from thee I learn
>
> (57–60)

The poet fulfills the father's desire because the poet, keeping the incident intact, translates it into "better lore."

The father has murdered in order to dissect the child's pleasures, but, at least as Wordsworth described in the Fenwick note, the impulse for this poem is not merely the personal relation of father and son. The Fenwick note on "Anecdote for Fathers" begins: "This was suggested in front of Alfoxden. The Boy was a son of my friend Basil Montagu, who had been two or three years under our care" (Butler and Green 346). The note does not identify the "father" in the poem, and the assumption has generally been that it was Wordsworth himself (see Moorman I: 289). But, as Basil

Montagu visited his son at Alfoxden, his character might also shape the narrator, especially if his overpossessiveness is taken to compensate for his absences.[23] Basil Montagu was a struggling lawyer caught between his Godwinian notions and his desire for a successful legal practice when his son came to live with the Wordsworths. Accounts differ as to who suggested the scheme,[24] but Dorothy quickly anticipated that his father would "see a great improvement in Basil" (LEY 161, 30 November 1795). Later, she wrote that "we teach him nothing at present but what he learns from the evidence of his senses" (LEY 180, 19 March 1797); whatever the father can learn from the son is a result of what the poet's family enabled the son to learn from nature.

The Fenwick note offers another narrative about Wordsworth's inspiration for the poem which serves, from the perspective of a reader, as commentary: "I remember, once when Coleridge, he ["the famous John Thelwall"], and I were seated together upon the turf on the brink of a stream in the most beautiful part of the most beautiful glen of Alfoxden, Coleridge exclaimed, 'This is a place to reconcile one to all the jarrings and conflicts of the wide world.'—'Nay' said Thelwall 'to make one forget them altogether'" (Butler and Green 346).[25] This prose exchange is set as an idyll (embedded in six prepositional phrases) with a tone of easygoing indolence resembling the narrator's opening mood in "Anecdote." Especially as supplemented by Coleridge's account in which "the jarrings and conflicts of the wide world" become the explicitly political and legal subject of "treason," this fragment of a debate offers two different relations between the social and natural worlds, one in which distance makes analysis more possible, and the other in which distance makes analysis irrelevant. Thelwall's position resembles the child's; Coleridge's, the father's; and Thelwall gets the last word. This biographical material suggests that the poem concerns not just how an "art" may "be taught" but how an artistic discourse can represent other speakers—fathers, lawyers, public lecturers, radicals—in order to teach them. Even though Coleridge corroborates this story, the Fenwick notes are reconstructions by Wordsworth long after, and his decision to connect Thelwall's visit to this particular poem is best understood as an interpretation, rather than an explanation.

The Fenwick note to "We Are Seven" points out that the first stanza (written last by Coleridge) was, in part, a joke in "hitching our friend James Tobin's name, who was familiarly called Jem" (Butler and Green 348). The published line, "A simple child, dear brother Jim" (revised from "A little child, dear brother Jem") suggests, if only in jest, the narrator as the brother of James Tobin (though "brother" is primarily a familiar). The poem was composed sometime between early March and mid-May, and on March sixth, Wordsworth had written to Tobin, who was staying with his brother John Tobin, an attorney and not-yet-successful playwright, at "Barnard's Inn, close to R[ichard] W[ordsworth]'s chambers"; the letter's closing paragraph contains the regards of Basil Montagu, the boy of "Anecdote" (LEY 210). Like "Anecdote for Fathers," then, the strong, logical parental figure is at least intermittently associated with the legal profession. His accurate calculation of the various bodies ("you are five") accords with his rendering accounts on words, as if they were commodities to be properly deployed: "'Twas throwing words away" (67). Jay Clayton has argued that the grown-up's disproportionate response to the child's obstinacy stems from the uncanniness by which the child maintains bonds with the dead, a connection that makes her proof against more arithmetic connections (*Romantic Vision and the Novel* 111). At the poem's beginning, the narrator's response seems stripped of anxiety (except perhaps for the narratively unneeded desire to assert a familial connection with the auditor). The narrative poise signaled by the framing first stanza, however, dissolves as the narrator's "sheer exasperation" (Clayton, *Romantic Vision* 111) returns, until the opening moral, as well as rhetorical distance, is forgotten, leaving the girl the last word. Again, like "Anecdote for Fathers," the poem that preceded "We Are Seven" in the first edition and followed it in the second, a narrative control based on a legalistic understanding of reason and social bonds gives way before other, more powerful, and more original bonds. The understanding of such poems as debates between types of discourses is enhanced by encountering "Expostulation and Reply" first, but the Preface provides the clearest articulation of the nature of the poetic bond.

The New Contract

The Preface to the *Lyrical Ballads* originally stood as a defense of a specific set of poems; its subsequent revisions reveal a trajectory toward generalization, toward claiming the Wordsworthian doctrine as *the* poetic doctrine. W. J. B. Owen and J. W. Smyser indicate that "in 1836 and subsequent editions . . . the pronoun of the first person, especially in the form 'I', is fairly rigorously excluded" (*Prose* I: 111). This process of generalization is a common feature of Wordsworth's career, and certainly part of the interpretive impulse of the Fenwick notes. Its success is marked by the Preface's canonical status within twentieth-century anthologies independent of the poems it initially addressed. In this section, I recontextualize the first appearance of the Preface to restore a polemical character of Wordsworth's theorizing consistent with changing the opening poem from "Ancient Mariner" to "Expostulation and Reply."

Kurt Heinzelman notes the language of contract in the Preface. My reading accepts the operations Heinzelman has demonstrated, and suggests that, in response to reviews of the first edition and in anticipation of future critics, Wordsworth shapes the Preface as a legal argument. In this doubling of legal forms, Wordsworth first excludes the critic from the contract between reader and writer, and then defends that exclusion before the bar of the critic—where it becomes a claim about lack of jurisdiction. Paul Michael Privateer, concurring with Heinzelman's assessment that "Wordsworth regarded 'poetry itself as part of an economic transaction,'" notes that the opening of the *Prelude* both "speaks for and challenges the ideology of autonomous individuals," and, more particularly, that "contractual obligation is implicit in this form of individual freedom [i.e., the 'enfranchisement' of being outside of London, itself the site of enfranchisement]" (*Romantic Voices* 115, 122). In the Preface, similar contractual obligations accrue "from yon city's walls set free" (*Prelude* I: 7).

Wordsworth's contract in the literary marketplace eschews the usual protection by the court afforded an economic contract, and substitutes a common law of poetry that permits the poem (or poet) to secure a contract with the reader at the moment of articulation. The poetic contract and the legal contract are both analogues and rivals within the economic sphere because each attempts to regulate that sphere by constituting norms of public interactions. Wordsworth announces the rivalry wittily. Despite his claims to speak to the common man, he chooses an epigraph in Latin, the language of legal maxims. R. L. Brett and A. R. Jones translate it "Something not at all to your taste, Papinianus,"[26] and explain it as a private joke against the lawyer James Mackintosh (*Lyrical Ballads* 124). As such, it has both political and aesthetic dimensions. First, the political: Mackintosh's *Vindiciae Gallicae* was a powerful defense of the French Revolution, but in the summer of

1799, he had undertaken to refute his earlier work in thirty-nine lectures, "The Law of Nature and Nations." Both Godwin and Hazlitt heard these lectures with dismay, the latter writing, "To be a hawker of worn-out paradoxes, and a pander to sophistry denotes indeed a desperate ambition" (quoted in Herschel Baker, *William Hazlitt* 100).[27] In this context, the epigraph implies that the politics of the *Lyrical Ballads* remain true to ideals Mackintosh deserted. Next, aesthetic: Mackintosh's erudite style and refined taste are not suited for a reader of the *Lyrical Ballads*. This private reference, however, remained unavailable to most readers, and those of sufficient learning could find a more public gloss.

The line comes from the legal historian and antiquarian John Selden, in his foreword to Michael Drayton's *Poly-olbion*.[28] Aemilius Papinianus, a Roman jurist (140–212 AD), wrote a *Responsa*, a nineteen-volume work that served as the basic curriculum of postclassical law schools; third-year students were consequently called Papinianistae. Wordsworth does not write for the hack lawyers and defies the taste of especially those lawyers who saw themselves as the arbiters of taste: Papinianus' stature as a commentator was confirmed by an imperial decree that, should jurists disagree on a point, his view was authoritative. Robert Chambers, in his *Lectures on the English Law* (1767–1773), had identified Papinianus as "the greatest of Roman lawyers," and, as a defender of English jurisprudence, noted with pride that the jurist had "presided in Britain as prefect" (1: 95). The epigraph establishes a distance between poetic production and legal tradition, a gesture preparing the claim for the propriety of poetic social regulation.

The opening of the Preface reworks the terms of the Advertisement's second paragraph. In 1798, Wordsworth had described his poems as an "experiment": "They were written chiefly with a view to ascertain how far the language of conversation in the middle and lower classes of society is adapted to the purposes of poetic pleasure" (*Lyrical Ballads* 7). The issue is whether specifically rustic speech can be adapted. The Preface widens both the stakes of the experiment and the range of the poet's interest: "It [the first edition] was published, as an experiment which, I hoped, might be of some use to ascertain, how far, by fitting to metrical arrangement a selection of the real language of men in a state of vivid sensation, that sort of pleasure and that quantity of pleasure may be imparted, which a Poet may rationally endeavour to impart" (*Lyrical Ballads* 241). The "selection" comes from the language of "low and rustic life," for historical and potentially transitory reasons, but now that choice occurs within the general exploration of the "real language of men."

By "real," Wordsworth does not mean the words of actual speakers, since merely reshuffling those words into verse results in "triviality and meanness both of thought and language . . . more dishonorable to the Writer's own character than false refinement" (246). Instead, "real language" is associated with the Latin root, *res*, "thing" ("Expostulation"'s "Things for ever speaking"). Johnson's three definitions of "real" are pertinent: "1. Relating to things not persons; not personal"; "2. Not fictitious; not imaginary; true; genuine"; and "3. In law, consisting of things immoveable, as land."

1. "Relating to things not persons; not personal": The real language of men speaks about things—land, cloth, natural objects—and it comes from a communicating relationship with these things, rather than from an abstracted property interest in them. Wordsworth chooses the rustic as his source of real language "because such men hourly communicate with the best objects [things] from which the best part of language is originally derived" (*Lyrical Ballads* 245). Wordsworthian poetry, then, attempts to reinvest language with objective origins. Further, these origins do not exist only in the past, as in the legal doctrine of prior possession, but persist through constant renewal. In his note to "The Thorn" (1800), Wordsworth argues that a "chief" reason for the beauty and value of "repetition and apparent tautology" in poetry is "the interest which the mind attaches to words, not only as symbols of the passion, but as *things*, active and efficient, which are of themselves part of the passion" (Butler and Green 351).[29]

The repetitions in "The Thorn" itself, including the near echoes of "Misery" and "Martha Ray," are part of the attempt to make the thorn as "impressive" an "object" to a reader as a storm had made it to him (Butler and Green 350). Describing the poem as "Wordsworth's most extreme experiment in pathos," James Averill associates the exacting terrain of the poem's scene with the "uncertain ground between the misery we read about" (whether in this poem, in the "true" story of Martha Ray, Basil Montagu's murdered grandmother, or in the belabored prose explanation of the narrating sea Captain in the 1800 edition) and "that which we see too clearly in the world around us" (*Suffering* 168). The intruding auditor, who catalogues details like the narrator's second self, seems to have caught more than just the "narrator's obsessive iterations" (Averill, *Suffering* 174). He interrupts just after the narrator offers Martha Ray's direct discourse of "Oh woe is me! oh misery" ("The Thorn" 66, 77), and his own "wherefore" (five times), "why" (twice), and "what" (four times) reenact, in the agony of not knowing, Martha Ray's "woe" with which these interrogatives are associated by alliteration.[30] The accumulation of the narrator's "numerical" details and testimony (catalogued by Susan Wolfson, *The Questioning Presence* 55) does not solve a mystery, but complicates it. When the narrator returns in the final stanza to the "plain" facts (244), they are in stark opposition to the possibility of legal discovery: "And some had sworn an oath that she / Should be to public justice brought / . . . I cannot tell how this may be" ("The Thorn" 232–33, 243). For Wordsworth, this uncertainty constitutes an experiment not just in pathos, but in the real. Real language, deriving from objects, is not personal. It does not express the passion of an individual, but produces a passion accessible to and exchangeable between poet and multiple readers.

2. "Not fictitious; not imaginary; true; genuine": Real language does not necessarily describe actual events. In the Advertisement, Wordsworth announces that except for "Goody Blake and Harry Gill," all the poems "are either the absolute inventions of the author, or facts which took place within his personal observation or that of his friends" (*Lyrical Ballads* 8). These three sources equally adapt real language to the extent that they successfully "make the incidents of common life interesting by tracing in them, truly though not ostentatiously, the primary laws of our nature: chiefly as far as regards the manner in which we associate ideas in a state of excitement" (*Lyrical Ballads* 244–45). The discourse of poetry and the lived experiences of the farmer both reflect primary laws, although the former is corrupted when it lacks social autonomy and grounds itself in affected (unreal, moveable, illegal) language, while the erosion of the latter concerns economic disruptions. To be true, then, is to be lawful, and these laws are rooted in nature, but this nature itself gains existence in the poetic procedure of encountering and interpreting real language.

The theory of natural law was a commonplace already used by two sides, Blackstone and Burke, Paine and Godwin, to justify opposed views of English Constitutionalism. From Wordsworth's perspective in the late 1790s, however, these theorists either perverted nature by falsely asserting that the existing human laws in fact derived from nature (as Blackstone did) or falsely believed that nature's laws could be derived by an inspection of only the human soul (as Godwin's Platonism implied). In "Lines Written in

Early Spring," Wordsworth argued that the laws of association of thought corresponded to (and become intelligible through) natural phenomena: "To her fair works did nature link / The human soul that through me ran" (5–6). As Wordsworth recalls these lines in the Fenwick note, they were "actually composed while I was sitting by the side of a brook" (*Lyrical Ballads* 287). Despite the many natural objects depicted—a grove, primrose tufts, birds, breeze—the poem never mentions a brook; the human soul, in the fluidity expressed in line 6, replaces it, or prepares for its eventual appearance as the older Wordsworth's recollection of the *actual*.[31] The human soul and Nature's fair works are linked, but the soul that "through me ran" is not identical with the individual. It is, rather, impersonal, that which compels the poet to thought, as in the last stanza:

> If I these thoughts [that twigs have pleasure, etc.] may not prevent
> If such be of my creed the plan,
> Have I not reason to lament
> What man has made of man?
>
> ("Early Spring" 21–24)

In this rhetorical question, man is both producer and material, but the product is the negation of the effortless production of pleasure that impresses itself on the speaker. The vague lament refers as easily to the fall of the ancient regime as to the English response to the French Revolution. In any case, man has manufactured himself in his own image and his language is no longer real.

3. "In law, consisting of things immoveable, as land": Beyond the actual protection of copyright, Wordsworth seeks a deeper claim, that language is a continual product of the poetic "occupation," a word that, with the senses of both work and occupancy, joins labor and property. To be occupied by language, or to occupy it, does not make language private, any more than the solitary work of the farmer remains secluded; both must be brought to market. Here, however, a difference between poetic labor and agrarian work becomes apparent. While language does literally circulate—volumes are bought, magazines distributed—the meaning remains fixed at a virtual origin, the Poet's sensibilities (William on the stone). What the farmer sells no longer names him. The paradox here of motion and stability is not unique to Wordsworth's aesthetics, but emerges in most ideological attempts to represent the marketplace to itself, since the market is itself stable in order to authorize motion within it. Words-

worth, however, hermetically seals meaning, and therefore economic value, into the poet as the (re)producer of the real by his discussion of "purpose."

WORDSWORTH OFFERS a contemptuous version of marketing poems, in describing poets who "indulge in arbitrary and capricious habits of expression in order to furnish food for fickle tastes and fickle appetites of their own creation" (*Lyrical Ballads* 246). In the next paragraph, Wordsworth distinguishes his poems from those usually encountered in that "each one of them has a worthy *purpose*" arising from "the habit of meditation." The name "Poet" and its instantiation "Wordsworth" secure this remark: "If in this opinion I am mistaken, I can have little right to the name of Poet." The right to that name is a *copy*right, the right to copy himself throughout the social text. The reissue of the *Lyrical Ballads*, combined with the unexpected success of the first edition, has materially established the right to the name and even a communal duty toward it: "Several of my friends are anxious for the success of these Poems" (242).

The purpose of the poems turns out to be their own expression. Wordsworth notes that "my descriptions of such objects as strongly excite those feelings, will be found to carry along with them a *purpose*" (246). The purpose appears to be ancillary to the feelings, or derived from their successful rendition, but in the next paragraph, Wordsworth collapses the distinction. The purpose "will be found principally to be: *namely* to illustrate the manner in which our feelings and ideas are associated in a state of excitement" (247; my italics). The laws of association both validate the poetry and are validated by it. Wordsworth repeatedly articulates the same circle in which origin is at once manifested and veiled. The definition of poetry is a crucial example:

> I have said that Poetry is the spontaneous overflow of powerful feelings: it takes its origins from emotion recollected in tranquility: the emotion is contemplated till by a species of reaction the tranquility gradually disappears, and an emotion, similar to that which was before the subject of contemplation, is gradually produced, and does itself actually exist in the mind. In this mood successful composition generally begins, and in a mood similar to this it is carried on. (266)

The passage begins as already having been said, so that the condition of spontaneity itself can be contextualized, revealed not as spontaneous but enmeshed within the poetic labor that it both overflows and fills by overflowing. The "origins" of Poetry arise in the midst of making poetry, in the habits of meditation: the emotion that validates the labor precedes and is preceded by poetry, and it is, then, constructed by poetic intention. The space of tranquility is occupied and consumed. The process of recollection presumes something previous made again to "actually exist," and this recreation becomes an original act that preserves re-collected emotions. The origins of poetry are not so much obscure as late; poetry begins already made. The second sentence of the quotation locates the definition of poetry given in the first ("Poetry is . . .") *as* the "mood" in which poetry "generally begins." The referent to "this mood" is uncertain, or, to turn it around, by describing the shifts of poetic composition as a single mood, Wordsworth asserts a homogeneity in the transitions between emotion, tranquility, and emotion again.

The recreated emotion is "similar" to some more primal feeling; and is capable of recreating itself in the reader. This recreation allows the Poet to become analogous to Nature: "Now if Nature be thus cautious in preserving in a state of enjoyment a being thus employed [the Poet], the Poet ought to profit by the lesson thus held forth to him, and ought especially to take care, that whatever passions he communicates to his Reader, those passions, if his Reader's mind be sound and vigorous, should always be accompanied with an overbalance of pleasure" (*Lyrical Ballads* 266). By "preserving" the "employed" poet in "a state of enjoyment," Nature protects the labor of the Poet who repays the debt indirectly by providing an "overbalance of pleasure," to the reader. This pleasure, a reciprocation enacted by circulation akin to that in a gift economy, contracts the reader into the labor of reading, on behalf of both writer and nature. The reader's necessary qualities of soundness and vigor recall the "better soil" of the working rustic, but overlaid with the city's sense for profit.[32] Wordsworth shifts between imagery of gifts and purchase. The Poet intends to profit from Nature and this accumulation overflows into the act of reading. Reading, then, like composition, begins already begun. The quoted sentence, however, can be emphasized in two ways. The first centers the poet's obligation ("care") toward the Reader as a contract, with Nature replacing Law as the horizon of enforcement. The second way repositions the obligation of the reader. Since poetry arose with an overflow of emotion, the reader ought to feel pleasure, unless his mind is not "sound and vigorous," which would implicate that reader in the "multitude of causes" that "blunt the discriminating powers of the mind" (249). Wordsworth defends his poetry with this appeal.

Finally, the systemization which he apparently rejects is present within the framework of that rejection. Even the specific reason he offers for not presenting an entire system locates literature at the heart of social interaction; the full defense would require "retracing the revolutions not of literature alone but likewise of society itself" (243). As I argue by example in the next chapter, this "retracing" is the task of the poems that the Preface authorizes.

Wordsworth's friends have suggested that "if the views with which [these poems] were composed, were indeed realized, a class of Poetry would be produced, well adapted to interest mankind permanently, and not unimportant in the multiplicity and in the quality of its moral relations; and on this account they have advised me to preface a systematic defence of the theory, upon which the poems were written" (*Lyrical Ballads* 242). The systematic defense would operate, at a metalevel of analysis, on a reading public (mankind) as the writing of a single poem at the level of emotional engagement does on the reader. The poet produces simultaneously poetry (as poems and as "a class of Poetry") and the laws of poetry (theory), and this self-sustaining, double production "interest[s] mankind" in both the "multiplicity" and "quality" of its "moral relationships." The rules of poetic discourse structure moral relationships just as the legal system regulates society while and by regulating itself through the science of jurisprudence. That Wordsworth refuses the task of this defense even as he presents it suggests the danger of the territory he invades, and Francis Jeffrey's continual public attacks, despite private claims of enjoying Wordsworth's work, represent a predictable response.

But why a preface at all?

Wordsworth wishes to avoid the "impropriety in abruptly obtruding upon the Public . . . Poems so materially different from those, upon which general approbation is at present bestowed." As with "real," the full range of "materially" is called for. The poems are of a different fabric, a different texture. This remark has a rhetorical dimension emphasizing Wordsworth's originality, but it also situates a new contract between poet and reader, secured by a new property. In the next paragraph, Wordsworth presents the traditional contract: "It is supposed that by the act of writing in verse an Author makes a formal engagement that he will gratify certain known habits of association, that he not only apprizes the reader that certain classes of ideas and expressions will be found in his book, but that others will be carefully excluded" (*Lyrical Ballads* 243).

Supposed by whom? Or rather, where does the power to assert such suppositions lie? At one level, Wordsworth is appealing to the common practices of poetry, but such practices have gained regulative force because of their commonness. So, the supposition resides in the laws of association. Because he will later argue that poetry can regulate those laws, Wordsworth contradicts these rules of inclusion and exclusion in the manner common law is challenged, by arguing that the rules have been inconstant and not in force from time immemorial: "This exponent or symbol held forth by metrical language must in different areas of literature have excited very different expectations: for example, in the age of Catullus Terence and Lucretius, and that of Statius or Claudian, and in our own country, in the age of Shakespeare and Beaumont and Fletcher, and that of Donne and Cowley, or Dryden, or Pope" (243). Wordsworth articulates these ages by the poets who, he claims implicitly, typified them. These poets name their ages, exerting a copyright over them by representing the condition of their historical intelligibility; without naming Shakespeare, the Shakespearean renaissance cannot be written. While these authors become the source of difference rather than of continuity, a continuity of difference is implicit in linking the Latin writers with the English, since the Roman conquest of England is taken as a civilizing origin grounded in Roman law introduced by prefects such as Papinianus.

This consolidation prepares for Wordsworth's consideration of the current age and his relation to it: "I will not take upon me to determine the exact import of the promise which by the act of writing in verse an Author in the present day makes to his Reader; but I am certain it will appear to many persons that I have not fulfilled the terms of an engagement thus voluntarily contracted." The certainty with which he interprets the response of "many people" implies that Wordsworth is capable of the determination that he declines. By refusing an analysis of the "promise" that the "act of writing in verse" *de jure* inflicts on an Author, Wordsworth opens a space to rewrite the contract himself while distinguishing "the Reader" (his reader) from the "many persons": "I hope therefore the Reader will not censure me, if I attempt to state what I have proposed to myself to perform, and also (as far as the limits of a preface will permit) to explain some of the chief reasons which have determined me in the choice of my purpose: . . ." Wordsworth avails himself of the widening range of contract which the convertibility of the marketplace permitted. But in the usual terms of a contract, the voluntary entry into it is not sufficient to validate it; the court must also be willing to enforce it. Wordsworth presents the contract—the preface itself—as self-validating and self-limiting, hence the parenthetical phrase in which form constitutes license. The proposal between Wordsworth and himself scripts the contract between reader and writer. Wordsworth completes the sentence by justifying this appropriation with a consideration balanced for both parties: "that at least he [the Reader] may be spared any unpleasant feeling of disappointment, and that I myself may be protected from the most dishonourable accusation which can be brought against an Author, namely, that of indolence which prevents him from endeavouring to ascertain what is his duty, or, when his duty is ascertained prevents him from performing it" (*Lyrical Ballads* 243–44). The contract of the Preface provides its own protection without recourse to its enforcement by an outside agent. Rather, a proper reading of the Preface (contract) constitutes both the meeting of the minds and the consideration necessary for the contract to have force.

After clarifying his purpose of exploring the associations of the mind by brief descriptions of several poems, Wordsworth details "the general importance of the subject": "to endeavor to produce or enlarge this capability ["of excitement without the application of gross and violent stimulants" in the reader] is one of the best services in which, at any period, a Writer can be engaged" (249). The metaphors of productivity invoke an economic horizon, but Wordsworth provides a critique of that horizon as having inadvertently created a need the poet can meet. The solution is not supplying the lacking "gross stimulants," which deepen the lack, but recalling the mind to its more delicate possibilities: "A multitude of causes unknown to former times are now acting with a combined force to blunt the discriminating powers of the mind, and unfitting it for all voluntary exertion to reduce it to a state of almost savage torpor" (249). Wordsworth recognizes that forces have "combined," have managed to accumulate into their own structure, and oppose the mind's delicate powers.[33] The term *the mind*, however, develops its own accumulative force—it is not the particular minds of individuals that are at stake, but the objective mind to which real language speaks. The oxymoron of "savage torpor" catches the frenzy of the economic marketplace madly creating the products (civilization) that sustain it by virtue of (and not despite) their inadequacy.

Wordsworth outlines the causes of the savage torpor: "the great national events which are daily taking place, and the encreasing accumulation of men in cities, where the uniformity of their occupations produces a craving for extraordinary incident which the rapid communication of intelligence hourly gratifies" (249). This market consolidation opposes the poet's craft. Where these forces accumulate men, the poet acts in solitude to join men together in the disparate act of reading. Where the men are made uniform by occupation, the poet differentiates the "more subtle windings" of the mind and insists on the individuation implicit in the unalienated labor. Where the economic structure of the city creates a craving, the poet fulfills an obligation. Where the men of the city require "the extraordinary incident," the poet provides "the fluxes and refluxes of the mind when agitated by the great and simple affections of our nature." Where the structure of communication must be rapid to meet the craving, the poet's purpose arises from having "thought long and deeply" (246–47). And where the city creates and gratifies the needs of workers by molding them into a "uniformity," the poet offers a contract obligating the reader to use the mind's capacity for excitement as a mode of self-knowledge.

The charge against the great national events demands that writers take sides, and Wordsworth laments that "to this tendency of life and manners the literature and theatrical exhibitions of the country have conformed themselves" (249). This conformity is double, at the levels of both content and form; these works ("frantic novels," "deluges of idle and extravagant stories in verse") provide the extraordinary incidents that are craved and constitute an accumulation of writers with a uniformity of occupation. This moment represents a radical challenge to the condition of literature, but Wordsworth retreats from it. For his poetry to succeed, it must act within a field of language that it cannot, of itself, sustain. Writing about diction, he presents a less confrontational attitude: "Not but that I believe that others who pursue a different track may *interest* [the reader] likewise: I do not *interfere* with their *claim*, I only wish to *prefer* a different claim of my own" (251, my italics; each italicized word appears in *Black's Law Dictionary*). The metaphor of interference and preference is from a bankruptcy action, a suitable image for the danger in which readers now discover themselves. Wordsworth does not interfere with other claims, that is, he does not inquire into the validity of the agreement between readers and other authors. Since these authors respond to the contingencies of the market, the readers who constitute the market have an interest in them. In preferring his claim, Wordsworth demands a priority on the capital (reading time, money, thoughtfulness) of the reader. The image doubles the reader as the creditor (or party of the contract) and the judge who must enforce the claims. The assertion of priority and the contention that his poems disclose the fundamental laws of association form a single argument.

Wordsworth's poems, then, perform a critical function of providing the regulations by which human behavior can be understood and poetry judged: "I have taken as much pains to avoid [poetic diction] as others ordinarily take to produce it; this I have done for the reason already alleged, to bring my language near to the language of men . . . [my good sense] has necessarily cut me off from a large portion of phrases and figures of speech which from father to son have long been regarded as the common inheritance of Poets" (251). By explicitly invoking the "real language of men," but dropping the adjective, Wordsworth suggests the success of his argument: only the "real language of men" is a language of "men"; other languages serve other masters. The production of false language, as in refined eighteenth-century wit, creates a personal property interest that can be inherited as a commodity. The image of the father passing it on to the son cuts off poetry from the production of a real language recreated by labor, and so Wordsworth refuses his inheritance. Not that he refuses a property interest in his poetry, but that he wants one of greater durability.

The old hereditary structure of primogeniture, with its analogue of monarchy, remained a vital legal metaphor despite having been abolished in all cases except for intestacy in 1669. Godwin and Paine questioned the validity of such inheritance by demonstrating its conventional basis. Paine, to mock the absurdity of hereditary titles, imagined "the ridiculous insignificance into which literature . . . would sink, were [it] made hereditary" (*Rights* 176); and Godwin, admiring the joke, specified it to the court-appointed office of Poet Laureate (*Enquiry* 468). Wordsworth has omitted many "proper and beautiful" expressions because they "have been foolishly repeated by bad Poets till such feelings of disgust are connected with them as it is scarcely possible by any art of association to overpower" (*Lyrical Ballads* 251). As words are seized by bad poets, they become inaccessible to good ones. This gives the reader a stake in eliminating bad poets, because it is the reader's associations that are being abused. The turn of the Preface at this point is to move from a defensive posture to one of mutual compliance. The interests of poet and reader merge into a contractual agreement that excludes critics who merely apply laws of poetry.

Wordsworth highlights this exclusion in the continued discussion of poetic style. Many critics, he says, find a line which, "though naturally arranged and according to the strict laws of metre, does not differ from that of prose," and they "imagine they have made a notable discovery, and exult over the Poet as over a man ignorant of his own profession" (252). He rebuffs this charge by illustrating his competence not in poetry but in criticism.

In reading Thomas Gray's poem, "Sonnet on the Death of Richard West," Wordsworth co-opts the point of the poem—that the solace of the overblown language ("reddening Phoebus lifts his golden fire") pales before the grief packed into such simple lines as "My lonely anguish melts no hearts but mine"—in order to establish his own authority. He claims that only the prosaic lines are "of any value," as if the observation criticizes, rather than subscribes to, the poem's own values.[34] By this strategic co-option, Wordsworth reverses Wrangham's comment that a good critic must be a poet also; instead, as a professional, a poet has the self-consciousness that allows the best criticism—precisely because critical rules do not precede poetic instances.

He objects to rigid laws of poetic diction because they arbitrarily place "the Reader utterly at the mercy of the Poet," but he veers from an appeal for anarchy. The meter and rhyme, in contrast to diction, "obey certain laws, to which the Poet and Reader both willingly submit because they are certain, and because no interference is made by them with the passion but such as the concurring testimony of ages has shewn to heighten and improve the pleasure which co-exists with it" (*Lyrical Ballads* 262). The willing submission to law presents law as a kind of contract, grounded in tradition, and opposes the idea that the law creates contract. David Hume had already demonstrated that the notion of an original contract was not well founded in history, law, or philosophy, and that people submitted to the regulations into which they were born because of a horizon of coercion; from his perspective, as a defender of the newly forming marketplace, this coercion was not malicious but a historical circumstance. Wordsworth has recognized this point in describing the usual marketplace for "idle and extravagant stories in verse," but here he suggests that poetry can introduce a new covenant that retains the forms (meter) of the old one, but enforces new content.

In his prose, Wordsworth has reworked the mutual agreement sought by the narrator of "Simon Lee":

> O reader! had you in your mind
> Such stores as silent thought can bring,
> O gentle reader! you would find
> A tale in every thing.
> What more I have to say is short,
> I hope you'll kindly take it;
> It is no tale; but should you think,
> Perhaps a tale you'll make it.
>
> (73–80)

Just as Wordsworth adds "to my stock of poetry" (LEY 215, 12 April 1798)[35] in order to deploy it into books, readers must call on their "stores" to recuperate the poems. The echo of "stores" in this stanza to an earlier description of Simon Lee ("Few months of life has he in store"[65]) suggests the seriousness of the matter; life itself must be stored in such a way that labor remains inscribed on the store and can be reactivated. A reader who has lived in the proper way can make a tale that is the tale the poet has made. Although the narrator of "Simon Lee" does not recognize the implications of his incident—he cannot interpret Simon Lee's tears nor his own consequent "mourning"—the reader presumably can, and must. The reviews of the first edition largely skipped "Simon Lee"; Burney, who commented on every poem, ignores the "Incident."[36] Not until Wordsworth appears by name do the two narrative levels of the poem emerge, the first in which Simon Lee and the narrator engage in a misguided contract of misunderstood labor, and the second in which the reader and Wordsworth mutually construct from that misunderstanding a genuine tale.

A serial relationship between the critic and reader is implicit in the structure of the reviews. One does not read alone, but in a matrix of readers who judge or defer to the readings of others. A consensus of judgment can be achieved, a verdict rendered through the jurisdiction of the reviewers. Wordsworth denies the validity of such a verdict and the claim of jurisdiction. In the closing argument of the Preface, Wordsworth requests "that in judging these Poems he [the Reader] would decide by his own feelings genuinely, and not by reflection upon what will probably be the judgment of others." Wordsworth's appeal aims at individual reviewers, asking them to respond like "my Reader" and not in the "mode of criticism so destructive of all sound unadulterated judgment" (*Lyrical Ballads* 270). Wordsworth rhetorically disrupts the reviewing institution by relocating its participants in a poetic, not critical, relation to the poet.

In his concluding sentence, however, he structures a serial relationship back into the Reader/Poet exchange: "From what has been said, and from a perusal of the Poems, the Reader will be able clearly to perceive the object which I have proposed to myself: he will determine how far I have attained this object; and, what is a much more important question, whether it be worth attaining; and upon the decision of these two questions will rest my claim to the approbation of the public" (272). Wordsworth has presented his evidence, the poems, and his rationale, the Preface, and from these, the reader can determine the result of two claims. In resting his defense, Wordsworth transforms the reader (consistently an individual in contrast to the critics who have been a teeming mass throughout the Preface) into a "public," a poetic institution. The labor of the individual reader, like that of the poet, can accumulate, can form a marketplace, and provided the critic does not manipulate that market, can do so without losing the individual character of reading.

Wordsworth's contractual approach eschews the usual protections of a contract—lawyer and critic—and instead insists on a mutuality between reader and writer; this very procedure, however, reveals a tension, if not a contradiction, in his work. Individual readers can accumulate into a market, and indeed must to the extent that books are sold, discussed, reissued, and so on; but they do so, in Wordsworthian terms, by denying the collective market character of their endeavors as readers and poets. The property Wordsworth creates is at once a poem and a way of reading which cannot be contained in the market yet can claim to represent the market while being a perfectly transparent exchange product between reader and poet.

THE SECOND EDITION garnered few reviews, but its Preface became the object of critical execration for the next decade. In the first issue of the *Edinburgh Review*, Francis Jeffrey used the occasion of Southey's *Thalaba* to attack Wordsworth's aesthetics, "the perverted taste for simplicity," and its results, the commemoration of "the chattering of Harry Gill's teeth" (1 [October 1802]: 68). Jeffrey's own agenda, his resistance to Wordsworth's system making, depends on his situation as a Scottish lawyer dedicated to legitimizing the market economy in a way that positions the courts as the arbiters of contracts, and, by corollary, the critics as the arbiters of a taste "long established like the doctrines of religion." Jeffrey knew that religion had a long and bloody history of doctrinal disputes, but he represents the doctrines as transcending their own history and, like common law, persisting from time immemorial. Such a view, seemingly a middle ground of political, aesthetic, and legal debate, unified a wide range of discourse. By controlling what constituted legitimate discourse, Jeffrey's reviewing procedures set the political standards and limits for the discourse of the reviewing industry. These limits were depicted as aesthetic judgments but also represented the ideological supports and possibilities of the marketplace.[37] They excluded discussions that radically questioned the marketplace; what they included allowed a range of disagreement but referred back to fundamental tenets. As a concrete example, two politically opposed journals, the *Satirist* and the *Poetic Register*, used the terms of Jeffrey's review against Wordsworth.

Despite Wordsworth's claim that the Preface was not a systematic defense, critics insisted that he was a builder of systems. Reviewing *Poems, in Two Volumes*, the *Satirist* recalled: "This gentleman published two volumes of Lyric Ballads [sic] some years ago, which were composed on a system of his own: as if poetry was a mechanical art, and performed its operations by certain regulated processes, and not an appeal to the hearts and feelings of mankind" (1 [November 1807]: 188). The impulse to dismiss this reading as stupid since Wordsworth does emphasize emotions misses the reviewer's rhetorical situation. The distinction between the mechanical and the emotional denies both the associationalist psychology that invigorates much of Wordsworth's work and the role that the market's regulative processes take in developing poetry. This is the image of the romantic poet, inspired, effusive, unbusinesslike. Since the claim secures the domain of the analytic for the critic and the critic's analysis can adjudicate the presence of genuine emotion, the poet's role becomes subordinate. The review, upending Wordsworth's Preface, satirizes his "grand system of poetry," which separates him from other poets and even from himself: "The gossipping style of those productions, in which his practice corresponded with his theory, was the object of universal ridicule; but whenever he forgot his system, and consulted his feelings, he displayed genuine talent" (189).

Without denying, in fact praising, Wordsworth's poetic talents, the reviewer condemns Wordsworth's critical abilities, both in themselves and for their effects on his poetry. While not explicitly political, the review signals the ideological implications of Wordsworth's effort to center himself at the expense of the critic: "If a certain *ex-chancellor* were to write a book of the same size, it could not contain a greater number of *I*'s and *me*'s. Almost a ludicrous contrast is produced between the swelling self-sufficiency of the writer, and the extreme insignificance of the object described" (189). The chancellor (who did not remain out of office for long) was Lord Eldon, who had aided the prosecutions of Thomas Paine as well as heading the prosecution against the members of the London Corresponding Society; he had declared his conservative values early and often. On the bench, his self-importance had manifested itself in the meticulous attention with which he approached cases, "however marginal or insignificant" (Nicholas Underhill, *The Lord Chancellor* 166). By ridiculing both Wordsworth and Eldon, and suggesting that their mistakes are systematic rather than aberrant, the reviewer bolsters the current Lord Chancellor, Erskine, who had defended Hardy and Horne Tooke.[38] The struggle against Wordsworth's false innovations intersects the effort for reform.

Wordsworth's political position was not read universally as reactionary, and critiques from the other side also invoked Jeffrey's terms. The notice of *Poems, in Two Volumes* in the *Poetical Register for 1806–07* (1811), produced by "the high-church publishers of the British Critic" (Reiman, *Romantics Reviewed* A2: 814) describes the volume as "calculated to excite disgust and anger in a lover of poetry. The drivelling nonsense . . . is insufferable, and it is equally insufferable that such nonsense should have been written by a man capable, as he is, of writing well" (*Poetical Register* [1811] 540–41). The insistence on calculation establishes a guilty intent, and this reviewer finds the same cause as does the *Satirist*: "But Mr. Wordsworth is a System maker . . . on the altar of that system he sacrifices melody, elegance, spirit, and even common sense. Whenever he deviates from his monstrous system he writes like a man of genius" (541). The metaphor of idolatry, signifying the effort to establish a religion and a ritual marking its inauguration, indicates that the central worry of the reviewer is not that Wordsworth lacks melody and common sense, but his effect on these qualities in society generally. In the notice following this one, the reviewer praises Mrs. Opie by implicitly contrasting her work with Wordsworth's: "Still less . . . does she imitate those persons who present to us an idiot in rags, as a specimen of native grace and decorum" (541). The concern of the critics was not, then, only aesthetic but involved questions of economic power, both literally, in the promotion of poems and review vehicles, and ideologically, in the manner in which critics and poets presented society to itself. In the next chapter, I turn to Wordsworth's presentation of society in the 1800 poems, the evidence of his system's success or failure.

SIX

Evidentiary Poems: The Second Edition

But we are press'd by heavy laws,
And often, glad no more,
We wear a face of joy, because
We have been glad of yore.
—"The Fountain, A Conversation"

WORDSWORTH'S genius as a poet was rarely disputed. In damning reviews, it was an aggravating circumstance by which to condemn the Wordsworthian system. While many poems, especially those in a register of simple language, were ridiculed, other poems that Wordsworth presented as reliance for his poetic contract became counterevidence in the court of Francis Jeffrey and other reviewers: the persuasiveness of the poem's power regarding human nature announced the superfluousness of the poet's theorizing, which distractingly and unaesthetically located that nature in a social context.[1] By turning to a range of poems from the second volume of the 1800 *Lyrical Ballads*—from classics of the anthologies ("The Old Cumberland Beggar") to one Wordsworth dropped from his collected editions after 1815 ("Andrew Jones")[2]—I argue the interrelationship between Wordsworth's commentary in his poems about legal/economic issues and his presentation of the poet's role as a mediator between various social locations across class and geography. In particular, the mediation between local and national customs, properties, and relations, culminating in "Michael," are explored throughout the second volume.

These readings, not exhaustive even in terms of their legal allusions, open a vista on the entire volume through the accumulation of evidence. I have chosen a sample (comprising roughly half the lines of the volume) in which fairly definable legal and professional issues surface, although certain omitted poems would have done as well. For example, "Ruth," the only long poem not discussed, turns on the crime of abandonment by Ruth's lover, whose attractiveness, however, derived from stories of his "lawless" state that could not be preserved in the legalizing institution of marriage. Failing to see Ruth's affinity to the lawless state (she escapes from a "prison" for the insane) and the extent to which her life mirrors her lover's, the narrator offers her the legalistic consolation of a "hallow'd" (224) burial in compensation for the inability of the proper form ("in the Church our faith will plight" 98) to secure the marriage.[3] An expanded reading of this poem could relate legal and interpretive boundaries in the construction of Ruth's identity to her mythic function in the local community as exemplar or scapegoat.

Two other sets of poems require notice; I discuss neither the Lucy poems nor the Matthew poems (which provides the epigraph to this chapter). Both groups, as has been frequently noted, concern boundaries and memory (see, for example, Hartman, *Wordsworth's Poetry* 158–60 and Tilottama Rajan, *The Supplement of Reading* 138–39). While the genres of lyric and eulogy obscure the institutional antagonists that make competing claims on memory and boundary, these poems are indirectly illuminated by their placement amid the poems I do discuss.[4]

The Right to Name: "Hart-Leap Well"

Geoffrey Hartman comments that "it is striking that many [of the *Lyrical Ballads*] are built around a 'spot,' whether in nature or in the psyche" (*Wordsworth's Poetry* 141). "Expostulation and Reply," in this context, revolves around the stone from which William will not budge. Equally striking, these spots themselves are built around, or become visible through, stories or what might be regarded as protopoems. Neither "spot" nor narrative has an extractable priority, but, like nature and property, they emerge simultaneously in a sustaining tension of inscription.[5] "Hart-Leap Well" revolves around the well built to commemorate the death of the Hart, but it becomes visible only through the story. As Wordsworth explained to Isabella Fenwick: "Both the stones and the well are objects that may easily be missed; the tradition [i.e., the story] by this time may be extinct in the neighbourhood: the man who related it to us was very old" (*Lyrical Ballads* 298).

As Hartman has suggested (*Wordsworth's Poetry* 142), Wordsworth encounters the tale upon his return to Grasmere and embeds in the Hart's return to the well a powerful nostalgia that mirrors his own attachment to the Lake District. This correspondence allows Wordsworth to preserve a tradition, even as it dies out locally. To the extent that Wordsworth relied on an intersection of land and imagination (spot and time), his work was positioned against other ways of claiming land. The Advertisement for "Poems on the Naming of Places" reads:

> By Persons resident in the country and attached to rural objects, many places will be found unnamed or of unknown names, where little Incidents will have occurred, or feelings been experienced, which will have given to such places a private and peculiar interest. From a wish to give some sort of record to such Incidents or renew the gratification of such Feelings, Names have been given to Places by the Author and some of his Friends, and the following Poems written in consequence. (*Lyrical Ballads* 217)

In small, this announcement repeats the poetic technique detailed in the Preface. It begins with "Persons" attached directly to "rural objects," but to maintain and to duplicate that attachment within the lives of the poet and his friends, names must preserve the "Incidents" and the "Feelings." The renewal of the feelings result in the poems which then recapitulate the triadic process of recounting the incident, creating the name, and invoking the feelings.

The double move of constructing human habitats and decomposing them into nature is a consistent theme in Wordsworth, mirroring the double movement of developing a space of tranquility and dissolving that space in creative labor. This double movement typifies the "Poems on the Naming of Places," poems that denote property, yet acknowledge and celebrate nature's unrestrained character. "There is an Eminence," for example, brings a cliff high enough that "The meteors make of it a favorite haunt" (9) under the name of the poet, but at the purchase cost of troubling his own social relations:

> 'Tis in truth
> The loneliest place we have among the clouds.
> And She who dwells with me, whom I have lov'd
> With such communion, that no place on earth

Can ever be a solitude to me,
Hath said, this lonesome Peak shall bear my Name.
(12–17)

The same relation (with his sister) by which the poet evades solitude generates his association with the "loneliest place [they] have among the clouds," an image that at once asserts and eludes possession. For a reader knowledgeable of Grasmere, the poem enacts this ambiguity through the poetic license of placing the cliff under the poet's constant gaze; within the poem, Wordsworth and Dorothy "can behold it from our Orchard-seat" and "at evening" when they "pursue our walk / Along the public way" (3–5). The first image, of private possession, is, as Wordsworth informed Fenwick, not true. The second offers the Eminence to all viewers (and potential renamers) on the public way. The claim is also troubled by the cliff already having a name which is not, as the prefatory note suggests, "unknown." In overwriting "Stone-Arthur" with the poet's name, Wordsworth both claims possession and foregrounds the entailments possession carries; these are not of a legal nature, but reside in the constant labor necessary to negotiate private and public relations.

The "Poems on the Naming of Places" demonstrate the poet's ability to claim the land by entering it in the record of his work; these poems contrast to legal discourse which, by regularizing property, obscures specific relations to land. Francis Jeffrey recognized in such a position an appropriation of legal discourse, since a reader's specific relation to land is mediated by Wordsworth. In branding Wordsworth, Coleridge, and Southey a "certain brotherhood" who "have haunted for some years about the Lakes of Cumberland" (*Edinburgh Review* 11 [October 1807]: 214), he attempts to meet head on Wordsworth's assertion that his poetry, while being local, can negotiate within and represent the literary marketplaces of London and Edinburgh. The widespread critical adoption of the term *Lake Poets* to join writers of disparate literary sensibilities and objectives indicates Jeffrey's qualified success. Jeffrey's label confines the poets within geographic boundaries, and resists Wordsworth's "Poems on the Naming of Places" that enact both communal and national interest in the Lake District by establishing a mutuality between place and poem.

The location of the poems on the naming of places at the conclusion of the second volume gives them special import. Strictly speaking, "Michael," the last poem, is not part of the series, but a variant in which the poet recounts the story by which he learned, rather than invented, the name of a place. Within the context of the *Lyrical Ballads*, however, such learning, transformed by the poetic labor of teaching, has claims identical to those of nominal invention, since names are a shorthand for Incident and Feelings inscribed on the land. The poems on naming end the second volume but also frame it, since the first poem, "Hart-Leap Well," has an introduction explaining that "[Hart-Leap Well's] name is derived from a remarkable chace, the memory of which is preserved by the monuments spoken of in the second Part of the following Poem, which monuments do now exist as I have there described them" (Lyrical Ballads 127). The "Naming" poems themselves constitute validating monuments that both alter (by disclosing origins) and stabilize the names given to various locations, which range from the public "Point Rash-Judgment" ("A narrow girdle . . ." 86) to the private nook "we have named from You" ("To M. H." 24). Unlike the final series, "Hart-Leap Well" is written in a ballad-like form of rhymed iambic quatrains (with frequent slant and exact rhymes linking stanzas) and uses archaisms to provide a medieval cast appropriate to the construction of property implicit in the poem.

"HART-LEAP WELL" divides into two schematic parts, a narrative and a dialogue. The first tells of Sir Walter's victory over the hart and his exultation expressed by inscribing himself yet more upon nature by building a pleasure dome. The second foregrounds the poet's encounter with the tale, reimagined from nature's perspective in his mutual contemplation with the shepherd of the pleasure dome's remains. By responding to the tension between the first and second parts, the reader performs a labor of interpretation similar to the poet's labor of composition.[6]

In the Preface Wordsworth warned readers that "in order to entirely enjoy" the *Lyrical Ballads*, it would be necessary to forgo "much of what is ordinarily enjoyed" (*Lyrical Ballads* 272) and this poem enacts that transfer. A common formal structure invokes, Wordsworth contends, "the blind association of pleasure which has been previously received from works of rhyme or metre of the same or similar construction" (266), and Wordsworth avails himself of this association in part one. Maintaining the same form for the second part, distinguished both as "matter for a second rhyme" and as "another tale" (95–96), Wordsworth undoes the "blind association of pleasure" and reaches for an antithetic pleasure of sensitivity. Thus, as the poem (ex)poses the feudal relations of property and power, it establishes a rhetorical covenant between reader and writer.

The first lines of the poem invoke the Red Crosse Knight meandering in his sluggish quest for good: "The Knight had ridden down from Wensley moor / With the slow motion of a summer's cloud" (1–2). Like Red Crosse, the Knight is on a pursuit, but, where Red Crosse seeks to free Una's lands from the dragon, Sir Walter roams his own dominions pursuing a Hart. Given the debates in the 1790s on the contribution of the poaching laws to the poverty of common people (P. B. Munsche, *Gentlemen and Poachers* 123–25), the choice of a deer suggests a royal (or, more recently, a propertied)[7] right of dominion. In a chapter devoted to the "Rise, Progress, and Gradual Improvements" of English law, Blackstone noted that a "violent alteration in the English constitution consisted in the depopulation of whole countries, for the purposes of the king's royal diversion; and subjecting both them and all the ancient forests in the kingdom, to the unreasonable severity of forest laws imported from the continent" (*Commentaries* 4: 408). He contrasts this state to the modern one: while "the forest laws established only one mighty hunter throughout the land, the game laws have raised a little Nimrod in every manor" (4: 409). In both cases, Blackstone recognizes that the laws regarding hunting regulate status by controlling access to resources, and, unusually, expresses reservations about legitimacy, because these laws drastically restructure, rather than reinforcing, the property relations that legitimate the system of status that has evolved from feudal categories.

Wordsworth selects a middle position, a baron who must operate with the king's grant and is, perhaps, a medium-size Nimrod. The Knight's name, Walter, derives from "'*waltan*' to rule." Read as a contemporary analogue, the abuses of Sir Walter are the abuses of a landholding class wantonly exercising legal power without regard to local conditions; Blackstone points out that a "freeholder of less than 100 *l.* a year is forbidden to kill a partridge on his own estate" (*Commentaries* 4: 409). The hunt reinforces Sir Walter's grip on the lands and the people of those lands. When he changes horses, he exerts power at "a Vassal's door"(3):

And "Bring another Horse!" he cried aloud.

"Another Horse!"——That shout the Vassal heard,
And saddles his best steed.

(4–6)

By not naming him, the poem constructs the Vassal as a property like the horse, but this valuation is concealed by the Vassal's immediate willingness to provide his best steed. The difference between what Sir Walter cries ("Bring another Horse!") and what the Vassal hears ("Another Horse!") is telling; the Vassal does not need the verb to understand what he must do. The announcement of an object amounts to the demand for it, and the demand to its acquisition. The Knight exchanges his linguistic power for a material force which is reconverted into the symbolic power of the "Pleasure-house." The Vassal, like the Hart and like the paramour and dancers who ornament the pleasure house, exhaust their freedom in the naming of the Lord. Where Red Crosse falls three times in his battle, Sir Walter dismounts as often, always to rise up stronger, not through faith but through the depletion of his vassals.

Wordsworth's critique is leveled not against feudalism per se, but against the perversions of power intrinsic in the overaccumulation of property. When Burke appealed to the days of chivalry to bolster his argument for the virtues of great accumulations of property, Wordsworth responded scornfully: "Mr. Burke, in a philosophical lamentation over the extinction of Chivalry, told us that in those times vice lost half its evil, by losing all its grossness; infatuated moralist!" ("A Letter to the Bishop of Llandaff," in *Prose* 1: 35–36). Wordsworth rejects Burke's chivalric code as one of aesthetic appearances ("grossness").[8] As Wordsworth interprets Burke, vice lost its grossness by being institutionalized into despotism cloaked in justice. Wordsworth replaces Burke's vision with a new, ironic chivalry that expresses disdain for Burke as compassion for Watson, who, having over-imbibed Burke, is victim to intellectual despotism. "Hart-Leap Well" acknowledges the force of Burkean appearances in Sir Walter's endurance and strength, yet forces them to yield—not as in the "Letter to Llandaff" to Godwinian rationalism but to a critique by "nature," or more precisely, by the "nature" that emerges through retellings.

A first reading of the opening stanzas highlights the Vassal's loyalty, the Knight's fortitude—exactly the traits needed, at least in the historical Burkean myth, for the feudal state. A second reading, shadowed by the second part, recasts these lines. Where first attention settles on such happy phrases as "Joy sparkled in the prancing Courser's eyes / The horse and horseman are a happy pair," a second reading weights the line closing that stanza: "There is a doleful silence in the air" (12). The word "doleful" anticipates the Poet's description of Hart-Leap Well: "More doleful place did never eye survey" (114). The silence is inscribed by nature that mourns the Hart, despite Sir Walter's elaborate and loud decree for his pleasure house.

The race at first seems a celebration of the Knight's ability to outlast all his men, horses, and dogs until he reaches a kind of solemn communion with the Hart:

> A rout this morning left Sir Walter's Hall,
> That as they gallop'd made the echoes roar;
>
> . . . .
>
> breath and eye-sight fail, and, one by one,
> The dogs are stretch'd among the mountain fern.
>
> (13–14; 23–24)

The primary meaning of "rout" is the archaic one, "a company of people or animals, especially of knights or wolves" *(OED)*, but, from nature's perspective, the modern legal meaning of an unruly, unlawful assembly is to the point. As Sir Walter rides on, he strips himself of society and of nature. This secondary reading in which the Knight's company decomposes into unlawful assembly becomes evident from the perspective of part two. The hints laid in part one are concealed by the conventions of the ballad and the medieval hero, and are unveiled when the new Poet meets the older Shepherd.

Like Kent, the speaker of part one can mar a curious tale in the telling:

> The poor Hart toils along the mountain side;
> I will not stop to tell how far he fled,
> Nor will I mention by what death he died;
> But now the Knight beholds him lying dead.
>
> (29–32)

Caught up in the race, the narrator has no time to narrate it. As a consequence, he conceals the climactic moment of man's victory over nature, and allows the reader to draw images from the Knight's exultation, "too happy for repose or rest" (45). But a trap has been laid, for the Shepherd retells the moment of death by displacing a legend:

> Some say that here a murder has been done,
> And blood cries out for blood: but, for my part,
> I've guess'd, when I've been sitting in the sun,
> That it was all for that unhappy Hart.
>
> What thoughts must through the creature's brain have passed!
> (137–41)

Against the narrative haste of the first version, we are given the Shepherd's deliberate stillness as he guesses. In rejecting the charge of murder (homicide), he does not deny that "blood cries out for blood." His own thinking recreates the thoughts of the Hart, precisely the labor that earns the poet his reader and at which the Knight failed. Sir Walter experiences the "stone-dead" (77) Hart as a monument, lifeless as the stone he proudly commands to "receiv[e] the living well" (82). Wordsworth does not propose a mystical formulation in which the Shepherd's sympathy literally duplicates the Hart's being; rather, as human beings, both Walter and the Shepherd assimilate the Hart to their world views through a process of association. That Walter chooses the stone (and the hunt), and the Shepherd chooses his own heart (that which circulates/cries out blood) is the telling distinction.

From the perspective of the Shepherd's version of the tale, Walter is indifferent to the mysteriousness of the well. The Hart is not running there to escape Walter, but because he wishes to die there. The race, which, in the first part, "look[ed] not like an earthly race" (27) is now, in the Shepherd's words,

> a desperate race;
> And in my simple mind we cannot tell
> What cause the Hart might have to love this place,
> And come and make his death-bed near the well.
> (145–48)

The shift of pronouns between "*my* simple mind" and "*we* cannot tell" (146) signifies a different sense of community boundaries from Walter's ecstatic solitude.

In the first part, the Knight's crime does not diminish his power, although after the shooting of the albatross in "The Ancyent Marinere" a reader might suspect the worst.[9] Sir Walter builds the pleasure house because he has caused, "Such sight [as] was never seen by living eyes: / Three leaps . . . / Down to the very fountain" (54–56).[10] Sir Walter's palace is reclaimed by "Nature" which "in due *course of time*, once more / Shall here put on her beauty and her bloom" (171) while Sir Walter "died in *course of time*, / And his bones lie in his paternal vale" (93–94, my italics). The course of time is nature, it is mortality, and it chastens pride. Sir Walter's decree, trying to hold his realm as a unity fully inscribed by human power, is antipoetic. The damage he does must be recouped by the Shepherd and Poet together composing the second part as a dialogue, and, as in "Michael," the Shepherd's version is the enabling oral precursor of the poet's inscription. The poem ends by pointing the moral:

> One lesson, Shepherd, let us two divide,
> Taught both by what she shews, and what conceals,
> Never to blend our pleasure or our pride
> With sorrow of the meanest thing that feels.
>
> (177–80)

Here, the Poet accomplishes what Sir Walter cannot. The titled name that proliferates in the first part ("Sir Walter" recurs eleven times) exists in the second part only as a trace within nature: "'Here in old time the hand of man has been.' . . . And Nature here were willing to decay" (112, 116). Similarly, the repeated deictic "here" replaces Walter's naming/arranging of Hart-Leap Well. The single lesson is divided, and then infinitely divided with each reader, but in each dividing, wholeness is reasserted. Finally, what nature teaches is the poet's office, a spiritual feudal lord, bounded and bonded by nature into the community he protects. In the figure of the poet himself, the power of the ruined well is recouped, quenching a different thirst.

The Economics of Interpretation: "The Brothers"

"The Brothers, a Pastoral Poem" is a measured account of both the powers and inadequacies of rural economy, expressed in the Priest's communal recollections and sketched in the cottage industry of his family. It tests various forms of authority, in terms of their abilities to preserve those stable relationships between men and land which, in the Preface, constitute the origins of the "real language of men." As with "Michael," however, these relationships emerge as the product of competing narratives and economic pressures which are not merely imposed on the vale, but are embedded in its history as the possibility of nationalistic identity and expansion. Although it is true that the moral bookkeeping of the Priest is not equivalent to law, Blackstone, Hume, Adam Smith, and others had already articulated the continuity between them through the concept of habits and manners; Burke, for example, wrote that manners "are more important than laws. Upon them, in great measure, the laws depend" (quoted in Eagleton, *Ideology* 42). Law is constituted by the formalization of such manners, but the process of formalization occurs when those manners are under stress and their preservation requires the importation of an authority that can announce itself as derived from the moral status of those manners. From the Priest's perspective, such formalization would be as unneeded as tombstones in the graveyard, but the narrative of the plot is to expose the precariousness of his position, linked as it is to a dissappearing local economy.

The pastoral plot of "The Brothers"—a wanderer arriving home unrecognized to hear the story of his own life—recalls Odysseus weeping at his own story in the Phaiakian's palace as well as his arrival in Ithaca, where he is not recognized by Eumaeus. But more like Dante's Odysseus who must sail to the ends of the earth, Wordsworth's seafarer finds his home inadequate. The necessary condition for his return to "his Father's Land" was that he became "rich" (330–31), but his wealth, a foreign acquisition, makes him a "Stranger." William Galperin places Leonard's alienation from his homeland, occurring through the medium intended to bring reunion, within "contractions with respect to selfhood—specifically, that the authority of the individual is never more than an imitation of authority" (*Revision and Authority* 128). The competing authorities in the poem—priest, mariner, poet—all imitate the institutional authority that creates their selves, and those selves are consequently imitations of authority. But further, to invoke Jean Baudrillard's analysis of the simulacrum ("Simulacra and Simulations" 177–81), the institutions of authority are no more powerful than their replications within the imitations that enforce them. Finally, in the last line of the poem, power devolves to the simulacrum of the forever-speaking "grey-beard" Ancient Mariner ("Rime" 15), a silent "grey headed Mariner" whose sea has all along been a reflection of a home he now knows is not there ("Brothers" 449). I begin with this ending, to anticipate the trajectory of the various lines I now present.

The Priest, the local, nearly parodic version of the professional moralist and record keeper, cannot withstand the erosion of his community; he barely sees it. He recognizes the cataclysmic changes, like the lightning which destroyed one of two Springs; of a more gradual change, a "dark cleft" that "does not seem to wear the face / Which then it had," he can only say, "for aught I know, / That chasm is much the same" (132–36). Wordsworth argues for the benefits of linking a moral vision of the community with a record of its past—the essential rationale for common law. Yet, in revealing the Priest's inability to synthesize unexpected alterations into the vision, he suggests that the poet, as a stronger interpreter of both the past and the land, can better integrate a community in the midst of economic diaspora. If Leonard is twice lost to the Vicar, he has never left the eye of the poet.

"The Brothers" opens with an ejaculation, a mock prayer:

> These Tourists, Heaven preserve us! needs must live
> A profitable life: some glance along,
> Rapid and gay, as if the earth were air,
> And they were butterflies to wheel about
> Long as their summer lasted; some, as wise,
> Upon the forehead of a jutting crag
> Sit perched with book and pencil on their knee,
> And look and scribble, scribble on and look,
> Until a man might travel twelve stout miles,
> Or reap an acre of his neighbour's corn.
>
> (1–10)

This view, one of local prejudice, is naive, but the naivety does not emerge until the poet disassociates himself from the narrative voice by indicating the Priest as the speaker, talking to his wife. In an initial reading, the description seems of amateur writers flitting about to be self-consciously inspired by a nature that is only an imitation of his own expectations. When the speaker is identified, the lines shift from being by the poet to being about him.[11] It is not an amateur writer but a professional, being observed by an inadequate observer. Wordsworth has already announced himself as a tourist, in "Tintern Abbey," one who traveled "five summers" ago. For him, the tour, which ended with the poem that concluded the first edition of the *Lyrical Ballads*, constitutes successful work.[12]

The Priest's thoughts are somewhat contradictory: in the first lines, walking is idleness, while in the portrait of the scribbler, his idleness is contrasted with walking, constituted as a labor equivalent to reaping. The poet can resolve this; his activity is at once idleness and labor, because it is capitalizing, weaving sight into words, words into sight. The chiasmatic exchange of scribbling and looking is the distrustful version of the Preface's definition of the poet as an observer of life, but the poem eventually validates writing as truth-revealing. The Priest does not recognize Leonard until his letter, and the poet, at first inside the scene, moves beyond it to the far future of the poem, when he can state, with the prosaic clarity of a postscript and nearly the prose cadence of *cursus tardus*, that Leonard "is now / A Seaman, a grey headed Mariner" (448–49).[13]

The Priest's remarks on tourists have come from the associations inspired by the sight of Leonard:

> But, for that moping son of Idleness
> Why can he tarry *yonder?*—In our church-yard
> Is neither epitaph nor monument,
> Tomb-stone nor name, only the turf we tread,
> And a few natural graves.
>
> (11–15)

There is, for the stranger, nothing to read, nothing interpretable, but at the same time, the Priest cannot interpret the stranger. Labeling Leonard as the "son of Idleness" is particularly inept, since his Grandfather worked himself to death while "buffeted with bond, / Interest and mortgages" (217–18). The limited view of "Only the turf we tread" foreshadows the fate of Walter's cottage:

> For five long generations had the heart
> Of Walter's forefathers o'erflow'd the bounds
> Of their inheritance, that single cottage.
>
> (207–9)

The image is of the family thriving, spreading out beyond the cottage into the community, and thereby strengthening the claim on the cottage. But this free movement is checked by economic change barely noticeable:

> Each struggled, and each yielded as before
> A little—yet a little—and old Walter,
> They left to him the family heart, and land
> With other burdens than the crop it bore.
> (212–15)

Wordsworth's own family estate at Falthwaite had, "through embarrassment arising out of surety and speculation in mines" been broken up early in the eighteenth century (Moorman I: 8). The details of Walter's patrimonial failure are unclear, and the broken syntax suggests that its dynamics are beyond the Priest. Stated generally, the expansive image of overflow constricts into incorporeal burdens; to have "o'erflow'd the bounds" may now mean to have overspent.[14] Leonard, as a trader and mariner, can negotiate within the mercantile economy, and yet, in overcoming the poverty that drove him from his ancestral home, he contributes to the marketplace in which bonds, mortgages, and interest burden the uninitiated. According to contemporary economic theorists, sailing ventures underwritten by corporate speculators drove up both interest rates and taxes. Unlike Wordsworth's seagoing brother John, who asked the East India house to assign Dorothy 20 pounds a year (Moorman I: 512), Leonard could not arrange for his earnings to support his sibling, who moves from one charitable home to another. The difference between Leonard, whose existence finally becomes reduced to his occupation, and John Wordsworth, whose generosity and encouragement enabled Wordsworth's poetry (LEY 563), is encapsulated in one of Wordsworth's epitaphs for his brother: "A Poet in everything but words" (Moorman I: 471).

One slender line suggestively describes Leonard's fortune: it was "Acquir'd by traffic in the Indian Isles" (64). Leonard would thus have traded in the West Indies sometime in the late 1700s. If, as Leonard's shyness suggests, Wordsworth had his own brother in mind as a model (Moorman I: 480), then Leonard's sailing west deserves scrutiny as a deliberate shift from biography, since John sailed for the East India Company.[15] During the period of the poem, the West Indies were major exporters of sugar, and since the plantations "were cultivated mainly by slave labor they were important centres of slave trade" (Holdsworth 11: 39). Although Leonard surely did not truck directly in the slave trade, he does operate in a slave-based economy, in contrast to the agrarian community glanced in the Vicar's suggestion that an idler might reap his "neighbour's corn."[16] The rumor that the Priest has heard that Leonard was "in slavery among the Moors / Upon the Barbary Coast" (324–25) does not accord with the narrative facts, but is a likely enough transposition of details, in which Barbados becomes Barbary and an enabler of slavery becomes slave.

In a "Lecture on the Slave-Trade," given at Bristol in 1795 (published the following year in revised form in *The Watchman*), Coleridge's first argument describes the inequity of the slave trade, not for the slaves, but for the English laborers. The "Slave Trade & West India Commerce," Coleridge contends, generates a market of luxury items to be traded for domestic necessities.[17] Consequently, "the poor with unceasing toil first raise and then are deprived of the comforts which they absolutely want in order to procure Luxuries which they must never hope to enjoy" (Coleridge, *Lectures* 237). This argument, and those that follow, are not unique, and Wordsworth would have had ample opportunity to encounter them,[18] not least through his friend Thomas Clarkson, an avid abolitionist.

The design of Coleridge's lecture enforces the connection between English liberty and the abolition of slavery. He notices that the same House of Commons that would not abolish the slave trade suspended the Habeas Corpus Act "with an ease and rapidity which might have astonished the oldest Turnkey in Newgate!" (*Lectures* 246).[19] His description of the free Africans corresponds to a nostalgic preindustrial England: "The Africans . . . cultivate their fields in common and reap the crop as the common property of all. Each family like the peasants in some parts of Europe, spins weaves, sews, . . . [makes] the implements of agriculture, and this variety of employment gives an acuteness of intellect to the negro which the mechanic whom the division of Labour condemns to one simple operation is precluded from attaining" (*Lectures* 240). The fluidity of occupation, idyllic in this vision, recurs in the description of the Priest's family:

> His wife sate near him, teasing matted wool,
> While, from the twin cards tooth'd with glittering wire,
> He fed the spindle of his youngest child,
> Who turn'd her large round wheel in the open air
> With back and forward steps.
>
> (21–25)

The family unit is emphasized as a single economic entity. The imagery of nourishment and openness recognizes the value of the labor not only in terms of monetary gain but in terms of sustaining the family structure which, written small, is the community structure. The daughter may be "sent to service" just as a "web is spun" (160): both events attach the family to the community, and substitute for calendars. From the Priest's view, the family regulates the wheel, around which the family work is organized. The poet, however, is aware of the reversibility of the situation and that the demands of the external economy (as well as traditional local law in many parts of England) can drive a daughter to service with the same fury that the storm "send[s] twenty score of sheep / To feed the ravens" (154–55).

The level of detail demonstrates the poet's knowledge of the operations of making wool; the Wordsworths were fairly self-sufficient at Grasmere, although Wordsworth's writing (like the Priest's ministry?) was the most important industry. From a psychological view, however, the extent to which Wordsworth identifies with Leonard and not the Priest contributes to his own uneasy relation to national markets. Galperin has suggested that "the paradox of being obligated to the reader and opposed to the reader following that obligation, is reflected in the almost protean character of 'Leonard' 's guilt" (*Revision and Authority* 131). In a similar paradox, Wordsworth's own labor of memorializing the Lake District, like Leonard's trafficking, is a potential betrayal of the Lake District by its contribution to the national economy and tourist industry.[20] But Wordsworth, after turning the Priest's satire about poets against him, compresses any consideration of Leonard's occupation into one line, easily overlooked against the much more ambiguous abandonment of the Vale, an act compelled rather than a crime chosen.

Without claiming that Leonard was a slave trader, I believe that the presentation of Leonard's business complicates a reading in which Leonard's rejection of the Vale stems from either his brother's death or his own guilt concerning that death. His guilt is also of a more general nature, a recognition that he has, in a certain way, betrayed his community (represented by the Priest's exuberant trust) by his co-option, however necessary, into the mercantile economy. Wordsworth welcomed the money John proposed to make for his family, but a poem such as "The Brothers" suggests that such wealth would need to be purified into poetry in order not to become a betrayal. The professional status of the poet allows such a purification to operate simultaneously as investments into the literary market, Grasmere, and the Wordsworth household.

The sight of the "Stranger" intrudes on the economy of the Priest's household, since he puts aside his task of "[feeding] the spindle of his youngest child" in order to "accost / The Stranger" (23, 35–36). Like the "abrupt" opening which needs reinterpretation, the third verse paragraph begins with a false recognition: "'Twas one well known to him in former days" (37). After the poet has recounted the history of Leonard's sailing, it becomes clear that closer inspection has not actually revealed Leonard's identity to the Priest. Against the poet's knowledge of Leonard's inner life as rooted in his community even while "the regular wind . . . blew with the same breath through days and weeks, / Lengthening invisibly its weary line" (46–49), Wordsworth places the Priest's inadequate reading of Leonard's body:

> 'Tis one of those who needs must leave the path
> Of the world's business, to go wild alone:
> His arms have a perpetual holiday,
> The happy man will creep about the fields
> Following his fancies by the hour, to bring
> Tears down his cheek, or solitary smiles
> Into his face, until the setting sun
> Write Fool upon his forehead.
>
> (103–10)

Not Leonard's but the Priest's fancy generates this scene. He naturalizes his own projection by making it the setting sun's inscription ("Fool") as a response to the idler's effort to inscribe his own face with simulated emotions. In contrast, Leonard's imagination, during a fever,

> saw the forms of sheep that graz'd
>
> . . . .
>
> And Shepherds clad in the same country grey
> Which he himself had worn.
>
> (59–62)

Wordsworth appends a footnote pointing out that the description of the calenture is "sketched from an imperfect recollection of an admirable one in prose." The imagination does not make up stories, but views the forms of reality: Leonard recalls his pastoral life, and the poet recalls an "admirable" description. The sentimental vision that the Priest attributes to Leonard, in which tears and smiles are superficial effects of trivial adventures, opposes

Leonard's association of inner sight to external stimuli when he looks into the "broad green wave" (53) and sees the "verdant hills" (60).

Just as the Priest has misunderstood Leonard's emotions, he has misconstrued his wealth. Leonard has not left the "path of the world's business" but retraced it. With his money, he returns not in idleness but in pursuit of "his paternal home" (65). Further, the wealth, from a worldly perspective, is "small," but it overwhelms the Priest's view of Leonard. If the message in the poem for Charles Fox is that small landowners can feel deeply (LEY 315), the message to the local Vicar is that travelers may also feel deeply, and may not be the strangers they appear.

Leonard's habit of staring—"[he would] gaze and gaze" (52)—until the sea changes into hills is repeated in a displaced way beside the graves:

> He had found
> Another grave, near which a full half hour
> He had remain'd, but, as he gaz'd, there grew
> Such a confusion in his memory,
> That he began to doubt, and he had hopes
> That he had seen this heap of turf before.
> (82–89)

Like the narrating poet in the previous poem, "There was a boy," Leonard stands at the grave "A full half-hour . . . / Mute" ("There was a Boy" 31–32); but where that encounter empowers the poet to confront the death of the boy of Winander, Leonard's vigil allows his imagination to invent doubt about what it knows to be true.[21] Simultaneously knowing and not knowing about James's death, Leonard constructs two motives in approaching the Priest, first, the enabling fiction of learning whether James is dead, and second, the need of a story to assess (and abate?) his guilt in that death.

The poem continually uses paired images, the "two Springs which bubbled side by side" (141), the "two bells" which would ring if Leonard returned (320), the two brothers "like two young ravens on the crags" (283), and the "pair of diaries" (164). The "diaries" are, one, the ledgers of family Bibles, particular to each family, and, two, the dramatic changes in the landscape available to all. Each pair, however, is disrupted. One spring has been destroyed; the bells will "never sound" for Leonard (322); one brother is dead, the other disguised, and ravens are the ensigns of death.[22] Lastly,

Leonard has taken away his Bible, its fate merely the speculation of the Priest's wager of "twenty pounds" (288), a bet only possible in idle but capitalistic speculation. The Ewbanks' unmarked graves are so indistinguishable that Leonard cannot decide (or at least can refuse to decide) if one grave is new or forgotten, and yet the unmarked progression evokes a terrible mortality.

The Priest ends with a highly suggestive image. James has died in a fall and

> midway in the cliff
> It [his staff] had been caught, and there for many years
> It hung—and moulder'd there.
> The Priest here ended—
> (417–19)

Although to the Priest a fact, a natural oddity, this is an image of suspension. The Priest ends his narrative with this fact as the grounds for communal interpretation ("we all conjectured" 409; "We guess" 416). Partly because the abrupt ending—marked by the mid-line paragraph break that ends the dramatic form of the "dialogue" (118)[23]—turns the reader's attention toward Leonard's response, a turn thwarted by Leonard's silence, the temptation to interpret the staff is nearly irresistible:[24] the lost or continuing leadership of the (potential) shepherd; the inability to speak since the staff, with rank and right, remains in sight of but beyond the reach of the local people; the lost support of a brother who, in carrying James "through the fords" (262) was as a staff to him; the suspended judgment on Leonard's responsibility for James's death, which, though repudiated by the Priest, remains as plausible as the conjecture about James's sleepwalking to his death; Leonard as caught between his past as a Shepherd and his future as a Mariner; a foreshadowing of the staff Michael makes and passes on to Luke without transmitting its symbolic power as talisman.[25] These could be woven endlessly, but settling on any one or combination would be too facile, for the poem itself discloses that no interpretation could stand apart from the authority—and the economic and moral investments of that authority—proposing the interpretation.

Wordsworth thus describes the origins of "The Brothers": "The poem arose out of the fact, mentioned to me at Ennerdale, that a shepherd had fallen asleep upon the top of the rock called The 'Pillar,' and perished as here described, his staff being left midway" (*Lyrical Ballads* 299). Wordsworth began with a fact and constructed a story that transformed it into a metaphor without surrendering any of its factuality (and with the Fenwick note, he integrated that factuality into the textual history of the poem). Around that image, the reader must construct an interpretation, just as the poet constructed the poem. Whether or not the Fenwick note is an accurate reconstruction (Christopher Wordsworth offers some corroboration; Butler and Green 380), it suggests at least how an older Wordsworth wanted the poem read. The ending of the poem, projecting to the old age of Leonard, hints at the Priest's death, and with that death, the end of his stories. The staff, both fact and image, indicates the poetic labor as at once the psychic labor of mediating between the Priest and Leonard and the public labor mediating private guilt and social transformation.

For Leonard, his labor as a mariner becomes the simultaneous expression of his "protean" guilt (in Galperin's phrase) and of social transformation. When the Vicar invites Leonard to "partake his homely fare," Leonard declines, "add[ing] that, the evening being calm, / He would pursue his journey" (430–31). The verb "pursue" suggests that the journey has a definite course, and its etymological link to "persecute" (both from the Latin *prosuqui*) gives shape to the poem's final passages. He does not pursue any real journey at first, but travels "not long" before he "stopp'd short" (432–33) and "review'd /All that the Priest had said," like so much evidence. Resolving that he could not bear to return to the vale, he travels to Egremont where he writes to the Priest asking "to be forgiven" for concealing his identity and, in a temporal condensation in which his self-banishment is enacted immediately, "This done, he went on shipboard, and is now / A Seaman, a grey headed Mariner" (447–48). In his banishment, he becomes the self toward which he had unknowingly been directing himself all along; where before, he was on board ship in order to return home, now he is thoroughly identified with the very labor that foreclosed his return.

Interpreting Criminal Law: "Andrew Jones" and "The Two Thieves"

The juxtaposition of "Andrew Jones" and "The Two Thieves" comments on the relation between what is criminal and what is evil. The first poem is a narrator's explanation of his hatred for Andrew Jones by describing that greedy man's encounter with a crippled beggar. The narrator is a common type in Wordsworth's ballads: he reacts against a situation but, because he is within the social framework that produced the situation, he duplicates it in a displaced way. The poem is "hewn" from "Peter Bell," with added first and last framing stanzas (Moorman I: 432; Butler and Green 388). The peculiar rhyme scheme, abccb, repeats in all seven stanzas, and the unrhymed first lines are never end-stopped except for the climactic penultimate stanza. Each stanza, consequently, has an unbalanced feeling, as if the narrator is striving for an arbitrary regularity, a legal rather than organic unity. Attempting to be a moralist without being careful of his craft, the narrator calls down upon Jones the same arbitrary power by which Jones justifies keeping the cripple's penny. Alternatively, the stanza is suggestive of the irregular lyrics of "rough music" that performed many local disciplinary functions, including managing domestic matters, protesting "enclosure" as well as "upholding common rights" and local "custom" (E. P. Thompson, *Customs in Common* 519). The poem both performs a disciplinary function (by exposing Andrew Jones) and defers the discipline by summoning the national music of the "drum / With its tantara sound" (3–4, 33–34).[26]

The climax of the poem is a legal interpretation:

> He stooped and took the penny up:
> And when the Cripple nearer drew,
> Quoth Andrew, "Under half-a-crown,
> What a man finds is all his own,
> And so, my friend, good day to you."
>
> (26–30)

Jones cites a common-law principle regarding abandoned money. The rationale, superfluous since the beggar cannot prevent Jones's action, acts as a self-justification. Since Jones is merely applying the law, and therefore giving the law its due, he can wish the beggar a good day and call him friend. The illusion that money has a stable value determined by law is replicated. Jones does not consider that to the beggar the coins are worth more than to him, in direct proportion to the ease with which Jones can scoop them up and the effort the beggar must expend merely to gather them together; for Jones, value is determined in relation to the legal threshold of "half-a-crown."

The narrator does not dispute the status of the law; he asserts that applying the law is base. Jones's behavior is in contrast to the humane treatment Wordsworth applauded in "The Old Cumberland Beggar":

> The sauntering horseman-traveller does not throw
> With careless hand his alms upon the ground,
> But stops, that he may safely lodge the coin
> Within the old Man's hat.
>
> (26–29)

The benefactor in "Andrew Jones," "Some Horseman who was passing by" (12) has followed an established custom. The concept of throwing the money down was a mock abandonment, so that the beggar could claim it of his own volition and the almsgiving would be, in some sense, anonymous and of greater credit to the benefactor. The "Horseman" does not respond to the obvious needs of "this poor crawling helpless wretch" ("Andrew Jones" 11), while the "horseman-traveller" ("The Old Cumberland Beggar") breaks custom to preserve the proper circulation of the money. The horseman's action allows for Jones's legalistic interpretation of the situation, and indeed, they understand money in similar terms. Both the horseman and Jones conceive of the money in terms of its value—the horseman throws down "A penny" (13) and Jones picks up "the penny" (25); the beggar, however, experiences the money in its material reality as "halfpennies" which must be "brought . . . together" (19–20).

Jones has construed the law to his advantage (an action in keeping with his source, Peter Bell). By an alternative interpretation, Jones could claim the money only if it was not in possession of the beggar or had been manifestly abandoned; and since the beggar had "brought / the halfpennies together . . . at his feet" (19–20, 24), he could have been deemed by such an action to have taken and retained possession. Jones's action, in this model, would have been illegal. Like the Old Cumberland Beggar, the Cripple must contend with natural elements:

> Inch-thick the dust lay on the ground
> For it had long been droughty weather:
> So with his staff the Cripple wrought
> Among the dust.
>
> (16–19)

The emphasis on the dust may, as parody, deliberately recall Locke's formulation in which property emerges from mixing labor with the earth. "Wrought," an alternative past tense of "work," is a favorite term of Wordsworth for labor; it recurs throughout "Michael," for example, as a description of interactions with natural elements. But in "Andrew Jones," the word's implications are lost on their speaker. The beggar's gathering is not recognized as labor by either Jones or the narrator. That beggars perform no labor is a fiction necessary to preserving the extralegal value of a charity circumscribed by the laws that permit the accumulation of wealth in particular configurations. The mock abandonment of the penny is taken as real, and Jones acquires possession before the beggar.

The narrator's solution is neither to give the beggar money nor to befriend him, "A friendless Man" (10). The beggar becomes an occasion to justify the narrator's hatred for Andrew Jones, just as the law served as Jones's justification. The poem begins with the narrator's strident declaration:

> I hate that Andrew Jones: he'll breed
> His children up to waste and pillage.
> I wish the press-gang or the drum
> With its tantara sound would come,
> And sweep him from the village!
>
> (1–5)[27]

According to E. P. Thompson, "No institution was as much hated, in the eighteenth century, as the press-gang" (*Working Class* 88). The constitutionality of this royal right had been debated for a century (see Hume's "Three Remarkable Customs" in *Essays Moral*) but with the war against France, it was in force as a public necessity. In the poem, however, it is figured as a curse and a punishment rather than as an obligation toward the nation. The narrator is calling on the arbitrary power of the crown to inflict harm, and thereby invokes a common myth (affirmed by Burke and opposed by Paine) about the origins of criminal law as a replacement for the blood feuds of early cultures. This reconstructed history helped institutionalize the opposition between law and disorder, despite the violence implicit to both.[28] But the poem, by staging the narrator's confusion between criminal law and other state police powers, exposes how this opposition of law and disorder can be one of ideological convenience, consistent with the suspension of *habeas corpus* and with impressment.

In 1797, conditions in the navy were so appalling that sailors mutinied at Spithead, the place from which on 17 November 1795 another naval expedition had sailed toward disaster. Dorothy wrote: "[My] brother saw the West India fleet sailing in all its glory before the storm had made such dreadful ravages" (LEY 162). Seven of eight naval vessels went down, and a dozen miles from where the Wordsworths were living, the shore "had been strewn with hundreds of corpses" (LEY 162n). What effect this event had on Wordsworth is unknown, but perhaps it helped form his view of the total desolation implied in the image of Jones's being swept from the village as before a great and naturalizing wind.

LIKE "ANDREW JONES," the poem that follows it disturbs the question of criminality. Titled like a medieval exemplar, "The Two Thieves, or The last Stage of Avarice" tells about an old man and his grandchild who steal their way through the town, ignorant that the old man's daughter repays the value of the stolen goods. In the Preface, Wordsworth identifies "The Two Thieves" as an "attempt to sketch characters under the influence of less impassioned feelings . . . characters of which the elements are simple, belonging rather to nature than to manners . . . and which from their constitution may be distinctly and profitably contemplated" (*Lyrical Ballads* 242). "The Two Thieves" opens with a peculiar introduction about storytelling, which complicates this schematic description by making the narrator one of the characters described by the Preface:

> Oh now that the genius of Bewick were mine
> And the skill which He learn'd on the Banks of the Tyne;
> When the Muses might deal with me just as they chose
> For I'd take my last leave both of verse and of prose.
>
> (1–4)

The depth of allusion is difficult to reconstruct. Bewick's inborn "genius" and learned "skill" seem to have natural origins; the genius he was born with, and the skill was learned on the Tyne. Muted is the seven-year apprenticeship in Newcastle learning the trade of engraving that made him famous. The first volume of his *History of British Birds* was published in 1797. The joke of Wordsworth's remark might be that the woodcuts of rural scenes carried the volume, so the text did not matter.

In addition, Bewick had begun engraving banknotes for local institutions in the mid-1790s. Since his work immediately became money, he had no need of muses. He had developed a self-sustaining art for the market economy; his representation of monetary circulation was part of the circulation itself. He engraved only for the local banks, and strongly supported traditional agrarian economies that interacted with London as little as possible. When contacted by the Bank of England in 1801, he responded that "though my plate would do well for country banks, it would not do for the great number wanted for the Bank of England" (Thomas Bewick, *A Memoir*, chap. 14); while Wordsworth does not, of course, allude to this anecdote in 1800, it is consistent with Bewick's public persona.[29] In the next stanza, the reference becomes yet more convoluted:

> What feats would I work with my magical hand!
> Book-learning and books should be banish'd the land
> And for hunger and thirst and such troublesome calls
> Every ale-house should then have a feast on its walls.
> (5–8)

What is meant by banishing books? Perhaps the narrator would use Bewick's talents to make prints for walls, like Hogarth's, rather than the small illustrations Bewick preferred. Alternatively, these lines signal the prescriptive force of certain moralistic writing (in a prepublication version, MS 29, the narrator imagines specifically the vicar's illiteracy). In "Rob Roy's Grave," "books" actually refers to acts of law,[30] such as the poor laws designed to feed the impoverished by keeping them on the parish rolls (more books "for hunger and thirst and such troublesome calls"), but ideological and legalistic works such as Burke's *Reflections* and Godwin's *Enquiry* also come under this narrator's prohibition. The narrator himself, in invoking banishment, attempts a judicial enforcement. He would substitute for books something on the ale-house walls, presumably scenes of rural life like the tailpieces that adorn *Birds*.

The third stanza, the last before the "tale" begins, adds another dimension:

> The Traveller would hang his wet clothes on a chair
> Let them smoke, let them burn, not a straw would he care,

For the Prodigal Son, Joseph's Dream and his Sheaves,
Oh what would they be to my tale of two Thieves!
(9–12)

The phrase "not a straw would he care" can refer either to his smoking and burning clothing or to "the Prodigal Son" and other biblical stories; the punctuation argues the former interpretation, while the use of "For" in line 11 suggests the latter. These alternatives cannot be resolved until the final line, an exclamation structured as an interrogatory, is parsed. In effect, the Traveller cares neither about his clothes nor about the biblical stories, since both wane before the pictorial "tale of two Thieves." Christ's parable of the profligate child and Joseph's dream of his brother's sheaves bowing both require several levels of interpretation. The words spoken by the father of the prodigal son must be interpreted at least by the older son, Jesus' audience, and a reader of the Gospel; Joseph's dream must be read by himself, by his brothers and father, and then by a reader of Genesis within the context of a narrative in which dream interpretation leads to professional advancement. Both stories revolve around proper familial behavior as governed by the legal traditions of the Old Testament. Joseph's brothers should not bow to him, because of primogeniture; and the prodigal son, having "wasted his portion," should not be given more of his father's estate. In both cases, the moral is the inadequacy of the traditional law, and the consequence of a proper interpretation is a profit—the older son realizes that all his father has is his, and Joseph rules his brothers as a great people.

The "tale of two Thieves," in the context of the biblical references, invokes the two thieves who died with Christ, an example of the inadequacy of law. Wordsworth's local tale, however, concerns a toddler and an old man who "go a stealing together" (16). Throughout the seven stanzas describing their activity, the illusion is that the grandfather, in the last stages of avarice, is a consummate thief. His victims are laborers ("the Carpenter" 17) and people engaged in transactions ("Is a cart-load of peats at an old Woman's door?" 18) and, from the perspective of the free market, he is a criminal. In reality, however, the community sanctions his thefts, because his daughter makes good the damages.[31] So long as the economy is kept in balance, all is well; the daughter would pay treble damages (44), actually the correct civil remedy (Holdsworth 2: 453), but no one asks, as that also would disrupt the local economy.

In terms of English law, the community's response is problematic. Thefts are acts against the king's peace, and the community abets the crime. By interpretation, the community's action can be rendered correct if the restored damages are figuratively tripled and they are. First, the actual restoration; second, the old man's sense of self is retained; and finally, he has a communal function as exemplar:

> I love thee and love the sweet boy at thy side;
> Long yet may'st thou live, for a teacher we see
> That lifts up the veil of our nature in thee.
>
> (47–49)

The vision of these final lines features a slide between the narrator's loving as an individual ("I love") and learning as part of a community ("a teacher we see"). Often, in Wordsworth's work, a narrator encounters a beggar, a soldier, or other marginalized figure, and learns from the experience. Without abating their suffering in any substantial way, the narrator finds his own is lifted yet deepened, and the poem thereby becomes a source of teaching. There is an extralegal exchange, economic in the widest sense of the word, but the exchange itself becomes productive in generating the poem that allows for the further exchange between the poet and the reader.

"The Two Thieves," like "Andrew Jones," has a narrator distinct from the persona of Wordsworth invoked in "The Old Cumberland Beggar" and the "Poems on the Naming of Places." In "The Two Thieves," Wordsworth deliberately mars the force of the narrator's tale, yet the conclusion fits the matrix of encounter just outlined. The difference, however, is that Dan is only apparently marginalized; he is actually at the center of the community trying to maintain its local economic and legal standards against the encroachment of the national market. The narrator and the community of "The Two Thieves" have not accepted (noticed?) the governmental powers of the press-gang and of the determination of value that the narrator of "Andrew Jones" exploits in his curse.

Wordsworth is not advocating illiteracy in his own voice at the beginning of "The Two Thieves," but using a narrator who sees in pictures and faces unmediated stories (Old Daniel's "look . . . tells a plain tale" 23–24) to expose the problematic category of the unmediated. The choice to append to this problem a tale about habitual criminality, in which the village shields

Daniel from legal scrutiny, argues for the difficulty in applying (imposing) law not derived from within the community. Late into the eighteenth century, according to Holdsworth, many local variations of parish governing were permitted, and where the population was small, "government fell into the hands of the principal inhabitants—the clergyman, the squire, the innkeeper, the miller, and the principal farmers." At the same time, increasingly, larger structures of overseeing vested in "larger liberties [that] might have a separate commission of the peace" (Holdsworth 10: 137–38). If, as the Webbs argue, "official relationships between parties were inextricably woven into the economic relationships that existed between the same individuals in their private capacity" (quoted in Holdsworth 10: 139), to unify English customary law meant changing communities and altering the meanings and legibility of their stories.[32] If this is a story about local meddling, it is also a warning, like the "The Old Cumberland Beggar," about the difficulty of anticipating the effects of nationalized meddling.

LAW, ECONOMICS, AND MEMORY: "THE OLD CUMBERLAND BEGGAR, A DESCRIPTION" AND "RURAL ARCHITECTURE"

Harold Bloom has proposed that Wordsworth "does not think of [the Old Cumberland Beggar] in social and economic terms, but only as a human life" (*The Visionary Company* 180). I suggest that Wordsworth defines the "human" only through a forceful, visible, and necessary negation of particular legal and economic terms, in order to claim a certain (natural) right, with economic consequences, for the poet. As in "Michael," Wordsworth uses these other professional discourses to authorize his position beyond them. Quoting only the first line, Bloom states that "nothing could be simpler than the poem's opening" (*Visionary* 178): "I saw an aged Beggar in my walk, / And he was seated by the highway side" (1–2). The poetic complexity of these lines (the slant rhyme of "aged" and "Beggar"; the assonance of "saw" and "walk"; the two internal rhymes and assonance of the second line—"he" and "seat"; "by," "high," and "side"; perhaps even the eerie mirroring of "saw" and "was," which obliquely announce the poem's visual ontology) augments the effect of the pseudoparallel structure of the two prepositional phrases that end the lines. The delicate question of possession, signaled by the disjunction between the informationally redundant "in *my* walk" (as the poet's sight) and "by the *highway* side" (as societal location), underscores the institutional debate as to who ought to regulate the Beggar.

Although, in his letter to Charles Fox, Wordsworth commends two other poems, "The Brothers" and "Michael," because of their concern with proprietors of small properties, his language more closely recalls "The Old Cumberland Beggar."[33] Like the letter, the poem announces itself as an argument. Where the verse paragraphs of "Michael" are marked as narrative by the opening temporal phrases—"And in a later time" (169), "And when" (187), "While" (217), "Next morning" (314, 434), "Three years" (482), and see also lines 80, 147, 215—the last three of the five verse paragraphs of "The Old Cumberland Beggar" begin with rhetorical argumentative gestures: "But deem not" (67), "Yet further" (125), "Then [i.e., therefore] let him pass" (155).

Wordsworth praises Fox for his "sensibility of heart": "Necessitated as you have been from your public situation to have much to do with men in bodies, and in classes, . . . you have not thereby been prevented from looking on them as individuals . . .. This habit cannot but have made you dear to Poets" (LEY 313). As a poet, Wordsworth sets out a similar relationship between class and individual in the juxtaposition of the poem and preamble of "The Old Cumberland Beggar." The prose introduction declares: "The class of Beggars to which the old man here described belongs will probably soon be extinct. It consisted of poor, and, mostly, old and infirm persons, who confined themselves to a stated round in their neighbourhood, and had certain fixed days, on which, at different houses, they regularly received charity; sometimes in money, but mostly in provisions" (*Lyrical Ballads* 205). Wordsworth elides the death of the individual by extinguishing the entire class in the shift from the present tense of the first sentence to the past tense of the second. The poem reverses this, and revitalizes, at least in its first gesture, the man as an individual.

It opens in the past tense ("I saw . . . he was seated" 1–2). When the narrator thinks back to his past, the present is recovered: "Him from my childhood have I known, and then / He was so old, he seems not older now" (22–23). The beggar is an image of continuity, not seeming to age, but someone by whom the poet can measure his own growth. After the argument for the beggar's beneficial effect on the community, the Statesman is asked to care for the future:

> Then let him pass, a blessing on his head! . . .
> . . . .
> As in the eye of Nature he has lived,
> So in the eye of Nature let him die.
> (155, 188–89)[34]

Despite the claim in the subtitle of being a "Description," the poem does little to particularize the beggar's appearance beyond the adjectives used in the preamble.[35] Repeatedly, he is called "aged Beggar" and "old Man"; he has a "palsied hand" (16) and is "Bowbent" (52); the wind "Beat[s] his grey locks against his wither'd face" (169), signs of infirmity, age, and poverty. A reader could not distinguish him from any other male of his class. What then individualizes him, a quality crucial to both poet and the idealized legislator that the implied reader of the letter to Fox represents? Not what he looks like, but who looks at him.

In the broadest structure, the poem shifts from the narrative "I" looking on the beggar, to the beggar's living and dying "in the eye of Nature." Sight is transformed from an activity to a location, a property over which the beggar has a right of occupancy against the claims of the Statesman and his statutory Poor laws.[36] Since, as Wordsworth tells Fox, "the most calamitous effect, which has followed the measures which have lately been pursued in this country, is a rapid decay in the domestic affections among the lower orders of society" (LEY 313), the Cumberland beggar's ability to maintain such affections by recalling the past establishes his right to nature's eye.

After the description of the beggar's efforts to eat, the poet narrates the beggar's encounters with three other people on the road, "The sauntering horseman-traveller" (26), "She who tends / The toll-gate" (32–33), and "The Post-boy" (37). This sequence is framed on either side by the line "He travels on, a solitary man" (24, 44). The three disturb neither his travels nor his solitariness, but are themselves slowed in their work. Taken as a group, they represent the newly developed occupations of the improved roads, a component of the "spread of manufactory" about which Wordsworth complains to Fox (LEY 313). The traveler has surplus wealth, and so he gives money—not the usual "provisions"—to the beggar. The woman regulates the flow of traffic by operating the toll, and the post-boy uses the roads for the improved communication necessary for economic development. The sight of the beggar "stops" the traveler. If the woman "sees / The aged Beggar," she "quits her work" (34–35); and the post-boy "Turns . . . to the road-side" (41). Implicit in this combination of a man, a woman, and a child is a domestic unit, and I would stress the synonymous connection of "domestic" and "economic," both having "house" as a root. Wordsworth, in his letter to Fox, shifts from his description of economic evil, "the encreasing disproportion between the price of labour and that of the necessities of life, the bonds of domestic feelings among the poor" to a scene of domestic disruption: "the wife no longer prepares with her own hands a meal for her husband, the produce of his labour" (LEY 313–14). The beggar checks temporarily the economic expansion, recalling its agents to their domestic roots.

From those who see the beggar, Wordsworth moves to what the beggar sees, and does not see:

> [His eyes] move along the ground; and evermore,
> Instead of common and habitual sight
> Of fields with rural works, of hills and dale,
> And the blue sky, one little span of earth
> Is all his prospect.
>
> (47–51)

The common sights are the common lands, and the rural works are both the activities of workers (shepherding, building) and their artifacts, such as the "low structure of rude masonry" on which the poet first sees the beggar. The previous rude structure a reader of the second volume would have encountered is the "hillock of misshapen stones" of "Lines Written with a Slate-pencil," a poem also in blank verse. It is not, the speaker tells the implied reader (the "Stranger" of the first line),

> a ruin of the ancient time,
> Nor, as perchance thou rashly deem'st, the Cairn
> Of some old British Chief.
>
> ("Slate-pencil" 2–4)

This ruin, a "pleasure-house" (6) abandoned by a Sir William and made visible by the inscription/poem serves as a middle term of a series of structures, from the opening Hart-Leap Well to the final image of Michael's unfinished sheep-fold.[37] With all these structures, the insistence that objects retain the traces of their making is crucial to Wordsworth's aesthetic and moral vision. Without these sights, the world is not open to interpretation, and even with them, habits of reading attuned only to grandeur (the "British Chief") cause misreadings. Just as these sights disappear for the beggar because of his infirmity, so also are they absorbed into enclosures of regulated space, until, like the beggar, the rural laborer has only, in Wordsworth's dismal pun, a prospect of one little span of earth. The result must be domestic disaster.

The morbidity of the "span of earth" is underscored by its unchanging status for the beggar, despite available differences:

> He plies his weary journey, seeing still,
> And never knowing that he sees, some straw,
> Some scatter'd leaf, or marks which, in one track,
> The nails of cart or chariot wheel have left
> Impressed on the white road, in the same line,
> At distance still the same. Poor Traveller!
> His staff trails with him, scarcely do his feet
> Disturb the summer dust.
>
> (53–60)

The beggar is like a cursed figure, the image of plying a journey perhaps recalling the Ancient Mariner.[38] To see without seeing is death-in-life, and these lines do not celebrate "irreducible natural man" who is "tenaciously alive," to use Bloom's phrases (*Visionary* 178–79). Rather, the beggar is an object of the poet's sight, a poet who can interpret "marks" in the road and has the perspective to compare the track of the wheel near and "At distance." Condemned to an utterly local vision, the beggar suffers for the community and for the poet, except that he is beyond suffering (or, to recall a line from "Animal Tranquility and Decay," "All effort *seems* forgotten" 9; my italics). The juxtaposition of the wheel that makes an impression on the "white road" and the beggar's feet, which scarcely "Disturb the summer dust," cuts in two directions. Taking Locke's property idea literally, in not mingling with the earth, the beggar gains no property interest, while the cart driver leaves his mark. The beggar has no claims other than to charity, and that has no legal status. But, as a consequence, the beggar does not damage the road but merely uses it.

The beggar is outmoded; his days of unintentional prophecy are done, as "His staff trails with him." He is passed even by the "slow-pac'd waggon" (66). But more important, though less obviously, he is passed by the poet, for in the next lines, the poet speaks to the political locus of London:

> But deem not this man useless—Statesmen! ye
> Who are so restless in your wisdom, ye
> Who have a broom still ready in your hands
> To rid the world of nuisances . . . deem him not
> A burthen of the earth.
>
> (67–73)

"Nuisance," for the lawyer, was a specific term, for "something that incommodes the neighbourhood" (Johnson),[39] and his "broom," a deliberately domestic image, is no more effective than the beggar's staff held in a "palsied hand." Like the beggar, the statesmen lack perspective, but not power. The statesmen's eagerness for social engineering extends historically at least back to the rise of insane asylums, and the corresponding legislation in 1618, which authorized a five-pound fine for the failure of a justice of the peace to provide housing for the indigent ("Commission . . . for Wards, Ideots, and Lunaticks"), and forward to the utilitarian legislation of the 1830s, including the Reform Bill of 1832 and New Poor Law of 1834. In 1795, the justices of Berkshire met in Speenhamland and handed down a recommendation that "subsidies in aid of wages should be granted in accordance with a scale dependent on the price of bread." Although never enacted by Parliament, "very soon [the Speenhamland scale] became the law of the land over most of the countryside" (Polanyi, *Transformation* 78). Joseph Townsend had already cautioned against such acts in his *Dissertation on the Poor Laws:* "A wise legislator will endeavor to confirm the natural bonds of society, and give vigour to the first principles on which political union must depend . . . . But our laws tend to weaken these bonds, and to destroy this subordination [of servant to master] by compelling the occupier of land to find employment for the poor. . . . The wisest legislator will never be able to devise a more equitable, a more effectual, or in any respect a more suitable punishment, than hunger is for a disobedient servant" (26–27).

The beggar is not, strictly speaking, a servant, but his regular rounds are dictated by hunger, and, not being "useless," he does serve the community. In the opening verse paragraph, he is trying to eat what he has gathered, "the dole of village dames" (9). The narrator does not impute appetite to the beggar, but describes his eating as a form of thriftiness. First, he "scann'd [his scraps and fragments] with a fix'd and serious look / Of idle computation" (10–11); and as he eats, he attempts "to prevent the waste" of spilling crumbs (17). It is as if he is reckoning for the community, just as statesmen attempt to do.

Against the plans of the statesmen, the poet sets natural law:

> 'Tis Nature's law
> That none, the meanest of created things,
> Of forms created the most vile and brute,
> The dullest or most noxious, should exist
> Divorced from good.
>
> (73–77)

The narrator argues that nature has created a niche for the beggar within the community. He reasons from a Platonic or Godwinian position, that "things" and "forms" always partake in good. Evil, then, amounts to misuse or misappropriation. For a Burkean perspective, human legislation should not, and ultimately cannot, violate natural law. Consequently, from either a conservative or radical position, the beggar's position has value. Speaking of the "small independent *proprietors*," Wordsworth tells Fox that "their little tract of land serves as a kind of permanent rallying point for their domestic feelings, as a tablet upon which they are written which makes them objects of memory in a thousand instances when they would otherwise be forgotten" (LEY 314–15). In similar fashion, the villagers view the beggar:

> the Villagers in him
> Behold a record which together binds
> Past deeds and offices of charity
> Else unremember'd, and so keeps alive
> The kindly mood in hearts which lapse of years,
> And that half-wisdom half-experience gives
> Make slow to feel, and by sure steps resign
> To selfishness and cold oblivious cares.
>
> (80–87)

Wordsworth again stresses the beggar's reified quality as something readable and available to inscription, just as the "tracts of land" are for small property owners. As Bloom contends, this is not "the vicious and mad doctrine that beggary is good because it makes charity possible" (*Visionary*

180), but neither is it far from that.[40] Charity is good, yet the beggar's value is less in being an object of charity than a record of it. Without such a record, half-experience would chill the heart. A world without poverty, in its full sense, would have to be one without half-experience, and so beggars would be unneeded, although other possibilities of charity could still be available; however, as Wordsworth had neither an economic nor a religious doctrine available that contemplated the elimination of poverty, such a vision would be mere abstraction. Thus, the argument is not for the necessity of charity; rather it is for the necessity of communal records, one device of which is charity and another of which (in the letter to Fox) is unalienable property. As it stands, the Cumberland Beggar (like the Statesman) performs an administrative service:

> let him bear about
> The good which the benignant law of heaven
> Has hung around him, and, while life is his,
> Still let him prompt the unletter'd Villagers
> To tender offices and pensive thoughts.
>
> (159–63)

The "good" is "hung" like the Mariner's albatross ("Rime" 138), symbolic of the life of the community. The villagers must read the beggar partly because they are "unletter'd" (162); they cannot read, for example, the *Lyrical Ballads*, a record of tender offices such as the misguided aid given "Simon Lee," the helpful poet of "The Idle Shepherd Boy," and the generous people of "The Old Cumberland Beggar" and of pensive thoughts, such as the Lucy or Matthew poems.

The beggar's functions within the community are passive, regular rather than regulative:

> Where'er the aged Beggar takes his rounds,
> The mild necessity of use compels
> To acts of love; and habit does the work
> Of reason, yet prepares that after joy
> Which reason cherishes. And thus the soul . . .
> By that sweet taste of pleasure unpursu'd
> Doth find itself insensibly dispos'd
> To virtue and true goodness.
>
> (90–97)

The social necessity for charity teaches the habit of goodness. Wordsworth again escapes the moral necessity for charity by offering two routes to the same joy, habit and reason. The beggar's presence provides the method of habit, but one could reason out the need instead. As with the meter of poetry providing an overlay of pleasure for the transmission of ideas and feelings, here the fact of the pleasure coming "unpursu'd" augments its value, sweetens its taste. The contrast of this sweetness to the beggar's insentient hunger figures the regular rounds of the beggar as a kind of labor necessary in order for the pleasure to be unpursued. Seemingly a continuation of the argument of lines 80–87, in these lines Wordsworth exalts half-experience in the guise of an insensible disposition. That habit was a form of unexamined life was a commonplace Wordsworth would have encountered in Godwin's *Enquiry* (bk 1 chap. 5).

The mechanical reproduction of good achieved by the beggar duplicates Bentham's contention that in the panopticon, the guards who watch are as subject to social improvement as are the prisoners watched. But where the guards are products of wage labor, the beggar's beneficiaries are equivalent to the community itself. In the context of an address to statesmen, this argument suggests that the beggar has the same effect as the panopticon, but it is experienced more widely because it is determined by his wide-ranging walks, and not by the enclosure of the prison, or its analogues, the workhouses. Later in the poem, Wordsworth connects these two institutions directly:

> May never House, misnamed of industry
> Make him a captive; for that pent-up din,
> Those life-consuming sounds that clog the air,
> Be his the natural silence of old age.
>
> (172–75)

By breaking up the phrase "House of industry" across a caesura (and avoiding Bentham's formulation, "Industry-House"; M. I. Zagday, "Poor Law" 65), Wordsworth creates a momentary ambiguity in which the Cumberland Beggar should never have any house,[41] and indeed, he must, like the Mariner, continue on his rounds. Rather than the punishment of the House, the "Struggle with frosty air and winter snows" (167) is atonement enough. Bentham's Industry-Houses, proposed in 1797 to displace Pitt's bill to reform the Poor Law, were designed "on the Panopticon plan—five storeys in twelve sectors—for the exploitation of the labor of the assisted poor . . . [and] were to be ruled by a central board set up in the capital and modeled on the Bank of England's Board, all members with shares worth five or ten pounds having a vote" (Polanyi, *Transformation* 107).[42] In arguing against the House, Wordsworth simultaneously resists the reinforcement of a stock-market economy (Burke's metaphor for the distribution of human rights in the *Reflections*, and Bentham's for the organization of the Industry-Houses). By keeping the beggar free, yet doomed to extinction, the poet anticipates a gap in the moral structure of the community which he can fill.

The narrator also reminds the statesmen that when other men see the beggar, they recognize their own advantages. In particular,

> The easy man
> Who sits at his own door, and like the pear
> Which overhangs his head from the green wall,
> Feeds in the sunshine . . .
> . . . .
> all behold in him
> A silent monitor, which on their minds
> Must needs impress a transitory thought
> Of self-congratulation, to the heart
> Of each recalling his peculiar boons,
> His charters and exemptions.
> (108–11, 114–19)

The language of this passage is a curious blend of the pastoral and the legal. The easy man beneath his pear tree evokes the tranquility of Micah's vision, "they shall sit every man under his vine and under his fig tree" (Mic. 4:4) As in the biblical passage, Wordsworth shifts from a collective plural "their minds" to individuals alone in contemplation "the heart / Of each." Micah's utopia, in which the law from out of Zion assures every man his property, is displaced into the reality that property is scarce. The man at ease recalls his boons, charters, and exemptions; these are the terms of legal entitlement.[43] Not until these gains are described as transitory does Wordsworth explicitly invoke a religious frame:

> and perchance,
> Though he to no one give the fortitude
> And circumspection needful to preserve
> His present blessings, and to husband up

The respite of the season, he, at least,
And tis no vulgar service, makes them felt.
(119–24)

These lines combine the two dangers to the small property owner, threats from the economy and threats from the weather. The beggar's presence is no talisman against either, but only makes a man feel the value of what he has. This raises the question of who can provide "fortitude" and "circumspection." Not the Statesman, who, like the easy man, "contemplate[s]" a triad, in this case, his "talents, power, and wisdom" (72), that is transitory. Perhaps the poet.

Between the two social benefits of the beggar, the habit of caring (90–97) and the recognition of one's own blessings (108–19), Wordsworth places another benefit, the development of the poet's mind:[44]

. . . To virtue and true goodness. Some there are,
By their good works exalted, lofty minds
And meditative, authors of delight
And happiness, which to the end of time
Will live, and spread, and kindle; . . .
(97–101)

The "good works" which exalt are not equivalent to almsgiving, nor to the activities of the community, the "rural works" (49). They are achieved by conscious "authors of delight / And happiness," a role the Statesman might like, but available only to the "meditative" as opposed to those "restless in [their] wisdom" (68). The expansion through spreading and kindling is mildly suggestive of revolution, but a revolution of traditional values moving beyond the local community into the national economy, of local customs gaining statutory force. This vision is not utopian, but historically specific, possible only during the time of the beggar's decline:

minds like these,
In childhood, from *this* solitary being,
This helpless wanderer, have perchance receiv'd,
(A thing more precious far than all that books
Or the solicitudes of love can do!)
That first mild touch of sympathy and thought
In which they found their kindred with a world
Where want and sorrow were.
(101–8, my italics)

The repetition of the specifier "this" locates the scene both temporally and geographically. Because the beggar is "helpless," he is doomed; interference by the statesmen, the community, or the poet is useless. While the poet recoups him in the generalized sympathy with "a world / Where want and sorrow were," he cannot thereby produce others of equal sympathy through either books or love. But he can warn the statesmen of his lacks and insist on the inadequacy of laws, even "the Decalogue" (127), if not guided by moral sympathy.

In his letter to Fox, Wordsworth describes a couple, "both upwards of eighty years of age." He is confined, and she recently lamed and unable to supply him with food. This couple can be read against "The Old Cumberland Beggar" in two ways. First, she recalls the narrator's neighbor who feeds the beggar every Friday, and then

> from her door
> Returning with exhilarated heart,
> Sits by her fire and builds her hope in heav'n.
> (152–54)

Her heart is exhilarated by the movement between feeding the beggar and returning to her domestic situation. The woman in the letter represents this same situation gone awry. With her lameness, she fears being boarded out, that is, becoming utterly the object of sympathy, rather than one who, to a small extent, can afford to feel it. Losing a "house kept together so long," she is sure, "would burst her heart" (LEY 314); like the poor woman in the poem, she retains "an almost sublime conviction of the blessings of independent domestic life" (LEY 314).

Since, as Wordsworth mentions parenthetically, she is supported by the parish, "independence" does not amount to ownership, but to the ability to walk. Her lameness will destroy her independence. In this guise, the couple can be figured as the beggar, and the parish as the woman in the poem. They support her independence so long as she can walk, just as he will survive "long as he can wander" (165). Wordsworth does not ask Fox for aid for this couple; they are an example of the "spirit" that the community bolsters. Rather, he directs Fox's attention to "The Brothers" and "Michael," poems about "small independent *proprietors*" (LEY 314). This "class of men is rapidly disappearing," but is not doomed to extinction; depicting for the statesmen their ability to "feel deeply," the poet hopes to rescue them.

Not so the beggar, who will die and whose class "will probably soon be extinct."

Until his death, however, the narrator says, "let him, *where* and *when* he will, sit down / Beneath the trees" (184–85). A plea for a right of use, this "let," one of nine directed to the statesmen, hovers between entreat and command. The emphasis is determined by the implied reader. Despite the address to "Statesmen," this poem is directed to those who might exert pressure on statesmen, not to the government itself. When Wordsworth actually addressed Fox, a statesman, he wrote "with the highest respect and admiration" (LEY 315).[45] Propertied readers are pushed to accept the value of charity as directly linked to their right of property, while disenfranchised readers, at least those accepting Wordsworth's characterization of the Statesmen which is consonant with contemporary radical satires (see Marcus Wood, *Radical Satire* chap. 2), adopt a derived sympathy for the Cumberland Beggar that associates them through their literacy with the community of property.

The poem becomes the record of that community, and yet the poet is not absorbed into the role of the beggar. Although he does not want the statesman to speed the process with social engineering, the poet is content to let the beggar, and his class, die. In its own time, the agrarian society will blend into the national one. This is perhaps tragic, but it is a tragedy from which the poet, unlike the beggar, is safe: he can see the tracks down the road.

"RURAL ARCHITECTURE," an anapestic poem written in four stanzas of aabccb rhymes, follows "The Old Cumberland Beggar." It names a rural work constructed by children, and is itself inelegantly assembled as if in imitation. Three boys build "Ralph Jones" out of stones, and after the wind blows "the Giant away" (16), they rebuild him. In contrast to their Frankenstein creature, the children are small, "the highest not more / Than the height of a Counsellor's bag" (2–3). This metaphor is peculiar. Perhaps the image recalls the bulk of a lawyer's briefcase, capable figuratively and, in some visual satire, literally of swallowing children. Alternatively, it refers to a famous counselor's bag, the budget of the Chancellor of the Exchequer, which contained the expenditures and revenues of the nation and was held up to the waiting crowd once the national budget was determined, a symbol of English stability. Wordsworth uses the word *bag* only twice in his published poetry,[46] once here, and once at the beginning of "The Old Cumberland Beggar," and the nearness invites comparison:

> from a bag
> All white with flour, the dole of village dames
> [The beggar] drew his scraps and fragments, one by one,
> And scann'd them with a fix'd and serious look
> Of idle computation.
>
> (8–12)

Like the budget of the exchequer, the beggar's bag contains the revenues of the day, which are by necessity, and in sharp contrast to the government's budget, exactly equivalent to the day's expenditures. The scraps are mostly bread, since the bag is "all white with flour," and with the Speenhamland Acts, the values of bread and of money were legally interconnected.

The verse paragraph ends with the food slipping through the beggar's shaking hands to the waiting scavenging birds. In the context of "The Old Cumberland Beggar" alone, this image is sad, but recalls a cycle of life between human beings and nature which the beggar mediates. But juxtaposed with the metaphor from "Rural Architecture," the scene becomes one of waste, perhaps shadowed by the huge national debt caused by the war waged against France, which left Britons to be the pickings of scavengers.[47] It suggests the beggar's ultimate inadequacy to his community role, just as the children cannot build a man to withstand the ravages of the wind. Like the Hebrews working without straw, they build without "mortar or lime" (5) and need intervention to succeed.

According to the Fenwick note on the poem, "These structures, as everyone knows, are common among our hills, being built by shepherds as conspicuous marks, occasionally by boys in sport" (*Lyrical Ballads* 306). If we accept the historical accuracy of this remark, the children, twice called "School-boys" (2, 17), are being educated in the ways of the village and especially in marking out its terrain. Their fortitude in rebuilding inspires the poet to join them, yet to outdo them, or at least to educate them beyond the power of the village custom. The effect is similar to the inspiration the Cumberland Beggar provides for "authors of delight":

> —Some little I've seen of blind boisterous works
> In Paris and London, 'mong Christians or Turks,
> Spirits busy to do and undo:

At remembrance whereof my blood sometimes will flag.
—Then, light-hearted Boys, to the top of the Crag
And I'll build up a Giant with you.

(19–24)

They build, not rebuild, the Giant, because it will be a new Man, better than either the boys' earlier work or what has been achieved in the big cities. Whether the line reads in parallel, pairing Paris with the Christians, or as a chiasmus, linking revolutionaries with infidels, depends on the reader's politics. In either case, the poet's empowerment constitutes the empowerment of the village amid the social changes inevitably arising from the conflicts between Paris and London, both actual and ideological. The poet's blood is restored by his return to the village, and in exchange, he helps the boys to build giants of themselves, and so outgrow the counselor's bag.

THE POET'S PROPERTY: "A POET'S EPITAPH"

"A Poet's Epitaph" combines two themes that occur frequently in the second volume of the *Lyrical Ballads*. First, a marker of death, most often a grave, is associated with some story.[48] Second, wandering provides a chance encounter with either a story of death or death itself. "A Poet's Epitaph," however, is the only poem labeled an epitaph in the volume; in it, the wanderings of professional men toward the poet's grave are prohibited, while the approach of the "idler" is allowed.[49] The various professional men appear before the grave as though before a judge, but their punishment is not that to which the "Statesman" would condemn the Old Cumberland Beggar, imprisonment. Rather, it is banishment. They are told to "come not near," reversing "the invitation, 'Pause, Traveller!' so often found upon the monuments," as Wordsworth points out in his "Essay on Epitaphs," composed around 1810 and appended to *The Excursion* (*Excursion* 448).[50] In that same essay, Wordsworth explicitly connects the dead as the implied author of his own epitaph with a judicial function: "The departed Mortal is introduced telling you himself that his pains are gone; that a state of rest is come; and he conjures you to weep for him no longer. He admonishes with the voice of one experienced in the vanity of those affections which are confined to earthly objects, and gives a verdict like a superior Being, performing the office of a judge, who has no temptations to mislead him, and whose decision cannot but be dispassionate" (*Excursion* 454).

The occasion of the poet's death, and more specifically the site of the poet's grave, serve to validate a particular social order against competing institutional structures. Replaying the tension between the narrative ballad and the epiphanal lyric from the volume's title,[51] in this poem, wandering (as searching and, etymologically, as "erring") and death (as resolution) allow Wordsworth to stage a confrontation between the poet retired in the Lake District and other professionals—statesmen, lawyers, etc.—characterized by a whirlwind of wasteful motion. By his formal choices, Wordsworth appropriates what is most enabling to the other professions, in order to provide to the rustic—the final internal audience—a vantage point of repose, the poet's grave. Wordsworth achieves this appropriation by invoking the language of property, inheritance, and economics, and finally by reworking the image from "Ellen Irwin," in which "Without a groan on Ellen's grave / His [Bruce's] body he extended" (45–47), into the invitation to the idler to "stretch thy body at full length" ("Poet's Epitaph" 59) upon the poet's grave.[52]

The definition of the poet himself is achieved through the modulation of wandering and death. The poet is gradually described by his social connections, but in the satirical outlook of the poem, those connections are constructed as absences and avoidances. Most literally, it is the poet's death that allows the poem. Speaking of Wordsworth's imagining his own death in "Tintern Abbey," Clifford Siskin has remarked that Roland Barthes's observation on the death of the author appears as "a narrative feature of the Romantic lyric: the interpretative search for transcendent meaning can end only with the 'birth of the reader . . . at the cost of the death of the Author.'" (*The Historicity of Romantic Discourse* 111). In a psychological reading, Wordsworth's imagining his own death as a trope for his absence from the realm of "public business" empowers the poem. But this absence is also structurally based, developed through the poet's antagonistic relation to statesmen, lawyers, moralists, and other writers of society.

The title, "A Poet's Epitaph," is cryptic. Its article remains ambiguous: if the epitaph is suitable for any poet, then it defines poetic activity generally, yet the individuation of death insists on a specific poet. Like Hume's man of letters, Wordsworth's poet acts specifically on behalf of his general type. Or, to recall the Preface, the question of what is poetry is isomorphic with the identity of the poet.[53] The second enigma of the title is the location of the epitaph. Is it actual carved words over "Some mute inglorious Milton" (Thomas Gray, "Elegy Written in a Country Churchyard" 59), or is it the poem itself?[54] This ambiguity says much about Wordsworth's method; the poem itself is positioned both to be what it represents (it is the epitaph which beckons from outside itself), and, further, to duplicate within the poem the structures that make the poem possible. To recast this ambiguity, is the epitaph composed about, or by, the dead poet? The fictional first-person of the epitaph, evident in the quotation above in which Wordsworth links the dead to a judge, provides the tradition in which the poem functions.

The reviewer for the *British Critic* divided "A Poet's Epitaph" into two parts; "an effusion of good-humoured satire, is succeeded by this picture of an animated and engaging sensibility" (17 [February 1801]: 129). He then quoted with approbation the last six stanzas (the "engaging sensibility") concerning the idler.[55] The division between the characters who are not welcome at the poet's grave and the rustic who is called to the grave employs specific stereotypes; the lawyer's "sallow face" and "coward eye" could be out of Hogarth's "Marriage à la Mode." At another level, however, the poem explores the social structure which produces such characters as the Statesman in order to suggest an alternative society characterized by the economy of a poetic, and not an industrial, marketplace.

The poem's design is simple, four-line abab stanzas of iambic tetrameter. Given the wider context of the *Lyrical Ballads*, with its use of narrative personae, this formal construction suggests the presence of the dead, rustic poet. Later, in his "Essay upon Epitaphs, II" Wordsworth describes the homely characteristics of "Country"epitaphs: "the strangeness of the illustrative images, the grotesque spelling, with the equivocal meaning often struck out by it, and the quaint jingle of the rhymes. These have often excited regret in serious minds, and provoked the unwilling to good-humoured laughter. Yet, for my own part, without affecting any superior sanctity, I must say that I have been better satisfied with myself, when in these evidences I have seen proof how deeply the piety of the rude Forefathers of the hamlet is seated in their natures" (*Prose* 2: 68–69).

Thus, Wordsworth's formal choices locate the epitaph within a rural economy, and associate the monument on which it is composed (if it is composed) with the rough stones of "Rural Architecture" and of the sheep-fold in "Michael." In the context of Wordsworth's musing on epitaphs, it tests the reader through its form and by providing a series of projected identities. The poem begins:

Art thou a Statesman, in the van
Of public business train'd and bred
—First learn to love one living man;
Then may'st thou think upon the dead.
(1–4)

These lines open to an entire horizon of "public business" that includes legislation and economic management. The hierarchical nature of professional politics divides men into the positions of subordination the poem satirically exploits. The statesman, then, cannot deal with individuals nor formulate a nation of humanity, the two valences of "one living man," neither of which he has "learn[ed] to love." Rather, he is caught in the factionalism of government. The poet, by contrast, achieves an understanding of the individual concurrently with a grasp of the general type.

The last line of the first stanza is double-voiced. To "think upon the dead" is both to approach the poet's grave and, more politically, to invoke tradition, precedent, and the laws of property, which, taking Burke and a Whig tradition as a model, describes the methods of statesmanship. Wordsworth does not reject statesmanship but appropriates it in order to criticize contemporary statesmen and their temporal institutions. The poet, at once narrative and lyric, capable of joining disparate individuals and humanity as a whole, is the better statesman.

The connection to tradition creates a transition to the next stanza:

A lawyer art thou?—draw not nigh;
Go, carry to some other place
The hardness of thy coward eye,
The falsehood of thy sallow face.
(5–8)

The interrogative form—"art thou"—which will be used again with both the soldier and the physician serves to link these various professions. (For the lawyer and philosopher Wordsworth uses the inverted interrogative structure, perhaps because both these professions, more than those of clergy and statesmen, depend on convoluted, that is, specialized, language.)

The interrogative form suggests that the professions are not quite distinguishable, or rather, that they are joined by the system in which they operate. While the lawyer's hardness and falsehood are written on his face, they do not originate there. They are figured as personal property to "carry." They are derived from the judicial system, or, within the hierarchy of the poem, they are given by the lawyer's position of subservience to the statesman. The traits of cowardice and sallowness, by contrast, are native to face and eye, and perhaps suggest the natural tendencies that make a person suitable to be called to the bar. Despite this satire, however, the poem employs a legalistic method of interrogation and sentencing; once again, the specific rejection is mediated by a structural appropriation.

The next possibility is a cleric. Resembling Chaucer's monk, this man seeks comforts and, since the sinecures of the church provide them, he is "plump" and "rosy" (9–10). Like the lawyer, his social station is written into his body. Next, a soldier:

> Art thou a man of gallant pride
> A Soldier, and no man of chaff?
> Welcome!—but lay thy sword aside
> And lean upon a Peasant's staff.
>
> (13–16)

Wordsworth invokes a variant on the admonition to beat swords into plowshares, and the metaphor of "chaff," calling up its counterpart of grain, indicates that the Soldier is not doomed to soldiering. Unlike the earlier professions, this is one created by conscription [*conscribere*, to write together, enter into a list], or the economic necessity of enlisting (an implicit conscription). Once the soldier is brought into the poem, the military imagery of the Statesman's "in the van" can now be reread; the statesman leads soldiers into war by controlling "public business," but he does so from a safe distance. While the biblical image generalizes the soldier, the more local reference to the contemporary war inscribes an opposition between the soldier and the man who becomes a soldier. Wordsworth rewrites, or unwrites, the conscripted soldier into a prototype of the idler. Denoting this man, the only character whose labors are in any sense tangible (albeit suppressed), as an idler points toward Wordsworth's image of the poet's idle wanderings (in such poems as "The Brothers" and "A narrow girdle of rough stones and crags") as a mode of labor.

Readings similar to those for the lawyer and soldier can be constructed for the philosopher and for the moralist, who is told not to "lose ten tickings of thy watch, / Near this unprofitable dust" (35–36). Connecting morality both to time keeping and to profit making reasserts the national economic horizon in which the poem is constructed, and provides a juxtaposition with the final stanzas that assert a local economy in the person of the idler. He is introduced thus: "But who is He with modest looks, / And clad in homely russet brown?" (37–38) While in earlier stanzas, the profession—Lawyer, Soldier—was capitalized, here the pronoun is. The adversarial question is not "art thou?" to which Christ has already given the conclusive reply at his trial, but "who is He?" By shifting into the third person, Wordsworth brings his reader into the poem as the person addressed. We are asked to look on this man, and consider. The rapid alteration of the professions gives way to sustained contemplation by both poet and reader.

This triangle of poet, rustic, and reader constitutes a rival economy of symbolic exchange, an alternative mode of enquiry from that of the court, one grounded in correspondences with nature: "He murmurs near the running brooks / A music sweeter than their own" (39–40). Through four more stanzas, the poet compares the idler with the environment. In the penultimate stanza, he is "Contented if he might enjoy / The things which others understand" (55–56). The "others" include those professions shunted from the grave, who, with only "understanding" and not enjoyment, understand nothing. Enjoyment is a prerequisite for understanding, but not sufficient to achieve it. This distinction separates the rustic and the poet. The former is a potential victim of the system—the enclosure acts had already demonstrated as much—and his strength is itself a weakness in its inability to capitalize itself: "—Come hither in thy hour of strength / Come, weak as is a breaking wave!" (57–58).

While this exploits a traditional comment on the vanity of human strength generally, in the context of the poem, it poses the specific problem of unprofessional labor which cannot sustain (store and redeploy) itself. By 1834, a Manchester silk weaver was able to articulate with both precision and acrimony the difference between labor and capital to the Select Committee on Hand-Loom Weavers' Petitions: "These two distinctions between the nature of labour and capital, (viz. that labour is always sold by the poor, and always bought by the rich, and that labour cannot by any possibility be stored, but must be every instant sold or every instant lost,) are sufficient to convince me that labour and capital can never with justice be subjected to the same laws" (in E. P. Thompson, *Working Class* 329). Labor cannot be stored for more favorable market conditions, cannot be deployed in other markets without cost if at all, and is not regulated by its own knowledge or needs. This last condition is not inevitable, but was secured by legislation such as gaming and anti-combination laws.

The poet can, in Wordsworth's representation, protect the idler because his facility with language (not the murmuring of running brooks) allows him to travel in both worlds. He resembles the Wordsworth who sent a copy of the second edition of the *Lyrical Ballads* to Fox. In addition to this letter, Wordsworth signed (authorized what Coleridge authored) letters to several other "persons of eminence," including William Wilberforce (LEY 312). The poet acts as advocate, and places the reader in the role of judge. The letter to Fox, however, demonstrates that Wordsworth's satirical position in this poem is mitigated by practical economic and institutional realities.

In the final stanza of "A Poet's Epitaph," Wordsworth employs two different figures to register the support the poet can offer the rustic: "Here stretch thy body at full length; / Or build thy house upon this grave" (59–60). In the first image, the rustic's temporal rest imitates the poet's eternal sleep from which he receives rejuvenation. Against this metaphysical vision is one of property. The poet grants land to the idler who then, in building a house, enlarges and enriches the grave, protecting it from the encroachment of the new society. The poem has become a will, and the poet's death is worked into a cycle equally natural (or at least naturalized) and linguistic. Common law required a will to exclude by name anyone with an apparently superior claim on property; thus, the poet's first nine stanzas.

The final line, granting property, plays against one from the previous stanza: "[The rustic] Hath been an idler in the land" (54). The phrase echoes the biblical phrase, "sojourner in the land." His status is temporary; moreover, he cannot inherit land, and, as a laborer, is always on the verge of enslavement from a landowner who "knew not Joseph." Within the system of the statesman and the lawyer, such was the historical reality: the peasants' lands were held in common, and thus any individual was as a sojourner, but the land was being rapidly sucked into larger estates. Furthermore, wages were in many places falling, but more to the point, were being wrenched from the traditional methods by which they were set in favor of a supply-and-demand model, one consequence of which was a steep climb in unemployed agricultural labor. A more distant echo from one of Christ's parables reinforces the economic dimension of this line: "And [an householder] went about the third hour, and saw others standing idle in the marketplace" (Matt. 20:3). Here, the landowner controls the price of labor and effects exactly the switch that, in Adam Smith's theory of political economy, the marketplace must be protected against: "So the last shall be first, and the first last" (Matt. 20:16). In "A Poet's Epitaph," the poet offers this transformation by granting a property at once spiritual and material, the grave upon which a house can be built.

To read the poem as a will, however, requires common law, and, at first glance, reinstates the ideological scribes of the legal system. Alternatively, however, the deed of the grave emphasizes the "commonness" of tradition as something natural, and as inscribed directly on the land ("The outward shews of sky and earth" 45) and not mediated by the courts. Instead, the buried poet, no longer distinct from the earth, is at once the mediator and the object of mediation. But all this is metaphoric: Wordsworth is alive, and building a house on a grave is, like building a church on a rock, to produce another institution. Where, then, does the reader stand? Given that readers, at least as represented by the circulation of a book printed in London and reviewed by the London and Edinburgh press, are city dwellers who rely on lawyers and statesmen, what is their activity in reading the poem? What speech act do readers experience the poem as performing? Such questions duplicate the problem produced by the poem—where do we locate the ownership of the poem's meaning, what kind of economy of exchange can be fabricated out of the exchange of poetry? In this context, the *British Reviewer*'s remark, splitting the poem into satire and sensibility, rhetorically disarms the poem's force.

The parabolic enigma of the final stanza cannot be interpreted, only reread in an effort to approach a grave that awaits a name. The mechanism of control that the poem enforces, however, depends not on the poet's being dead, but on the recognition that we only imagine Wordsworth's death as the enabling fiction by which we also imagine that Wordsworth continues to live and thus has not yet ceded his grave to the rustic/critic. The ending of this poem, like that of "Tintern Abbey," resists Barthes's formulation of the death of the author, but rather, in allowing readers to imagine themselves as the perpetual (and perpetually deferred) heirs of the author, maintains the poet's life through the continual revision of his works, a process that duplicates the revisionary processes by which Wordsworth both maintains a perpetual copyright and eschews the protection of the court in doing so. In my conclusion, I argue that the effort of self-assertion within a field of legal discipline overextended Wordsworth, and that the final revisionary moment of his career was to bring it into line with the legal discourse he had gained so much by opposing. But first, he would offer his most systematic excursus, the only epic poem he published in his lifetime. To this poem, we now turn.

SEVEN

The Excursion: Revision and Review

WORDSWORTH desired that readers take *The Excursion* seriously by extracting a system from the poem. I follow this suggestion but place the system against other competing systems—not only to notice the gaps in romantic systemization but to restore its polemic character. Reading *The Excursion* against "The Ruined Cottage" and reviews by William Hazlitt and Francis Jeffrey clarifies the political stakes of Wordsworth's aesthetics. This reading situates the poem within a political debate that centered on the valuing of labor and nature, issues that move toward Wordsworth's conception of rights. In the subsequent chapter, I relate the central trope of the poem, Wandering, to the central trope of legal society, Property, in order to explore implications of that conception of rights. While law and economics remain the primary focus, I widen the lens to locate in these discourses, as in *The Excursion*, a totalizing drive that rhetorically subsumes other voices.

The Pedlar's Retirement, Gothic Structures

Usurping the Pedlar

In *Wordsworth and* The Recluse, Kenneth Johnston demonstrates that the "history of *The Recluse* is one of repeated beginnings" (285): "The Ruined Cottage," the early *Preludes*, the sketches of "Home at Grasmere," the published *Excursion* with a preface highlighting an otherwise imperceptible fragmentary status, subsequent editions and revisions seen through the press by Wordsworth, and the posthumous publication of the *Prelude*. This series deliberately structures works so that wholeness and priority become interpretive issues. New beginnings are fashioned not as false starts but as repetitions and purifications, the same real language represented yet again and recalling readers to the task set for them in the *Lyrical Ballads*, making a tale, and a judgment, from scraps of evidence. At the same time, the poetic career, as an activity of publication and self-reference, revises the poems into a continuum of self-interpretation. New beginnings, thus, are also revisions and contaminations of earlier work. Wordsworth's composing procedures make this point clear: the 1,300 lines that "began" *The Recluse* in 1798 were dispersed into at least "The Old Cumberland Beggar," "Old Man Travelling" (described by Wordsworth as an "overflow" of "The Cumberland Beggar," although published two years before it), a section condensed into the Discharged Soldier episode concluding book IV of the *Prelude*, and a version of "The Ruined Cottage" that evolved into the first book of *The Excursion* (Johnston, *Wordsworth* 5–6). Dorothy, exasperated at the complicated state of the manuscripts, welcomed the publication of *The Excursion* as a hedge against Wordsworth's death, since she believed only Wordsworth could see them through the press; publication appears not as the end of a work, but as a resting place in the poet's development akin to the rock on which William sits in "Expostulation and Reply." The appropriate analogue is once again the common law, reinterpreting itself as a critique of its earlier versions in such a way as to erase them, or conform them to the contemporary version. And like the common law, the earlier versions remain not as overlooked, incidental traces but as the antithetical foundations that structure the movement of the published text.

Jonathan Wordsworth portrays Wordsworth's incorporation of "The Ruined Cottage" into *The Excursion* as a co-option that violates the aesthetic terms of the earlier poem, as, in a word, a mistake.[1] William Galperin revalues this violation, this taking, as a critique. For example, Galperin discusses the figure of the dreamer in both texts: "In *The Ruined Cottage*, the differences separating the Poet and dreamer help to unite the poet with the reader. . . . [In *The Excursion*] roughly the same experience actually accentuates the gap between self and community or between subject and object" (*Revision* 36–37).[2] Consequently, the authority established by the poet at the opening of *The Excursion* becomes unstable and must be reinstated through the secondary (yet also unstable) authority of the Wanderer. From "The Ruined Cottage" (in the earliest versions that contained the Pedlar's history) to *The Excursion*, Wordsworth expands the Wanderer's failure as a school teacher; the resulting choice to become a peddler emphasizes that his value (and consequently authority) is dependent on his location within a vanishing economy, rather than in a rising profession.[3]

The revisions of the Pedlar and the narrator in "The Ruined Cottage" into the Wanderer and the poet in *The Excursion* detail Wordsworth's struggle with poetic sovereignty. Like the Leech-gatherer, the Pedlar of "The Ruined Cottage" is engaged in an occupation on the verge of extinction; his retirement occurs within the textual history of the poem in the gap between "The Ruined Cottage" and *The Excursion*. The general tenor of *The Excursion* is one of orderly inheritance—the poet, educated by the Wanderer, will take up his tasks as educator, mediator, and judge. The disjunction between "The Ruined Cottage" and *The Excursion*, however, inscribes usurpation—a professional revolution, bloodless but socially violent—in the text.

Here is the description in "The Ruined Cottage" of the narrator coming upon the Pedlar:

> He lay, his pack of rustic merchandize
> Pillowing his head—I guess he had no thought
> Of his way-wandering life. His eyes were shut;
> The shadows of the breezy elms above
> Dappled his face. With thirsty heat oppress'd
> At length I hailed him, glad to see his hat
> Bedewed with water-drops.
>
> (44–50)

His pack is the means of his work and of his rest; at the end of the poem, "The old man [will rise] and hoist[] up his load" (534), the first movement reasserting a human presence among the noises of nature that "people[]" (533) the air. The narrator's guess that "he had no thought / Of his wandering-way life" is plausible because the Pedlar has no need to think about a life he always lives. This is the old (mythic) mode of labor; work is not carved out of life but integrated into it, unifying a landscape of human interaction. By the Humean formulation, there is a constant assertion of property relations maintained by his intersticial position between maker and user. His circulation mirrors and authorizes the circulation of local, not national, moneys marked by localizing engravings.

In *The Excursion*, Wordsworth substantially changes this description:

> Supine the Wanderer lay,
> His eyes as if in drowsiness half shut,
> The shadows of the breezy elms above
> Dappling his face. He had not heard the sound
> Of my approaching steps, and in the shade
> Unnoticed did I stand some minutes' space.
> At length I hailed him, seeing that his hat
> Was moist with water-drops.
>
> (I 438–45)

"At length," initially delineating the struggle for the narrator to approach within hailing distance, now indicates a period of gazing. The pack is gone, and the narrator's guess, a tautology within the Pedlar's economy, becomes a privileged gaze: not the occupation of unalienated labor, but the silent transforming profession that capitalizes on observation. In "The Ruined Cottage," the fifteen lines between the narrator's spotting the Pedlar and his going for water contain four emotional expressions ("instantaneous joy" 36, "dear to me as is the setting sun"[4] 39, "now / Delighted" 42–43, "glad" 49); in the later poem, these are all deleted and the poet's thirst is underscored by the opposition between his lips "parched with thirst" and the Wanderer's having "found relief" (I 449–50). In "The Ruined Cottage," the Pedlar points the way to water without prompting. In *The Excursion*, he does so "at the word" (I 450); a symbolic exchange becomes necessary.

In the difference between these two scenes, a resistance in the poet emerges: he seeks to outdo the Wanderer, but cannot without the Wanderer's aid. The most significant difference in the scenes is that in *The Excursion*, the first-person actor wishes to become a professional poet and needs tales, such as "Michael," those implicit in "The Old Cumberland Beggar," and the Parson's eulogies in *Excursion* VI, which can be turned to profit. As the Wanderer/Pedlar puts it in both versions, neither he nor the narrator is

> contented thence to draw [from the misery of the dead]
> A momentary pleasure, never marked
> By reason, barren of all future good.
>
> (I 629–31)

The "misery / Even of the dead" (I 628–29) is, like the unadorned tale of "Simon Lee," a store of potential value described in the language of capital investment. The good reader, like the good poet, does not (with)draw present (i.e., "momentary") pleasure but invests it in the mark(et) of reason. At the same time, "reason" marks emotions, such as misery, with value, just as money is validated by its markings. Consequently, reason both outlines the market of emotional investment and provides its central marking of value.

But the nature of "reason" needs clarification. Wordsworth is not rearticulating the eighteenth-century rhetorical center of logic, but appropriating its key trope, reason, to describe the procedures of plausible narrative; in book V, the Priest locates "reason" as a driving market force and the authorization of intellectual property when he delineates it as "An effort only, and a noble aim; / A crown, an attribute of sovereign power / Still to be courted" (V 502–4). That courtship, that flux of desire and attainment, of regulation and transgression, becomes the method by which stories become legible. We need pause only briefly to recall that the legal system, as it shifted to written forms of complaint and to independent juries, used a matrix of "reason" to construct the competing narratives of litigants. The reasonable man was a standard of behavior, and reasonable doubt, the threshold state-of-mind.[5] Both were, of course, fictions, as Bentham had pointed out and Blackstone reluctantly acknowledged, but my point is that legal and poetic representations contested control of the term "reason," and so enacted an economy of reason, at precisely the period in which economists delineated the relentless reason (invisible hand) of the national economy.

Further, the reasonability and coherent narrative were explicitly linked. Charging a jury in 1781, Judge Buller reiterated a legal commonplace: "that a presumption which necessarily arises from circumstances is very often more convincing and more satisfactory than any other kind of evidence, because it is not within the reach and compass of human abilities to invent a train of circumstances which shall be so connected together as to amount to a proof of guilt, without affording opportunities of contradicting a great part if not all of these circumstances" (quoted in Barbara Shapiro, *"Beyond Reasonable Doubt" and "Probable Cause"* 219). This is the legal rationalism that Godwin critiques in *Caleb Williams* in his representations of trial scenes and the advice Forester gives to Caleb to construct a coherent narrative.[6] Margaret's story, unlike the textually laden narratives Caleb manages, is "A tale of silent suffering, hardly clothed / In bodily form" (I 638–39). Just as the Pedlar provides raiment by merchandising and Robert by production, the poet clothes the story by wrapping it into first the Pedlar's history (bodily form) and then into the volume of *The Excursion*, and still again, into the collected editions of Wordsworth's work from 1820 onward. This is the layered investment that replaces the peddler's itinerant market, and that displaces the free-market economy, which through direct and indirect acts legislated the peddler's profession out of existence. At the same time, the reiterated versions preserve the nearly naked connectedness of the tale's circumstances.

In an 1802(?) revision of the 1799 "The Ruined Cottage," the Pedlar

> was slow
> In gathering wealth he had an open hand
> That never could refuse whoever ask'd
> Or needed.

The attempt, which replaced the observation that the Pedlar was "impelled / By curious thought" to "toil" in his "poor calling," and was itself rejected with horizontal slash marks ("The Ruined Cottage" 359), never congeals grammatically into an explicit connection between the Pedlar's generosity and his slow accumulation of wealth. It is as if Wordsworth cannot decide quite how to meet the narrative necessity of this speaker's poverty, although, as Alan Liu remarks, such lines in full context veer relentlessly toward the Pedlar as "intertextual dealer" (*Sense* 346). In these lines, the economic reality of local need coincides with the Pedlar's personal generosity, a generosity which, in *The Excursion*, is distributed over acts of charity, efforts at healing the Solitary, and his gift of the story of Margaret, a gift which reviewers like Francis Jeffrey and De Quincey declared not his to give. These lines do not survive into the published version, because they perhaps too easily pinpoint a dilemma of the poet's relation to the Pedlar. The Pedlar's sympathy, like his money, is spent in communal subsistence; the poet would invest that very sympathy whose mark is its localized, uninvested, and continually divested character.

My reading cuts against most of *The Excursion*, which asserts a sympathy between the Wanderer and the poet, but I suggest this sympathy derives from the perspective of the poet who, having subsumed the Wanderer, can now "*afford* to suffer / With those whom he saw suffer" (I 370–71). He can preserve, or at least represent as preserved, old modes of exchange within the new market, not least because that new market eliminated competitors such as peddlers who speak to customers and deliver real objects, rather than represent the "real language of men" to an anonymous audience. Wordsworth's procedure in *The Excursion* is to elide this difference between "The Ruined Cottage" and *The Excursion*, by periodically restoring to the relation of poet and Wanderer the continuity disrupted by the differential between the two versions. By doing so, he articulates the poet's authority in juridical, rather than sovereign form, to use terms Jerome Christensen invokes to discuss Byron.[7] If the *Prelude* is a personal epic that struggles to establish a sovereignty over self, *The Excursion* is a juridical work seeking to locate both self and other in a corporation under the "law / Of conscience" (IV 224–25) and its external manifestation, "The law of duty" (IV 1036). But this effort requires the constant overcoming of the claims of other juridical interpreters, whether critics or judges; the usurpation of the Pedlar is a trope for these other usurpations.

Gothic Spaces

The spaces Wordsworth opens for the poet are simultaneously enclosed. The conversion of Dorothy's mind into a "mansion for all lovely forms" and her memory into "a dwelling place" ("Tintern Abbey" 141–42), the invitation to build a house upon the poet's grave in "A Poet's Epitaph," and the psychic completion of the sheep-fold in "Michael" are prototypes for the building that Wordsworth announces provides the shape of his poetic career.

In his preface to *The Excursion*, Wordsworth presents the established interrelationships of his poems; their core is the incomplete *Recluse*, and the center of that is the volume in the reader's hand, *The Excursion*.[8] Wordsworth uses the architectural metaphor of a gothic church, the social functions of which overspill its confines into the courts, the shops, the farms, the day-to-day life of the town, and which, because its construction takes centuries, is used before completion and requires its occupants to complete it imaginatively.[9] It is Tintern Abbey reinvested, its contemporary passive function as a hideaway for vagrants displaced by its medieval, socially vital mode:

> The two Works [the unpublished "biographical poem" posthumously produced as the *Prelude* and the never completed *Recluse*] have the same kind of relation to each other, if he may so express himself, as the ante-chapel has to the body of a gothic church. Continuing this allusion, he may be permitted

> to add, that his minor Pieces, which have been long before the Public, when they shall be properly arranged, will be found by the attentive Reader to have such connection with the main Work as may give them claim to be likened to the little cells, oratories, and sepulchral recesses, ordinarily included in those edifices. (*Excursion* 2)

The development of such a church was subject to shifts in labor supply, weather, materials, and aristocratic and papal support, and yet the final product presented itself as a harmonious whole, mirroring both the ordered heavens and the continuity of social life. The Wordsworthian career, the metaphor implies, is also centrally located, weathering storms of criticism and reorganizing by accretion.

The metaphor of the gothic church was not original, and some of its resonance can be understood by examining Blackstone's use of another gothic edifice: "[Our system of remedial law resembles] an old Gothic castle, erected in the days of chivalry, but fitted up for a modern inhabitant. The moated ramparts, the embattled towers, and the trophied halls, are all magnificent and venerable, but useless. The inferior apartments, now converted into rooms of convenience, are cheerful and commodious, though their approaches may be winding and difficult" (*Commentaries* 3: 268). For both Wordsworth and Blackstone, the metaphor unites disparate writing and accounts for their appearance as discrete, disunified, even contradictory objects.

For Blackstone, new remedies did not indicate a new system, but adjusted a single constitution to the variations of history. The archaic aspects of the law, those associated with feudalism and discord ("moated," "embattled," "trophied") retain their sublime character and exert a unifying aesthetic pressure on the whole. Theresa Kelley has demonstrated Wordsworth's management of the sublime and the beautiful as tendencies toward inspiration and guardianship respectively (*Wordsworth's Revisionary Aesthetics* 44–45). Blackstone's position is similar: the "inferior apartments" that are "cheerful and commodious" are in "use," while the sublime structures are "magnificent" but "useless." The jurist, who as a student at Pembroke had circulated a manuscript on architecture, turns to an aesthetic mode to confront historical disjunctions which both threaten the grounds of the common law and, in the myth of law as a civilizing influence, must reside at the pre-original moment of that law. Demonstrating the nobility and order of law, Blackstone defined for the lawyer a right to police that nobility and order, combined with a loyalty to the aristocratic class that provided the empirical (or at least theatrical) basis of nobility as a psychic and economic commodity.[10]

The poet, Francis Jeffrey would maintain, does not compete for the same stakes as the jurist, but Wordsworth, as a professional determined to sing, as he put it in the Prospectus to *The Excursion*, "Of Truth, of Grandeur, Beauty, . . . / Of joy in the widest commonality spread; / . . . and the law supreme / Of that intelligence which governs all" (14–22) insists on those stakes and addresses exactly those disunities of history that vexed common law. In the middle of the middle book of *The Excursion*, the Parson delineates the essential incompleteness of human nature, and the Wanderer then paraphrases the Parson's "judgment" that

> Moral truth
> Is no mechanic structure, built by rule;
> And which, once built, retains a stedfast shape
> And undisturbed proportions.
>
> (V 562–65)

Moral truth, like the gothic cathedral and the poetic career, undergoes constant readjustment. Such readjustment is not done according to established laws, but dialectically responds to and creates such laws. This dialectic receives its initial explanation in the adherence to the discipline of reason:

> We may not doubt that who can best subject
> The will to reason's law, can strictliest live
> And act in that obedience, he shall gain
> The clearest apprehension of those truths,
> Which unassisted reason's utmost power
> Is too infirm to reach.
>
> (V 517–22)

From the initial prohibition, "we may not doubt," to the self-enforced "obedience" that allows a transcendence of reason, this passage is an inward spiral of restrictions. As such, it points to the incompleteness of juridical structure itself, whether in the domain of moral philosophy or of common law. If, as Peter Manning suggests, part of what irks Francis Jeffrey about *The Excursion* is Wordsworth's constant undercutting of his own authority, it is because the Wordsworthian self-critique is equally a critique of those discourses he appropriates. In the argument that "reason" is infirm, legal argument—its form constituted by the logical deduction here mimicked, and its vocabulary in constant play throughout the poem—is transcended.

The use of architectural metaphors to discuss what might be regarded as merely representational, poetry, or merely performative, law, dissolves the margins between representation and performance by locating both at the nexus of a community, whether church or baronial castle. But the constitution of such a nexus was itself representational and simultaneously performative. Both Wordsworth and Blackstone hoped their writing could establish a communal center not within the landscape of architecture and geography, but bound by discourses that echoed, and destabilized, such landscapes. William Hazlitt's review recognizes Wordsworth's effort, and marks its political implications.

Hazlitt's review of *The Excursion* appeared in the *Examiner* crowded by commentary on the Irish peasantry and tax law, and he opens it by challenging the poem's imagery of unity. He insists on the fissure between Wordsworth's power over his materials and his skills in choosing materials suited to those powers: "Whether, as it is, this most original and powerful performance may not rather remain like one of those stupendous, but half-finished structures, which have been suffered to molder into decay, because the cost and labour attending them exceeded their use or beauty, we feel it would be presumptuous in us to determine" (*Examiner* 21 August 1814, 541). Wordsworth invokes the metaphor of the Gothic Church as a building in active use, as if his current poem holds the same place in contemporary society that the gothic church held in ancient time. Alert to the crush of history, Hazlitt reworks the metaphor to foreground the decay to which such edifices have become subject, and leaves to the reader the problem of whether the effort to get through the poem, commensurate with the author's labor of composition, will be adequately rewarded. Introducing a cost-benefit analysis, Hazlitt positions the poem in a competitive marketplace, in which time itself is a commodity (a point increasingly obvious in both wage-driven labor and time-bound investment instruments; see Thompson, *Customs* chap. 6 and E. J. Hobsbawm, *Labouring Men* chap. 5). Further, the *Examiner* presents itself as a competitor, so that Hazlitt's version of *The Excursion* (with his digression on country folk that parodies the Parson's excursus on his dead parishioners) substitutes for Wordsworth's. It was cheaper, shorter, and, as if to represent a complete *Recluse*, appeared in three sections, each with a different emphasis.

Committed to unraveling Wordsworth's contradictory structures, Hazlitt equates the poem with its sublime landscape: "We are surrounded with the constant sense and superstitious awe of the collective power of matter, of the gigantic and eternal forms of Nature, on which, from the beginning of time, the hand of man has made no impression. Here are no dotted lines, no hedge-row beauties, no box-tree borders, no gravel walks, no square mechanical enclosures. . . . we doubt whether [Wordsworth] would not reject a druidical temple, or time-hallowed ruin, as too modern and artificial for his purpose" (541). Jerome McGann has argued that in both "Tintern Abbey" and "The Ruined Cottage" (and one could add the Matthew and Lucy poems), the "method is to replace an image and landscape of contradiction with one dominated by 'the power / Of harmony'" (*The Romantic Ideology* 86). To the extent that enclosed land shadows the opening landscape of "Tintern Abbey," then the landscape itself operates within a symbolic discourse. Approximately forty percent of the costs of enclosure were legal expenses. Which gesture—the legal documentation or the hedgerow ("hardly hedge-rows" ["Tintern Abbey" 16]) which surrounded the enclosed property—was symbolic, and which performative, depended upon how the audience read the acts. The replacement of one landscape with another is not merely a shifting from a historical paradigm to an aesthetic one, but an effort to replace the horizon of legal discourse with that of poetic system. Hazlitt displaces Wordsworth's displacement, and restores to the Wordsworthian landscape the hedgerows of enclosure.

Scenes like the churchyard or the Pastor's house contradict a literal reading of Hazlitt's point, and his next paragraph clarifies his position. Wordsworth's poem "is not so much a description of natural objects, as of the feelings associated with them, not an account of the manners of rural life, but the result of the Poet's reflections on it" (541). The occurrence of human objects and natural objects is ancillary to the poet's use of them, and indeed, the objects do not fully exist until the use is exerted. "An intense intellectual egotism swallows up every thing. . . . The recluse, the pastor, and the pedlar, are three persons in one poet" (542). Hazlitt's trinity attacks the illusion of heteroglossia in a text that subsumes all variety into one system, the poet's imagination. Dorothy Wordsworth's defense, in a letter to Catherine Clarkson, clarifies the terms of the debate: "[Hazlitt's] opinion that all the Characters are but one character, I cannot but think utterly false—there seems to me to be an astonishing difference considering that the primary elements are the same—fine Talents and strong imagination" (LMY 2: 165, 11 November 1814). For both Wordsworths, the poet's imagination is an origin of difference, and the poem enacts the dramatic conflict between two notions of difference.

The first, the Hobbesian notion that Hazlitt accepts, is that difference is the state of nature, and the civilizing process is the institution of a sameness that disciplines difference by arranging it as culture. Hazlitt's final section contains the digression on country people, who all "hate each other" precisely because they cannot differentiate themselves; Hazlitt's list of the cultural implements of differentiation is telling: "There are no shops, no taverns, no theatres, no opera, no concerts, no pictures, no public buildings, no crowded streets, no noise of coaches, or of courts of law,—neither courtiers nor courtesans, no literary parties, no fashionable routes, no society, no books, or knowledge of books" (*Examiner* 2 October 1814, 637). The law courts take the climactic position in the first list, a list focused on public exchanges, whether of merchandise or culture; and the following list offers an ironic assessment of the necessity of false representations—in which courtiers are much like courtesans, and in which "knowledge of books," gained by reading the periodicals, provides as much social capital as reading the actual books.

Dorothy Wordsworth, who at the time of her letter to Clarkson had heard an oral report of the third part of the review, singles out the detail that Hazlitt "has the audacity to complain that there are no Courtesans to be found in the country" (LMY 2: 165). Embedded in this observation is the Wordsworths' sense that "Hazlitt had behaved disgracefully [and possibly criminally] in some sexual way" when he visited the Lake District in 1803 (Stephen Gill, *William Wordsworth: A Life* 304), but equally important is their refusal to accept the stagings of the city as meaningfully distinctive. In *The Prelude*, Wordsworth would load "Residence in London" (bk VII) with metaphors of undifferentiated activity—"monstrous ant-hill" (149), "the roar" (168), "mighty concourse" (219)—even as he catalogued distinctions of nationality, occupation, social class, and physiognomy. He eventually moves his reader's eye "from entertainments, that are such / Professedly, to others titled higher," namely, "the brawls of lawyers in their courts / Before the ermined judge, or that great stage / Where senators, tongue-favoured men, perform" (486–92). He moves from a language announcedly representational to one performative, and discovers no substantial difference. Finally, the speech of law and legislation "Grows tedious even in a young man's ear" (511), and Wordsworth must seek another theory of difference.

The second notion of difference posits that prehuman nature (a temporal impossibility for Wordsworth, but a threat glimpsed in the "savage torpor" decried in the Preface of the *Lyrical Ballads*) is sameness, and that the introduction of the human imagination brings difference, variety, and beauty into existence. Variety for its own sake is devalued as not a species of difference at all; it resembles the gothic novels Wordsworth disparages in the Preface to the *Lyrical Ballads.* As Hazlitt remarks, Wordsworth refuses "the common vantage-grounds of popular story, of striking incident, or fatal catastrophe as illegitimate or vulgar modes of producing an effect" (*Examiner* 21 August 1814, 541). To rephrase Hazlitt's remark, Wordsworth refuses to make his story interesting by evoking the clichés of interest and depends instead on the reader's labor to operate the shifts from sameness to difference. Moreover, Hazlitt's continuity between the "illegitimate" and the "vulgar," in the context of his quarrel with legitimacy, marks his suspicions about both the implied aristocratic values of Wordsworth's system and the bad faith of its economic consciousness.

This argument between Hazlitt and Wordsworth was not about simple aesthetic choices, but about the relation between aesthetics and other public systems. Hazlitt spends what he himself indicates is an inordinate amount of time on Wordsworth's references to the paradigmatic figure of enlightenment ferment, Voltaire.[11] After quoting forty lines from book IV concerning the relationship between ancient and modern science (IV 941–78; 991–92), Hazlitt points out that "from the chemists and metaphysicians our author turns to the laughing sage of France, Voltaire." In the next paragraph, Hazlitt invokes Rousseau as a negative image of Wordsworth: "We shall not affirm with Rousseau (his authority would perhaps have little weight with Mr. Wordsworth)—*Tout homme reflechi est mechant*" (28 August 1814, 556). This framing recalls the French intellectual nexus of science, metaphysics, and politics that coalesced in the French Revolution.

To draw one example that concerns the concept of difference, Lavoisier sought to mark the arrival of a new chemistry with a new nomenclature: "A well-composed language, adapted to the natural and successive order of ideas will bring in its train a necessary and immediate revolution in the method of teaching and will not allow teachers of chemistry to deviate from the course of Nature; either they must reject the nomenclature or they must irresistibly follow the course marked out by it. The logic of the sciences is thus essentially dependent on their language" (quoted in Thomas Hankins, *Science and the Enlightenment* 109). Language replicates a "natural . . . order of ideas" and forces teachers to remain on the "course of Nature." This order and this course, in their strict correlation, constitute the logic of science and, when expanded into other domains, the reason of man, which is not open to the whims of individuals but is subject to the regulation of language as a collective human endeavor. Lavoisier himself insisted on the implications of classification and ordering for the regulation of weights and measures as simultaneously scientific and economic. But, in 1794, Lavoisier died under the guillotine, a victim of what Wordsworth, by 1814, saw as the result of pushing man's reason until it challenged nature as the builders of Babel challenged the heavens. The mistake was the reification of reason abstracted from its empirical origins.

In *The Excursion*, Voltaire is the named symbol of such reification, his *Candide* propping up a miniature city built by children. Wordsworth marks the egotism of the work by two images; first, the book "open[s] of itself," as if utterly independent, and second, it is "swoln / With searching damp" (II 439–40). The book, literally ruined by moisture, has absorbed more nature than its philosophic machinery can process.

Candide is discovered at the moment the Wanderer believes that the Solitary is dead, and the mistaken eulogy ends with this comparison:

> When change of times
> Hath summoned kings to scaffolds, do but give
> The faithful servant, who must hide his head
> Henceforth in whatsoever nook he may,
> A kerchief sprinkled with his master's blood,
> And he too hath his comforter. How poor,
> Beyond all poverty how destitute,
> Must that Man have been left, who, hither driven,
> Flying or seeking, could yet bring with him
> No dearer relique, and no better stay,
> Than this dull product of a scoffer's pen,
> Impure conceits discharging from a heart
> Hardened by impious pride!
>
> (II 474–86)

Although the reference to the servant's kerchief stained in blood invokes the executions of Louis XVI and Charles I,[12] the French Revolution itself plays the king within the metaphor, and *Candide* becomes the symbolic kerchief to which the Solitary can cling. The metaphor, however, emphasizes differences between the contained sovereignty within English law—in which a king can be "summoned," and in which the servant accepts, and symbolically preserves, a hierarchy—and the death of an abstract, and so anarchical, sovereignty of the revolutionary government, destroyed not by an evolution of power but by confusions in which "flying" and "seeking" become indistinguishable. This is, of course, a rather engaged interpretation of the meaning of 1649, one consistent with Burke's claim in *Reflections on the Revolution in France* that it served as a moment in which the English affirmed the monarchy. What is crucial here is that the Wanderer, and in Hazlitt's view, Wordsworth, finds the blood-stained kerchief comforting, and *Candide* "dull": "We cannot however agree with Mr. Wordsworth that *Candide* is *dull.* It is, if our author pleases, 'the production of a scoffer's pen,' or it is anything, but dull" (556). Staging the wide variety of human experience, *Candide* displays Hazlitt's notion of difference—which, for Wordsworth, mirrors the tedium of London. Charles Lamb spends considerable effort in a letter to Wordsworth about *The Excursion* in diffusing Hazlitt's argument in two contradictory ways. First, he recounts a dialogue in which he defends the Wanderer's remarks based on Wordsworth's "principle of its being a characteristic speech," and not one to attribute to the author. Then he adds, as if an afterthought, "I tried to get through [*Candide*] about a twelve-month since [i.e., before he could have read *The Excursion*], and couldn't for the dulness" ("Letter to William Wordsworth," 29 August 1814, 790).

Hazlitt's own aesthetic judgment of *Candide* replays the political assessment that Wordsworth has introduced by the antithetical structure of the introduction of the novel:

> [The book] I found to be a work
> In the French tongue, a Novel of Voltaire
> His famous optimist. 'Unhappy Man!'
> Exclaimed my Friend.
>
> (II 442–45)

The lines enact a struggle between Voltaire's words, "famous optimist," and the Wanderer's "Unhappy Man," the referent of the second being severalfold: the Solitary, Candide, Voltaire, and generalized man (i.e., reader of this most popular tale). This ambiguity resolves to focus on the Solitary:

> here then has been to him
> Retreat within retreat, a sheltering place
> Within how deep a shelter!
>
> (II 445–47)

The tedium of *Candide* works itself out in the disavowal by the reader (here played by the Solitary) of politics because of the failure of revolutionary sovereignty; in this sense, London and Paris are equated as they were in "Rural Architecture." But the task of *The Excursion* is to construct an alternative model, a juridical model in which interpretation, rather than force and declamation, constitutes power. Wordsworth marks the necessity for such a new model by immediately unraveling the Wanderer's own eulogy with the discovery that the Solitary is still alive. Such private speeches are, the Wanderer acknowledges, less reliable than the public songs of community; speaking of the funeral march, he says:

> We heard the hymn they sang—a solemn sound
> Heard anywhere; but in a place like this
> 'Tis more than human! Many precious rites
> And customs of our rural ancestry
> Are gone, or stealing from us; this, I hope
> Will last forever.
>
> (II 548–53)

This is the sort of moment in *The Excursion* that Hazlitt finds sentimental because it constitutes value (what is "precious") at an intersection of place and time, and it constitutes difference as a refinement of similarity—the song becomes "more than human" as an expression of the precisely human. Hazlitt "wish[es]" that Wordsworth had eliminated the "ambiguous illustrations" (termed in the next sentence, "particular illustrations") because they encumber the "general truth" (*Examiner* 28 August 1814, 555). Hazlitt variously asks that Wordsworth's poem be more historical and less so, because Wordsworth's aesthetic, in querying authority, queries the history that founds Hazlitt's professional project.

Francis Jeffrey and the Wanderer

"This will never do."

The line is familiar enough; Wordsworth himself, slightly misquoting, labeled them "these elegant and decisive words" (LMY 2: 182), and, reproduced in a hyperbolic version ("THIS WON'T DO!"), they provided a focus for Coleridge's passively hostile defense of Wordsworth's poetry (*Biographia Literaria* 2: 115). They are Jeffrey's infamously acceptable response to *The Excursion*,[13] published a few months after Hazlitt's review, as the lead article of the *Edinburgh Review* 24 (November 1814).

What will never do, and why? And do what? What speech act did Jeffrey, a lawyer who considered writs and reviews as performative, fear the poem might accomplish? Jeffrey objects to several claims about the ability of the poet to dictate the English intellectual economy, and consequently influence the monetary economy and the notions of property. Jeffrey recognized in Wordsworth's didactic poetry the effort to seat the poet in the chair where Jeffrey himself had placed the critic and the lawyer. Walter Scott had named that chair "the Scorner's chair" (Judson Stanley Lyon, The Excursion: *A Study* 2–3), and Wordsworth reluctantly granted its power, even as that which he would defy. A letter to R. P. Gillies,[14] like a review from the *Edinburgh*, begins discussing Gillies's poetical theory, considers his recent *Exile*, and then contextualizes the poem within English letters. Eventually, Wordsworth turns to Jeffrey's review: "I am delighted to learn that your Edinburgh Aristarch has declared against the *Excursion*, as he will have the mortification of seeing a book enjoy a high reputation, to which he has not contributed" (LMY II 180, 22 December 1814). Wordsworth's language positions a book's reputation as a joint-stock for readers; and the joke focuses on Jeffrey's bad investment, coupled with an allusion that recalls the moral terrain of their dispute.[15] The market will overturn its self-appointed regulator.

After his opening witticism, Jeffrey continues: "It [*The Excursion*] bears no doubt the stamp of the author's heart and fancy: but unfortunately not half so visibly as that of his peculiar system. His former poems were intended to recommend that system, and to bespeak favour for it by their individual merit;—but this, we suspect, must be recommended by the system—and can only expect to succeed where it has been previously established" (*Edinburgh Review* 24: 1). Although he shifts its architectonics, Jeffrey recognizes Wordsworth's project in which the poetry constitutes a career, and not free-standing productions. "System" was a common description of Wordsworth's method, and his propensity to deny it—as in his refusal of a "systematic defence" of the *Lyrical Ballads*—marked his willingness to engage the debate on those terms, much as Burke, who renounced French theorizing and abstract systems, constructed a system grounded in English tradition, a tradition formally institutionalized in common law and advertised as "custom."

In his formulation of Wordsworth's "particular system," Jeffrey is objecting to Wordsworth's claim in the Preface that "it is not the Author's intention formally to announce a system: it was more animating to him to proceed in a different course; and if he shall succeed in conveying to the mind clear thoughts, lively images, and strong feelings, the Reader will have no difficulty in extracting the system for himself. And in the meantime the following passage, taken from the conclusion of the first book of The Recluse, may be acceptable as a kind of *Prospectus* of the design and scope of the whole Poem" (*Excursion* 2). This is the language of contract. The lines from the "first book" are offered as consideration for an agreement of conveyance, in which the Author agrees to deliver "clear thoughts, lively images, and strong feelings." The nature of such consideration is slippery, when placed against the actual exchange in which a reader is brought into possession of a text. When a reader purchases a book, that reader owns not the text but a specific duplication of it. A reader neither buys the rights to reproduce it nor acquires the ability to destroy it. What is given up, money, is equally only a representation of a distant source, marked by the money's stamp. Wordsworth asserts that another contract, between Author and Reader, occurs in the Reader's activity of suiting himself to that title, that is, in his actual reading. The singularity of "Reader," reinforced by the reflexive pronoun "himself," casts the agreement between two individuals; in this way, Wordsworth makes a claim for the presence of the author within the particular readings by given individuals. The professional poet is entailed by his poetry, just as, in feudal law, the owner of a property is entailed by the property.

To view Jeffrey's judgment as solely aesthetic—merely right or wrong, agreeable or disagreeable—may be tempting. But a deviation from his usual method of presenting the relationship between critic and poet curbs this temptation. In his reviews of *Thalaba*, Crabbe's *Poems*, and Wordsworth's *Poems, in Two Volumes* (1807), Jeffrey positions the critic either as the judge or as the lawyer arguing before the bar of the public. In his review of *The Excursion*, he shifts the metaphor to another profession: "The case of Mr Wordsworth, we perceive, is now manifestly hopeless; and we give him up as altogether incurable, and beyond the power of criticism. We cannot indeed altogether omit taking precautions now and then against the spreading of the malady;—but for himself, . . . we shall watch the progress of his symptoms as a matter of professional curiosity and instruction" (*Edinburgh Review* 24 [November 1814]: 2). Figuring himself as a doctor (after the initially ambiguous phrase "The case of . . ."), Jeffrey obviates the need for argument and adopts, albeit sarcastically and obliquely, the Wordsworthian position that poetry, at least this particular poetry, is natural—like decay. Divorced from the social institutions on which Jeffrey believes communication depends, such nature is tantamount to disease and to abuse. It rejects the progress of humanity evident in every institution, but particularly the sciences (including jurisprudence and economics), the advances of which were both a staple subject of the *Edinburgh Review* and the magazine's lens for social development. The Lake Poets constitute a threat to other poetry in that they live outside the system of literary distribution—neither in London nor Edinburgh—and yet they deploy their works through those systems and threaten contamination.

Wordsworth also insists on a relation between nature and society, but one with a different structure. Jeffrey's rhetoric marks both this similarity and difference, since he has adopted the metaphor by which the Wanderer, the economic and moral center of the poem, understands the Solitary, who lives on the margins of the community. After telling the story of the Solitary, the Wanderer concludes by associating the Solitary's choice of occupation (i.e., where he lives) with illness:

> Tormented thus, after a wandering course
> Of discontent, and inwardly opprest
> With malady—in part, I fear, provoked
> By weariness of life—he fixed his home,
> Or, rather say, sate down by very chance
> Among these rugged hills.
>
> (II 304–9)

The Wanderer considers the Solitary as sick, but, unlike Jeffrey's view of Wordsworth, curable. The cure entails restoring the Solitary's intentional self, undoing the revision of "fixed his home" into "sate down by very chance." The Wanderer sees the Solitary's choice of habitation as a symptom of an inner malady; more precisely, his relation to the land has become one of mere possession, and no longer of property as an imaginative intersection of land and human intention. Jeffrey reverses this view in considering Wordsworth, whose sickness proceeds from his association with the Lake District. Jeffrey had long since claimed that Wordsworth was dominated by the land, figured as a company of misguided poets striving to break "loose from the bondage of ancient authority" (*Edinburgh Review* 1 [October 1802]: 63). As a consequence, Jeffrey maintains, Wordsworth loses the human dominion which, as Blackstone had asserted, is the divine foundation of property rights and hence of human government itself. Both Jeffrey and Wordsworth (or the Wanderer) make appeals to the past, but for Jeffrey, such history is firmly rooted in the procedures of precedent; it provides not objects of interpretation but interpretive templates. Wordsworth's history, like land, is always accompanied by the visibility of its own storytelling and retains the need for interpretation.

In asserting Wordsworth's incurability, Jeffrey denies his ability to present a moral methodology by which the Solitary could be cured. In essence, Jeffrey denies to Wordsworth the labor that is the central action of the poem, curing the illness of despair which the recent history of England and France has inflicted on early enthusiasts of the French Revolution. Jeffrey himself had attempted similar mediations, starting with the first article of the *Edinburgh Review*, his essay on Mounier's "Influence of the Philosophes . . . on the French Revolution,"[16] and continuing throughout his tenure as editor of the *Edinburgh Review;* and his attack against Wordsworth and other Lake Poets, therefore, is professionally defensive. Nonetheless, it marks a genuine philosophical difference about the scope of poetry. Even in acknowledging Wordsworth's genius, a typical move in Jeffrey's reviews of the poet,[17] Jeffrey disempowers it by limiting the scope of poetic investigation to truths derived from other institutions.

Peter Manning has identified in Jeffrey's review the "contradiction inherent in accusing *The Excursion* of being both simplistic and incomprehensible" ("Francis Jeffrey Reads *The Excursion*" 7). In a paragraph foregrounding this contradiction, Jeffrey's effort to dismantle the effect of the work is evident:

> The doctrine which the work is intended to *enforce*, we are by no means certain we have discovered. In so far as we can collect, however, it seems to be neither more nor less than the old familiar one, that a firm belief in the providence of a wise and beneficent Being must be our great stay. . . . If there be any deeper or more recondite doctrines in Mr. Wordsworth's book, we must confess that they have escaped us;—and convinced as we are of the truth and soundness to those which we have alluded, we cannot help thinking that they might have been better *enforced* with less parade and prolixity. His effusions on what may be called the physiognomy of external nature, or its moral and theological expression, are eminently fantastic, obscure, and affected.—It is quite time, however, that we should give the reader a more particular account of this singular performance. (*Edinburgh Review* 24: 5–6, my italics)

Jeffrey's assessment reels between the obvious and the obscure, never allowing that the foundation of the obvious may itself be obscure. The repetition of "enforce" acknowledges the poem as a speech act, but dismisses its authority by suggesting that it merely rearticulates familiar doctrine. To an extent, Jeffrey is right; Wordsworth's characters do argue for the curative effect of a "firm belief" in providence. But they specifically reject the foundation of that belief in familiarity. Rather, the belief itself is constantly shown to have no foundation; it is the work of human beings to ground their belief continually by asserting a relationship through what Jeffrey calls "the physiognomy of external nature." By his abrupt turn to the poem's specifics, Jeffrey obscures the relevance of that "physiognomy" to the discussion of moral truth, even as the proximity of the two points acknowledges a connection. Put another way, Jeffrey denies the cultural work that produces the "obvious," while Wordsworth's project is a sustained experiment in translating the visible into the legible.

Defining the "grand staple" of the work as "a kind of mystical morality," Jeffrey claims to open the book randomly (and so avoids providing context) to demonstrate "the chief characteristics of the style," that is, "it is prolix and very frequently unintelligible" (9–10)—a charge aimed at invalidating the Wordsworthian contract. The sample is thirty lines, beginning mid-sentence, from book IV, "Despondency Corrected" (72–86, 94–99, 130–37), without indications of the omissions that confuse grammatical reference. Exhibiting the passage as "a fair sample of that rapturous mysticism which eludes all comprehension, and fills the despairing reader with painful giddiness and terror," Jeffrey offers his judgment as aesthetic. Such a presentation is deceptive and, like the mutilated quotation, a partial view concealing, even while enacting, Jeffrey's wider ideological goals.

The random "sample" adduced by Jeffrey is central to the proposed cure that restoration may be found in adherence to "Duty," but duty presented in an unfamiliar mode, equated with neither law nor custom, but discovered through intellectual labor. Duty amounts to the

> apprehension [of] those transcendent truths
> Of the pure intellect, that stand as laws
> (Submission constituting strength and power)
> Even to thy Being's infinite majesty!
>
> (IV 96–99)

The referent to "thy Being," as well as the grammatical antecedent to "thy," is "dread source, / Prime, self-existing cause and end of all" (79–80), and Wordsworth confronts his readers with a paradox of origins, since this Being is ruled. It is important to recognize what Jeffrey dislikes about this position. As a reviewer, Jeffrey maintained that "poetry has this much, at least, in common with religion, that its standards were fixed long ago, by certain inspired writers [critics or poets?], whose authority it is no longer lawful to call in question" (*Edinburgh Review* 1 [October 1802]: 63).

In the same issue as the review of the *Excursion*, the *Edinburgh* reviews a seventy-volume translation of writings by church fathers: "We had thought that the merits of the Fathers were beginning to be pretty fairly estimated . . . that the time of their authority over conscience and opinion was gone by; that they were no longer to be regarded as guides either in faith or in morals; and that we should be quite within the pale of orthodoxy in saying that, though admirable martyrs and saints, they were, after all, but indifferent Christians" (24 [November 1814]: 58). This condescending attitude emphasizes Whig notions of progress, and particularly notes the progress in secular law, lightly emphasized with the legal metaphor of the "pale." For Jeffrey, religion occupies those gothic portions of the common law which provide, as Blackstone had said, magnificence and veneration, but its day-to-day practice occurs in (legal) history.

He objects, in neither review, to the religious per se but rather to Wordsworth's organization of institutions. At issue is whether poetic productions can change the rules of poetry; but for Jeffrey much more is at stake, because poetry is a specific, and culturally privileged, form of discourse production. While law is also a form of discourse subject to rules, the concept of being rule-bound allowed Jeffrey to position law as the dominant discourse. It was law that, paradoxically, both returned society to origins and provided the space of progress. At the end of his review of Wordsworth's *Poems, in Two Volumes*, Jeffrey articulates this position in an argument that partly transposes the Whig position on poetry for the Tory position on the French Revolution, and in that form, silently apologizes for the excesses of that revolution: "Many a generous rebel, it is said, has been reclaimed to his allegiance by the spectacle of lawless outrage and excess presented in the conduct of the insurgents; and we think there is every reason to hope, that the lamentable consequences which have resulted from Mr. Wordsworth's open violation of the established laws of poetry, will operate as a wholesome warning to those who might otherwise have been seduced by his example, and be the means of restoring to that antient and venerable code its due honor and authority" (*Edinburgh Review* 11 [October 1807]: 231).

The dominant institution here (and in Jeffrey's opening salvo against the Lake Poets in the *Edinburgh*'s first issue) is the law, used figuratively to regulate both religion and poetry. Such a figure situates law as a regulator of nonlegal issues, and locates its authority in history. It is specifically a solution to the problem of origins, a solution lawyers had depended upon in coming to power, and on which Jeffrey, like Hume and Blackstone, continued to rely.[18] For Wordsworth, as the opening lines to the "Duty" passage (which Jeffrey omits) show, the uncertainty of history itself requires and authorizes the search for transcendent values, specifically those values which transcend institutions: "Possessions vanish, and opinions change" (IV 69). Jeffrey would not deny this mutability, but would depend upon the revisionary process of the law to contain such shifts so that, even when possessions change, property would not. As Philip Flynn points out, Jeffrey was "committed to the interests of 'property,' and he repeatedly described the dangers of violent social revolution"; in support, Flynn quotes a passage that might come as easily from Blackstone or Burke: "The international law with regard to power, is . . . like the municipal law with regard to property. Its object is, not to establish a fantastic and irksome equality, like the Agrarian schemes of antiquity, but to protect and secure the irregularities to which fortune has given existence: to make wealth and poverty alike safe and independent" (*Francis Jeffrey* 116; quoting *Edinburgh Review*, 1803).

This position is not far from the Wanderer's criticism of the French Revolution and its effect on the Solitary in book II, nor from the Wanderer's equanimity in absorbing the destruction of Margaret's family for his own pedagogic purposes. The difference arises at the point of regulating difference. The claim "Duty exists" positions duty beyond the institutions that enforce debt, and, in generalizing the critique of the French Revolution to one of history itself as a privileged (uninterpreted) discourse, Wordsworth sets those institutions at risk, not from revolution nor even from reform, but of becoming unfamiliar to the people they govern.

Surrendering Wordsworth as incurable, Jeffrey seeks to contain the malady and to develop new poets free of disease. The relation between Jeffrey and young poets is that of the educator, the theorizer, a position similar to the Wanderer's relation to the young poet in *The Excursion*. That Jeffrey resorted to this approach can be read two ways. First, it demonstrates Wordsworth's control over the mechanisms of poetic interpretation in a way that foreshadows the domination of the *Prelude* as the most influential piece of Wordsworthian criticism. Second, it demonstrates Jeffrey's ability to co-opt, incompletely but effectively, Wordsworth's methods for his own devices. That the second is Jeffrey's intent is clear in the patronizing reference to Wordsworth as "our patient" whom "we" offer "cordials and lenitives" rather than "harass" with "nauseous remedies." Neither of these readings, Wordsworth's domination and Jeffrey's co-option, exists alone; they participate in a debate within the fabric of poetic production, in the metaphors and invocations, the meters and tropes, the book sales, critical commentaries, and copyright legislation that adumbrate the literary marketplace. Jeffrey's own answer to his rhetorical question recognizes this point, as he slides from a medical metaphor to an economic analysis: "Inveterate habit must now have given a kind of sanctity to the errors of early taste; and the very powers of which we lament the perversion, have probably become incapable of any other application. The very quantity, too, he has written, and is at this moment working up for publication upon the old pattern, makes it almost hopeless to look for any change of it. All this is so much capital already sunk in the concern" (*Edinburgh Review* 24: 2).

The transformation of individual habit to market operation rearticulates Adam Smith's connection between "moral sentiment" and the "wealth of nations." Consistency of individual habits provided the basis of rationality which allowed the market to operate, and this consistency was articulated as the single market goal of maximizing profits, all else being externalities. Jeffrey's reading clarifies the economic shadings of the *Prospectus* (*Excursion* 2). "Prospectus" came into English usage during the eighteenth century as "a description or account of the chief features of a forthcoming work or proposed enterprise, circulated for the purpose of obtaining support or subscriptions" (*OED*). The word marks the literary endeavor as commercial, aligning it with Pope's translations of Homer and Johnson's *Dictionary*. This professional arrangement between Author and Reader is not actual—the Prospectus does not commit Wordsworth to completing his work, nor provide a means for the reader monetarily to assist in that endeavor. Instead, it acts as a figured contract in which the reader will acquire from the writer the raw materials out of which to compose a system. Near the end of his review, after some illustrations of Wordsworth's poetic merit, Jeffrey comments on them and his procedure of producing them:

> When we look back to them, indeed, and to the other passages which we have now extracted, we feel half inclined to rescind the severe sentence which we passed on the work at the beginning;—But when we look into the work itself, we perceive that it cannot be rescinded. Nobody can be more disposed to do justice to the great powers of Mr. Wordsworth than we are . . . we have uniformly testified in their [Wordsworth's powers] favour . . . our high sense of their value is the chief ground of the bitterness with which we resented their perversion . . . and while we collect the fragments, it is impossible not to lament the ruins from which we are condemned to pick them. (*Edinburgh Review* 24: 29)

The metaphoric movement of this passage is to begin as judge, then to become witness, and to end up as condemned man. Perverting Wordsworth's metaphor of a gothic church, this structure enacts the decay of judgment a reader risks in contemplating Wordsworth's usurpation of critical regulation. Rather than assembling a system, as Wordsworth asks of his readers, Jeffrey dismantles it in order to reveal the scattered poetic beauties that might mislead a reader into constructing the entire poem seriously.

To take Jeffrey's critique as only aesthetic misses the immediacy with which a reader at that time would understand the Wanderer's role as double, at once as the educator of the poet (who must, ultimately, supplant the peddler by creating a community characterized by distance; creating, in other words, a nation) and as the voice of a particular social structure—the cottage economy, the communal grazing lands of Cumberland—which depends upon a certain understanding of property. Although the word *Pedlar* never occurs in *The Excursion*, Jeffrey prefers it to *Wanderer*, Wordsworth's common term. "It will be asked," Charles Lamb notes in his lauding review, which side-glances at Jeffrey's, "why put such eloquent discourse in the mouth of a pedlar?" After pointing to comparisons with Piers Plowman's Creed and Robert Burns, Lamb offers this advice in his concluding sentence: "After all, if there should be found readers willing to admire the poem, who yet feel scandalized at a *name*, we would advise them, wherever it occurs, to substitute silently the word *Palmer* or *Pilgrim*, or any less offensive designation, which shall connote the notion of sobriety in heart and manners with the experience and privileges which a wayfaring life confers" (*Quarterly Review* 12 [October 1814]: 111). This witticism (a reader would never have the opportunity for the palliative substitution) is tactical. By obscuring the role of the Pedlar as a peddler, Lamb softens the economic dimensions of the poem and assures the dominance of the religious. The poem may seem amenable to such a reading; after all, the Pedlar is retired and after the first book, his profession is little discussed. But an insistence on the importance of the Pedlar as the embodiment of a dispossessed economy—a mode of community and communication that is being destroyed—clarifies the "system" Jeffrey fervently decried. That system was, among other things, a theory of property and of interpretation, two parts of the same machinery held together by the linchpin of Wordsworth's concept of duty.

LABOR AND NATURE

Thomas Moore records the following exchange in 1820 between Wordsworth and Humphrey Davy regarding the expensive publication of *The White Doe* (1815): "'Do you know the reason', Wordsworth asked suddenly, 'why I published The White Doe in quarto?' 'No, what was it?' 'To show the world my own opinion of it.'" (Moorman II: 285). Wordsworth contends that through the market, he can "speak" to the world by inverting the usual relationship in which, as Burke says of the price of labor, "[it] rises or falls according to the demand" ("Thoughts on Scarcity" 126). By publishing an expensive edition, Wordsworth proclaims the worth of his work.[19] The remark suggests both the hostility toward the purchasing public delineated in the 1815 "Supplemental Essay" (see Klancher, *Reading Audiences* 148–50 and Erickson, "Egoism" 43–45) and a desire to communicate with that public. Wordsworth had not despaired of finding his audience, as the repeated reissues of his works demonstrate, but neither was he sure of finding it. If, in 1814, *The Excursion* came out in quarto to show what Wordsworth thought of it, in 1820, it appeared in octavo so that readers could render their opinions.

In consequence of Wordsworth's particular commitment to the market, his poetry is shaped to deal with concrete experience, but the very work of poetry—for reader and writer—is how to render experience concretely. The Parson's wife poses the problem when whispering to the poet after one of the Wanderer's speeches:

> While he is speaking, I have the power to see
> Even as he sees; but when his voice hath ceased,
> Then, with a sigh, sometimes I feel, as now,
> That combinations so serene and bright
> Cannot be lasting in a world like ours.
>
> (IX 465–69)

The task of the poet is to instill that "power to see," and the corresponding task of the reader is to not let the poet's voice die. The Wanderer's words ("combinations") are rendered as visual and a source of vision in the metaphor of brightness, while the Parson's wife's reception—sight—of those words is reintegrated not into words but into a fading sound, a sigh, the linguistic marker of absent language. Only through continual speech can the combinations survive as a shared vision. This exchange of sight for sound is played internally with each encounter with storytelling: the cottage and Margaret's story; the graveyard and the tales of the dead; the fragile vision of the Ram poised above its mirrored image and the Parson's wife's lament.

Because Wordsworth has constructed the exchange between reader and writer to exclude the critic, he appropriates the critical function in the last book in a way that reveals much about his "system." The Parson's wife's commentary on the Wanderer's speech comes after all his major speeches, and reflects back to each of them, insuring their fragmentary and polemic character. The object of the critique, however, is equally the Wanderer's beguiling speech and "a world like ours." The world at stake is not the human world divorced from a stabilizing natural world, but one constituted at the intersection of the human and natural, an intersection metonymized by the Ram standing over his reflection, "his shadowy counterpart":

> Each had his glowing mountains, each his sky,
> And each seemed centre of his own fair world:
> Antipodes unconscious of each other,
> Yet, in partition, with their several spheres,
> Blended in perfect stillness, to our sight!
> (IX 447–51)

The centered Ram and its possession of the mountains and sky (and wider universes alluded to by "several spheres") are not illusionary but neither are they real; rather, they are relational. The metaphor of possession insists on the human overtones of the Ram, and simultaneously suggests the transitory duration of possession. Nonetheless, the character of the human gaze requires centering the subject from which the landscape can be demarcated. Put abstractly, human beings construct nature out of the recalcitrant being which is nature. As the Parson's wife observes, a breath (like her sigh) can disperse the sight.

The poet himself deepens the dilemma in electing not to describe the landscape as their journey continues:

> —Ah! that such beauty, varying in the light
> Of living nature, cannot be portrayed
> By words, nor by the pencil's silent skill;
> But is the property of him alone
> Who hath beheld it, noted it with care,
> And in his mind recorded with love!
> (IX 512–17)

As with the description of the Ram, the imagery of possession has, for the poet, explanatory value. But property here is radically unalienated, arising only to the extent of contact and not transferrable. What can the poet transfer? Not beauty, but the awareness of beauty, the desire for it. The poet creates, and markets, a lack that demands its own fulfillment.

LIKE BENTHAM, HUME, AND BLACKSTONE, Wordsworth integrates human experience with the laws that govern it, although where Bentham rarely used natural law—preferring statutory legislation and denouncing the common law as incoherent—Wordsworth follows Blackstone in positioning human law under the jurisdiction of nature and in making laws the institutional equivalent to habit. Consequently, the effort to develop or invent ideal human laws amounts to a usurpation of nature, and constitutes an effort beyond the bounds of human reason. As the Wanderer describes it, the mark of that overreach in the French Revolution was the collapse of distinctions and the renunciation of habit:

> That righteous cause (such power hath freedom) bound,
> For one hostility, in friendly league,
> Ethereal natures and the worst of slaves.
>
> (II 227–29)

The lines are constructed as a series of three antitheses, all constraining liberty in the effort to express it: power's freedom binds; a hostility is the site of the friendly league; and "ethereal natures" (i.e., free spirits) join with the sign of their own failure, slaves. This final contrast has additional antithetical power, since "ethereal nature" is a metaphor from natural sciences for the human spirit which evades its social constraints by virtue of a higher (lighter) nature, while "slaves" is a economic metaphor denoting the artificial invention of restraints.

Continuing the antithetical device, the Wanderer explicitly invokes a legal tribunal in order to suggest an extralegal status:

> [The cause] Was served by rival advocates that came
> From regions opposite as heaven and hell
>
> . . . .
>
> A proud and most presumptuous confidence [arose]
> In the transcendent wisdom of the age,
> And her discernment.
>
> (II 230–31, 235–37)

The wisdom does transcend the age in destroying it, and at the same time the age, in its wisdom, attempts to transcend its own historical situation. This argument is a version of Burke's objection against untested ideas. When Burke defends the English Restoration and Revolution, he asserts that, although "the nation had lost the bond of union in the antient edifice; they did not however, dissolve the whole fabric. On the contrary, in both cases they regenerated the deficient parts of the old constitution through those parts which were not impaired" (*Reflections* 106). For Burke, the Constitution is the living body and the task of human beings is its preservation; rights inhere in that body of law itself. The history he concocts for England in the *Reflections* links the Norman Conquest, the Revolution, and the Restoration into moments that affirm the status of the Constitution. In particular, the whole English revolutionary struggle came down to a legal distinction between modes of inheritance, neither a critique of inheritance nor a manifesto for democracy.

The polemical effect is to gain the power to determine what counts as the history or story of England, and what constitutes mere accident. In a nation governed by common law, determining history amounts to determining law. Burke makes this argument by using the metaphor of regeneration Blackstone used to validate legal corporations: "Our political system is placed in a just correspondence and symmetry with the order of the world, and with the mode of existence decreed to a permanent body composed of transitory parts" (*Reflections* 120). What appeared alterations were temporary aberrations, and were possible precisely because they were not institutional. Burke locates the emergence of human nature in the ability of the state to check the aberrations of individual psyches: "Through the same plan of a conformity to nature in our artificial institutions, and by calling in the aid of her unerring and powerful instincts, to fortify the fallible and feeble contrivances of our reason, we have derived several other, and those no small benefits, from considering our liberties in the light of an inheritance" (121).

Wordsworth does not accept the Constitution as a living body with its own rights, but as a mediation between natural law and human experience. It is necessarily opaque and the desire to transcend that opacity amounts to the usurpation of power, as when the discernment of the age attempts to meddle

> not alone in rights,
> And in the origin and bounds of power
> Social and temporal; but in laws divine,
> Deduced by reason, or to faith revealed.
> (II 237–40)

Wordsworth articulates the continuum of natural and human law analogous to Blackstone's introductory remarks, but creates a fissure in the continuum at precisely the moment when social and temporal laws—located in historical origins and bounds—move into the ahistorical "laws divine." The result, like the affliction of war which rent Margaret's life, is that a "Plague from this union spread" (II 243). Again, the structure is antithetical: disunion, spreading, and contagion arise from the unholy union of heaven and hell, ethereal natures and slaves.[20] The implicit question is how a mediation between the "laws divine" and human rights can be established, since deduction and revelation are imperfect methods, subject to the very contagion of exuberance: "The strongest did not easily escape; / And He, what wonder! took a mortal taint" (II 244–45). The question of whether the Solitary can be reborn after the false rebirth of the French Revolution corresponds to the question of the fissure between human and divine law, with both its aesthetic analogue in the disjunction between readerly meaning and poetic intention and its scientific formulation as the laws of nature and human reason as they intersect on the empirical plane of human experience.

The issue of *The Excursion* is not how to encounter nature or reality unmediated, but rather, what forms of mediation transform nature into the most humanly accessible form. Put in the terms of a debate that raged in both law and the sciences, what constitutes adequate evidence for establishing an experience?

Wordsworth's work shows a decided admiration for scientific investigations, including the advances of the Scottish Enlightenment, but this admiration is checked by the remembrance of the French Philosophes and the collapse of their ideas in the Terror. In comparing "men for whom our age / Unbaffled powers of vision have prepared" with Greek shepherds, the Wanderer insists that surely contemporary men can obtain more "From sense and reason." But the examples of their powers are cautionary:

> Ambitious spirits—
> Whom earth, at this late season, hath produced
> To regulate the moving spheres, and weigh
> The planets in the hollow of their hand;
> And they who rather dive than soar, whose pains
> Have solved the elements, or analysed
> The thinking principle—shall they in fact
> Prove a degraded Race?
>
> (IV 947–54)

This question is open. To regulate the moving spheres is the astronomer's madness in *Rasselas*, except when it is understood that such regulation is actually internalizing nature's laws. Like the shepherd boy who divides the sun with a dial, the scientists regulate the planets only as a metonymy for self-awareness.

One immediate consequence is the increasing problem of technology, which may materially determine the answer to the Wanderer's rhetorical question. The earth that has produced these scientists is now threatened by them, through her own generosity:

> The Earth has lent
> Her waters; Air her breezes; and the sail
> Of traffic glides with ceaseless intercourse.
> (VIII 111–13)

The use of economic imagery to describe the contributions of the elements to the development of economy recalls the ultimate dependence of any economic system on natural resources (such as the trees that the wood-chopper carelessly destroys), and the Wanderer fashions nature's retribution within the terms of justice:

> I grieve, when on the darker side
> Of this great change I look; and there behold
> Such outrage done to nature as compels
> The indignant power to justify herself;
> Yea, to avenge her violated rights,
> For England's bane.
> (VIII 151–56)

The violation of nature's rights is articulated in a Promethean myth in which "soothing darkness" and "punctual stars"—the adjectives reminiscent of natural order—yield to an unceasing light which, like hell's darkness visible, appears as an alternative order but only offers pandemonium:

> an unnatural light
> Prepared for never-resting Labour's eyes
> Breaks from a many-windowed fabric huge.
> (VIII 167–69)

Rather than the stars, artificial sound marks the time, and simultaneously recalls the Norman Conquest:

> And at the appointed hour a bell is heard,
> Of harsher import than the curfew-knoll

> That spake the Norman Conqueror's stern behest—
> A local summons to unceasing toil!
>
> (VIII 170–73)

The curfew William imposed required the dousing of all lights and an enforced rest; in response to opposition, Henry I repealed the law in 1103. The new economy reverses the curfew: toil is unceasing, and the light unending. This vision is radically different from, for example, the tireless labor of Michael, for this labor is organized externally by the contingencies of the factory itself:

> Disgorged are now the ministers of day;
> And, as they issue from the illumined pile,
> A fresh band meets them at the crowded door—
> And in the courts—and where the rumbling stream
> That turns the multitude of dizzy wheels,
> Glares, like a troubled spirit, in its bed
> Among the rocks below.
>
> (VIII 174–80)

The day shift and the night shift meet at the exchange point, and become one another. Their social order, even their religion, is organized around the dizzy wheels:

> Men, maidens, youths,
> Mother and little children, boys and girls,
> Enter, and each the wonted task resumes
> Within this temple, where is offered up
> To Gain, the master idol of the realm,
> Perpetual sacrifice.
>
> (VIII 180–85)

The relation of the unceasing work for this new idol and the unceasing meditation under older religion is fashioned not as a stark contrast, but rather as a continuum:

> Even thus of old
> Our ancestors, within the still domain
> Of vast cathedral or conventual church,
> Their vigils kept; where tapers day and night
> On the dim altar burned continually,

In token that the House was evermore
Watching to God.

(VIII 185–91)

Political economists were creating a religious virtue out of labor, and enforcing it through a wage system and a general ideological mobilization, into which Wordsworth's works could as easily be co-opted as positioned to resist.[21]

Wesley had already observed that "religion must necessarily produce both industry and frugality, and these cannot but produce riches . . . [consequently] although the form of religion remains, the spirit is swiftly vanishing away" (quoted in Thompson, *Working Class* 391). The Wanderer rejects the transformation of religious zeal into economic gain, but modulates into an alternative position, in which the powers of technology are viewed as liberating because they are guided by moral law. His authority for this is Archimedes:

—Call Archimedes from his buried tomb
Upon the grave of vanished Syracuse,
And feelingly the Sage shall make report
How insecure, how baseless in itself,
Is the Philosophy whose sway depends
On mere material instruments;—how weak
Those arts, and high inventions, if unpropped
By virtue.

(VIII 220–27)

Paine, in the introduction to part two of the *Rights of Man*, had already put the figure of Archimedes into political play: "WHAT Archimedes said of the mechanical powers, may be applied to Reason and Liberty: '*Had we,*' said he, '*a place to stand upon, we might raise the world*'" (159). But the grounding, the "place to stand," is, for Wordsworth, not an analogy for a moral grounding, but the same ground. The sovereignty of man was his ability to name and to understand, not his power to use:

Happy is he who lives to understand,
Not human nature only, but explores
All natures,—to the end that he may find
The law that governs each.

(IV 332–35)

The usual sense of "who lives to" is "who lives long enough to," but here another meaning is more central, "who lives with the intent to." A duration of life corresponds with an intent of life, since time itself, like other mathematical constructs, is fraught with human intentionality. The discovery of governing laws is an end in itself, a position validated by Blackstone's contention that courts discover, rather than create, law. The passage that follows is laden with legal terminology combined with scientific jargon:

> and where begins
> The union, the partition where, that makes
> Kind and degree, among all visible Beings;
> The constitutions, powers, and faculties,
> Which they inherit,—cannot step beyond,—
> And cannot fall beneath; that do assign
> To every class its station and its office,
> Through all the mighty commonwealth of things;
> Up from the creeping plant to sovereign Man.
>
> (IV 335–43)

This exploration of nature is part of the Wanderer's solution to despondency, because it reveals an order perpetually renewed by the active power of nature's laws which "assign" (from *signum*, sign and *signare*, to mark) "station" and "office." The legalistic and bureaucratic terms in the passage implicitly compare natural order and English government. The position of man in nature's order resembles that of the king in England's monarchy, specifically that he rules beneath, rather than above, the laws. Sovereignty is derived from position in the hierarchy, rather than the hierarchy being created by virtue (strength) of the sovereign. Further, since man's sovereignty exists within this hierarchy, human law is not merely an analogy to natural law but a subset of it. For the Wanderer's argument, the existence of natural bounds, limits of both "beyond" and "beneath," helps explain the failures of human sovereignty.

EIGHT

The Excursion: The Poet of Property

> "And how do you tell them, may I ask?" said Bosinney.
>
> "By their sense of property. A Forsyte takes a practical—one might say a commonsense—view of things, and a practical view of things is based fundamentally on a sense of property. A Forsyte, you will notice, never gives himself away."
>
> —John Galsworthy, *The Man of Property*, 1906

THE structure of the Wanderer's tale of Margaret is a series of circulations. The Wanderer, in the course of his profession, periodically returns to Margaret and registers her increasing economic troubles. It is not, however, merely that her poverty is increasingly evident, but that the Wanderer structures his story so that with each return, Margaret's plight is situated within more overtly political causes—less to explore those causes than to make visible to the poet (and reader) the social institutions that poetic practice transcends. The poem reveals that poetic transcendence requires a recognition not only of the historical conditions it purports to transcend but of the institutions that interpret and produce those conditions.

Book I

After describing Margaret, the Wanderer locates the tale in the poet's past:

> Not twenty years ago, but you I think
> Can scarcely bear it now in mind, there came

Two blighting seasons, when the fields were left
With half a harvest.

(I 535–38)

The Wanderer restores the poet's history to him, making him bear it in mind, just as the Pedlar bears his wares. Implicitly, the poet is incomplete without Margaret's story to vitalize his own past. The echo of the years of famine in Egypt is complicated by what follows:

It pleased Heaven to add
A worse affliction in the plague of war:
This happy land was stricken to the heart!

(I 538–40)

The conjunction of the blighting seasons and the plague collapses the distinction between human and divine will, a point emphasized by the war being figured as a divine affliction, despite its human causes.[1] The famine and war do not create the disunities, but bring them into historical action from their dormant position in years of peace and prosperity.

The structure of the economy becomes evident as it is threatened:

A Wanderer then among the cottages,
I, with my freight of winter raiment, saw
The hardships of that season: many rich
Sank down, as in a dream, among the poor;
And of the poor did many cease to be,
And their place knew them not.

(I 541–46)

The Wanderer's work continues, its form remaining the same, its content altering with local necessities. Moreover, as the wanderer amid rooted people, he denotes the economic stability that is the hope for recovery in such dire times. But their rootedness is itself nostalgic; the rich become poor (and, unmentioned, wealthier property holders consolidated their lands by forfeitures and enclosures), and the poor die or are displaced.

The Wanderer speaks generally about the working population, and describes specifically the fate of one group, the artisans:

shoals of artisans
From ill-requited labour turned adrift

Sought daily bread from public charity,
They, and their wives and children—happier far
Could they have lived as do the little birds
That peck along the hedge-rows.
(I 559–64)

While "daily bread" is a metonym for food generally and echoes the Lord's Prayer, the Speenhamland acts, which linked wages to the price of bread in 1795 (roughly when Margaret's story is placed), introduce another reference. With the collapse in wages that resulted from the Speenhamland relief, artisans found little market for their work and were forced to rely upon the very instrument, public charity, that had prompted the counterproductive government intervention initially (Polanyi, *Transformation* 78–80). The sufficiency of the birds pecking the hedgerow echoes the "hedge-row birds" from "Animal Tranquility" (1). In both poems, the birds, part of a different economy, can afford a pecking indifference, but the hedge-row, an emblem of enclosures, reminds human beings that indifference is not a human luxury. While the plight of Margaret and Robert is cast in personal terms, juxtapositions insist on the more general causes and consequences:

A sad reverse it was for him who long
Had filled with plenty, and possessed in peace,
This lonely Cottage. At the door he stood,
And whistled many a snatch of merry tunes
That had no mirth in them; or with his knife
Carved uncouth figures on the heads of sticks—
(I 566–71)

The parodic images of "uncouth figures" mimic both the landowner unable to sustain his property and the unskilled artisan carving without creating anything of value. When Robert can no longer fill the Cottage "with plenty," he fills it with nothing—carved sticks and snatches of tunes. The paragraph details Robert's manic idleness, and ends with Margaret's commentary: "Every smile . . . / Made my heart bleed" (I 589–91). Margaret is responding to Robert's futile effort to hold things together within the Cottage against the ravages of the world beyond. Jeffrey, who retells the story in one paragraph, emphasizes at once its "considerable pathos" (indicating Wordsworth's "knowledge of the human heart") and its "triteness" (emphasized by "mawkish sentiment, and details of preposterous minuteness") (*Edinburgh Review* 24: 7). At the root of this valuation is the implication that his cosmopolitan audience, without Wordsworth's aid, can already afford such vicarious suffering. Jeffrey resists translating Margaret's economic story into a crisis of public imagination. Wordsworth, by contrast, interweaves these elements as the pedagogical method by which one acquires the intellectual capital to suffer sympathetically.

Scarcity forces shifts in the distribution of labor which the return of good weather cannot rectify. The Wanderer returns "in the warmth of midsummer, [when] the wheat / Was yellow" (I 707–8), and Margaret's life has worsened. Breaking his narration, the Wanderer asks:

> Why should we thus, with an untoward mind,
> And in the weakness of humanity,
> From natural wisdom turn our hearts away;
> To natural comfort shut our eyes and ears;
> And feeding on disquiet, thus disturb
> The calm of nature with our restless thoughts?
> (I 599–604)

This question contains its own dissolution. Nature is figured as a nonhuman reality: natural wisdom resides outside "our hearts," only to be gazed upon; natural comfort is something observed, not felt; and the calm of nature is susceptible to the invasion of restless (wandering) thoughts. The Wanderer postulates the distinction between nature and humanity to overcome it.

The poet, beguiled by the question, temporarily forgets Margaret's tale. But the forgetting, an echo of the social indifference inscribed on the ruined cottage, shapes the subsequent conversation as "trivial" and "To me soon tasteless" (611–12):

> looking round
> Upon that tranquil Ruin, I returned,
> And begged of the old Man that, *for my sake*,
> He would resume his story.
> (I 622–25, my italics)

The ruined cottage and Margaret's tale each interpret the other. No primacy of past or present, word or thing, nature or humanity emerges. At this moment, this point serves as the precondition for the poet's own education. As *The Excursion* evolves, social structures, as in the local tales told by the Parson and in the diatribe about national education in book IX, become more prominent. In such passages, the personal is not forgotten, but is resituated as the foreground of the social. Unlike Bentham's panoptic plans, which both the Wanderer and the Parson ridicule in their descriptions of contemporary labor, the Wordsworthian gaze does not shape a human being by power but calls forth an unalienated labor often figured as imagination.

At the same time, this imagination must operate in a field of scarcity to acquire use-value, the unspoken something-more implied by the Wanderer's preamble before beginning again:

> It were a wantonness, and would demand
> Severe reproof, if we were men whose hearts
> Could hold vain dalliance with the misery
> Even of the dead; contented thence to draw
> A momentary pleasure, never marked
> By reason, barren of all future good.
>
> (I 626–31)

Although such a momentary pleasure is, presumably, not being drawn, the two men do extract some value that can be used for something, for some "future good," as well as for a defense against "Severe reproof." Rendering this argument both vaguely and through continued negations and conditionals—("It were . . .," "if we . . .," "vain," "never marked," "barren")—the Wanderer comes close to exposing that the use-value derived from the story is nothing more than its exchange value, which is within capitalism, as Jean Baudrillard argues, a core structure and illusion of value (*Mirror of Production* 22–25). The Wanderer's distance from Margaret, which gives him his purchase to moralize about the tale and to prevent it from slipping into sensationalism, only comes "for a price," as Karen Swann notes discussing the "Ruined Cottage." Exploring "Wordsworth's powerful and uneasy collusion with the nascent mass culture of the late 1790s," Swann persuasively specifies the price as "a sensationalizing of the abandoned woman" ("Suffering and Sensation in *The Ruined Cottage*" 84). Not only is the reciprocity between Margaret and the Wanderer striking—Swann catalogues the various correspondences to their circulations (85)—

but at the moment of the Wanderer's resuming the tale, money enters into it explicitly. If, literally, it comes from Robert, it is also a compensatory narrative gesture, the cost of the Wanderer's admission. Within Wordsworth's larger scheme of *The Excursion*, however, the compensation is a continual practice of storytelling and resisting the immediate ("momentary") pleasure of that telling to consolidate value by valuing consolation.

In the resumed tale, when the Wanderer returns to Margaret's cottage, Robert has enlisted and left money in his absence. In "The Ruined Cottage"

> Within her casement full in view she saw
> A purse of gold . . . "I knew it was his hand
> That placed it there."
>
> (263–66)

In *The Excursion*, the lines are recast to bring out an implicit second meaning in "his hand," that of inscription:

> Within her chamber-casement she espied
> A folded paper, lying as if placed
> To meet her waking eyes. This tremblingly
> She opened—found no writing, but beheld
> Pieces of money carefully enclosed,
> Silver and gold . . . "I knew it was his hand
> That must have placed it there."
>
> (I 666–74)

The revision is more intimate, located explicitly in the bedroom, and the verbs "espied" and "lying as if placed" emphasize Margaret's interpretive agency. At first the paper holds out the hope of writing, the poetic trope of presence. Instead, it is only money, not just gold as in "The Ruined Cottage," but silver and gold. This change might be read to lessen the actual amount, but it also suggests a more varied economy in which differentials such as that between writing and money are duplicated within the figure of money itself. Robert's hand, incapable of labor, cannot write but can only use the implements of writing to enclose money. Enclosing money in paper replays in a literalizing parody the rise of the national debt through the issuing of bills. After the wait of three days for news of Robert's enlistment, money substitutes for the sacrificed/resurrected Robert. Wordsworth connects the appearance of the money and the arrival of the news-bearing stranger who has co-opted the Pedlar's function. Unlike the Pedlar, however, his news is vitiating and characterized by the abstraction of money, rather than by the concreteness of worked objects. This event silences the Wanderer:

> I had little power
> To give her comfort, and was glad to take
> Such words of hope from her own mouth as served
> To cheer us both. But long we had not talked
> Ere we built up a pile of better thoughts.
> (I 683–87)

This passage, for Alan Liu, marks the economic position of the Pedlar in "The Ruined Cottage," and his comment can be extended to *The Excursion.* These lines indicate "the Pedlar's inability to contribute anything of value and, indeed, [he] need[s] to 'take' textual value—'words of hope'—from Margaret herself; and finally, through strange dealings in absence, a 'pile of better thoughts'" (*Wordsworth: The Sense of History* 347). These better thoughts, in the wider context of *The Excursion*, are the arguments against despondency that the Wanderer makes in the later books. If, as Liu suggests (*Sense* 345–47), the Pedlar's activities form a capitalistic black market, then the poet subsumes that capital investment into his own, within the legitimate market in which *The Excursion* is published. More precisely, the poet, not the Wanderer, converts the "purse" to "paper," and indeed it is the same poet who transplanted the names "Margaret" and "Robert" from the criminal economy of *The Borderers* to *The Excursion*. Margaret's narrative provides no mode to invest "words of hope," no juridical structure to stabilize paper, whether money or poem. When the Wanderer returns, Margaret's life has deteriorated and the economic landscape comes more into focus as an issue of circulation and symbolic exchange.

Encountering Robert's absence in every stranger, she nearly loses her self, a self whose being is attached to the cottage: "sometimes—to my shame I speak—[I] have need / Of my best prayers to bring me back again" (I 755–56). Words addressed to the religious patriarch who substitutes for Robert in an erotic displacement are all that maintain Margaret's "place," referring to her property, her sanity, and, as in the earlier use of "place," to her position within the social order. From her view, the stability of Margaret's home is destroyed when Robert leaves, but he can only join the army because of the hostilities that produce the initial economic instability that Robert viewed as having emptied their home of meaning.

Thomas De Quincey responded to Robert's desertion with derision and a practical remedy. He suggests that the Wanderer might have done better than sympathizing with Margaret by "inquir[ing] for the station of [Robert's] detachment [and] . . . [t]hat same night he might have written to the War-Office; and in a very few days an official answer, bearing the endorsement *On H.M.'s Service,* would have placed Margaret in communication with her truant" ("On Wordsworth's Poetry" 307). He also invokes institutional aid in discussing the younger child's death: "Had any one of us readers discharged the duties of coroner in her neighborhood, he would have found it his duty to hold an inquest. . . . The Wanderer himself might have been called, as a witness for the crown" ("On Wordsworth's Poetry" 307).[2] De Quincey calls down the law upon Margaret in the same move as he calls down the critical, even novelistic standard of realism on Wordsworth. But, from the Pedlar's perspective, what value is the endorsement "*On H.M.'s Service*"? What precisely would a finding of Margaret's negligence mean, given her own neglected status? The fact-finding methods De Quincey invokes would uncover nothing more—from the perspective of "The Ruined Cottage" as a tale within *The Excursion*—than what the reader already learns from the poet. The Wanderer is already a witness, not for the Crown, but for a perspective that can query the origins of criminality, nature as disclosed by human reason. This is not to suggest that Wordsworth is anarchistic like Godwin, even though the initial drafts of "The Ruined Cottage" began when Wordsworth was under Godwin's influence. Rather, as appropriated into *The Excursion*, an understanding of the story of Margaret, unmediated by the investigative powers of the state, is the precondition for the poet to educate not his own affections alone but also the state institutions which reify the structures by which such affections may be shown. What Wordsworth requires his poet to move beyond in order to see into the life of things, De Quincey reasserts as the primary material questions that must not be evaded.

From the unsuccessful wanderings of Margaret and Robert and the disruption of their marriage emerges the emotional and intellectual union of the Wanderer and the poet. The poet's sympathy for Margaret allows him to commune with the Wanderer, who, consequently, can teach him how to "*afford*" to suffer. Before hearing the story, the poet's own wanderings are difficult (toiling / With languid steps 21–22), disrupted, poised between haze and clarity:

> Southward the landscape indistinctly glared
> Through a pale steam; but all the northern downs,
> In clearest air ascending, showed far off
> A surface dappled o'er with shadows flung
> From brooding clouds.
>
> (I 2–6)

The indistinct glare of the south is caused by a sun too bright, and the clarity of the north is endangered and engendered by "brooding clouds." This distinction between north and south, which more than one reviewer recognized as a distinction between Scottish and English values, recalls Michael's understanding of the directional winds, but the poet of *The Excursion* is illiterate in the reading of nature. After uniting with the Wanderer and hearing the story of Margaret, the poet finds the return trip effortless:

> Together casting then a farewell look
> Upon those silent walls, we left the shade;
> And, ere the stars were visible, had reached
> A village-inn,—our evening resting-place.
>
> (I 967–70)

The two men share a single glance at the silent walls, the archetype of ruin and disruption unified by the common story. On one hand, this is a communion with nature, but a nature embedded by the tale of Margaret with economic and social meanings. The Wanderer shapes his narrative as a series of returns to Margaret's cottage, each sharpening the confrontation with economic underpinnings. This progression is designed to teach the poet to read nature; and to prepare the reader to see the category of nature as perpetually in need of interpretation. As Hazlitt puts it, Wordsworth has "a repugnance to admit any thing that tells for itself, without the interpretation of the poet" (*The Examiner*, 28 August 1814, 556). Such literacy, or interpretive skill, however, does not arise only against the object of interpretation, but against other competing systems of interpretation like those De Quincey puts in play.

Book II

Wordsworth's textual strategy of new starts is engraved onto the text itself; as Johnston comments, "Wordsworth's final and most extended period of work on it [the composition of the last books of *The Excursion*] . . . start[s] all over again, with a new character, the Pastor, and a new cast to whom he gives voice, the rural folk buried in his church yard" (*Wordsworth* 285). Book II begins afresh a journey for which the day trip of book I was the prototype. These new beginnings reflect, as Thomas McFarland puts it, the "phenomenology of human awareness" as an experience of discontinuities (*Romanticism and Forms of Ruin* 3); they equally engage and resist an argument about the totalizing efforts of law and economy, and the ability of any voice, within a poem or a society, to achieve hegemony. Like the forced metaphor of the "Counsellor's bag" in "Rural Architecture," the fragmenting renewals of *The Excursion* have a polemical violence. The invocation of book II looks backward, to journeys once permitted by a mythic social continuity but no longer possible:

> In days of yore how fortunately fared
> The Minstrel! wandering on from hall to hall,
> Baronial court or royal; cheered with gifts
> Munificent, and love, and ladies' praise;
> Now meeting on his road an armed knight,
> Now resting with a pilgrim by the side
> Of a clear brook;—beneath an abbey's roof
> One evening sumptuously lodged; the next,
> Humbly in a religious hospital;
> Or with some merry outlaws of the wood;
> Or haply shrouded in a hermit's cell.
>
> (II 1–11)

The minstrel's terrain is thoroughly humanized; social encounters are everywhere and each day begins a new excursion into a different stratum of life. The passage describes the Minstrel's wandering in the midst of medieval order, but with inversions that, even while expressing continuity, suggest fissures. The baronial halls and royal halls are interchangeable, recalling but mitigating the struggle between the ruling classes that resulted in the Magna Carta; the precise contents of the "love" and "ladies' praise" are a shade suspicious, given the chivalric tradition of adultery; the abbey, soon to be a ruin, is perhaps a touch too wealthy in contrast to the religious hospital; the outlaws are merry, recalling the tradition of Robin Hood and weakening the force of the royal corporation from which the passage derives its structure. Each encounter is with a figure of order, a baron who rules, a knight of sworn allegiance, the merry outlaws who defy King John in the name of Richard, the civil law of the abbey, and the religious stricture of the hermit's cell; however, the figure of the Minstrel himself maintains the order by calling forth human nature in a manner that deflects force. He moves with impunity, protected from both outlaw and soldier:

> Him, sleeping or awake, the robber spared;
> He walked—protected from the sword of war
> By virtue of that sacred instrument
> His harp . . .
>
> . . . .
>
> [which opened] from land to land an easy way
> By melody, and by charm of verse.
>
> (II 12–18)

This Godwinian formulation equates the robber and the knight who carries the sword of war in sworn allegiance to the king's peace. The Minstrel's authority is emblematic, not derived from the violence which was the guarantee and mechanism of, but also the threat to, feudal order, nor yet from the rights espoused by classical liberal theory and rooted in the 1689 Bill of Rights. The sacredness of the harp displaces the four different religious incarnations (pilgrim, abbey, hospital, hermit) of the previous lines and empowers the Minstrel not with truth or law but with charm. It remains for the Wanderer, and then the poet, to transform such claims into something more stable, more marketable.

The romantic vision of chivalry, as Byron noted in the addition to the preface of *Childe Harold's Pilgrimage*, is a fiction: "The vows of chivalry were no better kept than any other vows whatever; and the songs of the Troubadours were not more decent . . . than those of Ovid." Wordsworth's presentation of the myth is no more realistic than Byron's. Wordsworth's opening phrase, "days of yore" (altered from the 1804 MS X reading, "days of old"), suggests not merely times long ago, but times that never existed. The shading of the word was well established: Johnson defines *yore* as referring to the past, but his four citations are from poems in which the past is fictional. Where Byron records the nightmare of a chivalric knight made real, Wordsworth validates the myth by proposing a contemporary exemplar, the Wanderer:

> Yet not the noblest of that honoured Race
> Drew happier, loftier, more empassioned, thoughts
> From his long journeyings and eventful life,
> Than this obscure Itinerant had skill
> To gather, ranging through the tamer ground
> Of these our unimaginative days.
>
> (II 19–24)

Nothing has suggested that the Minstrel's task was to collect "thoughts"; rather, he gained gifts, ladies' praise, and food. Along the way, given the inevitability of his encounters, he accumulated thoughts effortlessly and, with a similar naturalness, returned them in song. When, after the fall from this intellectual Eden and gift-exchange economy, "thoughts" need to be gathered in a terrain of scarcity, like the Leech-gatherer's leeches that "have dwindled long by slow decay" ("Resolution and Independence" 125), their values increase; more precisely, they come to have value as a commodity when previously they were by-products of other primary exchanges. The Wanderer has the necessary "skill," a word suggesting a contemporary economy in which "thoughts" can be gathered, produced, and exchanged in commodified interactions consistent with "higgl[ing] about tape, or brass sleeve buttons" and "selling [of] flannel and pocket handkerchiefs," as Jeffrey exasperatedly describes the Wanderer's profession (*Edinburgh Review* 24: 30).

In part, Jeffrey was horrified that the Wanderer's intellectual skills would be viewed as consistent with selling wares, rather than as the specialized skills of the professional. His language, arbitrarily specifying objects where Wordsworth speaks of "load[s]," "wants," "wares" (I 324, 331–32), asserts the distinction between linguistic and material exchanges. He contends that the Wanderer's "lofty diction" would "frighten away all his customers." Jeffrey's own task in making this observation, however, is to frighten Wordsworth's customers to the *Edinburgh Review*. He suggests a privileged critical gaze, since after the customers are gone, there remain viewers who (like the Vicar of "The Brothers") can take the Pedlar "for a madman, or for some learned and affected gentleman, who, in a frolic, had taken up a character which he was particularly ill qualified for supporting" (24: 30). Jeffrey's own language, exploiting the Wanderer's mythic predecessors, locates the Pedlar as a displaced Don Quixote. The economic and class adumbrations of Jeffrey's language insist on the particularity of linguistic value adhering in words, whereas, for Wordsworth, the simulacrum between language and objects provided a method of situating meaning in both, and so provides the Pedlar's double function of supplying wants and pleasing fancies (I 331–32).[3] I would emphasize that Jeffrey's position and Wordsworth's are not far apart in proposing a linguistic management of objects; both are, after all, professional writers. Their division stems from where they locate the right and execution of such management.

By positioning the Minstrel as the Wanderer's prototype, Wordsworth prepares the poet as the Wanderer's heir. Neither the economic order of the minstrel/poet based on the gift nor that of the Wanderer (and his economic replacements, the monetary markets based on commodities) is original; they exist in mutual dependence, one myth building upon the previous even while providing the literary space in which to write that previous myth. Such a claim, which dominates the moral terrain of the entire poem, is reinforced by the judicial strength of the Wanderer, achieved not institutionally but through the natural affections of those on whom he passes judgment.

Despite his retirement, the Wanderer is greeted as though he still carries items of worth; Wordsworth articulates that worth not as platitudinous moralizing, as Jeffrey pretends, but as something more threatening—the power of judgment. The second verse paragraph turns from the invented Minstrel to the real (within the poem) Wanderer, and it divides into two parts. The first describes the ability of the Wanderer to read the landscape; nearly every house "yield[s] a remembrance" and "call[s] forth" a tale, while his encounters with nature are silent:

> And in the silence of his face I [the poet] read
> His overflowing spirit. Birds and beasts,
> And the mute fish that glances in the stream,
>
> . . . .
>
> The fowl domestic, and the household dog—
> In his capacious mind, he loved them all.
>
> (II 40–46)

The hierarchy is neither the thoroughly humanized one of the Minstrel nor utterly natural, but one that joins humanity and nature. The double reading, the Wanderer's of nature and the poet's of the Wanderer, demonstrates the sympathy of the two travelers, but also establishes the neophyte position of the poet. He cannot yet read directly (nor can he read the houses at all, except through the words of the Wanderer). Again, the prototypic position of the Wanderer's narration of the Ruined Cottage is evident, but here expanded into present interactions with tenants of "many a cottage-hearth" (II 59). The poet is a stranger, but because of the affection by which the Wanderer is met, he "at once forg[ets]" that status. Such a forgetting is psychologically empowering, similar to the possession the poet gains over the Ruined Cottage in receiving its tale, and the rights of citizenship granted correspond to the Wanderer's response to natural beings:

> Their rights acknowledging he felt for all.
> (II 47)

This line entails a characteristic Wordsworthian displacement, since the rights of animals, as established in the laws of chattel, do not exist. The Wanderer tacitly recognizes as much by merely watching and sympathizing with a "poor brute's condition, forced to run / Its course of suffering in the public road" (II 51–52), but his own suffering introduces a human cost to the abuse, and thus begins a rewriting of the language of rights as inscribed in the eighteenth-century understanding of chattel. Recognizing rights at this moment does not entail any specific action, but an internal feeling. It remains to the poet to transform that feeling into action by relocating it within readers in the political economy.

Line 47 admits another reading: their rights acknowledging *that* he did indeed feel for all. The human treatment of natural beings acknowledges that such beings have rights, and the subsequent refusal to recognize those rights is an alienation not just from nature but from self. It seems to me that here Wordsworth has anticipated Christopher Stone's arguments for the legal empowerment of "things": "We are inclined to suppose the rightlessness of rightless 'things' to be a decree of Nature, not a legal convention acting in support of some status quo. It is thus that we defer considering the choices involved in all their moral, social and economic dimensions" (*Should Trees Have Standing*? 6).[4] Wordsworth suggests that by the construction of rights from natural law, human beings tacitly acknowledge nature's rights, even if, subsequently, such rights are obfuscated through a marketplace of natural resources. Just as there is a "Right of a human Creature to be exempt from being considered as a mere Instrument" (IX, Argument), natural beings can only become "mere instrument" through human control. Thus, in book VII, the company sees a woodman:

> "Here," said the Pastor, "do we muse, and mourn
> The waste of death; and lo! the giant oak
> Stretched on his bier—that massy timber wain;
> Nor fail to note the Man who guides the team."
>
> (VII 546–49)

In the context of his funereal stories, this is less anthropomorphic than recognizing that human beings are isomorphic with nature. The Wood-cutter is a cheerful, inadvertent capitalist: "Year after year is added to his store / With *silent* increase" (VII 565–66) and his piety is marked by a regular commodification, as "every sabbath day," he hears "The Christian promise [of stores in heaven] with attentive ear" (VII 577–78). The Parson recognizes both his goodwill and his utility within a market language ("Many a ship / Launched into Morecamb-bay, to *him* hath owed / Her strong knee-timbers" [VII 602–4]), and yet in this enthusiasm, the Wood-cutter has forgotten the origins of his labor in the largesse of nature:

> the JOYFUL ELM,
> Around whose trunk the maidens dance in May [a fertility rite]—
> And the LORD'S OAK—would plead their several rights
> In vain, if he were master of their fate;
> His sentence to the axe would doom them all.
>
> (VII 620–24)

The function of rights, then, is not to preserve property but to remind us that what seems to be property may be other things as well.

The first half of the verse paragraph in book II has used a natural-rights theory as its horizon and the second half shifts to another legal metaphor, that of adjudication. The results are more performative, not because of the specific exertion of power—as in a literal court—but because the Wanderer's adjudication concerns the individual divided against himself:

—Nor was he loth to enter ragged huts,
Huts where his charity was blest; his voice
Heard as the voice of an experienced friend.
And, sometimes—where the poor man held dispute
With his own mind, unable to subdue
Impatience through inaptness to perceive
General distress in his particular lot;
Or cherishing resentment, or in vain
Struggling against it; with a soul perplexed,
And finding in herself no steady power
To draw the line of comfort that divides
Calamity, the chastisement of Heaven,
From the injustice of our brother men—
To him appeal was made as to a judge;
Who, with an understanding heart, allayed
The perturbation; listened to the plea;
Resolved the dubious point; and sentence gave
So grounded, so applied, that it was heard
With softened spirit, even when it condemned.

(II 62–80)

The admonition the Wanderer offers is obscured by the emphasis on the genre of the advice, the judicial decision: "as to a judge." Since jurisprudence is constructed on the view that the law treats similar cases similarly, the form of the poor man's "crime" is an inability to recognize similarity or dissimilarity. He cannot subdue his impatience because he does not perceive "General distress in his particular lot"; he cannot distinguish the "chastisement of Heaven" from the "injustice" of men. The adversaries in the case are the "poor man" and "his own mind"; thus, the divided self is an artifact of an isolated self, and the imposition of juridical order conjoins them in a sentence which is both punishment and absolution.

Wordsworth's choice of this metaphor is itself polemical. He asserts the ability to judge the thoughts of men and to work alterations on their spirit. This assertion enters a complicated debate on the status of criminal intent. Bentham, following Beccaria, had argued that the courts lacked the capability to examine intention and that the doctrine of *mens rea* was an incoherent fiction since the guilty mind of the criminal was established only through the act he committed. Criminality, for Bentham, was determined by the harm of an act within society and not by the moral status of the act;[5]

denying the relevance of intentionality girded Bentham's panoptical projects of surveillance.

Robert Chambers, by contrast, recognized in these same facts the invariable pressure that the law exerted on human intentions and the consequential ability to enforce judgment on that basis: "The great strength of human laws arises from the constitution of things ordained by Providence, by which man is so formed and disposed that he can suffer more than he can enjoy. . . . But such is the frame of man, that the dread of evil may be always made more powerful than the appetite of good" (*Lectures* 1: 309). In this model, the criminal law does not alter the basic drives of human beings, but adjusts the external world—by the imposition of penalty—to exploit the intentional structure of the human mind. To account for the obvious cases when the expected deterrence failed, Chambers followed Blackstone in describing passion as a mitigating circumstance, since in an impassioned state, the public individual was subsumed by the private. Blackstone's descriptions of intentionality are an element of a more general unifying principle, the balance of equity and law within a monarchy: "One of the great advantages of monarchy in general, above any other form of government [is] that there is a magistrate [the king], who has in his power to extend mercy, wherever he thinks it is deserved: holding a court of equity in his own breast, to soften the rigour of the general law" (*Commentaries* 4: 390). Monarchy legally places above the law an individual who can assure that the law maintains its just status. The king searches the heart; the court examines only the deed; between them, all human nature is under gaze.

In book II, Wordsworth's use of the adjudicative metaphor suggests another solution—that the initial division between intention and act is itself an artifact of criminality, disempowerment, breaks in human nature. The courts formalized disputes only between different litigants and, even for corporations (fictive individuals), denied the right to bring suit against one's self; Wordsworth, by contrast, insists on the continuity between disputes among parties and a dispute between a man and his mind. Communal obligation arises as a structure of the self, and precedes its institutionalization.

COMING FULL CIRCLE: PROPERTY AND WANDERING

For Wordsworth, the problem of property occasioned a dramatic moment in which the relationship between an individual and nature could be located as a social reality: by becoming part of one's land, one joined society, even in solitude. Furthermore, property was the intersection of land and human imagination, a continual transformation worked upon the land in constituting it as natural. For Jeffrey, this was madness, or worse, mysticism, reversing the logical priorities in which social contract created property, and in which ownership was an appropriation of nature to human use. As a lawyer, Jeffrey *knew* that only that which the law protected as property was property.

Byron's criticism of *The Excursion* in *Don Juan* presents a useful contrast: "A drowsy frowzy poem called the *Excursion*, / Writ in a manner which is my aversion" (III 94). Byron pretends that his boredom inheres in the manner of the poem and not in his own anxious response, but it is less the manner to which Byron is averse than the poetic implications of such verse. He condenses common complaints against Wordsworth into a sharp witticism that need not address, or even acknowledge, Wordsworth's rationale. Like Jeffrey, Byron sees a system at work to give the professional poet an economic status, precisely the position Byron's career repudiates or obfuscates. In the stanza above the specific reference to *The Excursion*, Byron explains Wordsworth's early radical views (in between trashing Southey and Coleridge): "Or Wordsworth unexcised, unhired, who then / Seasoned his pedlar poems with democracy" (III 93). The unlicensed ("unexcised") Wordsworth has no use for the monarchist government which provides licenses, but once established, Wordsworth no longer uses the spice of democracy because he has an investment in the government. Byron, living in exile for reasons that summed to the oppressiveness of English society, understands Wordsworth as having bought into the commercial system precisely because he insists on the status of a professional poet. The poems are not so much poems about peddlers, but poems actively peddled in the marketplace, and hence subscribing to exactly those values that Byron as a public persona despises.

In *The Excursion*, Wordsworth attempts to work out a solution to the problem of property dramatized in "Michael" by locating the concept of ownership as a duty, rather than as a right. "Duty," as a legal term, can be synonymous with debt or can denote the precondition of bringing a tort action. For Blackstone, a duty would inhere only in a property interest; thus, a master has by contract a property interest in his servant, so has a cause against harm to that servant, but not the reverse. Wordsworth, who would have been aware of the legal definitions as well as the religious dimensions of the word *duty*, understood ownership as a duty toward the land, and a consistent theme in his poetry is that a violation of that duty leads to a harm which then entails an action, not before the court of men, but before the laws of Nature. With the Parson's stories, the verdict of Nature is accepted by the social ceremony of burial, a literal mixing of ashes and dust.

Wordsworth's position on property opposed a recent but overdetermined and violently established tradition that understood property not only as a right but as the surety of all other rights. In part, Wordsworth's opposition to classical liberal theory arose from the failure of property to produce the social stability that its proponents argued was its natural consequence. With increasing capital, the distance between an owner and the item or land owned became arbitrary, and ownership became a method of making profits because a fundamental right of ownership was the right to transfer the property. Wordsworth's response is at once tinged with medievalism—the inscription of the owner on land, of the maker on personal property—and radicalism, the demand that the accumulation of property be checked by utility.

The classical liberal theory of property—which locates the right of property in the work performed by an individual and consequently opens out the possibility of ownership, in theory, not only to anyone but also of anything—reaches a comprehensive legal articulation in Blackstone's *Commentaries*. These *Commentaries* used the theory to offer an ideological justification for the economic structure of English society as it stood in the 1760s, and simultaneously to justify property law as being both a natural law and the highest evolution of social law. The self-regulation of the government was achieved through property structure; the two houses of Parliament "naturally drawing in two directions of opposite interest [that is, landed and commercial interests], and the prerogative in another [the king, who is a part of Parliament] still different from them both, they mutually keep each other from exceeding their proper limits" (1: 154). Furthermore, a stability of the English social terrain had been achieved by the creation of new alienable properties, such as a principal debt, "and thus the legislature of England has universally promoted the grand ends of civil society, the peace and security of individuals, by steadily pursuing that wise and orderly maxim, of assigning to every thing capable of ownership a legal and determinate owner" (2: 15). This owner was usually the Crown, or, as Bentham would insist, the king. Blackstone's sentence, which ends the first chapter of his second volume, *The Rights of Things*, balances words associated with natural law and those linked to legislation; "grand ends" pairs with "civil society"; "peace with security"; "wise with orderly." Wordsworth presents the interrelation of human and natural productions as something itself in need of interpretation.

Wordsworth, like Blackstone, envisions a society in which the natural underwrites the contractual, but, where Blackstone believed such a society was discoverable in the British Constitution, Wordsworth thought that it was discernible only through a continual contact with nature, and that the constitution was not an object of interpretation but a method of interpreting nature. At the opening of book III, the Wanderer, Solitary, and poet/narrator come upon "A mass of rock" which resembles "A stranded ship, with keel upturned." Is this the symbol of another journey gone astray, or one guided to safe shore by a divine will, like Noah's ark? The description which follows at first suggests the latter; among other rocks,

> a pair were seen,
> That with united shoulders bore aloft
> A fragment, like an altar, flat and smooth.
> (III 58–60)

And then, as with the story of Noah, transgression enters:

> A tall and shining holly
> . . . .
> stood upright,
> As if inserted by some human hand
> In mockery.
> (III 62–65)

The poet's description prepares for the argument between the Wanderer and the Solitary. The Wanderer goes first: "Behold a cabinet for sages built, / Which kings might envy!" (III 74–75). His language asserts the reality of what is beheld—the rocks were built—and interlocks the natural and the human. The Solitary acknowledges the resemblance:

> Some shadowy intimations haunt me here,
> That in these shows a chronicle survives
> Of purposes akin to those of Man,

but goes on to explain it:

The sport of Nature, aided by blind Chance
Rudely to mock the works of toiling Man.
And hence, this upright shaft of unhewn stones.
(III 88–90, 126–28)

The echo of "Michael" recalls not the struggle between man and nature, but the struggle to grasp what that relation is. Are the works of man sanctified by nature, or only by the power bestowed by the king's laws? This argument does not resolve the question, but locates it in the poem's future, in the fate of the Solitary and the fate of England.

To turn this dispute back toward the structure of poetry, the presence of these rocks calls into question the relation of intention, associated with an originating source, and meaning, derived from the empowered mechanisms of reading, metonymized as viewing. The structure of man, as a working being, is intentional, and his intentionality is present on and in his work to the extent that labor is unalienated. When the Pedlar sells a ware, with it is the story of its making and the reinstitution of relation between buyer and seller as user and maker. When nature produces such rocks effortlessly, man's intentional structure seems mocked, devalued. But poetry, in recouping the rocks within *The Excursion* itself, (re)creates the rocks as a poetic labor which then opens the way for meaning. Moreover, the Solitary's very expression creates meaning by endowing nature with intent. Man's intentional structure is the creation of the meaning of nature; the Solitary's "hence" constructs the causal relationship which invests nature with an intentional structure, a desire to mock. Like the Pedlar, whose labor is the display and circulation of other labor, the poet's work entails the management and representation of both labor and intentionality.

Blackstone had thought to settle the relationship of rights—the right to speak, act, be—with the rights of property once and for all. Any change in rights would constitute an attack on property, and hence on the fabric of English law, on security and peace, on order and wisdom. The French Revolution was, however, such an attack, and Burke, in repudiating it, turns to Blackstonean notions that locate natural order and rights within property interests: "The levellers therefore only change and pervert the natural order of things; they load the edifice of society, by setting up in the air what the solidity of the structure requires on the ground" (*Reflections* 138). Air was one of the few things Blackstone considered incapable of ownership. Against the air (and the airiness of new ideas), Burke pits property: "Nothing is a due and adequate representation of a state, that does not represent its ability, as well as its property . . . . [But to be] safe from the invasions of ability . . . [property] must be represented too in great masses of accumulation" (140).

Burke, however, adds explicitly a relation between rights and property which was only implicit, and indeed disguised, in Blackstone. Burke lays out a variety of natural rights, which include the rights to justice, to the means of profitable industry, and to the possessions of one's parents (which Blackstone viewed as a legal convenience, not a natural right). The list is itself formulated in terms of property, but then Burke's analogy shifts: "In this partnership [society] all men have equal rights; but not to equal things. He that has but five shillings in the partnership, has as good a right to it, as he that has five hundred pounds has to his larger portion. But he has not a right to an equal dividend in the product of the joint stock" (149–150). The analogy points out the way a capitalistic trade has created a new domain for property, and a new urgency for the alienability of that property. The exchange of money for ownership can be done without regard to the product, the workers, or the location of the work. Buying stock profitably requires the ability to sell it quickly, and selling is useful only if the money allows the acquisition of other property. The fallacy of Burke's argument immediately evident to Wollstonecraft, Godwin, and Paine, was that the wealthy had not invested their five hundred pounds in society, but in a market which Burke constituted as the site of social empowerment. The stability of property on which Burke insists is actually undercut by his own understanding of the circulation not only of ownership but of human rights. Wordsworth indicates the danger of obscuring the arbitrariness with which rights are located within property in his treatment of the Solitary. Here, the Solitary is relaying his domestic bliss by using a legal doctrine of occupancy:

> Seven years of occupation undisturbed
> Established seemingly a right to hold
> That happiness; and use and habit gave
> To what an alien spirit had acquired
> A patrimonial sanctity.
>
> (III 622–26)

But, "A claim . . . shattered all" (III 638). Death, it turns out, does not recognize property rights. Indeed, against this version of property, we can place Wordsworth's use of the word *tenant* in the poem. Book IV begins, "Here closed the Tenant of that lonely vale / His mournful narrative" (IV 1–2). (Like a Homeric epithet, the phrase "Tenant of that lonely vale" recurs three times, each time in the same metrical position of closing a line.) Similarly, the Wanderer ends his story of Margaret, "and here she died; / Last human tenant of these ruined walls" (I 915–16). In both these cases, the word *tenant* is encased in painful imagery which recalls the power nature has to reclaim itself. Against this greater power, even an owner in fee simple is but a tenant. But if Wordsworth rejected Burke's formulation, he found Godwin's response equally problematic.

Godwin was quick to seize on Burke's inconsistencies, and sought to formulate a different view of property, one in which rights precede property, and in which property is itself known through obligation. If property has been the foundation of English law, he argues in *Enquiry Concerning Political Justice* and in *Caleb Williams*, it has equally been the source of English crimes. Certain instances, the enclosure and gaming laws, are obvious examples, but his argument seeks a more metaphysical foundation in seeing that one man's property is experienced as lack by another. Paine, like Godwin, attempts to reverse the relationship between property and rights that Burke has set out in the metaphor of a stock company. Paine claims that all Englishmen own England, and that the right of property, then, only inheres in the improvement upon the land which an owner undertakes; thus, any English citizen is entitled to a land rent from those who occupy the land. Presence is not required, and at a first glance, this might seem to accord well with the Wanderer's freedom.

If, in at least the dominant readings of *The Excursion*, the moral center is a wanderer, almost all wandering in the poem is problematic. Indeed, as a central romantic trope, wandering is fraught with dangers. Childe Harold's nihilistic journeys have replaced the meaning-making pilgrimage of the Red Crosse Knight. This particular example is shadowed by Byron's own wasted journeying, but his choice to overwrite this biographical information into Spenserian stanzas with allusions to Duessa and ruin and the loss of "One" (Una) illustrates a shift in the valuation of wandering. The Ancient Mariner's travels end in a condemnation to roam, and that roaming is experienced as arrest: "He holds him with his glittering eye— / The wedding guest stood still" ("Rime" 13–14), The Mariner's intrusion threatens the ceremonies of civilization, the negative allusion being to Christ at Cana (John 2:1).

Wordsworth was himself a great wanderer, but his travels were also fraught with ambiguity; the mixed emotions of "Tintern Abbey" resonate with his travels through France and leaving Annette Vallon and their child—a story told in the mirror image of the Ruined Cottage. The vagrants and beggars and the "Old Man Travelling," who recalls Priam crossing Ilium to ransom the body of Hector, define the terrain of the *Lyrical Ballads*. Poems which follow *The Excursion* are similarly marked, none more forcefully than Byron's *Don Juan*, or Shelley's *Alastor*, a journey that remaps Wordsworth's poetic territory. The appearance of wandering in literature is not new to Romanticism; Henry Fielding's novels typically operate by the wanderings, more or less arbitrary, of individuals through recognizable social constructions—the inns of *Joseph Andrews*, the bailors prisons of *Amelia*—and as I have already suggested, the journeys of the Knights in *The Faerie Queene* tantalize with the dangers to which the romantic counterparts such as Childe Harold and Cain succumb. The change in the values of such journeys reflects the historical conditions of increased vagrancy, of conscription into the army, of improved road conditions which made travel easier but also increased the economic necessity of intranational importing. Other displacements, of impoverished aristocracy and disowned farmers, contributed to this historical background.

More recently, roughly a year before *The Excursion*'s publication, Wordsworth accepted a job as the Distributor of Stamps for the county of Westmoreland. The post was secured by William Lowther, Earl of Lonsdale, who had repaid his predecessor's debt to the Wordsworth family. It seems appropriate for a poet to have charge of stamps, the symbols of circulation and authority for written documents: "The office of Distributor of Stamps was concerned with the collection of Inland Revenue duties. All legal documents, wills, licenses of all kinds, as well as pamphlets, books, papers, and insurance policies, came under its jurisdiction. . . . The Distributor was expected to make quarterly rounds of his district, collecting the takings and forwarding them to the Board of Stamps in London" (Moorman II: 244–45). As with the Spectator who himself circulates to empower the circulation of the *Spectator*, Wordsworth circulates through Westmoreland. When Wordsworth was given the chance to exchange this office for the Collectorship of Customs at Whitehaven, a considerably more lucrative post, he declined, being, according to his nephew Christopher Wordsworth, unwilling to surrender his retirement at Mount Rydal for a larger town (Moorman II: 253). At Rydal, his writing and official position formed a continuum, in which symbolic presence authorized circulation.

By his dedication to Lonsdale, Wordsworth underscores the parallel between this occupation and that *Excursion*, in which a smaller circle is walked and stories are collected, exchanged, and interpreted:

> Oft, through thy fair domains, illustrious Peer!
> In youth I roamed, on youthful pleasures bent;
> And mused in rocky cell or sylvan tent,
> Beside swift-flowing Lowther's current clear.
> —Now, by thy care befriended, I appear
> Before thee, LONSDALE, and this Work present,
> A token (may it prove a monument!)
> Of high respect and gratitude sincere.
>
> (1–8)

The roaming, echoing the narrator's early days described in "Michael," provides the opportunity for musing, and so prepares for the profession of poetry. Lonsdale's domains are neither completely natural nor civilized, but a careful balance between "rocky" and "cell," between "sylvan" and "tent." Condensed into these phrases is Wordsworth's notion of property as the intersection of civilization and nature, and as such the product of the human imagination. The debt, poetic or otherwise, to Lonsdale for use of the land is heavily mediated until the exchange between the lord and the poet takes on the aspect of mutual gifts. Not explicit about the latest demonstration of "care," Wordsworth casts his wandering into his past. He elides the point that he had roamed the domains not of this Lonsdale but of the previous, less illustrious one. Wordsworth erases—leaving sharp erasure marks—the painful treatment to which the peer's family had subjected Wordsworth's by not paying John Wordsworth for his legal services.[6] Wordsworth figures the gift of the distributorship as an advance against his own accomplishment, which begins as a "token" but, by circulating in the literary marketplace, might become a monument. For Wordsworth, then, the issue is whether wandering could be made to hold social value within the historical disruptions of which wandering was a sign.

Many Wordsworthian wanderings differ from the Pedlar's (and Wordsworth's in his distributorship) in that they are characterized by flight, by either the avoidance of duty or the inability to locate duty. The Pedlar himself, by finding a profession in wandering, is able to give his wandering a regularity. He is associated with the sun throughout the poem. The opening verse paragraph, moreover, describes in detail how the sun structures the land:

> shadows that lay in spots
> Determined and unmoved, with steady beams
> Of bright and pleasant sunshine interposed.
> (I 6–8)

As the sun gives shape to the earth, the Pedlar structures the economic environment of his community. The function is becoming obsolete:

> And their hard service, deemed debasing now,
> Gained merited respect in simpler times;
> When squire, and priest, and they who round them dwelt
> In rustic sequestration—all dependent
> Upon the PEDLAR's toil—supplied their wants,
> Or pleased their fancies, with the wares he brought.
> (I 327–32)

Through the Pedlar, the community supplied its wants. The wording carefully maintains power in the community, and makes the Pedlar the means through which the community can express itself to itself. Where work is translated into money, then work becomes interchangeable and so do individuals. But with the Pedlar's "steady" function, a myth of the specificity of work is preserved. He brings items, and with those items, he brings their origins. He is Walter Benjamin's storyteller.

Wordsworth had once before used a peddler as the meeting point of a community, in "Michael": "wherewith the Neighbours bought / A Basket, which they fill'd with Pedlar's wares." Richard Bateman, however, takes these wares "up to London," exchanges them for his master's merchandise, and grows "wondrous rich." He has outgrown the peddler's limited market. In *The Excursion*, the threat is that the entire community has done so, and in doing so, lost itself, commodified itself. The Pedlar forestalls this outcome by retiring, and signifies at once the economic binding of the community and the replacement of that binding with a poetic, or natural, binding. By natural, I mean—and believe that Wordsworth often meant—a binding that inheres in the structure of the land. The key to the Pedlar's successes, as salesman, as minstrel, and as educator lies in his ability to find the community at home. (His educational designs on the poet/narrator need to be read against his having "essayed to teach / A village-school—but wandering thoughts were then / A misery to him" [I 312–14].) This requirement, then, entails a particular notion of property as obligation. The freedom of an individual to alienate property is a triple alienation, from society, from nature, and from self, since the self is seen in the concrete work, and not in the abstract return of work in the form of money. Further, it is an alienation disguised as freedom, and aligned to the failure of the French Revolution. By generalizing the "home" of the reader into England itself (and, in book IX, the empire), the mature Wordsworth can, in the myth of *The Excursion*, always find the reader at home, and thus continue the role of the peddler in an economy that has extinguished that role, and has substituted instead lawyers, critics, and merchants.

Goaded by the Solitary, who "playfully draws a comparison between [the Wanderer's] itinerant profession and that of the Knight-errant" (VIII, Argument), the Pedlar acknowledges the ruination of his profession and of the social order which permitted itself to be expressed through him:

> I have lived to mark
> A new and unforeseen creation rise
> From out the labours of a peaceful Land
>
> . . . .
>
> With fruitless pains
> Might one like me *now* visit many a tract
>
> . . . .
>
> Meanwhile, at social Industry's command,
> How quick, how vast an increase! From the germ
> Of some poor hamlet, rapidly produced
> Here a huge town, continuous and compact,
> Hiding the face of the earth for leagues—and there,
> Where not a habitation stood before,
> Abodes of men irregularly massed
> Like trees in forests.
>
> (VIII 89–91, 95–96, 117–24)

The images keep working out wider and wider and cannot hold. The purpose of property is not to obscure the face of the earth, but to show it; the function of habitation is that people may be grouped with regularity, not irregularly massed. The metaphor of the trees, playing off the image of "fruitless pains," is suggestive in recalling the ruined cottage which has been overgrown—here, increase and ruin have merged.

Wordsworth is writing a tragedy, which, in the full design of *The Recluse*, he intends to overcome, through the recovery of the Solitary and the triumph of the poet, and because of this intent, we read the equanimity of the Pedlar onto his maker. But Wordsworth never finished the work, and perhaps the contradictory goals set for the other parts preclude a conclusion. "The first and third parts of The Recluse," Wordsworth writes in his preface, "will consist chiefly of meditations in the Author's own person" (2). By contrast, the final lines of the poem promise more of the Solitary:

> How far [the Solitary's] erring notions were reformed;
> And whether aught, of tendency as good
> And pure, from further intercourse ensued;
> This—if delightful hopes, as heretofore,
> Inspire the serious song, and gentle Hearts
> Cherish, and lofty Minds approve the past—
> My future labours may not leave untold.
>
> (IX 790–96)

The poem's future and the Solitary's fate lie suspended between Wordsworth's inspiration and the poem's reception. Or to repose the issue, the reformation of the Solitary and the possibility of future good depend on the intercourse between poet and reader.

In any event, the critical history of the poem does not mark its narrator's triumph. By and large, the continuity between *The Excursion* and the *Prelude* has been rejected by an academic community which can accept the struggles of the latter, but not the critique of the former. Harold Bloom, for example, cites the following passage to "show clearly the decline of Wordsworth, the heavy frost that encrusted a spirit endowed by Nature with a vitality nearly the equal of Blake's" (*Visionary* 194–95):

> the care prospective of our wise
> Forefathers, who, to guard against the shocks,
> The fluctuations and decay of things,
> Embodied and established these high truths

In solemn institutions:—men convinced
That life is love and immortality.
(V 997–1002)

The rejection of these lines (Bloom quotes to the end of the book, l.1016), which in prose might well be a defense of the English Magna Carta or the United States Constitution—albeit one that raises to the surface difficult interpretive questions which those very institutions, losing sight of a relation between love and life, have buried—brings us to Judge Richard Posner's remark that "we do not require the poet to show us how to get from where we are to where in his imaginative vision he wants us to be" (*Law and Literature* 203). We do not require it, nor do we, taking our cues—as Posner inadvertently does—from Francis Jeffrey, allow it; yet, that was Wordsworth's goal. To derive the full system from *The Excursion*, as Wordsworth hoped his readers would do, was not to merely rediscover the Preface to the *Lyrical Ballads*, nor to achieve an aesthetic understanding, but to recognize the impossibility of ownership in fee simple. Human lives are entailed.

The Excursion has not done. For, in the guises of objectivism, of law and economics, even of romantic ideology, we cling to property as securing rights, even at the cost of denying those rights, spending them in the acquisition of property and its tropes of independence and genius. We live as if to agree with Blackstone: "So great moreover is the regard of the law for private property, that it will not authorize the least violation of it; no, not even for the general good of the community "*Commentaries* 1: 135).[7] But within the context of *The Excursion*, it becomes clear that private property is not an objective given; rather it arises as an interpretation, an act of textuality and of power. Wordsworth's *Excursion*, long as it is, needs to be felt as fragmentary, as voicing a vision of social structure at once antiquarian and revolutionary, but one which the legal/economic system, championed by Jeffrey, would not allow, because it might have done.

Conclusion

> As Justice Holmes explained, "[i]t would be a dangerous undertaking for persons trained only to the law to constitute themselves final judges of the worth of [a work], outside of the narrowest and most obvious limits. At the one extreme some works of genius would be sure to miss appreciation.
> —Souter, J., unanimous opinion in *Campbell v. Acuff-Rose Music, Inc;* considering 2 Live Crew's parody of Roy Orbison's "Oh, Pretty Woman"

DEATH and copyright were connected for Wordsworth in part because of the way his poetry asserted its force, and its propriety, in light of mortality: the poet's death allows for the grave in "A Poet's Epitaph"; Michael's death allows the poet to possess a literary sheep-fold; deaths surround the journey of the Wanderer and poet, from the story of Margaret to the funeral procession, from the graveyard stories the Pastor tells to the violence of the French Revolution. And Wordsworth's death sets in motion the long-awaited publication of the poem on the growth of a poet's mind. But copyright and death were also connected because of the way in which the author's death entered the formula for determining copyright; in a complaint that he made often, Wordsworth wrote to Gladstone that "within the last three years or so my poetical writings have produced for me nearly 1,500 pounds, and that much the greatest part of them either would be public property tomorrow, if I should die, or would become so in a very few years" (LLY 3: 536, 23 March 1838). In these few remaining pages, I do not intend a thorough investigation into either Wordsworth's engagements with death or those with copyright.[1] Instead, in the first part, I examine the difference between Wordsworth's and Hume's views on copyright to distinguish the terms of their professionalization. Then, to conclude, I wish to suggest something of what Wordsworth's encounter with law can teach us about the unnaturalness of death.

WORDSWORTH AND HUME ON COPYRIGHT

The eighteenth century established an alliance between publisher and writer, the producers, respectively, of the work and the text, contained by mercantile operations: "The booksellers were the other, the more public, half of the book business, and during the eighteenth century they, and particularly a small influential group known as 'the trade,' dominated the book publishing business, controlling both printers and writers" (Kernan, *Printing Technology* 62). The structure of the audience did not, in practice, require the resolution of a conflict over ownership between publisher and author. With the dissolution of a polite readership into a reading public which could absorb more than thirteen thousand copies of the monthly *Edinburgh Review* by 1818, the issue of the relation between a corporeal property and an incorporeal property was fought not as once, between sovereign and legal institution, nor even between book producers and "pirates," but now, within the procedures of book production itself, between publishers and authors. Who was to govern? That question turned on whether an authorial text dominated the physical work of the publisher, or whether, like an invention subsumed into industrialization, a text was consumed (or bought out) in the manufacturing process of making books. Publishers had brought the author's common-law right of copy into visibility as the naturalizing fiction for their own claims in the eighteenth century[2]; in doing so, they laid the groundwork for the rebellion of their own creature, the author.[3]

For sixty years, the Statute of Anne limiting copyright to twenty-eight years coexisted with a common law and trade-practice understanding that a copyright, being a property, must be perpetual, and it was in general under the common law that injunctions against piracy were sought in Chancery court.[4] In February 1774, this contradiction ended. The House of Lords ruled in *Donaldson v. Beckett* that Queen Anne's act had abolished the common law protection, and provided the only available protection to booksellers.[5] The Lords overturned the Court of Sessions decision by a 6-5 vote, with Mansfield (who would nearly certainly have sided with the minority) absent for ethical reasons, since it was his own ruling under consideration. The *Annual Register* offered this analysis: "Near £200,000 worth of what was honestly purchased at public sale, and which was yesterday thought property, is now reduced to nothing" (quoted in *Letters of David Hume*, 275). Hume, who as a writer presumably stood to lose money since the value of a limited copyright was less than that of a perpetual one, was not particularly bothered. He was sixty-three years old and only in fair health, which might have aided his indifference, although Wordsworth in 1839 indicated that his own age of "approaching 70" was one reason he was so concerned about reforming the copyright act.

Hardly matching Wordsworth's industry in writing letters to modify the copyright law, Hume wrote a letter that a lawyer for the booksellers introduced into the Commons in an effort to secure legislative relief from *Donaldson*. The lawyer described the letter as "containing the warmest wishes to the petitioners, lamenting the late decision of the House of Peers as fatal to literature, and hoping that the booksellers might get speedy relief" (quoted in *Letters of David Hume* 278). To Strahan, at whose request Hume probably wrote the public letter, he privately expressed a nearly indifferent opinion:

> I have writ you an ostensible Letter on the Subject of literary Property, which contains my real Sentiments, so far as it goes. However, I shall tell you the truth; I do not foresee any such bad Consequences as you mention from laying the Property open. The Italians and French have more pompous [i.e., splendid] Editions of their Classics since the Expiration of the Privileges than any we have of ours: And at least, every Bookseller, who prints a Book, will endeavor to make it as compleat and correct as he can. (*Letters of David Hume* 274–75, notes omitted)

In part, Hume expresses confidence in the bookselling cartel to regulate its own marketplace. The Edinburgh pirates cannot secure the best (i.e., most recent) editions, and their potential threat would prompt the London publishers to produce superior, and reasonably priced, editions.[6] For Hume, the publishing cartel is potent enough and unified enough that its own beliefs will determine the shape of the literary marketplace. Further, the introduction of support of the booksellers' petition by literary figures displayed the mechanism of production as a combination of publisher and writer. Johnson's *Dictionary* might be exemplary. His words were derived from the texts provided by his publishers, to whom he returned them through the agency of the printer, W. Strahan. Strahan was also Hume's publisher and a long-time correspondent, as well as the printer for Edward Gibbon, Adam Smith, and Tobias Smollett.

Hume's assessment seems, for a time, to have been correct. The cartel of English booksellers assembled by 1777 and, pooling their copyrights, agreed to produce "an elegant and uniform edition of *The English Poets* . . . with a concise account of the life of each authour, by Dr. Samuel Johnson" (E. Dilly to Boswell, *Life of Johnson*, 802).[7] But, by degrees, the cartel dissolved into individual concerns and the interests of writers and publishers divided. Thus the striking contrast between the battle over *Donaldson* and the debate over Talfourd's bill (introduced in 1838) to extend copyright to sixty years: the booksellers and the authors were on opposite sides of the latter bill.

The Wordsworthian view of literary property as the sign of a connection between reader and writer positioned the publisher as an agent of the writer. Wordsworth contracted with publishers on a profit-sharing basis and retained his copyrights. Wordsworth's view on copyright, in which he invokes the law against market practices, can be seen as the third in a series of positions on literary property. In the *Lyrical Ballads*, especially the Preface and "A Poet's Epitaph," the poet disdains the aid of the courts and relies on a doctrine of natural law substantiated not, as natural-law lawyers claimed, by the courts but by the poem itself. In *The Excursion*, Wordsworth still insists on a foundation in natural law for literary property, but locates it within a natural-law basis of property generally. In appropriating the role of judgment to the Wanderer, but marking his insufficiency to the task in the new marketplace, Wordsworth reestablishes the courts not as the authorizers of literary property but as the protectors of a value that inheres within the poem. By 1838, perhaps contemplating his own death, Wordsworth had lost most of his faith in the ability of the poet to regulate the market, and, like Hume's calling on the juridical powers by using his will to position "My Own Life," Wordsworth called on the legislature to protect his family's interest in the *Prelude*, as well as in his earlier works. This patrimony, like the encumbered land Michael receives, is not a simple gift of monetary value but a property of responsibility.

Wordsworth wrote letters to Members of Parliament (and their friends) calling for support on the second reading of Talfourd's bill in 1838 (see LLY 3: 535–47). As he tells Francis Lloyd, a Birmingham banker, "the Booksellers and Printers, in their rapacity, threaten a *very* strong opposition" (LLY 3: 547, 2 April 1838).[8] In addition to private correspondence, he published two letters in newspapers, one anonymously and the other addressed to Talfourd. Aware of his difficult position, Wordsworth was reluctant to present a petition although he eventually acquiesced to Talfourd's pleas.

Wordsworth's anonymous letter in the *Kendal Mercury* responded within a week point-by-point to a "petition against Sergeant Talfourd's Copyright Bill from compositors, pressmen, and others employed in the town of Kendal, to be presented to the House of Commons by the representative of that place" published in the *Mercury* on 7 April 1838 ("The Law of Copyright," in *Prose* 3: 309). Both Wordsworth and the employees of Kendal whom he was opposing had the curious rhetorical task of balancing arguments in favor of the public at large against their own self-interest. To conceal the latter completely would be patently false and would compromise integrity; to rely overly on self-interest would smack of greed. The petitioners declare that altering the copyright laws would be "highly injurious to the interests of the community, the literature of the country, and more particularly to the interests of the petitioners (*Prose* 3: 309). Wordsworth solves the rhetorical task by appropriating this quotation, which allows him to play the role of answering objections. Further, he uses another quotation to focus the issue on literature, and never addresses the question of the interests of the petitioners: "The effect of the extension of copyright proposed in Sergeant Talfourd's bill would, according to the words of the petitioners, be to render works having that privilege 'a mere dead letter, or confine them to the hands of the wealthy, and could not be productive of any real advantage'" (*Prose* 3: 309).

The protection of copyright, the petitioners argue, would prevent the republication necessary to keep a work vital. Against these dire consequences, Wordsworth suggests that the issue concerns a limited number of works, which have relatively little economic impact on printers in comparison to bestsellers: "It will be found that a book for which there is a great demand would be sure of being supplied to the public under any circumstances; but a good book for which there might be continued demand, though not a large one, would be much more sure of not becoming a 'dead letter,' if the proposed law were enacted than if it were not" (*Prose* 3: 309). These good books with only limited demand turn out to be the works central to English culture. Wordsworth points out that in America, where no copyright for English works exists, no publisher ventures to produce a decent edition, for fear it will be undersold by a "work incorrectly and meanly executed" (*Prose* 3: 309). The implicit argument is that without copyright, the economic currency, money, will overpower and debase the cultural currency, literature.

Where the petitioners set their interest in defeating the bill as parallel to the improvement of literature, Wordsworth argues that the self-interest of the writer, and the consequent obligation of the writer's heirs, guarantees the improvement of literature: "Who can doubt that [author's children and descendants] would be particularly prompted to extend the circulation of his works, not merely for their own pecuniary advantage, but out of respect or reverence for his memory, and to fulfil what could not but be presumed to be his wish?" (*Prose* 3: 310). This is a vision of familial obligation comparable to Michael's efforts to maintain his ancestral lands, but one that obscures the possibility of a Luke, not least because the moral education implicit in such works would help prevent such erring. This vision allows Wordsworth to integrate the writer's monetary interest into the family industry which revolves around the author's work.

After pointing out that neither Coleridge nor Southey made much money writing poetry, and only recently did "another author" (i.e., Wordsworth) make much, he declares: "Not one of them but is too highminded to repine; but the sense of justice is, I doubt not, sufficiently strong in them all to make them resent the denial to their posterity or their heirs of that moderate compensation which a rational view of their interests would lead them to aim at, and which the public might be ready to bestow" (*Prose* 3: 310). The last phrase is telling; by securing copyright, the public's judgment is preserved by making the works available for that judgment. Without it, the chaos of an America of books prevents proper judgment, fulfillment of family duties, and writers' achieving their best work by making it harder for them to imagine a future audience. After addressing two more arguments by the petitioners, Wordsworth concludes with a summary that ends by observing that this issue is not merely one of interest but of obligation: "And lastly, you violate a fundamental right, by leaving that species of property which has the highest claim to protection, with the least share of it; for as to the analogy, which has been elsewhere much dwelt upon, between literary property and mechanical inventions and chemical discoveries, it is, as might be shown in a few words, altogether fallacious" (*Prose* 3: 312). Literature has the "highest claim to protection" because as an act of culture, it most effectively protects culture.

At this point, it becomes clear why the bestsellers, ridiculed in the Preface to the *Lyrical Ballads*, are excluded from the need for protection; they do not acculturate as literature does. By way of anticipatory example for this point, Wordsworth had pointed out that authors with copyright protection (his example is "Mr. Wordsworth") do not deny to educators the ability to extract their work and republish it in a form convenient for teaching. In fact, he suggests that authors are more willing than publishers, since, in another example, "the publisher of [Mr. Wordsworth's] works threatened [the editor of a sonnet collection that contained 57 pages out of 300 of Wordsworth's poetry] with an application to the Court of Chancery for an injunction," but "Mr Wordsworth's immediate reply" caused the issue to be dropped (*Prose* 3: 312).

The letter to Talfourd, published in the *Morning Post*, outlined Wordsworth's argument on copyright and explained his reluctance to petition with a rhetorical feint belied by his torrent of private letters: "I am loth to think so unfavourably of Parliament as to deem that it requires petitions from authors as a ground for granting them a privilege, the justice of which is so obvious" (*Prose* 3: 313). The term *justice*, underscored by being "obvious," transforms what was a personal petition into Wordsworth's granting Parliament the ability to perform its task, the distribution of justice. He further defers by claiming that the bill at issue does not address the true nature of the argument, that literary property ought to be perpetual, as it was at common law.[9] The letter serves as evidence so that Talfourd will not be "treated as a volunteer intruding without wish or sanction openly expressed by any one of the class whose rights and interests you have so much to your honour stepped forward to maintain" (*Prose* 3: 314). Wordsworth's rhetoric obscures his personal interest, and positions himself as outside the skirmish—since only perpetual copyright would truly address the transcendent value of poetry.

Given Wordsworth's care in continually revising his work, his anxiety involves not only how much money his family will make from the *Prelude* but whether his family will be able to preserve the relationships of his poems against the literary marketplace's ability to dissolve his canon and open up interpretive gaps. Such gaps would not merely allow misreading but would make the correspondence of labor between reader and writer impossible. In "A Poet to his Grandchild: Sequel to 'Plea for Authors,'" Wordsworth uses the sonnet form explicitly to associate economic and literary motives. In the octave, he imagines his grandchild in want, the consequence of which is that his further descendants will be "left unfit . . . / even to feel or understand / My simplest Lay" (4–6). The sestet turns to the "Statutes of the Land," which, like Wordsworth's poetic work, need constant revision to approximate "nature's claim / Or Reason's" (8–11). From this broad vision, the sonnet closes on "hopes spun in timid line" (11), a phrase which shifts to a vision of cottage economy while punning on the poetic "line." The ultimate effect is to render interdependent the fates of poetic and genetic progeny.[10]

I am not concerned with how convincing these arguments were, a difficult historical question since the bill was withdrawn in 1838 and a variant of it was passed in 1842. Rather, I wish to stress that Wordsworth's campaign solidified the transcendent vision of the poet, but paradoxically located that vision squarely within the marketplace. This position revised the Wordsworthian view in the *Lyrical Ballads*, a revision that confronted the paradoxical requirement of transcendence itself—the necessity of a specific historical space to transcend that, unless shaped actively by the poet, would be structured through other mechanisms, such as law, economics, and industry. I am not suggesting that Wordsworth's poetry fails because its transcendence is a fiction, but rather that the fiction of that transcendence is precisely the space that permits the labor of the reader, who struggles to rewrite the poem not merely against the critic but against the author himself, in whose name the reader labors.

In part, the legacy of this strategy has been a transcendent discourse without political efficacy, and even, within a New Critical school that persists within the wider culture, without agency. It is, in an anti-Foucaultian sense, the death of the author by his enshrinement. Richard Posner, whom I have positioned as an heir to Francis Jeffrey, contends (not alone) that literary and legal texts are essentially different in that the former should be read without regard to the author's intentions, while readings of the latter should be guided primarily by authorial intention. Posner understands Wordsworth's "A Slumber Did My Spirit Seal" as a failed "hymn to pantheism," but suggests that if "we want to save it as an object of aesthetic value" our options include declaring that Wordsworth "intended to write a good poem rather than to spill his guts" (*Law and Literature* 234). This sense of "saving" resembles an aesthetic safe deposit box that signifies value but shrouds the valued object. The goal, "to write a good poem," prepares for the reader who "as he lays down the book, will be able to cry out with a tranquil soul, 'All this is only literature'" (Sartre, *What Is Literature* 28).

Posner offers the following hypothetical situation: "Imagine asking Wordsworth when he was alive whether he insisted that 150 years hence *A Slumber Did My Spirit Seal* be firmly understood as advocating pantheism, even if, as a result, people stopped reading the poem. I expect he would have answered that he was indifferent to the precise conditions for the survival of the poem for such an immensely long time" (*Law and Literature* 235). This hypothesis is difficult to respond to, first, because it glides from a reading that rejects Wordsworth's intended pantheism to a description of that reading as merely shifting "the *precise* conditions for the survival of the poem." A response is difficult, secondly, because Wordsworth did not intend "A Slumber" as "*advocating* pantheism." The poem poses a difference between "earthly years" (4) and "earth's diurnal course" (7) and, as Jerome McGann points out, "These are a set of human thoughts which lie too deep for tears."[11] McGann identifies "A Slumber" as a quintessential romantic work, a miniature which illustrates that "amidst the tottering structures of early nineteenth-century Europe, poetry asserted the integrity of the biosphere and the inner, spiritual self, both of which were believed to transcend the age's troubling doctrinal conflicts and ideological shifts. . . . Ecological Nature is the locus of what is stable and orderly, and it is related to Imagination as a set of vital hieroglyphs is related to an interpretive key" (*Romantic Ideology* 67–68, 69).

To respond in general to Posner's question, however, from Wordsworth's perspective: a poem not understood in the sense intended by the author was not the author's poem at all. Further, Posner posits the poet's authorizing a nonintentionalist reading, an authorization which can carry weight only from an intentionalist perspective; thus, encoded into his denial of intentionalism is a romantic assertion of the author as self-decomposing, as losing identity at the boundary of his text. It is, I suggest, deeply ironic that Posner's reading suffers from the same slumber—of not recognizing an author as an earthly thing—from which the speaker of the lyric is woken by death.

The Nature of Death

A natural-law theorist might attempt to illustrate our sense of death by Lear's observation near the end of Shakespeare's *King Lear:* "I know when one is dead, and when one lives" (V iii 261). Part of what is heartbreaking about this scene, however, is that the line—especially as performed on a stage in which the body of Cordelia is literally alive and as qualified by Lear's decision to use a scientific test of whether Cordelia's "breath will mist" a looking glass (V iii 263)—is false. False not merely for Lear, but for the audience. The basic truth of death, under the right conditions, is an interpretive problem (as Christianity posits in its core event), and such conditions will appertain at any moment language is summoned. Nature does not tell us of natural law, but, as Wordsworth's *Excursion* argues, our inventions of natural law tell us about nature. Wordsworth, in the slow process of recovering from his daughter Dora's death in 1847, ventured to visit his son Willy, and, describing Willy's wife, invokes the final scene of *King Lear:* "Her manners are quiet, gentle and mild, her voice sweet, which we have upon high authority is 'an excellent thing in woman'" (quoted in Moorman II: 602). The process of grieving over the death of a daughter involves a rewriting that death, complicating it by merging it with sentiments for a daughter-in-law, whose specific status within the family is only by virtue of law. The sad, if not tragic, overtones of this letter are both distanced and enforced by Wordsworth's misquotation (Cordelia's voice was "soft," not "sweet"). Wordsworth, who had been treated as something of a national relic for the last decade, could not miss that in placing his daughter/daughter-in-law as Cordelia, he positioned himself as Lear near the end of the play.[12]

Death cannot be rendered natural, or rather, death is rendered unnatural by its human particularity. More generally, *The Excursion* exploits the terms of the *Recluse*, "Man," "Nature," and "Human Life," not to demonstrate the transparency of any of these terms but the reverse: to demonstrate that they only arise in the mediation of language, human interaction, and political struggle. At a more local level, the significance of the parishioners buried in the Church-yard resides in how they are talked about, how their lives are reconstructed into narrative. The deaths in this work—the Solitary's wife, the parishioners, Margaret—are not deflected, but are subsumed into larger narrations, and poetry itself becomes the term mediating the naturalness of Death and the unnaturalness of any particular death.[13]

Let me put the matter at its most paradoxical to generations of Wordsworth readers: Wordsworth is less the poet of nature than is Francis Jeffrey. In Wordsworth, nature is a mediated term, one constructed within a debate of institutional jurisdiction. Jeffrey, by contrast, accepts the hegemonic position of law and legal metaphors, out of which he constructs a human nature that is immune to history and becomes the measure of poetry. Stanley Fish, considering a contemporary natural law theorist, points out that all theories of nature move at some point to a grounding in convention.[14]

In Wordsworth's "A Slumber Did My Spirit Seal," the significance of the rocks and stones is itself part of the mystery which law and science confront; the decision to apply one mode *a priori* from Wordsworth's perspective is to surrender the mystery and complexity of experience. Poetry, by intensifying the real language of men, resists such an *a priori* categorization. As Fish would be quick to point out, however, Wordsworth himself achieves this perspective only by constituting another set of interpretive strategies for his community; these interpretive strategies are often appropriated from the very fields of discourse—law, science, history—that romantic poetry seeks to master. This appropriation, in turn, forced Wordsworth's poetry to rely on the very structures it attempts to transcend as the ground of its intelligibility.

William Wordsworth did, as Klancher suggests (*Reading Audiences* 150), find his audience—and not posthumously. In the late 1830s, Wordsworth's poetry earned him fifteen hundred pounds (Owen, "Costs"). While a certain portion of this must be accounted for by purchasers who placed Wordsworth's complete works on their shelves beside Milton and Shakespeare as artifacts of culture, Henry Taylor's review (*Quarterly Review* 1841) of "The Sonnets of William Wordsworth" (1838) shows that Wordsworth was being read, and on his own terms. Taylor, for example, reads the sonnets in relation to *The Excursion*: "Taking the 8th Book of the 'Excursion' for a connecting commentary, the reader may be led by the Sonnets to trace the course of political liberty through some of its leading consequences in our own country" ("Wordsworth's Sonnets," *Quarterly Review* 69 [1841]: 24). Taylor interprets "The world is too much with us . . ." as a critique of the economics in which industry is balanced not by rest and repose, but by an "excitement of another kind—the excitement of spending," a word blending the waste of oneself with the acquisition of objects.

The conclusion of Taylor's essay introduces the sonnet sequence "On the Punishment of Death," which Wordsworth would publish under his own name for the first time in 1842. This joint venture, perhaps the first time any of Wordsworth's writings appeared originally in a review, and perhaps the first time original poetry appeared in the *Quarterly*, signals a shift from Wordsworth's earlier collaboration; here, Wordsworth deliberately allows his poems to be interrupted by historical and aesthetic remarks.[15] These sonnets overtly enter a political debate which Taylor outlines.[16] Taylor comments that Wordsworth offers his opinions "in poetry with as deep a solicitude as to their justness as if they were delivered from the bench or the pulpit" (69: 41). The first sonnet, "Suggested by the View of Lancaster Castle (on the Road from the South)," opens with a description of the beauty of the view: "This spot—at once unfolding sight so fair / Of sea and land . . ." (1–2). The diction here is typical for even the early Wordsworth, but the octave ends by asking a question that marks the incongruity between the sight and its effect on human beings: "Why bears it then the name of 'Weeping Hill'?" (8).

Wordsworth's strategy reverses the procedures of the "Poems on the Naming of Places," in which naming is used to make the "natural appearance" of a place evident. The sestet answers the question of whether Lancaster prison is the site of "lingering durance or quick death with shame" (11), and this spot represents the prisoners' first view of their future. It is a view that is, in a sense, not seen: "Their first look—blinded as tears fell in showers / Shed on their chains; and hence that doleful name" (13–14). Like the prisoners who are blinded, the reader cannot see the castle, until Wordsworth makes it visible through the explanation of the name, just as he had with the private site of Michael's sheep-fold. The arguments Wordsworth presents for capital punishment are by now, and were likely by then, platitudinous, but from a critical viewpoint, the relation these poems develop among the triad of state, people, and poet represents the end of the professional trajectory traced in the previous chapters.

The first two sonnets develop sympathy for the criminal, but equally suggest that the limits of that sympathy can be effective in ultimately eliminating capital punishment: "Strike not from Law's firm hand that awful rod, / But leave it thence to drop from lack of use" ("Conclusion" 12–13). The refusal to revise becomes its own revision. The final poem, "Apology" (which follows "Conclusion"), justifies the poet's turn to such a subject:

> The formal World relaxes her cold chain
> For One who speaks in numbers; ampler scope
> His utterance finds;
> . . . .
> And, serving Truth, the heart more strongly beats
> Against all barriers which his labour meets.
>
> (1–3, 6–7)

The image is of the poet and indeed all human beings as prisoners of the "formal World" but by appropriating form, the poet gains a freedom which is simultaneously a responsibility. Wordsworth does not seek to free us from a world too much with us, but to make the character of that "too much"—a by-product of necessary social institutions such as law and economy—apparent as, paradoxically, the lack which only the poet can fill.

NOTES

Introduction

1. Minow's perspective that legal discourse constitutes a mode of story-telling recognizes that, in part, the story is told by submerging narrative features within assumptions of rationality. Richard Posner, for example, begins his analysis of law and economics by stating that rationality is "a general and dominant characteristic of social behavior." At times, however, especially those in which rationality, the master narrative, is threatened, narrative features—metaphor, heteroglossia, complicated tense shifts, constructing hypothetical spaces, generating suspense—emerge; here Posner is discussing the right of privacy: "It is as if the [Supreme] Court had become infected with the student radicalism of the late 1960s and early 1970s, with its emphasis on candor at the expense of privacy, its slogans of 'doing your own thing' and 'letting it all hang out.'" (*The Economics of Justice* 345; note omitted). For critiques of Posner, see Martha Minow, *Making All the Difference* 159–63 and Robin West, "Authority, Autonomy, and Choice."

2. Bernard Jackson has suggested the extent to which Anglo-American law, at least as understood in the positivist tradition of Hart and Dworkin, should be regarded as a distinctive, and self-distinguishing, semiotic system: "Despite claims that the specificity of law resides only at the pragmatic level, both syntactic and deep semantic features of legal discourse stand out as peculiar to it. Legal discourse claims to regulate its own creation, and to practice self-interpretation. Monosemicity and restricted connotations are characteristic claims of legal discourse. The capacity to create 'inferior' semiotic objects, the special claims of the legal *acteur*, and the relation of 'recognition' to 'competence' also emerge from the Greimasian analysis as contributing to the specific appearance of law" (*Semiotics and Legal Theory* 283–84).

3. W. Schuchtler, quoted in Jurgen Habermas, *The Theory of Communicative Action*, vol. 1: *Reason and the Rationalization of Society* 258. Habermas suggests that, for Weber, when "modern structures of consciousness can be embodied in a legal system such as bourgeois private law," that law can be "distinguished primarily by three formal properties; positivity, legalism, and formality." Through "formality,"

"Modern law defines domains in which individuals may legitimately exercise free choice" (259).

4. Habermas argues that, although the tendency toward formalization "can be observed already in late medieval faculties of law," it "appears very unevenly in the legal developments of different nations"; and consequently, its development cannot be explained by primary reference to "its internal systemization" (*Reason* 256).

5. The particular forms of ideological transmission chosen by institutions are partly determined by the necessity of preserving power within the duplicating structure itself (the courts or the publishing industry), partly determined by the need to disguise this preserving function (by reference to, say, constitutional rights or a standard of taste), and partly determined by the material available to meet or assimilate threats to that power. External review may be substantially prevented by an aura of secrecy and difficulty, often an artifact of the professional language. Jeremy Bentham, for example, believed that William Blackstone's rhetorical strategies simultaneously equated and distinguished "law as it is" and "law as it ought to be" and argued that the result was an insistence on blind obedience by nonlawyers disguised as moral behavior. Bentham describes judicial procedure thus: "If he meets with a decision he does not like, it is well: he may overthrow it at his pleasure. Only let him be sure he does not say it was a bad law: let him call it no law, and everything is as it should be" ("A Comment on the Commentaries" 201). See also H. L. A. Hart, "Positivism and the Separation of Law and Morals" (1958) 51–52. The potential for internal critique in law may be limited by educational and licensing procedures; Duncan Kennedy, a Critical Legal Studies theorist, observes: "Implicit loyalty oaths have always been a condition of admission to the inner circles of legality. The enterprise of merely understanding the legal order is not likely to be taken up by a person radically opposed to the status quo. Opposition to the status quo does not easily survive the kind of identification with the legal system that seems to be a psychological precondition for really understanding it" (Duncan Kennedy, "The Structure of Blackstone's *Commentaries*" 218).

6. Tom Tyler, in an extended study of Chicago residents, found two main criteria for why people report that they obey the law. The first is procedural fairness, that is, the perception that the courts and police have acted in a fair way (apprising of rights; adequate opportunities to cross-examine, etc.), regardless of whether their decisions or the underlying law were fair. Second, respondents emphasized a normative perspective; that is, they matched legal proceedings to the norms that derived from a variety of institutional sources (*Why People Obey the Law* 161–66 and passim). These findings correspond to the Weberian conditions Habermas outlines for an authority to be recognized as legitimate: "(*a*) the normative order must be established positively and (*b*) those legally associated [with the authority] must believe in its legality, that is, in the formally correct procedure for the creation and application of laws. . . . [Habermas adds a third condition that] grounds for the legitimiz-

ing force of this formal procedure must be given" (Jurgen Habermas, *Legitimation Crisis* 98).

7. In *Hanover v. Ruch, 1991*, the Tennessee Supreme Court recently abolished the common-law tort of criminal conversation because it "is founded upon a property-theory [of marriage] which has no place in contemporary society"; in summarizing the history of criminal conversation, Justice Anderson turned to *Don Juan:* "In 1818 Lord Byron described the English judicial process of evaluating 'what a wife is worth'" (894–95). He then quotes Canto I, 13–14. This offers a clear, if somewhat superficial, illustration of a comment Stephen Greenblatt has made regarding New Historicist practices: "We need to develop terms to describe the ways in which material—here official documents, private papers, newspaper clippings, and so forth—is transferred from one discursive sphere to another and becomes aesthetic property. It would, I think, be a mistake to regard this process as uni-directional—from social discourse to aesthetic discourse—not only because the aesthetic discourse in this case [the literary narrative of Mailer/Abbott/state execution/murder] is so entirely bound up with capitalist venture but because the social discourse is already charged with aesthetic energies" ("Towards a Poetics of Culture" 11).

8. Justice John Paul Stevens has suggested that the study of poetry, and lyric poetry in particular, is the "best preparation for the study of law" (George Gopen, "Rhyme and Reason" 333).

9. For Addison's articulation of an explicit relation between the social audience of polite society and the legal institution of the Assize, see *Spectator* No. 122 (20 July 1710).

1. The Poet and Professional Patriarchy

1. Paul Fry, catching the contentiousness of the recent debate on Wordsworth and history (the roots of which are in Thomas De Quincey's and William Hazlitt's equally contentious remarks on the poet) comments: "Poetry is not, as it is so often said to be, a critique or evasion or suppression of *history*. . . . it is a critique, rather, and by no means an evasion or suppression, of *the historical*, of that will to explain which occupies the symbolic and iconic powers of language" ("The Diligence of Desire" 162).

2. Robert Rehder has argued that the "ten subjects" Wordsworth contemplates as the subject of his epic in the *Prelude* "reveal a great concern for history as a form, and Wordsworth in this poem becomes a historian" (*Wordsworth and the Beginnings of Modern Poetry* 72).

3. James Johnson provides an array of supporting quotations, including Swift, Johnson, Burke, and Mary Wortley Montagu; see The Formation of English Neo-Classical Thought chap. 2.

4. For a general history of historiography, see Ernst Breisach, *Historiography: Ancient, Medieval, & Modern*. Chapter 13 discusses the "eighteenth-century quest for a new historiography," while subsequent chapters explore the relation between historical narrative and various European nationalisms, with some attention to legal implications.

5. Bernard Jackson rehearses a "host of powerful devices, symbolic and otherwise" that project the "image of the unity of the English legal system"; in particular, he points to the metonymic accumulation of "The Law," derived from discrete and contradictory acts of legal and police action (*Law, Fact, Narrative Coherence* 133–32). Such a pervasive position has a history, largely indebted to the rise of *stare decisis*, made possible, according to Francis Bacon, by Coke's *Institutes* (J. C. Gray, *The Nature and Sources of Law* 448–67; Catherine Bowen, *Francis Bacon* 140).

6. Lipking continues: "In terms of jurisprudence, much becomes clear: the desire to preserve all documents regardless of their immediate relevance; the reliance upon ceaseless recital and revaluation of precedents; the urge to end every dispute by delivering a final verdict. The *History of Music* never allows us to forget how closely contemporary Hawkins was to Blackstone" (Lawrence Lipking, *The Ordering of the Arts in Eighteenth-Century England* 249, note omitted).

7. Clare Simmons, *Reversing the Conquest* 113. This book explicates the Whig interest in the history of the Norman Conquest.

8. See Clare Simmons, *Partial History* chap. 1. Simmons demonstrates the complex relationship between the political goals and historical productions of Victorian historians by showing the existence of a tory theory of history in debate with the whig notion that has subsequently become dominant.

9. A corollary of this position on history is David Haney's observation that "for Wordsworth, law is both a system of representation and a living, commanding voice, both an epistemological system of signs and an incarnational event" (*William Wordsworth and the Hermeneutics of Incarnation* 209).

10. James Chandler offers the following catalogue of a period Wordsworth claimed was barren of events: "his involvement with the French Royalists in Orleans, with Michel Beaupuy, and with the revolutionary societies in Paris; his complicated and painful affair with Annette Vallon in Blois and their natural daughter; . . . his plan to form a radical newspaper in London with William Mathews; his friendship with William Godwin, England's most important radical theorist of the mid-1790s; not to mention his friendships with Coleridge, Southey, Lamb, Thelwall, and others equally well known by 1801" (*Wordsworth's Second Nature* 8, note omitted). Wordsworth signals a disjunction between his life and its history in the disclaimer that "the history of my life is very short"; this temporal short-circuit by the 31-year-old is further emphasized by the overall route of his life, which circumscribes the extensive travel: "I was born at Cockermouth, about twenty-five miles from the place where I now dwell" (LEY 327).

11. For a sampling of "new historical" work, see many of the reviews (and the books reviewed) in *The Wordsworth Circle* 19:4 (1988), most centrally, Alan Liu's review of David Simpson's *Wordsworth's Historical Imagination*, which includes a list of the most "obvious" critics associated with "Romantic New Historicism" (180). For earlier work, see Simpson, *Wordsworth's Historical Imagination* 20. Peter Manning's analysis of "Poor Susan" and "The Solitary Reaper," with its careful attention to previous critics, underscores both the continuities and disjunctions of various new historicist, older historical, and nonhistoricist readings (*Reading Romantics* chaps. 11, 13). For a challenge concerned with New Historicist readings by "the sons of Karl [i.e., Marx] rather than with the sons (and daughters) of Michel [i.e., Foucault]," see M. H. Abrams's attack on Heather Glen, Marjorie Levinson, and Jerome McGann in "On the Politics of *Lyrical Ballads*" (*Doing Things with Texts* 364–91; quotation from 365).

12. To George Beaumont, Wordsworth offers a *biographia economical* that entwines the Lonsdale debt, Wordsworth's loan to his brother John to outfit his trading ship, and the income received from the *Lyrical Ballads*. It begins: "My Father, who was an Attorney of considerable eminence, died intestate" (LEY 546, 23 February 1805).

13. Marks of this reinscription have been delineated by Susan Eilenberg in her discussion of Wordsworth's proprietary conception of the second edition of the *Lyrical Ballads* (*Strange Power of Speech* chap. 1).

14. Bateson overstates the case, since Wordsworth mentions his father in the *Prelude* I (1805), discussed below, in "To a Butterfly" and "The Sparrow's Nest" (1802; pub. 1807) and in at least two of the Itinerary Poems of 1833, most notably the sonnet "In sight of the Town of Cockermouth," with the explanatory note "(Where the Author was born, and his Father's remains are laid)." That poem opens: "A point of life between my Parent's dust, / And yours, my buried Little-ones! am I." References to Wordsworth's father in William and Dorothy's letters, excepting discussion of the Lonsdale debt, are rare. One might sense a running anti-allusion in the poetry of dead and abandoned parents. In almost every case, the father is either the only parent who or the first one who dies or abandons the family; an exception is the Vaudracour and Julia episode of the *Prelude*.

15. J. G. A. Pocock recognizes two trends in the historical conceptions of property leading to the eighteenth-century notions: "First and foremost, there is the tradition begun by Aristotle and continued by Aquinas, in which property appears as a moral and political phenomenon. . . . Property was both an extension and a prerequisite of personality." The citizen, in this model, possessed property for an autonomy necessary to civic behavior and emphatically not "in order to engage in trade, exchange or profit." Pocock sees as the other face, of equal importance to understanding property, the "language of jurisprudence, inaugurated by the Roman civilians, strongly present in Aquinas, and carried on by a succession of jurists and

natural-law theorists into the age of Locke." In this view, property "was defined less as that which makes you what you are than as that to which you have a right." This model was less hostile to trade since "property became a system of legally defined relations between persons and things, or between persons through things." With the "collapse of civil authority" and the attempt to reconceptualize it after 1649, Thomas Hobbes came to represent the latter view and James Harrington the former (J. G. A Pocock, *Virtue, Commerce, and History* 103–6).

16. Thomas De Quincey describes Lowther as "a true feudal chieftain" ("On Wordsworth's Poetry" 149). The DNB quotes the following couplets from the *Rolliad:*

> E'en by the elements his pow'r confess'd
> Of mines and boroughs Lonsdale stands possess'd
> And one sad servitude alike denotes
> The slave that labours and the slave that votes.

See Joanne Dann, "Some Notes on the Relationship between the Wordsworth and the Lowther Families" 80–82, for details of John Wordsworth's work: "The election of 1768 [in which John Wordsworth was almost certainly involved] was the eighteenth-century substitute for armed skirmishes between opposing lords of the manor" (80). She also notes that he aided in "serving some 400 ejectments of tenants" in 1769 (82). Stephen Gill, citing Dann, describes John Wordsworth's tasks as including "dealing with grievances, and keeping loyalties in good repair" (*William Wordsworth: A Life* 14).

17. See Thomas Hartwell Horne, *The Lakes of Lancashire, Westmorland, and Cumberland* 28; Thomas West, *Guide to the Lakes in Cumberland, Westmoreland and Lancashire* 78–81. Of the fifteen places named in the letter to Taylor, only Grasmere is underlined, a graphological choice consistent with guidebook italics.

Gill points out that Wilberforce had compared Grasmere to "Rasselas's happy Valley," and Gray had called it a "little unsuspected paradise" (*A Life* 179, note omitted). Wordsworth, who knew that Thomas West's *Guide to the Lakes* made heavy use of Thomas Gray's descriptions of the lakes, including Grasmere (79), perhaps had on his mind the future fame the place would achieve from the first part of *The Recluse*, "Home at Grasmere." In 1790, the popular writer Charlotte Smith published *Ethelinde, or the Recluse of the Lake* which is set in the ruined and fictitious Grasmere Abbey; Kenneth Johnston suggests that Wordsworth may have derived his title for *The Recluse* from this work (*Wordsworth and* The Recluse 13). The paradisal description of Grasmere through the mediation of tourism and poetic language was made possible through such capitalistic mechanisms as enclosures, increased production expectations, and aggressive legal management of property. Grasmere remains quaint, to mark progress elsewhere and to provide a space of leisure that would not impede labor. While Cockermouth, as a "considerable borough and market-town, which is excellently situated for trade and manufactures," continued to grow in population and industry due principally to coal mining (Horne, *The Lakes* 56), Grasmere remained relatively stable, though increasingly popular for tourists (Kenneth MacLean, *The Agrarian Age* 91), as its use for West's frontispiece suggests. As David Simpson remarks: "Wordsworth had a very sophisticated though often implicit conviction about the human imagination as best thriving in a subsistence, agrarian economy of owner-occupiers. This ideal—for that is what it was—is a fusion of poverty and possessiveness, and work and leisure" (*Historical Imagination* 47).

18. On August 6–7, 1787, Dorothy reiterated to Jane Pollard: "My Br Wm . . . wishes very much to be a Lawyer if his health will permit" (LEY 7). Although the phrase "if my/his health will permit" is a common expression, it remains interesting that Dorothy established the same condition for Wordsworth's becoming a lawyer as he would set to "devote [his] life to literature."

19. As critics, biographers, and tourists have remarked, John Wordsworth's house (owned by Lowther) was, and is, "the most imposing dwelling in the main street of Cockermouth" (Gill, *A Life* 14; see also Moorman I: 5). The specificity of place in the 1805 passage is emphasized also by the description of the river "travelling . . . Near my 'sweet Birthplace,'" a line changed to "winding . . . Where I was looking on, a babe in arms" in 1850 *Prelude*. Though more explicitly and typographically marked in the first text, in both versions, Wordsworth is citing "Frost at Midnight," Coleridge's distinctly fatherly poem to his child.

20. First published in *Poems, in Two Volumes*, the version quoted here is from 1845. Both "The Sparrow's Nest" and the "Was it for this" passage end with Wordsworth far from the father's house; "Was it for this" concludes with the image of Wordsworth as an Indian who "from my mother's hut / had run abroad . . . a naked savage" (*Prelude* I 302–4).

21. In the 1799 version of the *Prelude*, nothing precedes "was it for this" (DC MS 15; 1), and so what is offered as a totalizing, vague anxiety (marked by the blank space and uncapitalized "w" that starts the half-line) in 1799 is given economic shape in its reworking.

22. Both Klancher, who cites part of this quotation, and Bakhtin insist on historically situating this point. Klancher locates the heteroglossic moment at the rise of the great reviewing industry following the French Revolution: "The late eighteenth century ushered in a confusing, unsettled world of reading and writing. Ideas, signs, and styles had to cross new cultural and social boundaries" (Jon Klancher, *The Making of the English Reading Audiences, 1790–1832* 3). See also Sartre's chapter in *The Critique of Dialectical Reason*, "Human Relations as a Mediation between Different Sectors of Materiality": "[Words] carry the projects of the Other into me and they carry my own projects into the Other. Language might well be studied on the same

lines as money: as circulating, inert materiality, which unifies dispersal; in fact this is partly what philology does. Words live off the death of men, they come together through men; whenever I form a sentence its meaning escapes from me, is stolen from me; meanings are changed *for everyone* by each speaker and each day; the meanings of the very words in my mouth are changed by others" (98).

23. In 1765–69, William Blackstone published the first volume of his *Commentaries on the Laws of England*, in which he boasted that the study of law "is the proper accomplishment of every gentleman and scholar; an highly useful, I had almost said essential, part of liberal and polite education. . . . [It] will go hand in hand with their [gentlemen's] other pursuits: it will obstruct none of them; it will ornament and assist them all" (1: 6 and 26). The work's reception, and Blackstone's corresponding rise in the legal community to the Queen's Solicitor, suggests its success. Mansfield, among other judges, praised the *Commentaries* from the bench, and Gibbons reports having read it three times (Holdsworth, *A History of English Law* 12: 702–37). Byron includes it in his list of books he had read before the age of fifteen, suggesting minimally that he recognized that he should have read it (Leslie Marchand, *Byron: A Portrait* 29).

24. "[W]ith what greater success could you carry on a suit against him, with his immense fortune, than against his predecessor? You will reply to this perhaps that Lord Lowther is a man of a fair character, and would have a suit conducted in a fair way. But will his agents Attornies and people about him be men of honour and principle? . . .

"What success was a poor man ever known to have against a very rich one in a Law suit—especially of a complex kind?" (LEY 370, 24 June 1802).

25. Wordsworth quotes Richard's letter back to him: "You say '*If I had the least doubt about the proper steps to be taken, I am sure I would instantly ask your advice.*' This I approve; but remember that it may happen to be a great misfortune, that you *have no* doubts about the proper method to be taken" (LEY 371–72).

26. In this letter, Wordsworth cannot resist adding, with the deference implied by redundant qualifiers, the suggestion that Richard prepare a brief prose *lyrical ballad:* "It might be proper perhaps respectfully to remind him that no money can ever make us complete amends for the loss which we have sustained; I do not speak of the hardships and anxieties &c these I leave entirely out of the question, but the mere comparative value of the money to us now when set against the service it might have done us 15 years back" (LEY 382–83).

27. A central argument of the "master pamphlets" involved the thematic relationship between rights and an economic system. Edmund Burke resorted to the language of the Rights of Man in order to underscore that "men have a right to live by that rule [the rule of law]; they have a right to justice; . . . to the fruits of their industry; and to the means of making their industry fruitful. They have a

right to the acquisitions of their parents . . . In this partnership [of society] all men have equal rights; but not to equal things. He that has but five shillings in the partnership, has as good a right to it, as he that has five hundred pounds has to his larger portion" (*Reflections on the Revolution in France* 149–50).

Like Thomas Paine and William Godwin, Mary Wollstonecraft understood "rights" differently. Locke, she writes, "recommended in a more methodical manner religious toleration, and analyzed the principles of civil liberty: for in his definition of Liberty we find the elements of *The Declaration of the Rights of Man*, which, in spite of the fatal errours of ignorance, and the perverse obstinacy of selfishness, is now converting sublime theories into practical truths" (*A Historical and Moral View of . . . the French Revolution* 16, notes omitted).

28. The collusion/collision of discourses, and Wordsworth's manipulation of that intersection, provides a useful test case for Louis Montrose's observation that "to speak of the social production of 'literature' or of any particular text is to signify not only that it is socially produced but also that it is socially productive—that it is a product of work and that it performs work in the process of being written, enacted, or read" ("Professing the Renaissance" 23). The characterization of writing as a particular kind of work, namely professional, is an enabling 18th-century development for Wordsworth's career.

29. In a similar displacement, Don José's death and subsequent probate replaced a divorce action:

> He [Don José] died: and most unluckily, because
> According to all hints I could collect
> From counsel learnèd in those kinds of laws
> (Although their talk's obscure and circumspect),
> His death contrived to spoil a charming cause.
>
> (I 33, 1–5)

Typically, Byron shows his aptitude with the "talk" he indicates as "obscure," by working in a variation on "contrivance," a legal term for certain deceptions. In *Don Juan* XI, he demonstrates a similar facility in criminal "flash" as it interrupts, and interprets, Juan's panegyric on British Constitutionalism (see Paul Elledge, "Never Say(ing) Goodbye" 19–22 for a contextualization on Byron's use of flash within his pattern of heteroglossic hijinks).

30. To demonstrate that he is "not actuated by any prejudice," he "*ha[s] signed the permissions & sent them to London addressed to Mr. Murray.*" Byron could easily predict his publisher's response to Galignani; Murray's refusal included the observation that "for the copyright of these works, which you print for nothing, I have given the author more than 10,000 pounds" (Byron, *What Comes Uppermost* 57).

31. Wordsworth complicates these lines by echoing them in a retrospective passage which locates the victory of the French Revolution "Not in Utopia,"

> But in the very world which is the world
> Of all of us,—the place in which, in the end,
> We find our happiness, or not at all!
> (*Prelude* XI 724–28)

32. See Arthur Beatty, *William Wordsworth:* "The play came from an impulse similar to those which produced all Wordsworth's most characteristic poetry—from that set of interests which he states so clearly in the Prefaces of 1800 and 1815, and which he states and illustrates with such fulness in *The Prelude* and *The Excursion*" (35). Writing about *Guilt and Sorrow*, Wordsworth explained its "object is partly to expose the vices of the penal law and the calamities of war as they affect individuals" (LEY 145). See Donald Hayden, *After Conflict, Quiet* for a succinct statement of the Godwinian influence on *The Borderers* (82–85) and its connection to *Guilt and Sorrow*.

33. In the later version, Rivers/Oswald's dupe Marmaduke approves the sentiment by framing this speech within the discourse of jurisprudence:

> These walls shall witness it—from first to last
> He shall reveal himself.
> . . . .
> here
> The truth shall be laid open, his guilt proved
> Before her face.
> (*The Borderers* 594–95, 599–601)

In both versions, Mortimer earlier laments the problem of jurisdiction: "There is no earthly law / That measures crimes like his" (*A Tragedy*, II i 34–35; *The Borderers*, slightly revised, 582–83).

34. Marilyn Butler describes Herbert as "a father-figure who might stand generally for the *ancien regime* or more specifically for Louis XVI himself" (*Romantics, Rebels and Reactionaries* 65). But see John Turner, *Wordsworth: Play and Politics* 65–72 for an argument for more generalized referent.

35. Hayden notes that the play articulates two distinct theories of property that straddled Godwin and Burke, but also "Lord Lonsdale [who] remained representative of the cruel hand of aristocratic tyranny" and "the Calvert bequest [that] involved Wordsworth, however slightly, in the defense of possessions" (*After Conflict* 93).

36. See David Simpson, *Irony and Authority in Romantic Poetry*, for a reading that suggests the limits of this transformation, as the poet's act of naming "simply repeats in finer tones the prior nomination of the old man as an emblem of idleness. The gesture of self-correction is thus surreptitiously implicated in the same problems as determined the initial crime" (74). Although "crime" is, of course, not precise, it neatly recognizes the public domain in which this seemingly private action occurs. Eilenberg sees the naming as possibly "a refusal to acknowledge the

landscape's potential meaning" (*Strange Power* 81), a reading which again points to the domains by which land and landscape are given meaning that pressure the poetic act of naming. For my analysis of the "Poems on the Naming of Places" see chapter 6 below.

37. Coleridge, writing to William Blackwood in 1819, explicitly links Wordsworth's labor-intensive composing to an expectation of payment: "I may adopt the words which Mr. Wordsworth once used to Longman: 'You pay others, Sir, for what they write; but you must pay *me* likewise for what I do not write: for it is in this [i.e., the omissions, erasures &c] that cost me most both Time & Toil'" (quoted in Lee Erickson, "The Egoism of Authorship" 43, his brackets).

2. Law, Labor, and the Shepherd's Household: "Michael"

1. See Peter Manning, "*Michael*, Luke, and Wordsworth" (*Reading Romantics* 41–42 and notes). For a reading that links these biblical textual precursors to "spiritual economics," see Marjorie Levinson, *Wordsworth's Great Period Poems* chap. 2. Kurt Heinzelman, *The Economics of the Imagination* 215–23, associates the poem as an "act of compensation" with Wordsworth's "Labor Theory." Susan Eilenberg adds another dimension to the economics of "Michael" by using its displacement of "Christabel" from the *Lyrical Ballads* to establish Wordsworth's sense of textual possession, a reading supported by the drafts of "Michael" written, like portions of *Home at Grasmere*, on "STC's *Poems on Various Subjects*" (Butler and Green xxiv–xxv) and by Dorothy Wordsworth's remark that nearly a month after it was "Determined not to print *Christabel*," "Wm. composed without much success at the sheepfold," and then, after Coleridge joined them for dinner, they read aloud *Ruth* and *Christabel* (*Journals* 1:64, 68–69).

2. Peter Gabel and Jay Feinman point out that "between the latter part of the eighteenth century and the middle of the nineteenth century, both the economic and political foundations of eighteenth-century contract law were, in Marx's phrase, 'burst asunder.' In this period the system of economic and social relations known as free-market capitalism achieved a full development begun several centuries earlier, and the political climate was explosively transformed in the service of those social and economic developments with the aid of violent revolutions in America and Western Europe. These changes dramatically transformed the life situations of people in Western society and brought about an equally dramatic transformation in contract law" ("Contract Law as Ideology" 174). Such a shift, as the contract theorist P. S. Atiyah points out, strained the boundaries of the individual, and as such, brought the force of the state into play in the maintenance of those boundaries; see *The Rise and Fall of Freedom of Contract* chap. 10.

The introduction of negotiable instruments into the local life of England transformed the mechanisms by which social structure was maintained. "Bills of exchange at first were extended only to merchant strangers trading with English merchants, and afterwards to inland bills between merchants trading with one another here in England, and then to all traders and business men, and lastly to all persons whether traders or not" C. J. Treby, *Bromwich v. Lloyd*, 1697 (quoted in Holdsworth 8: 169). Treby, writing just after the formation of the national bank that got England into the business of negotiable instruments, is tracing, and advocating, a trend of increasing legal availability of the means for negotiating. (In France, into the 18th century, "the place where a bill is drawn must be so far distant from the place where it is payable that there may be a possible rate of exchange between the two" [Chalmers, in Holdsworth 8: 169].)

Albert Hirschman studies the ideological shift in which 18th-century writers (including Montesquieu, Steuart, Millar, Smith) identified the "rise of commerce and industry" with "orderly government" and the control of Hobbesian passions (*The Passions and the Interests* 102).

3. Much twentieth-century discussion of the agreement or promise as the quintessential performative speech act derives from J. L. Austin, *How to Do Things With Words*. The problem of its application to contract law has been addressed by Clare Dalton, "An Essay on the Deconstruction of Contract Doctrine" and Jacques Derrida, *Limited Inc.*, esp. 31–43. In these two analyses, Derrida and Dalton note the slippage of meaning in Austin's requirement that a promise be "serious" and suggest how the adjudication of that term can constitute a crisis of interpretation.

4. See also John Galt's *The Entail* (1822), a Scottish example of the disruptive psychology by which the love of land and of progeny coalesce only to devour one another with contradictions internalized from legal strictures.

5. The term *contract* existed in legal use to describe "where a Debt lay," after *Slade's Case* (1602) and in the case law and court consolidations of the following fifty years the "modern sense of agreement" emerges (Kevin Teeven, *A History of the Anglo-American Common Law of Contract* 65). Other writs beside Debt, (e.g., *Assumpsit* and *Covenant*) were precursors to modern contract that had limited application because of strict forms of pleading and the difficulties of jury trials in which neither plaintiff nor defendant could testify. Adam Smith, in his 1762 *Lectures on Jurisprudence* looks toward the *Wealth of Nations* by explaining the recent force of contracts as the gradual stripping away of impediments, as if legal history were evolving inevitably toward the contemporary doctrine.

6. By contrast, Broom devotes book 2, "Of Contracts," in his four-book treatise *Commentaries on the Common Law* (1846) to the law of contracts.

7. Mansfield would appreciate the way in which such a case, as a notable precedent, would locate London at the center of international trade and economic colonization. The development of contract law was continually linked to the expansion of English influence.

8. The three other concurring judges reasoned differently. Two maintained that consideration had been given because Pillans gave up the right to call upon White for the payment of the 800£. Ultimately, such compromise positions, in which "consideration" was entailed in the exchange of promises via writing, prevailed through the 1870s (Atiyah, *Freedom of Contract* chaps. 14–15). In practical terms, this amounts to Mansfield's position, since a promise became a "thing" and so could be exchanged as consideration. See also J. J. Powell, *Essay upon the Law of Contracts and Agreements* (1790) v. ii; Atiyah suggests Powell's genealogy: "the views of Hobbes, reinforced, now, by those which were being attributed to Adam Smith, at last being imported into English law" (*Freedom of Contract* 450). The slide from promises determining value into their possessing it is a reification (consonant with Polanyi's "great transformation") in which words emerge as commodities.

Williamson v. Losh (1775) brings out a contradictory aspect of contracts relevant to "Michael" and the tension of familial affection. John Losh had promised, in writing, to his wife's niece, Jane Tiffin, 100£ and several pieces of furniture upon his death, "for the love and affection that I have for [her]" (James Milnes Holden 136). When Losh died, Jane Tiffin's husband, Williamson, sued for the money and property. The estate of Losh argued that the promise was not enforceable since there was no consideration, but this argument did not prevail since a written document existed. The written note was not a negotiable instrument because it referred to personal property (including "bedclothes and seven pudden-dishes"), and, given the language of familial affection, it was on the face of it not commercial; still, the courts read the family commitments as if they were commercial in essence.

Of particular importance in this case was an argument not made, despite its availability for a hundred years. Williamson could have argued, with the precedent of *Dutton v. Poole* (1677), that "the warmth of natural affections and the recollection of paternal care sufficed to generate obligations [that is, constituted consideration] between the members of a family" (C. H. S. Fifoot, *Lord Mansfield* 135). Williamson, therefore, could have maintained that the familial affection expressed in the document constituted consideration and that the writing should be construed as a simple contract which sought to actualize that affection. The choice not to use this reasoning suggests the success of Mansfield's court at subsuming social relations under the legalistic ones of contract. See also Anon., *The Laws Respecting Women* (1777): "Natural affection is a good consideration in a deed; and if one without expressing any consideration covenants to stand seised to the use of his wife, child, or brother; here, the naming them to be kin implies the consideration of natural affection whereupon such use will arise" (115, note omitted).

Lord Skinner, in *Rann v. Hughes* (1778), gave the contradictory nature of contracts within the free marketplace bald expression: "It is undoubtedly true that every man is by the law of nature bound to fulfil his engagements. It is equally true that the law of this country supplies no means, nor affords any remedy, to compel the performance of an agreement made without sufficient consideration" (101 ER 1014). This decision by the House of Lords denied the special status Mansfield accorded a written document. Two years later, despite this setback, Mansfield further insisted on the negotiability of a signature in *Russel v. Langstaffe*. Langstaffe "had indorsed his name on five blank 'promissory notes'" which were filled in by Galley who sold them to Russel. When the notes fell due, Galley dishonored them and Russel sued Langstaffe as the endorser. The trial court held that a signature on a blank note was a "mere nullity" and could not be transformed by subsequent writing. Mansfield overturned the ruling, arguing that the signature was not a nullity, but "a letter of credit for an indefinite sum" (Holden 141).

For the status of considerations concerning contracts of surety, see William Theobald, *A Practical Treatise on the Law of Principal and Surety* (1836) 8–14.

9. Mansfield's position alters the domain in which truth is investigated from the external world to the written document. This position reflects an increased reliance on writing by aristocratic and mercantile institutions, and provides a legal frame to empower writing generally. This transformation, in its technological dimensions, can be viewed within the "Logic of Domination" by which Thomas Spragens details the 18th-century inscription on Lockean man as "*tabula rasa* [cluttered] with sundry reservations and codicils" (*The Irony of Liberal Reason*, 95).

10. In the event, Richard Wordsworth ended up threatening Montagu with "coercive measures to enforce the payment of my debt" (LEY 678, 14 May 1799), perhaps because, shortly after being called to the bar, Montagu tried to "earn a living by his pen" (LEY 224n). The debt to Richard was in practice a restructuring of the initial debt to William.

11. "At the end of the seventeenth century, recorded marriages may well have borne little relationship to the proportion of the population who went through some informal and irregular marriage ceremony" (Bridget Hill, *Women, Work, and Sexual Politics in Eighteenth-Century England* 223).

12. Both Lawrence Stone (*Road to Divorce* 121–37) and John Gillis (*For Better, For Worse* 139–45) suggest the act's immense social impact. Stone concentrates on the impact of London Fleet marriages, which may have been the more dominant target, but Gillis points to its reverberating rural impact. Hill points out that nonlegal marriages persisted into the nineteenth century (206).

13. Carl Woodring observes that the Evening Star "was a true house of industry, in contradistinction from the work-house denounced in 'The Old Cumberland Beggar' as 'HOUSE, misnamed of INDUSTRY.' . . . [F]rom the community's social allusion to the lamp of unusual industry, the poet has made a radiant symbol" (*Wordsworth* 69, quoting a late edition of "OCB").

14. The textual history of this moment, partly encoded in the poem itself and partly in the note Wordsworth dictated to Isabella Fenwick, undercuts the implied

naturalness. Wordsworth justifies the minute details of the lamp because "there are no few / Whose memories will bear witness to my tale" (135–36). The local audience, bearing witness before the national audience, confirms Wordsworth's story. In the Fenwick note, Wordsworth recalls that the "Evening Star" was not Michael's cottage, but one nearby (*Lyrical Ballads* 308). Consequently, an actual local audience would have discounted Wordsworth's story. His invention of a local audience is self-validating. Rawnsley reported that the cottage, still standing in 1882, was called the "Village Clock" ("Reminiscences of Wordsworth amongst the Peasantry of Westmoreland," in W. Knight, ed., *Wordsworthiana: A Selection from Papers Read to the Wordsworth Society* [London, 1889] 100; cited in Simpson *Historical Imagination* 145); this change, if accurately reported, makes the effort of naturalization more evident.

15. This description of a newly formulated family corresponded to the development of a social bourgeois class which the "family," as a cultural ideal, could, through emergent strategies of representation, both epitomize and reproduce. *The Spectator*, as an early representative of commercial values, proposes for itself a diverse audience, the culmination of which, however, is "well regulated Families" which will serve up the well-regulating *Spectator* "every Morning for Tea and Bread and Butter" (*Spectator* No. 10, 1: 44–45). Although Addison is addressing himself to a middle class, in which as a secondary operation, servants may be regularized through the standardization of the family day, much literature and legislation was directed toward what David Levine has described as "reorder[ing] the division of labor *within* the domestic economy" of protoindustrial workers (*Family Formation in an Age of Nascent Capitalism* 12–13).

16. Bridget Hill, in her extended study of *Women, Work, and Sexual Politics* notes that "in the debate on the consequences of enclosure and the erosion of common rights, the experience of women, and more particularly wives of smallholders and cottagers, has so far played little part" (Hill 23). The same point can be made for the examination of labor in "Michael." Critics have generally agreed that "Michael" is a poem about labor, and about how the great changes wrought in the community are foreshadowed and entailed by the destruction of Michael's family industry. Carl Woodring has suggested that "Michael's family has been able to live 'in the open sunshine of God's love' ["Michael" 239] because Michael's industry has freed his patrimonial fields from all encumbrance" (*Politics in English Romantic Poetry* 97). Kurt Heinzelman has noted that when Michael's "agrarian economy" "disappears under the complexities of economic legalisms involving entailment and inheritance, the traditional methods of the pastoral genre are similarly compromised" (*Imagination* 218). Marjorie Levinson expands upon the household of Michael's self-sufficiency, arguing that "Michael's family seems not to engage commercially" with other members of the community (*Great Period Poems* 63). In all of these readings, Isabel has no distinct role. Wordsworth himself seems to have started off this interpretive lens for

the poem, highlighting to Fox the poem's emphasis on "*men* who do not wear fine cloaths" (my emphasis).

17. See Catherine Hall ("Strains in the 'Firm of Wife, Children and Friends?'" 11–12) for a cautious guess about the distribution of labor, and for the demographic problems of getting a full picture of gender roles.

18. In this type of arrangement, "production is no longer controlled by the household alone (even if usually it remains located within the home), but is controlled by agents operating on behalf of capitalist merchants who own the capital involved and provide the raw material. . . . If [wives] still owned spinning wheels or jennies, they no longer owned the raw materials and were no longer responsible for marketing the finished product. All control over the amount of work available was dictated by the agents of capitalist clothiers" (Hill 25, 48).

19. Levinson contends that "the cheese that the family eats is 'homemade' as are their 'oaten cakes,'" based on the enumeration of the family's tools (*Great Period Poems* 63). But the lines are, I think, less clear: "[The family] Sate round their Basket pil'd with oaten cake / And their plain home-made cheese" ("Michael" 103–4, quoted from Butler and Green 256). The "Basket" suggests marketing, just as neighbors buy Bateman "A Basket, which they fill'd with Pedlar's wares" (272).

20. The poem describes Isabel's work with greater specificity than Michael's. In a rejected expansion to the poem, "Many a sheep" DC MS 31, Wordsworth had sketched a day's journey of shepherding, probably by Michael and Luke; and in another effort "[The Matron's Tale]," (eventually trimmed of references to "Old Michael" and considerable details of labor for *The Prelude* VIII 222–311 [1805]), describes the herding of sheep and searching for a lost one. Wordsworth had also rejected an expansion of "Michael" 131–35 that balanced the description of the lamp with a detail of "Old Michael's manners and discourse" (20) by inserting into the domestic scene "The fancies of a solitary Man!" (16 from DC MS 31; Butler and Green, 333–38).

21. Citing *Cage v. Russel*, Erskine, as Lord Chancellor, notes "that a forfeiture should not bind, where a thing may be done afterwards, or any compensation made for it. Forfeitures are even odious in law. Courts of Law, circumscribed as their jurisdiction is, struggle against forfeiture" *Sanders v. Pope* (12 and 13 March 1806, 33 ER 111). Although the conditioned bond remained popular during the seventeenth and eighteenth centuries, it was under attack because the forfeiture, for the obligor's failure to meet condition, of typically twice the contract amount was beginning to be perceived for what it was: penal, rather than compensatory" (Teeven 85). Teeven goes on to outline an ambivalent attitude by the courts toward forfeiture. See also Andrew Lang, "Forfeiture in Interests of Land" 428–29. Eilenberg (*Strange Power* 241) and John Bushnell ("'Where is the Lamb for a Burnt offering?'" 248; cited by Eilenberg) note the peculiarity that, once Luke is gone, the debt is no longer mentioned. Both assume that Michael loses no land, but the settlement, like the legality

of the forfeiture, is elided; since he no longer worked the land, its loss may have been entirely incorporated into the grief of losing Luke.

22. This speech suggests another defense, that of collusion between the holder of the surety bond and the nephew, a possibility Michael sees without recognizing its legal implications. John Turner notes that "the fear of betrayal of family by family" is Michael's worst fear (*Play and Politics* 214).

23. See Heather Glen, *Vision and Disenchantment*, for the view that Susan "is clearly a victim of this environment, but her present situation is only obliquely registered" (103). Not so obliquely, however, that Charles Lamb missed the implications (Manning, *Reading Romantics* 311). The names in the poem, Manning notes, "would have suggested an entire world of mercantile activity" to contemporary readers (302); see also David Simpson, "What Bothered Charles Lamb About Poor Susan?" Of course, the difference of gender between Luke and Poor Susan (especially as it relates to the implied relationships with their fathers) precludes any easy comparison.

24. John Galt's *Annals of the Parish* (1821, written 1813) traces the transformation of a Scottish community through the importation of foreign goods and ideas, but his narrative strategy, which makes "placing" of the storyteller/minister the first invasion, provides the church (and the periodical industry, to which Galt contributed) as mediating structures by which the community can maintain itself with some success. Galt and Wordsworth share a material basis for social transformation.

25. Roger Sales argues that Wordsworth systematically ignores and evades "questions of economic agency" throughout the poem in order to divorce "real estate" from "concepts of estate" (*English Literature in History, 1780–1830* 57).

26. Karl Kroeber, though more focused on the relationship between the reader's time and the poet's, concurs: "Our consciouness of how time may be experienced by human beings has been intensified, as we become aware when we find ourselves once again where we turned off 'the public way'" (*British Romantic Art* 46).

27. Kroeber notes that this poem's "strokes of art are temporal rather than spacial. . . . [The] presentation of a span of time *as* a span of time is characteristic of the entire poem" (*British Romantic Art* 51). In the passage from "Michael", the phrase "long time to look back" spacializes the temporal "sixty years" as if the first is the medium through which the second is seen.

28. I return to the Preface in chapter 5.

29. "Up the tumultuous brook of Green-head Gill" (2) and "Beside the boisterous brook of Green-head Gill" (491).

30. This reiteration is, in an early form, the mark of ritual and orality, but, as Derrida has remarked, it becomes the juridical practice of writing and, in particular, the form that marks the logocentrism of contractual speech and police powers. See *Limited Inc.*, 70–72, 126–27, 131–33.

3. Marketing the Professions: Addison, Hume, Wordsworth

1. In Maria Edgeworth's *Castle Rackrent* (1800), the lawyer originates in the servant class; Jason is the son of the narrator, Thady. Trading on specialized knowledge, he schemes to take over the Rackrent estate, for which he is disowned by his father. The ending, which the pseudoeditor acknowledges could "readily" have been made "more dramatic and more pathetic" raises without settling the relation between property and profession: "she [my lady Rackrent] and Jason, immediately after my poor master's death, set about going to law about that jointure; the memorandum not being on stamped paper, some say it is worth nothing; others again it may do" (96). Regardless of who wins, the legal profession earns a victory as the domain of the decision. Although this was written in and about Ireland, Edgeworth thought the reference to stamped paper sufficiently obvious to an English audience that her glossary for the English edition offers no explanation. The movement of Jason from "a very 'cute lad" (22) to the corrupt lawyer is balanced with the decline of the lords of Rackrent during Thady's tenure and presages, without conceding, a new era of the middle class dominated by lawyers.

2. Max Weber traces the simultaneous transformations of the "formal qualities of modern law" and the character of the speaker of that law in *Economy and Society;* the "charismatic revelation of law by 'law prophets'" gives way to the "empirical creation and finding of law by legal *honoratiores,*" and, after several other stages, to "the systematic elaboration of law and professionalized administration of justice by persons who have received their legal training in a learned and formally logical manner" (882).

3. Michel Foucault, in *Madness and Civilization,* has explored 18th-century medical discourse through the construction and containment of mental illness. Foucault provides an analytic critique of developing discourses by recognizing their material precursors. For madness, there was the deserted leprosarium: "Leprosy disappeared, the leper vanished, or almost, from memory; these structures remained. Often, in these same places, the formulas of exclusion would be repeated, strangely similar two or three centuries later. Poor vagabonds, criminals, and 'deranged minds' would take the part played by the leper" (7). By resituating a range of social ills within the domain of medicine, the profession exerts influence while concealing the social causes of those ills under the guise of rationalistic medicine (on this point, see Foucault, *The Birth of the Clinic* chap. 5).

Hugh Ryder records his treatment for "A distracted Person, most violently raving and the maddest I ever yet beheld": "I that Afternoon had him by force of Men held down, and gave him a Glyster, which wrought him well; the next Morning, I bled him in the arm, kept him to a cooling spare dyet, bled him the next day in the Forehead, and imporsed cupping glasses with Scarifications to the neck and

Shoulders; but all to no purpose, for he remained mad still as before" (*New Practical Observations in Surgery* 225). The language of procedure implies scientific method, but in terms of the principle of causality that grounds Lockean science, it is without basis. What is described is akin to religious ritual; the madman (a symptom of whose madness is his "breaking what ever cords he was tied with") allows for the organization of social order, here figured in the "force of Men" who contain the madman, and the impulse toward madness, while the doctor excises it. The medical profession derives authority here from its alignment with the church, the institution with which, in other social arrangements, it would contend directly.

4. Blackstone observes that as early as the reign of Henry IV (1402), "it was enacted, that attorneys should be examined by the judges, and none admitted but such as were virtuous, learned, and sworn to do their duty" (*Commentaries* 3: 26), and particular courts regulated their membership. An observer in 1696 estimated the average income for a lawyer at £154, compared with £38 for a skilled laborer. By 1707 pamphlets appeared complaining about the number of attorneys (Holdsworth 12: 53) and Chief Baron Gilbert denounced the inadequate regulation which allowed the "odium that every broken tradesman turns solicitor" (in Holdsworth 12: 54). See also Teeven, *Common Law of Contract* chap. 3, for an analysis of the factionalism of the legal practitioners and subsequent chapters for details about the consolidations of the Law and Equity Courts.

5. See Jerome Christensen, *Coleridge's Blessed Machine of Language* (163), for the analysis of Coleridge as a man of letters that provides the suggestion that the metaphor can be taken and meant literally.

6. "The American Bar Association in its Code of Professional Responsibility describes as a basic ethical duty of lawyers the promotion of 'respect for the law'" (Sanford Levinson, *Constitutional Faith* 54). Levinson's work is an inquiry into the hegemonic iconography the Constitution has acquired in the United States, but finally, his critique reverts to an effort to sustain constitutional faith. His metaphor of a secular religion reaches an anguished formulation in his conclusion: "It would be essentially misleading to attribute to constitutional faith the longevity we associate with the great religious faiths that have provided the metaphors for this book, particularly Judaism and Christianity. We might think instead of the great Egyptian, Greek, and Roman religions that today stock museums with their treasures but are otherwise dead as informing visions of how we the living might structure our own lives" (193–94).

7. The quotation continues with this example: "the capitalist *entrepreneur* creates with himself the industrial technician" ("The Formation of Intellectuals" 118). While Gramsci is concerned primarily with a Marxist critique, his observation is relevant to 18th-century intellectuals.

8. Moreover, the "world of economic production" itself is an interpretive construct the essential nature of which, if currently beyond question, is equally beyond demonstration. As Jean Baudrillard argues, the "monopolistic stage [of economic development] signifies less the monopoly of the means of production (which is never total) than *the monopoly of the code*" (*The Mirror of Production* 127). Once codes are in social play, their mastery is a matter of struggle, and the determination of the "essential" is a spoil gained by the victors.

9. *Laissez-faire*, as a principle, required a mystification in which juridical and legislative intrusions were experienced as internal interpretations of preexisting material facts. Adam Smith describes as eternal some laws of human nature that were developed in recent history and were not universal even within England: "What are the common wages of labour, depends every where upon the contract usually made between two parties, whose interests are by no means the same. The workmen desire to get as much, the masters to give as little as possible. The former are disposed to combine in order to raise, the latter in order to lower the wages of labour" (*Wealth of Nations* 74). Presented as laws not only of the marketplace but of human nature (workmen desire, are disposed), each of these sentences contains historical fallacies. First, wages were not constructed by contract, but Smith wanted to claim that since they were produced analogously (i.e., by some vague consent), they were in fact contracts and thus freely chosen and subject to legal scrutiny. Second, the notion of gain or surplus was hardly the workers' motivation; most were concerned with subsistence. The origins of workers in combination—the incorporated city and the guild—were only incidentally concerned with wages; the main impulses were security for labor and limited competition. In part by preventing individual laborers entering into contracts, the corporation of the guild insured labor by preventing competition from independent workers. Smith's mixture of legal language and human nature suggests a continuum between laws human beings make (contract and contract law) and those to which they discover themselves subject (desire and disposition).

10. The Spectator "resolved to observe an exact Neutrality between the Whigs and Tories, unless I shall be forced to declare my self by the Hostilities of either Side" (*Spectator* No. 1, 1: 5). Such studied neutrality was already engaged in the crucial political move of the professional, controlling the discourse that constituted the neutral, the compromise, the midpoint of the debate. Alan Bewell has recognized Wordsworth's affinity for Enlightenment philosophical systems: "The idea of addressing moral topics with 'eloquence' and through 'images' emerged in the space left vacant by his expulsion of moral philosophical inquiry" *Wordsworth and the Enlightenment* 11). This project reiterated in poetry Hume's own project of refining prose and became possible through the romantic reconstruction of Hume as a philosopher rather than as a historian, the designation more common in his life.

11. The "oil which renders the motions of the wheels of trade more smooth and easy" (David Hume, *Essays Moral, Political, and Literary* 309), money is unnecessary to subsistence, but indispensable to industrialization and to the security of the government.

12. Drawing examples from Athens, Genoa, Holland, and elsewhere, Hume demonstrates that "*every new tax creates a new ability in the subject to bear it*" (*Essays Moral* 356) because increased taxes correspond to increased industriousness. Taxes provide a way for the economy, through the government, to regulate its own productivity.

13. Addison's Spectator had also wished for "Superintendants" of the English language equivalent to the "several Persons whose Business it is to watch over our Laws, our Liberties and commerce" (*Spectator* No. 165, 2: 149).

14. See Burke, *Reflections* 218–23; 265–74 and Thomas Paine, *Rights of Man* 132–39; 214–60.

15. Adam Smith distinguished commodities from labor but recognized that, "though equal quantities of labour are always of equal value to the labourer, yet to the person who employs him they appear sometimes to be of greater and sometimes of smaller value . . . to him the price of labour seems to vary like that of all other things" (*Wealth of Nations* 37–38). Godwin maintains that "every man may calculate, in every glass of wine he drinks, . . . how many individuals have been condemned to slavery and sweat" to supply that luxury. He argues against Burke that "it is a gross imposition that men . . . talk of the property bequeathed to them by their ancestors. The property is produced by the daily labour of men who are now in existence" (William Godwin, *Enquiry Concerning Political Justice* 711–12).

16. For an extended discussion on the "ethos of Letters," see Chandler, *Wordsworth's Second Nature* 140–55. For a sampling of what legally constituted original literary work (based on litigation from about Wordsworth's birth to the publication of *The Excursion*), see George Ticknor Curtis, *A Treatise on the Law of Copyright* (1847) chap. 5.

17. Erskine is not denying the significance of events such as the execution of Louis XVI or the French declaration of war against Austria; rather, he is interested in how these events are given meaning within English discourse.

18. See Kennedy, "Blackstone's *Commentaries*" 208–26 and Spragens, *Irony* chap. 4, "The Logic of Domination: The Origins of Technocracy."

19. "Robespierre and Saint-Just inevitably made more moderate speakers appear to be defending the monarchy, and in comparison the legal and constitutional concerns of the Girondins would certainly have appeared as 'indecision'" (Nicholas Roe, *Wordsworth and Coleridge* 78).

20. J. M. Thompson, in *The French Revolution*, notes that this event did not certainly occur but its narrative circulated widely. In either case, its meaning to Wordsworth would be clear.

21. Roe (*Wordsworth and Coleridge* 75–80) discusses this section of *The Prelude* in ways congruent with my reading.

22. This debate was not new, as E. P. Thompson's rehearsal of the levellers shows (*The Making of the English Working Class* 24–26); what was new was the ability of the corresponding societies to grow rapidly, and to provide the "ad hoc distribution" which helped put 200,000 copies of Thomas Paine's *Rights of Man* in circulation by 1793 (Jon Klancher, *The Making of the English Reading Audiences, 1790–1832* 27). Opponents portrayed this circulation as a chaotic explosion (Thompson, *Working Class*, 117–20).

23. Sartre, following Durkheim, argues that the act of collectivity transforms the individual will through practico-inert structures that maintain the collectivity at the expense of the expression of individual wills (*Critique* 405–7); critiques of the Sartrean position foreground the institutional role of producing the "subject" or "individual" itself (see Judith Butler, *Gender Trouble* chap. 3). What is crucial about Paine's ideas is not their abstract (im)possibility, but their sufficient plausibility to mobilize the sound and fury of a range of institutions that claimed to fulfill already the Painite project by *representing* a human nature which Paine claimed they actually *produced* through the perversion of a genuine rights-based human nature.

24. In referring to the stock market, both Paine and Burke were drawing on an established metaphor. In the debate on a bill to establish a sliding scale of representation based on wealth, William Robertson argued, "How can it be reasonable or just, that one who contributes to a fund only £5, should have as much power in the management of that fund, as he who contributes to it £100?" (*Remarks on the Bill Which Was Intended to be Brought into Parliament in 1775*; quoted in Paul Langford, *Public Life and the Propertied Englishman* 55).

25. "Are we," the attorney general asks as a commentary on a passage, "reduced back again to that savage state of nature?" And later: "Does not this passage stand insulated between the two parts of the connected story [of the Revolution and Act of Settlement], officiously and designedly thrust in for the purposes of mischief?" (*Proceeding against Thomas Paine* 383, 387) Close readings permeate the Attorney General's speech and Erskine's defense.

26. For an analysis of the Godwinian influence evident in this correspondence, see Roe, *Wordsworth and Coleridge* 175–85. For a discussion of the educational ideas in the correspondence as evidence of his knowledge of French schemes for education, see Chandler, *Second Nature* 104–7.

27. In Wordsworth's letters to Mathews, he generally opens with an apology for his slow response. His elaborate excuse in an early letter (17 June 1791) runs over 200 words, about a fifth of the letter. After confessing that "it is totally impossible to find any apology," he offers a mock legal argument instead: "Moralists inform us that whoever meditates any crime *facti crimen habet*. May not the observation be re-

versed, and may not we also say, that whoever thinks of and resolves to execute any good intention ought also to have the merit of the actual performance of it" (LEY 48). Wordsworth's witticism relies on the contested legal status of the doctrines of intentionality. In response to the treason trials (1794), Godwin would observe that though treason entails "compassing and imagining the death of the King," the law requires that these intents "be manifested by overt acts" (William Godwin, "Cursory Strictures" 5).

28. Wordsworth's letters are replete with examples of moving between professional and personal registers. Around the same time as the letters to Mathews, Wordsworth and his brother Richard exchange letters discussing a bond of indemnity to protect Wordsworth from a debt by his aunt so that Raisley Calvert will leave him a substantial legacy. Each of Wordsworth's letters ends with a doleful account of Calvert's health, both genuine and a spur to Richard to act quickly (LEY 130–34).

29. Wordsworth ends this section of the letter by involving Mathews in his poetic concerns: "As I am speaking on the subject, pray let me request you have the goodness to call on Johnson my publisher, and ask him if ever he sells any of those poems and what number he thinks are yet on his hands. This will be doing me a great favor" (LEY 120). Asking this favor expresses Wordsworth's confidence in Mathews more substantially than do the praises the letter offers, and underwrites those praises by investing their object with responsibility. Wordsworth is not condescending to Mathews's project, but linking it with his own, the career of a poet. That the letter ends by invoking his poems indicates that they remain on the horizon of his discussion, and that Mathews is not to mistake Wordsworth's enthusiasm for their project as overshadowing his purpose as a poet.

30. Hume, who was rich from his writing when Strahan quoted his sentiments back to him and who had bargained hard with booksellers, clearly wrote for money, but he understood money—or wished to represent it—as the transparent sign of ideological sway in the marketplace; he received money because his works did their job, not because he wrote for money. James Boswell's Johnson, by contrast, did write for money, having, according to Strahan, written *Rasselas* so that "with the profits he might defray the expence of his mother's funeral, and pay some little debts which she had left" (*Life of Johnson* 240); nonetheless, the theme of *Rasselas*, as Boswell distinguishes it from *Candide* in the next paragraph, was, "by shewing the unsatisfactory nature of things temporal, to direct the hopes of man to things eternal" (242), a gloss that minimizes the meaning of the funeral and temporal debts. Boswell further deflects the meaning of Johnson's writing for money by the metaphor describing his own reading of *Rasselas:* "The fund of thinking which this work contains is such, that almost every sentence of it may furnish a subject of long meditation" (242). The work is a depository of value, and the money Johnson received for it—immediately passed on in the fulfillment of filial duty—reflects only a fraction of the value

imparted to the reader. Like Hume, Boswell's Johnson writes for other things *by* writing for money, and their remarks reflect a difference in emphasis on the relation between money as representation and money as object, money as symbol of value and as commodity possessing value (see Karl Polanyi, *The Great Transformation* chap. 16).

31. A gesture such as this verifies Jeffrey's perception in labeling Wordsworth as part of a school of Lake Poets. The *Lyrical Ballads* constitutes an attempt to exploit this distance from London, in a way similar to Scott's situating primal struggles on the border of Scotland—not because they did not occur in cities but because they were, for him and much of his anticipated audience, more expressible beyond urban civilization.

32. The competing journals of the 1790s confirm this view; see Klancher, *Reading Audiences* chap. 1.

33. "So that we see emerging [at the end of the 18th century] as the organizing principles of this space of empiricities, *Analogy* and *Succession*: the link between one organic structure and another can no longer, in fact, be the identity of one or several elements, but must be the identity of the relation between the elements" (Michel Foucault, *The Order of Things* 218). Or, to use language of the period that employs this shift to construct a hierarchy of art forms, "In reality, poetry and rhetoric do not succeed in exact description so well as painting [a more primitive art] does; their business is to affect rather by sympathy than imitation, to display rather the effect of things on the mind of the speaker, or of others, than to present a clear idea of the things themselves" (Edmund Burke, *A Philosophical Inquiry into the . . . Sublime and Beautiful*, 172).

34. Five lines later, he writes: "Next come parliamentary debates, detailed as you have specified, and such state papers as are of importance" (LEY 126). This might locate the poetry within the hierarchy, but I would suggest this addition revises the original intention. Having dealt with his own profession, which needs no specific place, he turns to Mathews's profession and offers it pride of place, as the anchor, second in honor only to that which needs no place.

35. Sigmund Freud, *Totem and Taboo* 2–3; 155–57. I do not suggest Freud is historically accurate; only that Wordsworth's representation of poetry is totemic in positioning itself as a discourse that is at once an ancestor of other discourses and, by its own independence, structures those discourses.

36. In the final paragraph, Richard suggests burning his letter, as if opposing Lord Lonsdale were potentially seditious.

37. The acquittals, although greeted with enthusiasm, did not restore *habeas corpus*, and despite the outcome of the specific trial, the government continued to exercise a chilling effect: "In the next year the steady repression of reformers—or 'Jacobins'—was renewed. And by the end of the decade it seemed as if the entire

agitation had been dispersed. The London Corresponding Society had been outlawed. Tom Paine's *Rights of Man* was banned. Meetings were prohibited" (Thompson, *Working Class* 22).

38. A supplemental reading of this sentence takes the "oath" as a "threshold" gift, a moment of entry both physical and spiritual, or (in the imagining of terms I have already suggested) geographic and monetary. Drawing on an anthropological tradition, Lewis Hyde remarks that "threshold gifts may be the most common form of gift we have" (*The Gift* 41).

39. This metaphor parallels Hardy's trial, since the verdict on constructive treason depended on the jury's reading of the London Corresponding Society. In 1792, Fox's Libel Act shifted the power to determine whether a publication was a criminal libel from the judge to the jury. Previously, the jury would only determine the fact of publication (had the defendant willfully made a work available to at least one member of the public?). The question of whether the writing constituted a libel was a matter of law for the judge. Wordsworth's implied metaphor of the readers—common people, the pool of jurors—reflects this shift in the law, and, although the trial of Hardy concerned treason, rather than libel, the fear of an empowered jury that could ignore judicial instructions in returning a verdict haunted the prosecution.

40. Roe suggests that Wordsworth may have contributed to Daniel Isaac Eaton's *Philanthropist*, which appeared from March 1795 to January 1796 (*Wordsworth and Coleridge* 276–79). Kenneth Johnston ("Philanthropy or Treason?") and E. P. Thompson ("Wordsworth's Crisis") argue a Wordsworthian presence in Eaton's magazine.

4. Goody Blake and the Reviewers

1. In the documents of Longman & Co., the "only available record of *Lyrical Ballads* . . . seems to occur . . . in a Copyright Book, where, under the heading 'Cottles Copies', appears *inter alia*, 'Lyrical Ballads', deleted" (W. J. B. Owen, "Costs, Sales, and Profits of Longman's Editions of Wordsworth" 93).

2. The play of representation on title pages was an established 18th-century device; see A. D. Barker, "The Printing and Publishing of Johnson's *Marmor Norfolciense* (1793) and *London* (1738 and 1739)" for a discussion of the manipulations by Thomas Gardner, who published some of Johnson's work (esp. 288–93).

3. James Butler ("Wordsworth, Cottle, and the *Lyrical Ballads*") traces the confusions of the title page and its subsequent version which erased the name of the printer, and substituted instead:

London
Printed For J. & A. Arch, Gracechurch-Street.
1798

4. Eventually, the name William Wordsworth functions similarly, gaining cultural identity beginning with its announcement in the second edition of the *Lyrical Ballads*, and continuing as his career developed through a series of collected works. Longman, the publisher of *Poems* (1815), suggested that the title be *Lyrical Ballads and Other Poems, by W. Wordsworth* (20 May 1814, in W. J. B. Owen, "Letters of Longman & Co. to Wordsworth, 1814–36"). Wordsworth's desire to feature his name more prominently and to subordinate the term *Lyrical Ballads* suggests his care in reworking material. Longman apparently continued to prefer its suggested title, as a later letter refers to the edition as "Ballads" (5 August 1814, in Owen, "Letters").

5. Nearly every review of *Poems, in Two Volumes* (1807), a volume whose authorship is announced as "William Wordsworth, Author of the *Lyrical Ballads*," recalls the earlier work.

6. The reviewers take on this historical claim, not by denying the evidence of poets but by insisting on the critical evaluation of that evidence: "[Our author] is not singular in this unhappy decision of taste; we have had a multitude of rhimers who have looked into the earliest efforts of the art, for their model; and seem to have thought, that rudeness was synonymous to simplicity. Bishop Percy's publication of Reliques of Ancient Poetry, has been the fertile mother of a numerous and meagre race of *stanza-enditers*" (*New London Review* 1 [January 1799]: 33–34).

7. For a reading that indicates Wordsworth's continual anxiety with this correspondence, an anxiety that suggests the professional representational strategy implicit in the confident expression in the prose supplements to Wordsworth's poetry of that correspondence), see Charles Rzepka, *The Self as Mind* chap. 2, esp. 42–47, 63–69.

8. Demonstrating the political profile that shaped reviews in the 1790s and 1800s, Marilyn Butler cites the *Edinburgh*'s 1804 review of Edgeworth's *Popular Tales*, in which Jeffrey associates the "charitable endeavors of Messrs Wirdsworth [sic] & Co." with Thomas Paine's efforts to "bring disaffection and infidelity within the comprehension of the Common people" (*Romantics* 62).

9. Of seven notices in Donald Reiman, ed., *The Romantics Reviewed*, only the *AntiJacobin Review* (ten lines long) does not quote from the first three paragraphs of the Advertisement; it does quote the last paragraph.

10. A more typical use of the word appears in this review of Coleridge and Southey's *Fall of Robespierre*: "At the end of this work, Mr. Coleridge has subjoined, proposals for publishing . . . Imitations from the modern Latin Poets" (*Critical Review* 2nd Ser., 12 [November 1794]: 262).

11. Burney experienced the importance of the first encounter when Hawkins's complete *History of Music* (1776) appeared after only one volume of Burney's own

History of Music. The consequence was that his final version, published in 1789, encodes a running struggle with Hawkins's work, including silent borrowing and reappropriation of the sort Burney uses in his review of Wordsworth (see Lipking, *Ordering of the Arts* 229–31, 295–304).

12. In the Preface of 1800, Wordsworth answers this question in a footnote: "It is worth while here to observe that the affecting parts of Chaucer are almost always expressed in language pure and universally intelligible even to this day" (*Lyrical Ballads* 246).

13. Wordsworth answers (appropriates) this charge in the 1800 Preface with his analysis of the powerful lines of Thomas Gray's "Sonnet on the Death of Richard West": "It is equally obvious that except in the rhyme, and in the use of the single word 'fruitless' for fruitlessly, which is so far a defect, the language of these lines does in no respect differ from that of prose" (*Lyrical Ballads* 253).

14. Burney comments with exasperation on Coleridge's "The Dungeon": "Here candour and tenderness for criminals seem pushed to excess. Have not jails been built on the humane Mr. Howard's plan . . . at an expence which would have maintained many in innocence and comfort out of a jail, if they have been driven to theft by want?" (*Monthly Review* 29 [June 1799]: 207) The fourth edition of John Howard's *The State of Prisons* had come out in 1792, and Godwin used its descriptions of the wretched conditions of prisons to deride the claim that the English "have no Bastille" (*Things as They Are; or, . . . Caleb Williams* 181). Like Bentham's panopticon, Howard's proposed penitentiary house was approved by the government (1779), but not implemented until 1810–20 (Howard, *Prisons* 297 n E).

15. Despite the frequency of names, both proper ("Simon Lee") and descriptive ("The Mad Mother") in the *Lyrical Ballads*, only two titles take the form of "X and Y," "Goody Blake and Harry Gill" and "Expostulation and Reply," which takes the form of a debate both internally and in its relation to "The Tables Turned."

16. In "Simon Lee," Wordsworth gives us a perverted form, in which youth, trying to be helpful, overruns old age:

> "You're overtasked, good Simon Lee,
> Give me your tool," to him I said: . . .
> I struck, and with a single blow
> The tangled root I sever'd.
>
> (89–94)

"We Are Seven" and "Anecdote for Fathers" come nearer to Wordsworth's ideal, but the extreme youth of the respondents begs the issue of two able generations contending for limited status and resources.

17. None of Johnson's three definitions of *shepherd* or the supporting quotations acknowledge a market function.

18. Changed to "old" in 1800.

19. The phrase "Young Harry" may invoke its absent complement "Old Harry" and suggest, more than inheritance, usurpation.

20. The phrase "secular arm of the church" refers to the church's invocation of civil powers to punish offenders, as in the Inquisition.

21. See also Thompson, *Working Class*, esp. chap. 7, "The Field Labourers": "Enclosure (when all the sophistications are allowed for) was a plain enough case of class robbery, played according to fair rules of property and law laid down by a parliament of property-owners and lawyers" (237–38).

22. In his justification of meter in the 1800 Preface, Wordsworth uses the poem to argue the Burkean point, in language that answers these reviewers: "In consequence of these convictions [that verse invests a description with the appearance of passion] I related in metre the Tale of GOODY BLAKE and HARRY GILL, which is one of the rudest in this collection. I wished to draw attention to the truth that the power of the human imagination is sufficient to produce such changes even in our physical nature as might almost appear miraculous. The truth is an important one; the fact (for it is a *fact*) is a valuable illustration of it. And I have the satisfaction of knowing that it has been communicated to many hundreds of people who would never have heard of it, had it not been narrated as a Ballad, and in a more impressive metre than is usual in Ballads" (*Lyrical Ballads* 267).

5. The Contractual Basis for the *Lyrical Ballads*

1. The Preface itself steers a middle course. Coleridge's poems are included "for the sake of variety" and because they "in a great measure have the same tendency as" Wordsworth's poems. Eilenberg, who also favors the language of propriety, suggests that this "paragraph graciously reinterprets the origins of the *Lyrical Ballads*" and suggests Wordsworth's "reluctance to confront the real differences that lay between him and his friend" (*Strange Power* 8–9). I agree, but with the friendly amendment that this reluctance resided in the Wordsworthian prose, while the poetry and construction of the volume more aggressively highlighted the difference; as James Kissane suggests in his discussion of the replacement of "Christabel" with "Michael," Wordsworth's poem "may be considered an aesthetic alternative to 'Christabel' which stands as a commentary upon—a kind of 'admonitory tribute' to—the unfinished attempt it replaces" ("'Michael,' 'Christabel,' and the *Lyrical Ballads* of 1800" 57). Similarly, Marilyn Katz suggests that a "sharp private disagreement" existed between Coleridge and Wordsworth regarding poetic theory, and that it "surfaced in 1800" ("Early Dissent between Wordsworth and Coleridge" 50); I contend that the need to bring it to visibility had to do with Wordsworth's professional(izing) goals, but, as Eilenberg suggests in her discussion of the *Biographia Literaria*, Coleridge also implicates himself in the decision (*Strange Power* 88–89).

2. "I think publications in which we formally & systematically lay down rules for the actions of Men cannot be too long delayed" (*Prose* 1: 103). The essay continues with an attack against Godwin's method, but the attack itself develops the outlines of an associationalist system that grounds the Preface of 1800.

3. Even by 1806, Simpson contends, "Neither poetry nor the self that produced it were adequately individuated; Wordsworth had no true freehold on his work." Simpson offers this idea to explain Wordsworth's "over-strenuous images of individuation" (*Historical Imagination* 49). I would modify this evaluation to say that the individuation was a continual part of symbolically managing a copyright that Wordsworth literally circulated, but that was within a system of law that could provide no "true freehold." I take as a problem of career management and economic/legal pressures the self that Charles Rzepka, in *The Self as Mind*, has analyzed from psychological and ontological perspectives (62–71).

4. Laura Claridge notes, "Dorothy's comments [about Robinson having 'claimed the title' and both volumes being published by Longman; LEY 297] illuminate the very real professional anxiety William felt" (*Romantic Potency* 36).

5. In 1800, Cottle and Biggs printed 750 copies of the first volume and 1,000 copies of the second volume (Owen, "Costs" 94); the economic rationale was that many purchasers of the first edition would buy only the second volume. Wordsworth's decision, then, to place his critical polemic in the first volume where previous readers would not encounter it, rather than as an appendix to the second volume, suggests its superfluousness for those readers of the first edition able to sustain enough pleasure to buy the second in 1800.

6. That modern critics, Siskin notes, have been held in thrall by the discursive power of English Romanticism "dramatizes how completely and invisibly the psychologized 'reality,' of Romanticism has determined our understanding of ourselves and of our writing" especially as that reality requires such "artifacts" as "disciplinary boundaries (literary versus nonliterary), hierarchical differences (creative versus critical), aesthetic values (spontaneity and intensity), and natural truths (development and the unconscious)" and "also the distinction between the organic and the ironic/deconstructive that informs contemporary critical debate" (Clifford Siskin, *The Historicity of Romantic Discourse* 3). For Siskin, Wordsworth's revisionary practices reconstituted generic distinctions and instituted a developmental history that found its enabling trope in the individual; see especially chap. 5.

7. The recent attention given to Wordsworth's career as a series of revisionary acts by such critics as Siskin, Kenneth Johnston (*Wordsworth and* The Recluse), and William Galperin (*Revision and Authority in Wordsworth*) positions Wordsworth's career, and Romanticism, within a wider historical framework which was constructing itself through revisionary practices. What Siskin says about "the extratextual manifestations" of romantic work applies equally well to the reconstruction of contract

law during Wordsworth's lifetime: "This revisionary activity is intended to work not by altering what we read, but how we read it" (Siskin, *Historicity* 111).

8. "Author," in the legal discourse, denominates the authorial industry—writer, publisher, bookseller—but this legal fiction exposed the liberal fiction of the individual to whom property was consigned by virtue of signature. Ownership by deed depends upon the (st)ability of a name to authorize, and as a limiting case, of some names (Spectator, Dr. Johnson) to project identities as writers. To take a copyright was to offer a name (copyrights could not be anonymous), to put into circulation an inscription that exceeded being (e.g., that could become adjectival—Shakespearean, Wordsworthian, Derridean). Derrida observes that "the proper name has never been, as the unique appellation reserved for the presence of a unique being, anything but the original myth of a transparent legibility present under the obliteration; it is because the proper name was never possible except through its functioning within a classification and therefore within a system of differences, . . . that the interdict was possible" (Jacques Derrida, *Of Grammatology* 109).

The system of classification was, for the 18th century, part of a massive scientific enterprise which found its enabling metaphor in *Law*, itself a proper name masking conflicting identities in its own interdiction ("in the name of the law"). The Derridean force of the proper name adumbrated in *Of Grammatology* (113–17) has its iterate (and root?) in legal historical practice. See also Jean-François Lyotard, "Judiciousness in Dispute" 53–57 and Stephen Greenblatt, "Capitalist Culture and the Circulatory System" 260–62 on the disciplinary functions of using and taking a name.

9. See Blackstone, *Commentaries* 3: 3, citing Genesis 1:28. This is not Blackstone's only strategy, but one germane to a consideration of professional writers. For analyses of his treatment of property, see Daniel Boorstin, *The Mysterious Science of Law* chap. 9 and Kennedy, "Blackstone's *Commentaries*" passim. Laying the groundwork for Blackstone by combining a conceptual right and material object through the process of labor, John Locke offered a definition of property made famous by its dissemination through multiple discourses: "Though the Earth, and all inferior Creatures be common to all Men, yet every Man has a *Property* in his own *Person*. This, no Body has any Right to but himself. The *Labour* of his Body, and the *Work* of his Hands, we may say, are properly his. Whatsoever then he removes out of the State that Nature hath provided, and left it in, he hath mixed his Labour with, and joyned to it something that is his own, and thereby makes it his *Property*" (*Second Treatise*, "Of Property" 305–6).

Addison Swift, Blackstone, Burke, Godwin, Hume, Fielding, Pope, Johnson, Boswell, Mansfield, Adam Smith, and Horne Tooke are among those who refer to this particular passage. Locke's language reconciles two moments in Genesis, God's grant of dominion over the earth and the punishment that "In the sweat of thy face shalt thou eat bread" (3:19). A fortunate fall, God's punishment provides the occasion for individual rights. Locke argued that man's freedom derived from his inscription within property relations, which, with some circularity, began with the assertion of that freedom in the form of 'working' the land. Locke's extended interpretation of Genesis recurs throughout 18th-century property discussions. (As noted above, Genesis 1:28 is for Blackstone the only "solid foundation" for property. In his Vinerian Lectures, Robert Chambers, despite greater emphasis on Roman law, follows suit [2: 148].)

Hume, answering Locke, pointed out that "we cannot be said to join our labor to anything but in a figurative sense" (*Treatise* 505). In Hume's myth of social construction, property started as "this expedient that *every one continue to enjoy what he is at present possessed of*" (*Treatise* 503–4). The actual occupations of uncivilized man became property in the stroke of civilization. For Hume, nothing of modern society depends upon this, or any other, prehistorical formation, because property is overdetermined; in a footnote to the above passage, Hume points out that "there are, no doubt, motives of public interest for most of the rules, which determine property; but still I suspect, that these rules are principally fix'd by the imagination, or the more frivolous properties of our thought and conception" (*Essays* 71). "Properties" of the mind determine "property" in society, because the rules of association that govern ideas also govern property.

10. The grant of Genesis 1:28 does not explain the acquisition of specific property rights by individuals, which, Blackstone proposes, evolved as social roles became more specialized. Without such rights, "innumerable tumults must have arisen, and the good order of the world been continually broken and disturbed" (*Commentaries* 2: 4). Blackstone cites Isaac's interest in Abraham's well (Genesis 26:15 ff) and the division of Canaan and Jordan between Abraham and Lot as early rules of property. The reliance on these texts authorizes textuality itself as the method to trace property, but also marks a horizon Blackstone would not look beyond. Law itself discouraged further investigation; a libel of the Bible was seditious blasphemy because it de facto challenged a state authority based in biblical scripture. The subsequent history of property rights that Blackstone describes develops through the increasing power of written instruments; and through the romantic period, the specter of a textuality beyond legal regulation haunts the courts. In the trial of Daniel Isaac Eaton (1812), Lord Ellenborough refuses the defendant permission to read the "offensive passages" of the document whose offensiveness was at issue. In his summation, Ellenborough reminds the jury that Lord Kenyon has expressly determined that "the Christian religion was the law of the land, and must be protected as the law" (*Proceedings on the Trial of Daniel Isaac Eaton* 950). Ellenborough reiterates this point in the trial against William Hone, and goes further by disallowing as evidence previously published works which, though not prosecuted, should have been (Hone, *Three Trials*, Second Trial 13, 24–25).

11. In *Walcot v. Walker*, Eldon reiterates copyright theory from the 1780s that "publications may be of such a nature that the author can maintain no action at law, [and] it is not the business of this Court . . . to decree either an injunction or an account of the profits of works" (6 May 1802, 32 ER 1). The writer does not create a literary property, but rather, the text, when incorporated into a work, becomes the subject of juridical scrutiny. For a literary work to be a property, it must maintain a moral character that could sustain an action in court.

12. The act, not "primarily to benefit authors," was "a trade regulation" (Lyman Patterson, *Copyright in Historical Perspective* 143). Nonetheless, within twenty years of the act, and before the most prominent litigation regarding common-law copyright, authors had recognized their ability to exploit their initial ownership of a text; A. D. Barker has demonstrated, for example, Johnson's participation in the manipulations of the copyright of *London* ("Printing and Publishing" 297–98). See also Mark Rose, *Authors and Owners* and David Saunders, *Authorship and Copyright;* these works, along with Patterson's and Curtis's, detail the 18th-century debates about the nature of copyright in its relationship to authors. My argument here, though overlapping, is that the discussions of copyright filtered into another complicated debate about the nature of property itself. "Authors," declares a bookseller's pamphlet, "have ever had a Property in their Works, founded upon the same fundamental Maxims by which Property was originally settled, and hath since been maintained" (quoted in Rose, *Authors* 53). Arguing against this equation, Justice Yates writes in *Millar v. Taylor*: "But the property here claimed is all ideal; a set of ideas which have no bounds or marks whatever, nothing that is capable of visible possession, nothing that can sustain any one of the qualities or incidents of property" (20 April 1769, 98 ER 233). As Rose points out, one "crux of this argument was the premise that a literary composition was essentially a collection of ideas" (*Authors* 87); another crux was that a property was grounded in materiality and independent of the ideas through which it was discussed. Both pamphlet and justice assume this stability, but the fact that a text was arguably both a property and not a property (or once a property, and then not a property) demonstrates the rhetorical work of their assumption. Yates had continued to distinguish two uses of the word "property" as "the right of a person" and "the object itself" (98 ER 233) but, like Blackstone who was on the opposite side of the copyright debate, he insisted that the right could derive only from the object.

13. "[I]t may truly be said that public interest requires, and therefore the law allows, the king to be their [ancient books'] guardian and conservator. As the laws passed in Parliament are always accounted the king's laws, . . . the copies may justly be termed his property. The same may be said of the Common Prayer and English Bible, one of which was composed and the other translated by the king's authority and at his expense" (Chambers, *Lectures* 1: 174). Both Chambers and Blackstone

overstate the case for royal prerogative by sliding over the cases through which such ownership was articulated. See in particular *Roper v. Streater* (on whether the "crown" or the "purchaser of the author" held the copyright on Croke's reports; King's Bench decided for the "purchaser," and the ruling was reversed by the House of Lords); *Baskett v. University of Cambridge* (on whether the king's right was a prerogative or acquired by purchase); and Curtis, *Copyright* 116–33 (for a discussion of these and other cases and authorities).

14. Blackstone observes that Roman law held that "writing should belong to the original owner of the materials on which it was written" (*Commentaries* 2: 406); in the English 'improvement,' ideas rather than materials are constitutive. Blackstone solidified the boundary between these two concepts partly because it was murky for a variety of productions, such as translations and abridgments. To take one example, realistic work found a crisis moment in cartography. Was an accurate map a copy of another nearly identical map? Since, clearly, the value of either map depended on accurate representation, their near identicalness was a given; in 1785, in *Sayre v. Moore*, Mansfield found that mapmakers could, and ought to, "take advantage of all prior publications" (102 ER 139; see also *Cary v. Longman and Rees* [25 April 1801, 102 ER 138–40]). Accurate maps served the market best, and this concern overrode a cartographer's interest (Benjamin Kaplan, *An Unhurried View of Copyright* 16–17). Constructing what constituted literary labor, Mansfield reified the division between fact and fiction, the permeability of which provided much of the subversive play in early 18th-century literature (see Lennard Davis, *Factual Fictions*, and Michael McKeon, *The Origins of the English Novel, 1600–1740*).

15. This project is consonant with the ideological work several scholars have argued occurs in Blackstone's *Commentaries*. Daniel Boorstin, in *The Mysterious Science of the Law* (1941), explores how the *Commentaries* "employed the assumptions prevalent in its day about science, religion, philosophy, history, art, and reason, to give the legal system and the values embodied in it an appearance of rationality and acceptability" (vii). Duncan Kennedy concentrates on how the *Commentaries* mediate the "fundamental contradiction" of liberal thought that other human beings (including the state) are both necessary and inhibiting to personal freedom ("Blackstone's *Commentaries*" 213); in particular, Kennedy argues that Blackstone's "right/wrong distinction functioned to legitimate the 18th century legal system," and that "Blackstone's organizational scheme *also* functioned as a mediator between collective power and individual freedom, permitting him to deny the fundamental contradiction of the two" (222). Alan Watson chides Kennedy (correctly) for avoiding the historical and literary context of the *Commentaries* but concludes naively (in light of Boorstin) that since Blackstone "wished to set forth a systematic exposition of English law for teaching purposes" and was heavily influenced by the structures of Justinian's *Institutes*, of the tabular explanation by Dionysius Gothofredus, and of

Hale's *Analysis*, "it is difficult to imagine that there was also a particular and precise political ideological motivation for the structure of the *Commentaries on the Laws of England*" (Watson, "Structure of Blackstone's *Commentaries*" 810–12). Watson's work presents many instances (claims of objectivity, precedent as transparent and ideologically neutral, a natural "need for structure" for social interaction as if that structure were value-neutral) that Kennedy identifies as characteristic of liberal modes of denying contradiction. Richard Posner, in "Blackstone and Bentham," contends that Blackstone presented law "not as a speculative abstraction or a collection of rules but as a functioning social system . . . [which demonstrated] how those laws operated to achieve the economic, political, and other goals of the society" (571–72). The choice by the leading proponents of the Critical Legal Studies movement (Kennedy) and of the Law and Economics movement (Posner) to engage Blackstone's *Commentaries*, despite its irrelevance to most of contemporary American law, suggests the continuing ideological significance of the work.

16. See also Lucy Newlyn, *Coleridge, Wordsworth, and the Language of Allusion* chap. 2 and Eilenberg, *Strange Power* chaps. 1 and 2. Paul Magnuson's first chapter in *Coleridge and Wordsworth* provides earlier critics who recognized the collaborative/competitive nature of the dialogue.

17. In praising "The Old Cumberland Beggar," Lamb explicitly revels in the paradoxical nature of poetic mediation: "the delicate and curious feeling in the wish for the Cumberland Beggar, that he may have about him the melody of Birds, altho' he hear them not. Here the mind knowingly passes a fiction upon herself, first substituting her own feelings for the Beggar's, and, in the same breath detecting the fallacy, will not part with the wish" (Lamb 89)

18. Lamb himself was aware of this paradox, and, during his career as Elia, maintained his clerking job in the East India House—which situated his own writing as avocational. The creation of Elia, Lamb's persona in the *London Magazine*, "was itself an anagrammatic hoax ('a lie'), destined to rival in the literary sphere the scheme of the South-Sea Bubble whose centenary Lamb is here [in Elia's first appearance] wryly commemorating" (Gerald Monsman, *Confessions of a Prosaic Dreamer* 39). The bubble was the failed scheme to obtain a trade monopoly in the South Seas in exchange for buying up the national debt; the character of Elia is equally a bid for an undisputed claim—over a reading public—and equally doomed. But it is a failure Elia/Lamb cheerfully (rhetorically) admits by recalling to his readers his real (i.e., daytime) profession just when he describes his writing process in "Oxford in the Vacation" (*London Magazine*, October 1820): "The enfranchised quill, that has plodded all the morning among the cart-rucks of figures and ciphers, frisks and curvets so at its ease over the flowery carpet-ground of a midnight dissertation. It feels its promotion * * * * So that you see, upon the whole, the literary dignity of *Elia* is very little, if at all, compromised in the condescension" (Lamb 421).

The necessity of an extraliterary profession is emphasized by the metonym of the quill that serves both occupations. The final force of the apology belies its own claims—writing is done at midnight, hidden. Perhaps only a coincidence, on 29 March 1825, Lamb wrote Henry Crabbe Robinson this letter (Lamb 173 quoted entirely):

> I have left the d———d India House for Ever!
> Give me great Joy. C. Lamb

Within half a year, Elia appeared no more in the *London*.

19. Like Lamb, although only by way of passing example, Simpson glances at an economic continuity between Swift and Wordsworth: "What they share, I suspect, is a common sensitivity to the predicament of the bourgeois experience of authorship: radical uncertainties about readership, affiliation and determination" (*Historical Imagination*, 12).

20. See also Huntington Brown, "The Gloss to *The Rime of the Ancient Mariner*" for a reading of the fictive layers that provide McGann's point of departure.

21. The final sentence of the "Advertisement" does say that "the lines entitled Expostulation and Reply, and those which follow, arose out of a conversation with a friend who was somewhat unreasonably attached to modern books of moral philosophy" (*Lyrical Ballads* 8). While this gives a biographical configuration, the phrase "arose out of" is vague enough not to situate the poem's speaker as a poet, and the note in the "Advertisement" suggests Wordsworth's awareness that the poem, as positioned, did not accomplish the work he hoped it would.

22. The complex valence of the weathercock is suggested by a comment made by Dorothy Wordsworth about the boy on whom the poem is based: "He has played frequently an hour or two without appearing sensible that the rain was pouring down on him or the wind blowing about him" (LEY 166, 7 March 1796). The weathercock provides an objective measure for what the boy does not experience subjectively. It is, in this sense, like the father's legalistic insistence that there must be "some reason" ("Ancedote" 42) for the preference of Kilve.

23. The "fact" of the home at "Kilve" prevents any perfect correspondence between the narrator and Basil Montagu.

24, According to Dorothy Wordsworth, Montagu "proposed to William to allow him 50£ a year for his board provided I should approve of the plan" (LEY 147); according to Montagu, "Wordsworth proposed to take my child from my Chambers in London in[to] Dorsetshire, where he was to settle with his Sister" (LEY 147n). For their approach to teaching and disciplining the child, see LEY 160–61 and 180–81.

25. This event occured about a year before Wordsworth wrote the poem. Coleridge's version is different: "'Citizen John,' I said to him, 'this is a fine place to talk treason in!' 'Nay! Citizen Samuel,' replied he, 'it is rather a place to make a man forget that there is any necessity for treason'" (quoted in Moorman I: 328).

26. Wordsworth's interest in the motto is apparent from a postscript in a letter to Biggs and Cottle: "Be careful to print the motto accurately—Quam nihil ad genium, Papiniane, tuum!" (LEY 293). Butler and Green (*Lyrical Ballads* 377) translate "How utterly unsuited to your taste, Papinianus" and quote Derek Roper's summary: "Selden is voicing his scorn for ignorant critics, and his use of this quotation suggests that for him Papinianus represents the true learning which despises their 'barbarous glosses.' But in its new context the sentence must refer to the *Lyrical Ballads* themselves, and 'Papinianus' seems to stand for the unsympathetic persons who are here warned that the poems will not be to their liking" (Butler and Green 377).

27. By the *Spirit of the Age* (1825), Hazlitt's view of the manner of presentation, if not of its content, had altered: "The effect [of the Lectures] was more electrical and instantaneous [than his speeches in the House of Commons]. . . . Dazzling others by the brilliancy of his acquirements, dazzled himself by the admiration they excited, he lost fear as well as prudence. . . . The principles of Reform were scattered in all directions, like chaff before the keen northern blast. He laid about him like one inspired; nothing could withstand his envenomed tooth" (215–16).

28. J. W. Binns has traced the citation to the Dutch poet Jan Sousa's satire on legal commentaries and their deadening effect on poetic inspiration, "Epistola XVI" (1609), but believes that neither Wordsworth nor Coleridge was aware of this source ("The Title-Page Epigraph of the *Lyrical Ballads*" 222–24).

29. Drawing on *Prelude* V, Lucy poems, and Wordsworth's third "Essay on Epigraphs," David Haney argues that "the objective materiality of language . . . is very concretely envisioned in the notion, shared by Coleridge, that words should be treated as 'things'" (*Hermeneutics* 69).

30. Susan Wolfson aptly describes the eighth stanza as "recast[ing] a tentative report into interrogative form" (*The Questioning Presence* 54).

31. Whether Wordsworth's description of the composition is accurate determines if his act of writing performed this transformation by suppressing the external brook or if his act of reading invented the brook to unify the poem further through interpretation.

32. Poems such as "Goody Blake and Harry Gill" and "Simon Lee" from the first edition had already suggested that the city's sense of profit existed in displaced ways in the country. One interpretation of "The Last of the Flock" would be to understand the shepherd's error as the destruction of his capital, sheep, which should be used only to produce renewable wool and not taken to market themselves.

33. The Link between this argument and Wordsworth declining to "trade" in the "moving accident" in "Hart-Leap Well" connects Wordsworth with the economy of generic fiction and poetry, in which such denials are standard stock. James Averill uses the phrase "moving accident" to argue that Wordsworth put his sentimental "rivals at the level of eager shopkeepers spreading goods for potential cus-

tomers" (*Suffering* 182). Paul Magnuson, citing Averill, links the phrase to Wordsworth's desire to avoid the supernatural, such as in Coleridge's *Ancient Mariner* (*Coleridge and Wordsworth* 247). Granted, but this avoidance shadows an attraction since it occurs within a poem that centers on a "moving accident" that is mysterious and, in the shepherd's version at least, rife with superstition. Put another way, Wordsworth's "trade" depends upon making visible what it is not. Karen Swann ("Suffering and Sensation in *The Ruined Cottage*") makes a similar argument for the Pedlar's tale of Margaret—"a common tale / By moving accident uncharactered" ("Ruined Cottage" 231–32).

34. This co-option is almost certainly deliberate, as Wordsworth had, in a poem Averill describes as "a crude form of dramatic monologue" (*Suffering* 40)—an unpublished sonnet rich in Gray's sentimental diction ("curfew toll" 1; "midnight spreads her raven gloom" 4)—elaborated a metaphor of sunset and death. The poem ends awaiting "Heaven's bright Morn" that will "lead on the eternal day" ("Sonnet Written by Mr.———Immediately after the Death of his Wife" 14; composed 1787, in William Wordsworth, *The Poems* 1:47–48).

35. Presumed to be the earliest reference to the *Lyrical Ballads*.

36. "*Simon Lee, the old Huntsman*, is the portrait, admirably painted, of every huntsman who, by toil, age, and infirmities, is rendered unable to guide and govern his canine family" (*Monthly Review* 29:207). Burney declines to translate the scene into a "tale," insisting instead on it as a description of a generalizable inevitability and erasing the narrator's presence and action.

37. For a more extended analysis of how the term *system* operates within the periodical industry, see Mark Schoenfield, "Regulating Standards" 149–51.

38. For accounts of the rivalry between Eldon and Erskine, see anecdotes 53, 96, 173, and 174 in Eldon's *Anecdote Book*.

6. Evidentiary Poems: The Second Edition

1. Arguing that *The Prelude* "is an autobiography before it is a theory," Laurence Lerner, among others, continues a dichotomy championed by Francis Jeffrey between poetic and philosophical/political genres. Insisting on the incoherence of Wordsworth's theories of nature, he points out that, in the bird-snaring episode in book 1, "Nature suddenly seems more interested in the protection of property than in the sanctity of life" ("What Did Wordsworth Mean by 'Nature'?" 292).

2. The decision to omit "Andrew Jones" from the *Miscellaneous Poems* (1820) may have had more to do with the publication of its 'parent' poem *Peter Bell* in 1819 than with an aesthetic judgment.

3. The narrator's unreliability is established in his description of Ruth's wild life. At the "pleasant Banks of Tone," she dwells "Under the greenwood tree" (190–92), an echo to the fanciful, romantic space of *As You Like It*. Wordsworth,

however, drops a note to indicate that the woods by the Tone are a Coppice wood, i.e., "low woods cut at stated times for fuel" (Johnson). Some of the resonances of "coppice" are clear in the last of Johnson's quotations: "The rate of *coppice* will fall upon the discovery of coal-mines. —*Locke*"

4. Without agreeing on what constitutes a "Lucy poem," critics have concurred that, as David Perkins put it, "they are written in a half-private language of imagery" (*Wordsworth and the Poetry of Sincerity* 193; see also Geoffrey Hartman, *Wordsworth's Poetry* 190, Frances Ferguson, *Wordsworth* 178, Virginia Ireys, "Lucy as Pastoral Heroine" 391). In glancing at "Strange Fits of Passion Have I Known," I depend on the corollary to Perkins's observation that the poem relies on a half-public language, one discernible from both the poem's location in the *Lyrical Ballads* and its relation to the language of lunacy current in the popular press at the time of its publication.

As Susan Eilenberg points out, the "economy of the Lucy poems involves neither property nor, in any obvious sense, possession" (*Strange Power* 108). Moreover, the mortality that overhangs the poems seems a thorough denial of the very sense of possession that "Strange Fits" activates; the poem uses "my" six times, and third-person possessives four times (not including "Nature's gentlest boon" 18). Further, the play between "my way," "wayward thoughts" ("Strange Fits" 7, 25) and "th'untrodden ways" ("She Dwelt" 1) maps the uncanny—a favorite critical term for the Lucy poems—over physical space, and so contests the possibility of other claims of ownership. The rejection of possession, indeed the incapacity for possession during the "fit," becomes a refusal of agency and responsibility that is consonant with the law on property with regard to lunacy.

In "Ellen Irwin," Gordon "cannot bear the thoughts / That through his brain are travelling" (25–26) and so, in what would legally be called the "heat of passion" or a "fit of passion," he kills "Fair Ellen." As Chambers put it in his discussion of homicide, "To shed blood by design is never to be excused by any thing less than the violence of a sudden passion" (*Lectures* 2:401). Immediately after the horror tale of "Ellen Irwin," Wordsworth presents "Strange Fits of Passion Have I Known," a lyric which translates the public phrase "fit of passion" from a violent register to one of poetic "delicacy," the term the *British Critic* uses to characterize the poem (17 [February 1801]: 130). Susan Meisenhelder argues that the first stanza of "Strange Fits" "allow[s] the reader to expect the relation of a very mysterious and even macabre event rather than the revelation of a psychological insight" (*Wordsworth's Informed Reader* 37), and that the poem's placement in the volume after "Ellen" heightens this effect since both are "in the same meter and rhyme scheme" (*Informed Reader* 249). In moving from "Ellen" to "Strange Fits," the reader moves from a public scene (the Scots ballad *Helen of Kirkconnell* was "famous" [Butler and Green 382]; Bruce's grave, uncharacteristically for the *Lyrical Ballads*, has a visible text) to a private, "fond" musing. Simultaneously, the movement from "Ellen" to

"Strange Fits" reverses the escalation of "outrageous stimulation" that Wordsworth criticized in the Preface (*Lyrical Ballads* 249), and distinguishes "Strange Fits," in which feeling "gives importance to action and situation," from "Ellen," which the *British Critic* describes as "merely narrative" (17:128). Hartman could have been contrasting the two poems in his description of "Strange Fits" as "preferring mood to the ballad-mongers' stock-in-trade of supernatural or extraordinary incidents" (*Wordsworth's Poetry* 23). The effect in "Strange Fits," however, is achieved by invoking a term—*fit of passion*—that has a public currency connected with violence and its adjudication in terms of a defendant's state of mind, and then taming it in order to mark a difference. As we know—from the canceled final stanza in which Lucy does die as if from the speaker's thoughts; from the poem's continual associations with other "Lucy" poems and "Nutting"; and from the critical history of reading a subtext of guilt into these poems—the poem remains haunted by a violence structured through social possibilities (marriage, incest, confession, community). Bateson speaks of the "Lucy poems" as Wordsworth's "killing her [Dorothy] off symbolically" because of his incestuous desires (Re-interpretation 153); Richard Matlak also suggests a murderous wish directed at Dorothy, because she was a hindrance to his following Coleridge to Ratzeburg ("Wordsworth's Lucy Poems in Psychobiographical Context" 49); Richard Bourke cites "Bloom's thesis that guilt is repressed and concentrated in the person of Lucy" (*Romantic Discourse and Political Modernity* 195).

The association of "fits of passion" with the sleepwalking death of James in "The Brothers" is suggested by a shared textual precursor, Erasmus Darwin's discussion of "reverie" in *Zoonomia* (see Kent Beyette, "Wordsworth's Medical Muse" 94). Consequently, there is reason to see the convergence of the moon's and the speaker's inexorable approach to Lucy's cottage as a symbol of the speaker's lunacy. On the treatment of lunacy, the lunatic as a legal category, and the legal disempowerment of such an individual, see Kathleen Jones, *Lunacy, Law, and Conscience: 1744–1845*.

The disappearance of the moon, and the return from the fit, leaves the speaker with the vague foreboding of what he has done: "'O mercy!' to myself I cried, / 'If Lucy should be dead!'" (27–28). The pause added by the exclamation point suggests, however lightly, a plea. "Should she be dead, then mercy" is the precise paraphrase of the exclamation, despite the tendency to read it idiomatically as "For mercy's sake, do not let Lucy be dead."

Despite the seeming singularity of the scene described ("What *once* to me befel" 4, my emphasis), it is only a representative of repetitive "fits," only "*one* of those sweet dreams" (17, my emphasis). The recurrence of such fits is a definition of lunacy, as distinguished from idiocy, which is a continuous condition (for the history of this distinction and its eventual collapse, see A. Highmore, *A Treatise on the Law of Idiocy and Lunacy* [1822] 2–10). In part, what the poem occludes is precisely the content of "sweet dream," and it substitutes instead a description of his journey which shows he remains as aware as when he is not entranced. Aware of the details of the horse's gait, the speaker's mind is elsewhere. In this sense, the reverie severs consciousness and self-consciousness, a division made evident by the moment when "to myself I cried" (the inversion of the usual prose order emphasizes the presence of the two subjectivities, one of which remains capable of judgment).

Although we do not know whether the opening stanza was added to the poem before or after James Hadfield's attempted assassination of George III and Erskine's subsequent successful insanity defense, by the time the poem was copied out to be sent to Cottle, the issue of liability for the impassioned mind was certainly current. That the accused, who was the same age as Wordsworth, had suffered a head trauma while fighting in France gave the case yet another spectacular element. Erskine argued that, despite Hadfield's clear knowledge of his demonstrably premeditated act, of its wrongness and its consequences, Hadfield was still a lunatic because he acted at the command of God and felt himself entirely passive (he also sought to replicate Christ's "passion"; see *Rex v. Hadfield*, 26 June 1800, 27 *Howell's State Trials* 1323–24, 1341–42); the defendant's mind, Erskine contended, was filled with "inconceivable imaginations, wholly unfitting it for all dealing with human affairs according to the sober estimate and standard of reason" (1321). Erskine's successful defense constituted a crucial divergence from the older understanding of legal lunacy as requiring the total dissolution of a mind, so that new legislation was passed to accommodate this judicial change (see Hansard *New Parliamentary History* 35 [1800]: 389–90 for the brief debate on 39&40 Geo III c. 94). Erskine's defense emphasized the apparent sanity of many who are insane, perhaps even when a fit is upon them—when the manifestation may be only the slightest degree of plodding intensity. Although the phrase "fit of passion" never occurs in the trial, both words appear frequently, as do a number of synonymous phrases with identical grammatical structure. Hadfield's brother noted that his "various fits" occurred "about the hot season [and] at about the changes of the moon" (1338). This trial, further, provided for public reiterations (by both prosecution and defense) of the debilities of lunacy, in terms of both criminal and civil law. I am not arguing for this case or its publicity as a direct source for the new stanza (without better information about when the first stanza was added, this remains an open question); instead, I use it to point to the public resonances of "Strange Fits" for a contemporary reader.

5. Charles Lamb had denoted "Lines left upon a Seat in a Yew-Tree" as an "inscription." That genre, prevalent in the 18th century, Hartman explains, "was any verse conscious of the place on which it was written . . . [a] feature of the inscription, and perhaps the most intriguing, is related to this sense for a life (in nature) so hidden, retired, or anonymous that it is perceived only with difficulty" (*The Unremarkable Wordsworth* 32–33).

6. Susan Wolfson neatly catches this aesthetic function of this doubling: "To move the heart into thought, rather than 'To freeze the blood,' requires the reader to leave behind the physical action of the ballad world—'the throng, the tumult of the chace'—for the inward, meditative motions of lyric poetry" (*The Questioning Presence* 79).

7. In a similar metonymic shift, Richard Bateman's Chapel-floor in "Michael" is a modern version of the pleasure house, built not by a lord but by a merchant.

8. For more on the relation of Wordsworth to Burke in the unpublished "Letter," see Chandler, *Second Nature* 15–25.

9. As the poem develops, other similarities to Coleridge's ballad emerge, including the moral of kindness to living things delivered by a "Grey-headed Shepherd" who "hast spoken well" ("Hart-Leap" 161).

10. His find is comparable to the spot of the Khan's fountain in Coleridge's "Kubla Khan":

> Where Alph, the sacred river, ran
> Through caverns measureless to man
> Down to a sunless sea.
>
> (3–5)

Sir Walter attempts to impose his value, to measure out the "three leaps"; the Khan builds where nature's sacredness precedes him in an attempt to gird it. Their mistakes are reciprocal, and answered reciprocally. Kubla Khan hears "Ancestral voices prophesying war!" (30), and the well water sends "forth a dolorous groan" (136).

11. A footnote directs the reader's attention to the abruptness of the opening lines: "This poem was intended to be the concluding poem of a series of pastorals, the scene of which was laid among the mountains of Cumberland and Westmoreland. I mention this to apologise for the abruptness with which the poem begins" (footnote to title). Instead of coming last, "The Brothers" is the first of the five poems called pastorals in a volume containing several others that resemble the pastoral form. Strictly, the intended location for the poem does not explain its opening, which only becomes abrupt with prompting. Wordsworth portrays the poem itself as dislocated, shifted from its place, like Leonard. In later editions, Wordsworth drops the footnote and sets the initial lines with quotation marks. In a letter to Cottle, Coleridge indicates Wordsworth's desire that "The Brothers" "*begin* the volume" (LEY 290; 1 August 1800), but apparently the printing had already started and he had to be content with it appearing third. If it had begun the second volume, the sense of dislocation generated by the footnote would have been still increased. The framing of the volume by "The Brothers" and "Michael" would centralize Wordsworth's view that "men who do not wear fine clothes can feel deeply" (LEY 315).

12. The story that on finishing the poem, Wordsworth rushed it to his publisher, thus effectively ending the tour and the Lyrical Ballads simultaneously, emphasizes the poet's ability to convert idleness into labor. (See Butler and Green 357–58 for documentation and a critical survey regarding the composition of "Tintern Abbey"). For a detailed discussion of the ramifications of tourism as a political act, see Alan Liu, "The Supervision of the Picturesque" (in *Wordsworth: The Sense of History* 91–115), in which Liu argues the "importance for the picturesque of . . . actual as well as symbolic equivalence between scenery and property" that depended on a "peculiar" distribution "of property in the picturesque zones of Britain" (91–92).

13. Of the blank verse poems of the second volume, only this one ends on an unaccented (or slightly accented) syllable, an effect reinforced by commas breaking in the middle of the fourth foot of the previous line and the second of this one.

14. Simpson distinguishes the "bond / Interest and mortgages" from "tithes, fines and heriots, the semi-feudal obligations that were the traditional encumbrances of the customary tenant" in order to show that the Ewbanks "for laudable reasons indeed, have brought upon *themselves* the woes that now impinge upon the family" (*Historical Imagination* 144).

15. In a letter to Jane Pollard, 8 May 1792, Dorothy mentions that John is sailing to either "the West Indies or America, and next spring he goes out again to the East." John's involvement in the West Indies is twice diluted in this sentence, and he is dissociated from the slave trade by the postscript: "I hope you were an *immediate* abolitionist and are angry with the House of Commons for continuing to traffic in human flesh so long as 96" (LEY 73, 75).

16. Suppressing the exact years of Leonard's voyages, Wordsworth does not allow a reader to locate his involvement in the West Indies against the political agitation for the abolition of the slave trade, a position supported by Wilberforce and Pitt in the 1790s (see Holdsworth 13:157).

17. This exchange has an analogue in the transformation of the Lake District into a Tourist Industry, which the Priest decries. Land, while serving for local subsistence, is expended in becoming a tourist spot. See Simpson, *Historical Imagination* 75–77, for Wordsworth's resistance to a proposed railway through the Lake District in 1844 as a critique of the aesthetic of tourism.

18. See James Walvin, *England, Slaves, and Freedom, 1776–1838* chap. 5, as well as the notes to Coleridge's lecture.

19. A postmodern analogy would be the simultaneous attack on abortion rights and child care initiated by the Reagan reforms (see Patricia Williams, *The Alchemy of Race and Rights* 35).

20. In a short poem, possibly a fragment, composed "possibly around late July 1800" and "heavily lined out and cross-hatched," a narrator excoriates "some Tour-

ists of the Lakes" who "pass by reading; a practise very common." The overelaborate diction of the first lines suggests Wordsworth's discomfort: "What waste in the labour of Chariot and Steed! / For this came ye hither?" (*Poems, in Two Volumes* 535).

21. As Wolfson has written, "the power of Leonard's questioning lies in the very inevitability of the answer" (*Questioning* 84).

22.

> One roaring cataract—a sharp May storm
> Will come with loads of January snow,
> And in one night send twenty score of sheep
> To feed the ravens
>
> (152–55)

23. Wordsworth twice insisted to Cottle and Biggs that the "names of the Speakers" be printed "at full length in the middle of the page" (LEY 289; 290).

24. L. J. Swingle has noted how often in Wordsworth's poems a reader can reach "at several, and contrary, readings" (*The Obstinate Questionings of English Romanticism* 93); his discussion of "The Two April Mornings" focuses on the vision of Matthew "with his bough / Of wilding in his hand" (59–60), an image with affinities with James's staff ("The Brothers" 92–93).

25. Chandler discusses Michael's "inclusive" gesture as a rite of passage for Luke which, in duplicating himself, becomes a passage of rites for Michael (*Second Nature* 163–64).

26. Wordsworth worried over the precise sound of the drum, trying out "its rattling music" in MS 1800/02 and the published 1815 version (Butler and Green 184).

27. The final stanza restates all this in the past tense, starting with "And *hence* I said that Andrew's boys . . ." (31).

28. See Geoffrey MacCormack, "Revenge and Compensation in Early Law," for an effort to ground this transformation in legal doctrine. For a sampling of the scholarship on revenge, see Richard Posner, *Law and Literature* 26–27n.

29. For a sampling of Thomas Bewick's vehement dislike of Pitt, see his *Memoir* chaps. 15–16. Bewick earns his entry in the *Biographical Dictionary of Modern British Radicals* less because of his radicalism than by contrast with the conservative climate during the wars against France.

30. "Said generous Rob, 'What need of books? / Burn all the statutes and their shelves'" ("Rob Roy's Grave," *Poem, in Two Volumes* 21–22).

31. Lamb, writing to Wordsworth in 1815, spoke of that "delicacy towards aberrations from the strict path which is so fine in the Old Thief and the boy by his side, and always brings water to my eyes" (Moorman I: 481n).

32. See also E. P. Thompson, *Customs in Common* esp. chap. 3, "Custom, Law, and Common Right," which concludes "It is not that John Clare—nor the commoners for whom he spoke—were primitive communists. . . . Common right which

was in lax terms coterminous with settlement, was *local* right, and hence also a power to exclude strangers. Enclosures, in taking the commons away from the poor, made them strangers in their own land" (184).

33. The review in the *British Critic* groups these three poems as "of the highest order of Poems" in the volume (17 [February 1801]: 128). Stephen Parrish notes that the "Old Cumberland Beggar" would "have needed no more than a shift of focus . . . or the addition of a moving accident" to fit into Wordsworth's projected series of Pastorals that included "The Brothers" and "Michael" (*The Art of the Lyrical Ballads* 159–60).

34. Chandler has argued that the "eye of Nature" is "the eye of the villager whose perception is governed by the mild necessity of use" (*Second Nature* 89). This equation obscures the complexity of the various gazes through which the poem tracks the Beggar. I would suggest that the "eye of Nature" is a sight immune from the "mild necessity of use" which, in gazing on the Beggar, equally gazes on and admonishes the villagers.

35. The textual history suggests that Wordsworth began working on the poem as "only a description poem" as early as 1796; it was not until 1798, however, about when the political economists were "beginning their war upon mendacity" (as Wordsworth told Fenwick), that the poem discovered its intention (Butler and Green 393–94). Put in the poem's own language, the constant gaze (description) was given political shape by virtue of national changes. Wordsworth's choice, then, to retain the subtitle of "A Description" is indicative of the poem's mechanisms.

36. Averill, having catalogued the "verbs" of "visual perception," contends that "vision is the metaphor of encounter, of interaction between subject and suffering object" (*Suffering* 121). I agree with this assessment, but my argument concerns what other possible encounters, from legal and legislative discourses, this one replaces.

37. Citing Charles Du Bos, J. Hillis Miller argues that "stones play an important role in Wordsworth's poetry," both as found objects that function as a symbol for "inmost being" and as the site of inscription (*The Linguistic Moment from Wordsworth to Stevens* 81–82).

38. The beggar's perpetual oldness (22–23) has a cursed element (see "Song of the Wandering Jew") and, in the context of poems like "Ruth" and "Ellen Irwin" (whose first name recurs in the poem immediately preceding "The Old Cumberland Beggar"), one line hints at the beggar's past by negation: "His age has no companion" (45).

39. A gloss from the *OED* is more suggestive: "Anything injurious or obnoxious to the community, or to the individual as a member of it (esp. as an owner of property), for which some legal remedy may be found."

40. But see Anthony David Nuttall, who has contended that "Wordsworth is virtually saying that distress is good because it provides stimulus and scope for charity" (*A Common Sky* 131). Chandler suggests that Wordsworth may indeed be "closer" to that "mad doctrine," "perhaps, than many of us would like to believe" (*Second Nature* 86). Lerner, discussing lines 150–54 from the 1827 version, insists "there can be no doubt what this means: we need beggars so that we can give to them" ("What Did Wordsworth Mean?" 293). See Gary Lee Harrison, *Wordsworth's Vagrant Muse*, chap. 5, for a historicized account of the Wordsworths' practices of charity and their relation to the poem's ideological strategies.

41. In later editions, Wordsworth made the allusion to the social scheme more evident by putting both "House" and "industry" in full capitals.

42. Polanyi reports that 250 Industry Houses eventually held half a million inmates; the association between such houses and prisons recurs in discussions on either. "The Act for establishing penitentiary houses," composed by Blackstone and Eden, was intended to reform prisoners by "inuring them to habits of industry" (Howard, *Prisons* 260).

43. *Boon* is a general term, meaning "a gift, a grant; a benefaction; a present" (Johnson). Of the four quotations Johnson has, two are legalistic, e.g. "The blustering fool has satisfy'd his will; / His boon is giv'n . . . Dryden's Fables."

"1. A *charter* is a written evidence of things done between man and man. *Charters* are divided into *charters* of the king and *charters* of private persons . . . Cowel." All three additional quotations under this definition are explicitly legal, while both quotations under the second meaning, "Any writing bestowing privileges or rights," are doctrines of natural law, e.g., "God renewed this *charter* of man's sovereignty over the creatures. *South*." The two examples for the third definition, "privilege; immunity; exemption" are metaphors from Shakespeare, e.g., "I must have liberty / Withal as large a *charter* as the wind."

Both examples of "exemptions" are from discourses on law, e.g., "The Roman laws gave particular *exemptions* to such as built ships, or traded in corn. *Arbuthnot on Coins*."

44. Although verbal echoes are insufficient to claim a deliberate allusion, this movement from the pedestrian formation of habit to the development of the poet occurs in Godwin's *Enquiry* (bk. 1 chap. 5).

45. Even to the extent that Fox is included in the audience, he is located outside the Pitt government; Wordsworth emphasizes his awareness of this at the end of his letter: "Wishing earnestly that the time may come when the country may perceive what it has lost by neglecting your advice" (LEY 315).

46. He never uses the synonym *budget*. In an unpublished version of "Repentance. A Pastoral Ballad," the speaker recounts:

When the fine Man came to us from London, said I
Let him come with his bags proudly grasp'd in his hand
But Thomas, be true to me, Thomas, we'll die
Before he shall go with an inch of the Land.

(DC MS. 80, quoted in Parrish, *The Art;* for other versions see both *Poetical Works* 2: 46–47 and *Poems, in Two Volumes* 575–76)

The published version, altering "fine Man . . . from London" to "troublesome Tempter" and "bags" to "purse" suggests the economic overtones to "bags" (and to London). Parrish points out that "Rural Architecture," "Ballad Michael," and "Repentance" all share "the same sort of bouncing meter and homely manner" and so suggests thematic comparison (*The Art* 155).

47. That thoughts of the war hover over "The Old Cumberland Beggar" is clear from its compositional history; it once contained lines from "Old Man Travelling," in which an old man goes to see his son, dying of a battle wound.

48. "Hart-Leap Well," "There was a boy," "The Brothers," "Ellen Irwin," "'Tis said, that some have died for love," "To a Sexton," "The Two April Mornings," "A Poet's Epitaph," "The Danish Boy," and "Michael" all have encounters with graves, and "Lines Written with a Slate-Pencil" opens with a "hillock of misshapen stones" that are of initial interest because they resemble a cairn. Many other poems that allude to death and graves, in the context of the volume, are implicated in this theme; "It was an April Morning," for example, concludes:

Years after we are gone and in our graves,
When they [shepherds] have cause to speak of this wild place,
May call it by the name of EMMA'S DELL

(45–47)

Emma's Dell is a marker of deaths to come, even while it is the poet's "out-of-doors abode" (41); and in an earlier poem, "The Two April Mornings," a figure named Emma is already dead.

49. "A Poet's Epitaph" revises "Lines left upon a Seat in a Yew-tree," which begins with the eulogistic "—Nay, Traveller! rest." The poetic voice seeks in the traveller "one whose heart the holy forms / Of young imagination have kept pure" in order to admonish "Stranger! henceforth be warned; and know, that pride, / Howe'er disguised in its own majesty, / Is littleness; that he who feels contempt / For any living thing, hath faculties / Which he has never used" (44–50). He might be talking to someone, like himself, on the verge of choosing a profession; if "Lines" is the general admonishment, "A Poet's Epitaph" is a confrontation with the specific forms, or, more precisely, a refusal of confrontation, in order to regain the general. As Hartman points out, in "Lines" only "the poet's imagination . . . sees that pile of stones as a funeral pyre" (*Unremarkable* 34).

50. The paragraph in which this observation occurs begins with the comment that Wordsworth "could here pause with pleasure, and invite the Reader to indulge with me in contemplation of the advantages that must have attended such a practise" as burying the dead "beyond the walls of towns and cities" (*Excursion* 448). Wordsworth's rhetorical strategy is to coax his reader to pause, like a fellow traveller, to examine not an epitaph but a procedure of eulogy. The homology of reading a work and reading the procedure of its composition provides another version of the argument from the Preface to the *Lyrical Ballads*.

51. Robert Langbaum suggests the tension of these poles in his description of the Lucy poems. "Such poems are narrative to the extent that we read them as dynamic or moving through time. They are lyric to the extent that we read them as static, as organized around a moment of illumination" ("Wordsworth's Lyrical Characterizations" 319).

52. Although "A Poet's Epitaph" may have been composed a few months earlier than "Ellen Irwin," the reader encounters "Ellen" first in the *Lyrical Ballads*.

53. In the "Essay on Epitaphs," Wordsworth suggests that it is enough "that the trunk and the main branches of the worth of the deceased be boldly and unaffectedly represented. Any further detail . . . must inevitably frustrate its own purpose [and become] unaffecting and profitless" (*Excursion* 453).

54. In his note on "The Brothers" 183, Wordsworth had indicated that most churchyards have few gravestones, and in that poem, the Priest articulates the same notion as a potential economic threat: "The Stone-cutters, 'tis true, might beg their bread / If every English churchyard were like ours" ("Brothers" 177–78).

55. David Ferry suggests that the rustic's opposition to the professionals is simultaneously one "between imagination and the 'meddling intellect'" and between "the life of man in time and the life of man in eternity" (*The Limits of Mortality* 60).

7. *The Excursion:* Revision and Review

1. These comments typify Jonathan Wordsworth's analysis: "scarcely less disastrous is the expansion of the Pedlar's fourth visit in order to get in a reference to Margaret's spinning of hemp . . . . The process of revision goes on through MS.M. (1804) and MS.P.—responsible, for instance, for the deplorable lines on Robert" (*The Music of Humanity* 24–25). Rejecting the economic additions (Margaret's spinning as an "employment hereabouts" and Robert's "humble worth" and "keen[ ] industrious[ness]"), Jonathan Wordsworth presents a text transcendent in its concerns, while erasing the economic and historical parameters the poem presumes to transcend.

2. Galperin's most expansive statement locates Wordsworth's rewriting as the beginning of the revisionist trend exemplified by Levinson and McGann: "But

where the revisionists increasingly use Wordsworth to disabuse the liberal, humanistic values seemingly encoded by the poems of the Great Decade (and on which Wordsworth's reputation rests), it is the purpose of this study to show that Wordsworth was necessarily the first to understand this revision" (*Revision* 1–2).

3. In 1785, petitions were brought to ban peddlers in order to appease retail merchants who faced yet another new tax. As Alan Liu analyzes the debate, "the lack of proper documentation is itself a clue to the deep truth of the controversy: peddlers were holdovers from a system of production and distribution that, in the transition to modern production by wage labor and distribution by retail outlet, became objectionable precisely because it represented the undocumented, unaccountable, and unregulated" (*Sense* 345). The peddlers were too free for the free market because they did not function within either the physical or textual limitations of the market. Wordsworth replaces the peddler in two senses; first, as a poet, he preserves an unalienated exchange, but secondly, as a stamp distributor, he stretches the reach of the market through its documentary mechanisms until the margins that the peddler requires are subsumed.

4. The equivalent line in *The Excursion* described "a Man of reverend age" (I 33).

5. "The Anglo-American legal system developed a psychologically and politically satisfactory standard, 'satisfied belief,' in the late seventeenth century and its cognate, 'beyond reasonable doubt,' in the late eighteenth century for the jury trial" (Barbara Shapiro, *"Beyond Reasonable Doubt" and "Probable Cause"* 79). Shapiro details the dialogue between philosophy and law which shaped the notion of the reasonable. See also Douglas L. Patey, *Probability and Literary Form* chap. 2, "Probability and Signs: Reasoning from Effect to Cause" on the 18th-century relation between reasonability and representation, and Alexander Welsh, "Burke and Bentham on the Narrative Potential of Circumstantial Evidence" (608–11) on the use of inductive reasoning in trial narratives.

6. See also Patey, *Probability* chap. 3 "Conditions of Knowing in Augustan Fiction," (esp. 179–97 on Ferdinand's exploitation of the signs of narrative coherence in *Ferdinand Count Fathom*).

7. Christensen is borrowing from Foucault: "The contrast between Humean force and Byronic strength corresponds to Michel Foucault's distinction between a juridical notion of power in which 'power is taken to be a right, which one is able to possess like a commodity, and which one can in consequence transfer or alienate' and a [sovereign] power that 'is neither given, nor exchanged, nor recovered, but rather exercised[.']" (*Lord Byron's Strength* 4; quoting Foucault, *Power/Knowledge*, note omitted).

8. See also the "Preface to the Edition of 1815": "My guiding wish was, that the small pieces of which these volumes consist, thus discriminated, might be regarded under a two-fold view; as composing an entire work within themselves, and

as adjuncts to the philosophical Poem, 'The Recluse'" (in *Prose* 1:28). Typically Wordsworthian, what is whole from one perspective is partial from another, and the reader must hold both views simultaneously.

9. A gothic architect, usually anonymous and often multiple, was subordinate to the benefactor(s); and the 1814 volume begins with a dedicatory sonnet to "the right honourable / William, Earl of Lonsdale, K.G., / ETC., ETC." from "William Wordsworth," which asks for the lord's "favour" (13).

10. David Cottom describes an 18th-century attitude toward taste, championed by Hume and Burke, that regards "uneducated perceptions" as "pseudo-events": "The assurance with which an individual may report an experience is of no consequence if that report does not defer to the social prescriptions for the senses" (*The Civilized Imagination* 3, note omitted). Cottom outlines an economy of aesthetic experience that relied on aristocratic sensibilities, and demonstrates the relation between those sensibilities and aristocratic wealth and ownership.

11. In his letter to Wordsworth about this review, Charles Lamb produces a circulation of his copy of *The Excursion* that both implicates it in and disperses the economic impulse. First, in order to write his unfavorable review, Hazlitt actually borrowed Lamb's copy of the poem, and because Hazlitt "blowed us up about six months ago," it has only lately been returned—just in time, Lamb hopes, for him to review it in the *Quarterly*. The letter ends by posing *The Excursion* as a haven from business concerns; Lamb is "so fagged and dispirited" with "cursed India House work, I scarce know what I do. My left arm reposes on the *Excursion*. I feel what it would be in quiet." This sympathetic reading of the poem, because of its insistence on the poem's being uneconomic, rather than on its proposing an alternate economy, places Lamb's interpretation within Hazlitt's paradigm. From Wordsworth's view, that flaw is apparent in the ease with which Lamb can divide Wordsworth's identity, since, curiously, the whole of this letter is addressed "to W. W., Esq., Collector of Stamp Duties for the Conjoint Northern Counties, not to W. W., Poet" ("Letter to William Wordsworth" 789–90).

12. "Each tidbit of a relic saved from Charles's execution [including fragments of cloth stained with his blood] held for its possessor a whole story—a whole paradigm, we might say—about the King" (Patricia Fumerton, *Cultural Aesthetics* 17).

13. Matthew Arnold invoked Jeffrey's comment in regard to Wordsworth's poetic style: "although Jeffrey completely failed to recognize Wordsworth's real greatness, he was yet not wrong in saying of *The Excursion*, as a work of poetic style: 'This will never do'" (quoted in Judson Stanley Lyon, The Excursion: *A Study* 122). Edward Quillinan's estimation of *The Excursion* appears in *Henry Crabb Robinson on Books and Their Writers*: "It *will* do, in spite of my Lord Jeffrey, and its occasional defects" (Lyon, *Study* 140). The phrase "in spite" requires full weight; what the poem *does* sticks in Jeffrey's critical craw.

14. Wordsworth gave Gillies, whose essay on Solitude Wordsworth had praised the previous month, the role of the Solitary against his own Wanderer. Gillies had lost a small fortune in investments, and Wordsworth published a sonnet urging:

From the dark chambers of dejection freed,
Spurning the unprofitable yoke of care,
Rise, GILLIES, rise . . .
(*Misc. Sonnets* Pt. II, IV, 1–3, rpt. in *Poems*)

15. In *Caleb Williams*, after Caleb has fled both lawyers and thieves to seek a life of independence through writing in London, his "first productions . . . were rejected with contempt by the Aristarchus of" a newspaper (258). Philip Whithers (d. 1790) had taken up the name Aristarchus to argue the relationship between a "cultivated Mind" (3) and a command of the Principles of Composition: "Language is an Art and a glorious one, whose Influence extends over all the others, and in which finally all Science must centre. . . . The Importance of a correct Mode of Expression in BUSINESS is sufficiently obvious. . . . In the PULPIT, the SENATE, at the BAR, and in all public Assemblies, it is necessary to speak with Purity and Elegance" (*Aristarchus, or the Principles of Composition* 27, 30). Aristarchus of Samothrace (c. 215–c. 143 BC) headed the Alexandrian library and produced some of the earliest critical editions and commentaries of Homer, Pindar, etc.

16. "But though we conceive that philosophy [read: political economy, moral philosophy] is thus, in some degree, responsible for the French revolution, we are far from charging her with the guilt that this name implies. The writers may have produced effects very different from what they intended, and very different even from what their works might seem calculated to produce" (*Edinburgh Review* 1 [October 1802]:9).

17. "Wordsworth's *Poems*" (*Edinburgh Review* 11 [October 1807]:215); "Wordsworth's *White Doe*" (*Edinburgh Review* 25 [October 1815]:355); and "Wordsworth's *Tour*" (*Edinburgh Review* 37 [November 1822]:450), as well as the review of *The Excursion* all mention Wordsworth's "genius."

18. For a detailed discussion of the reliance by lawyers on case law as developed in Coke's *Reports* as a precursor to the establishment of an empowered legal profession within the seventeenth century, see Holdsworth 5:339–6:163.

19. Jeffrey had already associated literary and economic value of the poem by pointing to its expensive presentation, and Wordsworth was perhaps stinging from the review's opening: "This, we think, has the merit of being the very worst poem we ever saw imprinted in a quarto volume" (*Edinburgh Review* 25 [October 1815]:355).

20. For the established tradition of plague as a political trope and a bureaucratic experience, see Foucault, *Birth of the Clinic* chap. 2, "A Political Consciousness."

21. E. P. Thompson details the circumstances of the laborers in "Standards and Experiences," *Working Class* chap. 10.

8. *The Excursion:* The Poet of Property

1. In chiding Richard Watson's defense of Burke's position on the French Revolution, Wordsworth had written, probably in 1793, that "we are necessarily led also to conclude that you have no wish to dispel the infatuation which is now giving up to the sword so large a portion of the poor and consigning the rest to the more slow and more painful consumption of want" (*Prose* 1:49). The correspondence between consumption in Parliament and among the poor is both parallel—the war uses up both the physical resources of the poor and the talents of the politicians—and chiasmatic—the consumption (eating) by the government corresponds to the consumption (disease or the negative eating of "want" as if it were a substance) of the poor.

2. De Quincey may snidely allude to the poet's father, who held a post of coroner near, in both time and place, to Margaret's tale.

3. Jeffrey denies what Jean Baudrillard would later distinguish as the "sign-value" of brass buttons, a supplement to their "use-value" and "exchange-value" (*For a Critique of the Political Economy of the Sign* 65).

4. Decisions like *Pierson v. Post* (1805) upholding a fox under pursuit as the property of the pursuer, *Dred Scott* (1857) denying legal (and human) standing to a black human being, and *In the Matter of Baby "M"* (1987) confronting a contractual agreement to surrender a child, as well as recent litigation involving Indian burial grounds and the use of mummies in museums all show that rights are constantly being redrawn under a veneer of stability. Patricia Williams discusses most of these examples in *The Alchemy of Race and Rights*.

5. Bentham's mathematical metaphor suggesting a rigorous formulation, is typical: "Legislation has the same centre with morals, but it has not the same circumference" (quoted in Margery Fry, "Bentham and English Penal Reform," 26). This aphorism follows from 16th-century doctrines that the intention to commit a crime, though immoral, was not criminal, and that the commission of a killing during the course of a felony constituted murder and the presumption of intent. In the 14th century, by contrast, intent did constitute a criminal offence (see Holdsworth 8:433). More recently, the paradoxical nature of any division between act and intent has been explored by H. L. A. Hart in "The House of Lords on Attempting the Impossible." In *Haughton v. Smith* (1975) the House of Lords held that "one who handles goods, mistakenly believing at the time of handling that they were at that time still stolen goods, cannot be convicted of an attempt to handle stolen goods" (369). To hold otherwise, according to Lord Morris of Borth-y-Gest, would be "to convict [the respondent] . . . not for what he did but simply because he had a guilty intention" (quoted in Hart, "Attempting the Impossible" 370n12). But all unsuccessful crimes present this quandary: is firing an unloaded gun, believed to be loaded, attempted murder? A loaded gun that is broken and will not fire? A gun that fires but

sends the bullet wide? I am not concerned with resolving this question, but would point out that such a resolution will function by locating a distinction between the guilty intention and the guilty act at an arbitrary point. Essentially, it is an interpretive act and requires (or invokes) an interpretive theory of justification.

6. The dedication also elides the unsuccessful legal battle the Wordsworths waged to recover the debt and the eventual extralegal settlement. The repayment was, from the perspective of law, a gift; but from the perspective of natural justice Wordsworth championed, it was equity, and it would ultimately benefit all, including the heirs of Lonsdale, in precise proportion to the public value accorded Wordsworth's poetry.

7. Applauding the U.S. government's decision to use Individual Transfer Quotas for fishing, an editorial in the *Wall Street Journal* opined that "those who eat and those who commune with fish are going to want the results that only rules consistent with human nature—that is, with property—can deliver" (246: 12 [19 July 1995] A10).

Conclusion

1. The former are the subject, at some level, of nearly every book written on Wordsworth. On the subject of copyright, Wordsworth's own letters are the proper starting place. Besides the standard biographies, P. M. Zall sets out the historical and biographical context in "Wordsworth and the Copyright Act of 1842." Lee Erickson, in "The Egoism of Authorship: Wordsworth's Poetic Career" discusses the relationship between Wordsworth's professionalism and his use of copyright, while Susan Eilenberg's "Mortal Pages" explicitly links Wordsworth's dual obsessions of death and copyright by tracing the flux between "money" and "monument," words etymologically linked by the common ancestor of "*monere*, to warn or to remind" (356; rpt. in *Strange Power* chap. 8).

2. See John Feather "From Rights in Copies to Copyright" 460–66 and "The English Book Trade and the Law 1695–1799" 63–66.

3. See Marlon Ross, "Authority and Authenticity"; Mark Rose, *Authors;* and Trevor Ross, "Copyright and the Invention of Tradition" as well as Alvin Kernan, *Printing Technology, Letters & Samuel Johnson.*

4. After the lapsing of the licensing act, Queen Anne's statute set up a limited copyright which established the 28-year term on copyright. The bill, although it established a specific property right, did not allow the assignees of that right to set any price on the sale of works; that is, the act did not contemplate a free market in which competition would determine prices, partly because the act reduced competition, and partly because in 1709, local marketplaces functioned on traditional prices. The act included a provision to insure that it would not be construed as altering that tradition in regard to literary property: "A Court of Arbitration was established in case

'any bookseller shall set a price upon any book as shall be conceived by any person to be too high and unreasonable'" (*Letters of David Hume to William Strahan*, 278, quoting *Statutes at Large* xii, 84). This provision was repealed in 1738, suggesting that the literary marketplace offered sufficient constraints on prices by virtue of the difficulty in preventing piracies and the willingness of the public to purchase any specific work against a widening array of choices.

An advertisement, written by Johnson for the "proprietors of the paper entitled *The Idler*," suggests much about the book industry and its reliance on the common law and traditional notions of justice and power. (Johnson himself was, in a way, a proprietor, since "he was supposed somehow to share in the profits of the new paper"; he received about £300 for his *Idler* contributions, and an additional £84 when Newbury published the collected papers [James Clifford, *Dictionary Johnson* 192].) After forgiving previous trespasses since "the past is without remedy, and shall be without resentment," the advertisement announces that "the time of impunity is at an end":

> Whoever shall, without our leave, lay the hand of rapine upon our papers, is to expect that we shall vindicate our due, by the means which justice prescribes, and which are warranted by the immemorial prescriptions of honorable trade. We shall lay hold, in our turn, on their copies, degrade them from the pomp of wide margin [both profit and white space] and diffuse typography, contract them into a narrow space, and sell them at an humble price; yet not with a view of growing rich by confiscations, for we think not much better of money got by punishment than by crimes. We shall, therefore, when our losses are repaid, give what profit shall remain to the *Magdalens;* for we know not who can be more properly taxed for the support of penitent prostitutes, than prostitutes in whom there yet appears neither penitence nor shame. (Boswell, *Life of Johnson* 244n2)

5. Boswell's Johnson summarizes the argument for perpetual copyright simultaneously with describing the profession of writing as an amalgam of publishers and writers: "[Donaldson, who had printed Thompson's *Seasons*] is a fellow who takes advantage of the law to injure his brethren; for, notwithstanding that the statute secures only fourteen years of exclusive right, it has always been understood by *the trade*, that he, who buys the copy-right of a book from the authour, obtains a perpetual property" (*Life of Johnson*, 310). Johnson was explicit that this right derived from trade practices, and not from the law. More precisely, the market of booksellers operates independently of the law, and is contained enough to express its own practices. As noted in chapter four, the practical end to common law copyright did not utterly destroy its ideological usefulness.

6. The letter ends by alluding to one of Hume's own essays, probably "On the Origin of Government," which first appears in the posthumous 1777 edition of his work: "The Essay I mentioned is not so considerable as to [be] printed apart; yet

any pyrated Edition would be reckond incompleat that did not contain it" (*Letters of David Hume*, 275, addition by editor). Hume attempts to demonstrate the truth of his argument by reference to his own work, and the audience of that demonstration is his own publisher.

7. In addition, committees were formed to engage the best engravers, to choose the ideal paper, and, as a result, to establish the superiority of London publishing (Boswell, *Life of Johnson* 803).

8. Forms of the word *rapacity* recur throughout the letters, in reference to the booksellers. Lloyd's written response, no doubt, pleased Wordsworth: "Free Trade is all very plausible when reciprocity is its basis. If Booksellers cannot produce "Excursions" themselves they must pay a proportional duty" (LLY 3: 547).

9. In *The Sonnets of William Wordsworth*, Wordsworth had published a sonnet, "A Plea for Authors, May 1838," which made this argument in a sarcastic tone:

Failing impartial measure to dispense
To every suitor, Equity is lame;
And social Justice, stript of reverence
For natural rights, a mockery and a shame;
Law but a servile dupe of false pretence,
If, guarding grossest things from common claim
Now and for ever, She, to works that came
From mind and spirit, grudge a short-lived fence.
(1–8)

10. Wordsworth did not republish this poem, suggesting that he was not satisfied with its results, whether political or aesthetic. The argument that the poem fell into irrelevance after the 1842 Copyright Act is implausible since Wordsworth did republish "A Plea for Authors." Perhaps he felt that the economic motive, limited here to his family rather than to the heirs of authors generally (as in the "Plea"), served his opponents better than himself.

11. The debate on Wordsworth's position vis-à-vis pantheism is exemplified by Cleanth Brooks's expression of "agonized shock . . . of the girl's falling back into the clutter of things" and F. W. Bateson's delight in the poem's "pantheistic magnificence" (both quoted in Walter Benn Michaels, "Against Formalism: Chickens and Rocks" 221).

12. Mary Moorman, as she assembles snatches of his last years in her final chapter, follows Wordsworth's hint. In the paragraph previous to Wordsworth's letter referring to Lear, she tells a story of Wordsworth breaking into tears during a conversation with the Kent-like gardener, James, the "one person humble and gentle enough to speak to the stricken man on his prolonged and excessive grief" (Moorman II 602). The other quotations in the paragraph that contains the *Lear* reference are, first, from Mary who "wisely" says, "we must not yield to his inclination to keep

aloof from all contact", a contrast to Lear's comment to Cordelia, in refusing to see his other daughters, that "We two alone will sing like birds i'th'cage" (V iii 9); and second, Miss Martineau's denouncement of reports in "some newspapers that [Wordsworth] was failing in mind" as "'utter nonsense'" (603) and her recognition of Wordsworth's "fixed despondency (uncorrected)" for which she "love[s] him best" (Moorman II 603n3), comments which play against the miseries and madness of Lear and Edgar, as well as against Wordsworth's aborted attempt to reform the Solitary. The Fool had thought to go to bed at noon, and Wordsworth "breathed his last calmly, passing away almost insensibly exactly at twelve o'clock (this midday), while the cuckoo-clock at his bedroom door was striking the hour" (Edward Quillinan, quoted in Gill, *A Life* 494n129).

13. In such a schema, the ability to talk about one's self, to narrate one's own life posthumously, is tantamount to self-authorization; this is the canonizing work which the *Prelude* performs, and it is a function prepared by the publication of the *Biographia Literaria* within a year of *The Excursion*, in which Coleridge makes known to the general reading public the existence of the *Prelude*.

14. Michael Moore is considering the "legal" definition of "death," and suggests that interpreters (especially judges) attempting to establish whether someone is dead should be guided "not by some set of conventions we have agreed upon as to when someone will be said to be dead; rather, we will seek to apply 'dead' only to people who are really dead, which we determine by applying the best scientific theory we can muster about what death really is" ("A Natural Law Theory of Interpretation 294). Stanley Fish observes that in this passage Moore shifts from a convention of law to one of scientific definition (*Doing What Comes Naturally* 381).

15. On 3 November 1841, Taylor had written to Wordsworth that "I introduced them into my article with connecting comments chiefly expository,—such as I thought w[oul]d lead review readers to a more ready apprehension of their drift, and also by giving them a *prose* setting, relieve them of some disadvantages which I believe to be incidental to the reading of sonnets consecutively" (LLY 4: 258). Wordsworth's reply on 5 November makes no comment on this assertion, but begins, "You and Mr. Lockhart have been very kind in taking so much trouble about the Sonnets. I have altered them as well as I could to meet your wishes and trust that you will find them improved, as I am sure they are where I have adopted your own words" (LLY 4: 257–58). On 19 November, he writes Taylor that "for many reasons it would be better to leave these sonnets untouched [i.e., not interlaced with the prose] in your Review, but I leave the matter to your own judgment" (LLY 4: 263). Between these two letters, Wordsworth wrote to Dora Quillinan, "My sonnets on Capital punishment 14 in number are about to be printed in the Quarterly Review by Mr. Taylor, along with a general reviewal of my Poems in that form. Perhaps this

may give some stimulus to the six Volumes which as Moxon says they sadly want" (261–62).

16. In 1837, the punishment of death was removed from "about 200 offenses" and remained only "to high treason, murder and attempts at murder—rape—arson with danger to life—and to piracies, burglaries, and robberies, when aggravated by cruelty and violence" (Henry Taylor, "Wordsworth's *Sonnets*" 39). Taylor points out that in many cases, the punishment of death merely deterred juries from convicting, and in other cases was never invoked and remained as only "the dead letter of the law" (39). In 1841, legislation was introduced to abolish capital punishment entirely; the measure was defeated, although rape was made a noncapital offense. The issue, then, that Wordsworth addressed was whether capital punishment should be completely abolished.

WORKS CITED

Abrams, M. H. *Doing Things with Texts: Essays in Criticism and Critical Theory*. New York: Norton, 1991.

Addison, Joseph, and Richard Steele. *The Spectator*. 1709–1714. 4 vols. Ed. Donald Bond. Oxford: Clarendon, 1965.

Anon. *The Laws Respecting Women, as they regard their Natural Rights*. London: Johnson, 1777.

Atiyah, P. S. *The Rise and Fall of Freedom of Contract*. Oxford: Clarendon, 1979.

Austin, J. L. *How to Do Things With Words*. (William James Lectures delivered at Harvard University in 1955.) 2nd ed. Ed. J. O. Urmson and M. Sbisa. Cambridge, Mass.: Harvard University Press, 1975.

Averill, James. *Wordsworth and the Poetry of Human Suffering*. Ithaca: Cornell University Press, 1980.

Bacon, Francis. "Of Judicature." In *The Essayes or Counsels, Civill and Morall*. 1st ed. 1597, 3rd ed. 1625. Ed. J. Pitcher. London: Penguin, 1985.

———. *Elements of the Common Lawes of England*. London, 1636. In *Law Tracts*, vol. 4 of *The Works of Francis Bacon*, 10 vols. London: J. Johnson, 1803.

Baker, Herschel. *William Hazlitt*. Cambridge, Mass.: Harvard University Press, 1962.

Bakhtin, M. M. *The Dialogic Imagination: Four Essays*. Ed. M. Holquist, trans. C. Emerson and M. Holquist. Austin: University of Texas Press, 1981.

Barker, A. D. "The Printing and Publishing of Johnson's *Marmor Norfolciense* (1793) and *London* (1738 and 1739)." *The Library*. Sixth series 3 (1981): 287–304.

Bateson, F. W. *Wordsworth: A Re-interpretation*. 2nd ed. London: Longmans Green and Co., 1956.

Baudrillard, Jean. *The Mirror of Production*. 1973. Trans. M. Poster. St Louis: Telos Press, 1975.

———. *For a Critique of the Political Economy of the Sign*. Trans. C. Levin. St. Louis: Telos Press, 1981.

———. "Simulacra and Simulations." *Selected Writings*. Ed. M. Poster. Stanford: Stanford University Press, 1988.

Beatty, Arthur. *William Wordsworth: His Doctrine and Art in Their Historical Relations.* 2nd ed. Madison: University of Wisconsin Press, 1927.

Bentham, Jeremy. "A Fragment on Government," In *A Comment on the Commentaries and A Fragment on Government.* Ed. J. H. Burns and H. L. A. Hart. London: University of London Press, 1977. 393–501.

———. "A Comment on the Commentaries." In *A Comment on the Commentaries and A Fragment on Government.* Ed. J. H. Burns and H. L. A. Hart. London: University of London Press, 1977. 3–389.

Bewell, Alan. *Wordsworth and the Enlightenment: Nature, Man, and Society in the Experimental Poetry.* New Haven: Yale University Press, 1989.

Bewick, Thomas. *A Memoir of Thomas Bewick Written by Himself.* Written 1822–27, pub. 1862. Ed. Iain Bain. London: Oxford University Press, 1975.

Beyette, Kent. "Wordsworth's Medical Muse: Erasmus Darwin and Psychology in 'Strange Fits of Passion Have I Known.'" *Literature and Psychology* 23 (1973): 93–101.

Binns, J. W. "The Title-Page Epigraph of the *Lyrical Ballads,* 1800." *The Library,* Sixth series 2 (1980): 222–24.

Blackstone, William. *Commentaries on the Laws of England: A Facsimile of the First Edition of 1765–1769.* 4 vols. Chicago: University of Chicago Press, 1979.

Bloom, Harold. *The Visionary Company: A Reading of English Romantic Poetry.* 1961. Ithaca: Cornell University Press, 1971.

Bonsall, Brian. *Sir James Lowther and Cumberland and Westmoreland Elections, 1754–75.* Manchester: Manchester University Press, 1960.

Boorstin, Daniel. *The Mysterious Science of Law: An Essay on Blackstone's* Commentaries *showing how Blackstone, Employing Eighteenth-Century Ideas of Science, Religion, History, Aesthetics, and Philosophy, Made of the Law at Once a Conservative and a Mysterious Science.* Boston: Beacon Hill, 1941.

Boswell, James. *Life of Johnson.* 1791. Ed. R. W. Chapman. Oxford: Oxford University Press, 1985.

Bourke, Richard. *Romantic Discourse and Political Modernity: Wordsworth, the Intellectual and Cultural Critique.* New York: St. Martin's, 1993.

Bowen, Catherine. *Francis Bacon: The Temper of a Man.* Boston: Little, Brown and Co., 1963.

Breisach, Ernst. *Historiography: Ancient, Medieval, & Modern.* Chicago: University of Chicago Press, 1983.

Brest, Paul. "The Misconceived Quest for the Original Understanding." 1980. In *Interpreting Law and Literature: A Hermeneutic Reader,* edited by S. Levinson and S. Mailloux. Evanston: Northwestern University Press, 1988.

Broom, Stephen. *Commentaries on the Common Law.* London and Boston: n.p., 1846.

Brown, Huntington. "The Gloss to *The Rime of the Ancient Mariner.*" *Modern Language Quarterly* 6 (1945): 319–24.

Burke, Edmund. *A Philosophical Enquiry into the Origin of Our Ideas of the Sublime and Beautiful.* 1757. Ed. J. Boulton. Notre Dame: University of Notre Dame Press, 1968.

———. *Reflections on the Revolution in France.* 1790. Ed. Conor Cruise O'Brien. New York: Penguin, 1982.

———. "Thoughts and Details on Scarcity." 1795. In vol. 9 of *The Writings and Speeches of Edmund Burke.* 9 vols., edited by R. B. McDowell. Oxford: Clarendon, 1991. 119–45.

———. "Thoughts and Details on Scarcity." 1795. In vol. 9 of *The Writings and Speeches of Edmund Burke*, edited by R. B. McDowell. Oxford: Clarendon, 1991. 119–45.

Bushnell, John. "'Where is the Lamb for a Burnt Offering?': Michael's Covenant and Sacrifice." *Wordsworth Circle* 12 (1981): 246–52.

Butler, James. "Wordsworth, Cottle, and the *Lyrical Ballads*: Five Letters, 1797–1800." *Journal of English and Germanic Philology* 75 (1976): 139–53.

Butler, Judith. *Gender Trouble: Feminism and the Subversion of Identity.* London: Routledge, 1989.

Butler, Marilyn. *Romantics, Rebels and Reactionaries: English Literature and its Background, 1760–1830.* Oxford: Oxford University Press, 1981.

Byron, (George Gordon, Lord). *The Poetical Works of Byron.* Boston: Houghton Mifflin, 1975.

———. *Don Juan.* 1819–1824. Eds. T. G. Steffan, E. Steffan, and W. W. Pratt. New Haven: Yale University Press, 1973.

———. *Byron's Letters and Journals.* 12 vols. Ed. L. Marchand. London: John Murray, 1973–82.

———. *"What Comes Uppermost": Byron's Letters and Journals, Supplementary Volume.* Ed. Leslie Marchand. Newark: University of Delaware Press, 1994.

Cage v. Russel. (1681) 2 Ventris 352; 86 *English Reports* 481.

Cairns, John. "Blackstone, an English Institutist: Legal Literature and the Rise of the Nation State." *Oxford Journal of Legal Studies* 4 (1984): 318–60.

Campbell v. Acuff–Rose Music, Inc. 114 Supreme Court Reporter (1994): 1164–82.

Canfield, J. Douglas. *Word as Bond in English Literature from the Middle Ages to the Restoration.* Philadelphia: University of Pennsylvania Press, 1989.

Carey v. Kearsley. 4 Espinasse 168; 170 *English Reports* 679–80.

Cary v. Longman and Rees. 25 April 1801. 1 East 358; 102 *English Reports* 138–40.

Chambers, Robert (in association with Samuel Johnson). *A Course of Lectures on the English Law, Delivered at the University of Oxford, 1767–1773.* 2 vols. Ed. T. M. Curley. Madison: University of Wisconsin Press, 1986.

Chandler, James. *Wordsworth's Second Nature: A Study of the Poetry and Politics.* Chicago: University of Chicago Press, 1984.

Christensen, Jerome. *Coleridge's Blessed Machine of Language.* Ithaca: Cornell University Press, 1981.

———. *Practicing Enlightenment: Hume and the Formation of a Literary Career.* Madison: University of Wisconsin Press, 1987.

———. *Lord Byron's Strength: Romantic Writing and Commercial Society.* Baltimore: Johns Hopkins University Press, 1993. 3–31.

Claridge, Laura. *Romantic Potency: The Paradox of Desire.* Ithaca: Cornell University Press, 1992.

Clark, J. C. D. *English Society, 1688–1832: Ideology, Social Structure and Political Practice During the Ancien Regime.* Cambridge: Cambridge University Press, 1985.

Clayton, Jay. *Romantic Vision and the Novel.* New York: Cambridge University Press, 1987.

Clifford, James. *Dictionary Johnson: Samuel Johnson's Middle Years.* New York: McGraw-Hill, 1979.

Coleridge, Samuel Taylor. *Lectures 1795: On Politics and Religion.* Ed. L. Patton and P. Mann. Princeton: Princeton University Press, 1971.

———. *Biographia Literaria or Biographical Sketches of My Literary Life and Opinions.* 2 vols. 1817. Ed. J. Engell and W. J. Bate. Princeton: Princeton University Press, 1984.

———. *Statesman's Manual; or the Bible the Best Guide of Political Skill and Foresight: A Lay Sermon.* Burlington: Chauncey Goodrich, 1832.

"Commission with instructions and directions granted by his Maiestie to the Matter and counsaile of the Court of Wards and Liveries, For compounding for Wards, Ideots, and Lunaticks, and given under His Highnesses great Seale of England. 1618." In *Three Hundred Years of Psychiatry, 1535–1860: A History Presented in Selected English Texts*, edited by R. Hunter and I. Macalpine. Oxford: Clarendon, 1963.

Cornish, W. R., and G. De N. Clark. *Law and Society in England, 1750–1950.* London: Sweet and Maxwell, 1989.

Cottom, Daniel. *The Civilized Imagination: A Study of Ann Radcliffe, Jane Austen, and Sir Walter Scott.* Cambridge: Cambridge University Press, 1985.

Curtis, George Ticknor. *A Treatise on the Law of Copyright in Books, Dramatic Material . . . with some Notices of the History of Literary Property.* London and Boston, 1847.

Dalton, Clare. "An Essay in the Deconstruction of Contract Doctrine." *Yale Law Journal* 94 (1985): 997–1114.

Dann, Joanne. "Some Notes on the Relationship between the Wordsworth and the Lowther Families." *Wordsworth Circle* 11 (1980): 80–82.

Davis, Lennard. *Factual Fictions: The Origins of the English Novel.* New York: Columbia University Press, 1983.

De Quincey, Thomas. "On Wordsworth's Poetry." In vol. 11 of *The Collected Writings of Thomas De Quincey,* edited by David Masson. 14 vols. Edinburgh: Adam and Charles Black, 1896–97.

———. *Recollections of the Lakes and the Lake Poets.* Ed. D. Wright. New York: Penguin, 1985.

Derrida, Jacques. *Of Grammatology.* 1967. Trans. G. C. Spivak. Baltimore: Johns Hopkins University Press, 1976.

———. *Limited Inc.* Trans. S. Weber. Evanston: Northwestern University Press, 1988.

Doody, Margaret. *Frances Burney: The Life in the Works.* New Brunswick: Rutgers University Press, 1988.

Eagleton, Terry. *The Ideology of the Aesthetic.* Cambridge, Mass.: Basil Blackwood, 1990.

Eaton v. Lyon 8–14 March 1798. 3 Vesey Junior 690–696; 30 *English Reports* 1223–26.

Edgeworth, Maria. *Castle Rackrent.* 1800. New York: Oxford University Press, 1969.

Eilenberg, Susan. "Mortal Pages: Wordsworth and the Reform of Copyright." *ELH* 56 (1989): 351–74.

———. *Strange Power of Speech: Wordsworth, Coleridge, and Literary Possession.* New York: Oxford University Press, 1992.

Eldon, John Scott, Lord. *Lord Eldon's Anecdote Book.* Ed. A. L. J. Lincoln and R. L. McEwen. London: Stevens and Sons, 1960.

Elledge, Paul. "Never Say(ing) Goodbye: Mediated Valediction in Byron's *Don Juan* XI." *Byron Journal* 20 (1992): 17–26.

Erickson, Lee. "The Egoism of Authorship: Wordsworth's Poetic Career." *Journal of English and Germanic Philology* 89 (1990): 37–50.

Fagles, Robert. "The Serpent and the Eagle: A Reading of 'The Oresteia.'" In Aeschylus, *The Oresteia,* edited by Robert Fagles and W. B. Stanford and translated by Robert Fagles. New York: Penguin, 1979.

Feather, John. "The English Book Trade and the Law 1695–1799." *Publishing History* 12 (1982): 51–75.

———. "From Rights in Copies to Copyright: The Recognition of Authors' Rights in English Law and Practice in the Sixteenth and Seventeenth Centuries." *Cardozo Arts and Entertainment Law Journal* 10 (1992): 455–73.

Ferguson, Frances. *Wordsworth: Language as Counter-Spirit.* New Haven: Yale University Press, 1977.

Ferry, David. *The Limits of Mortality: An Essay on Wordsworth's Major Poems.* Westport, Conn.: Greenwood, 1959.

Fifoot, C. H. S. *Lord Mansfield.* Oxford: Clarendon, 1936.

Fish, Stanley. *Doing What Comes Naturally: Change, Rhetoric, and the Practice of Theory in Literary and Legal Studies.* Durham: Duke University Press, 1989.

Flynn, Philip. *Francis Jeffrey.* Newark: University of Delaware Press, 1978.

Foucault, Michel. *Madness and Civilization: A History of Insanity in the Age of Reason. Folie et déraison; histoire de la folie,* 1961. Trans. R. Howard. New York: Random House, 1965.

———. *The Birth of the Clinic: An Archaeology of Medical Perception.* 1963. Trans. A. M. Sheridan Smith. New York: Random House, 1975.

———. *The Order of Things: An Archaeology of the Human Sciences. Les Mots et les choses,* 1966. New York: Random House, 1973.

———. *Discipline and Punish: The Birth of the Prison.* 1975. Trans. Alan Sheridan. New York: Random House, 1979.

———. *Power/Knowledge: Selected Interviews and Other Writings, 1972–1977.* Ed. C. Gordon, trans. C. Gordon, L. Marshall et al. New York: Pantheon, 1980.

Freud, Sigmund. *Totem and Taboo: Some Points of Agreement between the Mental Lives of Savages and Neurotics.* 1912–13. Trans. J. Strachey. New York: Norton, 1950.

Fry, Margery. "Bentham and English Penal Reform." In *Jeremy Bentham and the Law: A Symposium.* Ed. G. Keeton and G. Schwarzenberger. London: Stevens and Sons, 1948. 20–57.

Fry, Paul. "The Diligence of Desire: Critics on and Around Westminster Bridge." *Wordsworth Circle* 23 (1992): 162–64.

Fumerton, Patricia. *Cultural Aesthetics: Renaissance Literature and the Practice of Social Ornament.* Chicago: University of Chicago Press, 1991.

Gabel, Peter, and Jay Feinman. "Contract Law as Ideology." In *The Politics of Law: A Progressive Critique.* edited by D. Kairys. New York: Pantheon, 1982.

Galperin, William. *Revision and Authority in Wordsworth: The Interpretation of a Career.* Philadelphia: University of Pennsylvania Press, 1989.

Galt, John. *Annals of the Parish: or the Chronicle of Dalmailing.* 1821. New York: Oxford University Press, 1972.

———. *The Entail, or The Lairds of Grippy.* 1822. Ed. Ian Gordon. New York: Oxford University Press, 1984.

Gill, Stephen. *William Wordsworth: A Life.* Oxford: Clarendon, 1989.

Gillis, John. *For Better, For Worse: British Marriages, 1600 to the Present.* New York: Oxford University Press, 1985.

Glen, Heather. *Vision and Disenchantment: Blake's Songs and Wordsworth's Lyrical Ballads.* Cambridge: Cambridge University Press, 1983.

Godwin, William. *Enquiry Concerning Political Justice and Its Influence on Modern Morals and Happiness.* 1st ed. 1793, 3rd ed. 1798. New York: Penguin Books, 1985.

———. "Cursory Strictures on the Charge Delivered by Lord Chief Justice Eyre to the Grand Jury, October 2, 1794." In Godwin, *Uncollected Writing.* Gainesville, Fla.: Scholars' Facsimiles, n.d.

———. *Things as They Are; or, the Adventures of Caleb Williams.* 1794. New York: Norton, 1977.

Gopen, George. "Rhyme and Reason: Why the Study of Poetry Is the Best Preparation for the Study of Law." *College English* 46 (April 1984): 333–47.

Gramsci, Antonio. "The Formation of Intellectuals." In *The Modern Prince and Other Writings.* New York: International Publishers, 1959.

———. *An Antonio Gramsci Reader: Selected Writings, 1916–1935.* Ed. D. Forgacs. New York: Schocken, 1988.

Gray, J. C. *The Nature and Sources of the Law.* 2nd ed. New York: Macmillan, 1929.

Greenblatt, Stephen. "Capitalist Culture and the Circulatory System." In *The Aims of Representation: Subject/Text/History,* edited by Murray Kreiger. New York: Columbia University Press, 1987.

———. "Towards a Poetics of Culture." In *The New Historicism,* edited by H. A. Veeser. New York: Routledge, 1989.

Gregory, C. A. *Gifts and Commodities.* London: Academic, 1982.

Habermas, Jurgen. *The Theory of Communicative Action.* Vol. 1, *Reason and the Rationalization of Society.* Trans. Thomas McCarthy. Boston: Beacon Press, 1984.

———. *Legitimation Crisis.* Trans. Thomas McCarthy. Boston: Beacon, 1975.

Hall, Catherine. "Strains in the 'Firm of Wife, Children and Friends'? Middle-class Women and Employment in Early Nineteenth-century England." In *Women's Work and the Family Economy in Historical Perspective,* edited by P. Hudson and W. R. Lee. New York: Manchester University Press, 1990.

Haney, David. *William Wordsworth and the Hermeneutics of Incarnation.* University Park: Pennsylvania State University Press, 1993.

Hankins, Thomas. *Science and the Enlightenment.* Cambridge: Cambridge University Press, 1985.

Hanover v. Ruch. 809 South Western Reporter, 2nd ser. (Tenn. S. Ct. 1991) 893–98.

Harrison, Gary. *Wordsworth's Vagrant Muse: Poetry, Poverty, and Power.* Detroit: Wayne State University Press, 1994.

Hart, H. L. A. "Positivism and the Separation of Law and Morals." 1958. In *Essays in Jurisprudence and Philosophy.* Oxford: Clarendon, 1983.

———. "The House of Lords on Attempting the Impossible." 1981. In *Essays in Jurisprudence and Philosophy.* Oxford: Clarendon, 1983.

Hartman, Geoffrey. *Wordsworth's Poetry 1787–1814.* 1964. Revised with "Retrospect." New Haven, Conn.: Yale University Press, 1971.

———. *The Unremarkable Wordsworth.* Minneapolis: University of Minnesota Press, 1987.

Hayden, Donald. *After Conflict, Quiet: A Study of Wordsworth's Poetry in Relation to His Life and Letters.* New York: Exposition, 1951.

Hazlitt, William. *Spirit of the Age: or Contemporary Portraits.* 2nd ed. London: Henry Colburn, 1825.

Heinzelman, Kurt. *The Economics of the Imagination.* Amherst: University of Massachusetts Press, 1980.

Highmore, A. *A Treatise on the Law of Idiocy and Lunacy.* ("First American from last London Edition") Exeter, N.H.: G. Lamson, 1822.

Hill, Bridget. *Women, Work, and Sexual Politics in Eighteenth-Century England.* New York: Basil Blackwell, 1989.

Hirschman, Albert. *The Passions and the Interests: Political Arguments for Capitalism Before Its Triumph.* Princeton: Princeton University Press, 1977.

Hobsbawm, E. J. *Age of Revolution: 1798–1848.* New York: New American Library, 1962.

———. *Labouring Men: Studies in the History of Labour.* London: Weidenfeld and Nicolson, 1964.

Holden, James Milnes. *The History of Negotiable Instruments in English Law.* London: University of London Press, 1955.

Holdsworth, William. *A History of English Law.* 17 vols. London: Methuen, 1938.

Hone, William, publisher. *The Three Trials of William Hone for Publishing Three Parodies.* London: William Hone, 1818.

Horne, Thomas Hartwell. *The Lakes of Lancashire, Westmorland, and Cumberland.* London: T. Cadell and W. Davies, 1816.

Howard, John. *The State of the Prisons.* 1st ed. London, 1777, 4th ed. 1792. Ed. Ernest Rhys. New York: E. P. Dutton, 1929.

Hume, David. *Treatise of Human Nature.* 1739. Ed. L. A. Selby-Bigge. Oxford: Clarendon, 1896.

———. *Essays Moral, Political, and Literary.* 1742–52; 1777. Vol. 2 in *Essays and Treatises on Several Subjects,* 2 vols. Edinburgh: Bell & Bradfyte, 1817.

———. *The History of England from the Invasion of Julius Caesar to the Revolution in 1688.* 1778. 6 vols. Ed. W. B. Todd. Indianapolis: Liberty*Classics,* 1983.

———. *Letters of David Hume to William Strahan.* Ed. Birkbeck Hill. Oxford: Clarendon, 1888.

Hyde, Lewis. *The Gift: Imagination and the Erotic Life of Property.* New York: Random House, 1983.

Ireys, Virginia. "The Death of the Muse: Wordsworth's Lucy as Pastoral Heroine" *Papers on Language and Literature* 24 (1988): 384–403.

Jackson, Bernard. *Semiotics and Legal Theory.* New York: Routledge and Kegan Paul, 1985.

———. *Law, Fact and Narrative Coherence.* Chippenham: Deborah Charles, 1988.

Jacobus, Mary. *Tradition and Experiment in Wordsworth's* Lyrical Ballads *(1798).* Oxford: Clarendon, 1976.

Johnson, James. *The Formation of English Neo-Classical Thought.* Princeton: Princeton University Press, 1967.

Johnson, Samuel. *The Plan of an English Dictionary.* 1747. Facsimile repr. Menston: Scolar, 1970.

———. *A Dictionary of the English Language in which the Words are deduced from their Originals, and Illustrated in their Different Significations by Examples from the Best Writers to which are prefixed a History of the Language and an English Grammar.* 1755. 2 vols. New York: Arno, 1979.

———. *The History of Rasselas, Prince of Abyssinia.* 1759. Ed. W. L. Fleischauer. New York: Barron's Educational Series, 1962.

Johnston, Kenneth. *Wordsworth and* The Recluse. New Haven: Yale University Press, 1984.

———. "Philanthropy or Treason? Wordsworth as 'Active Partisan.'" *Studies in Romanticism* 25 (1986): 371–409.

Jones, Kathleen. *Lunacy, Law, and Conscience, 1744–1845: The Social History of the Care of the Insane.* London: Routledge and Kegan Paul, 1955.

Jordan, John. *Why the* Lyrical Ballads? *The Background, Writing, and Character of Wordsworth's 1798* Lyrical Ballads. Berkeley: University of California Press, 1976.

Kaplan, Benjamin. *An Unhurried View of Copyright.* New York: Columbia University Press, 1967.

Katz, Marilyn. "Early Dissent between Wordsworth and Coleridge: The Preface Deletion of October, 1800." *Wordsworth Circle* 9 (1978): 50–56.

Keats, John. *The Complete Poems.* Ed. Miriam Allott. New York: Longman, 1970.

Kelley, Theresa. *Wordsworth's Revisionary Aesthetics.* Cambridge: Cambridge University Press, 1988.

Kennedy, Duncan. "The Structure of Blackstone's *Commentaries.*" *Buffalo Law Review* 28 (1979): 205–382.

Kernan, Alvin. *Printing Technology, Letters & Samuel Johnson.* Princeton: Princeton University Press, 1987.

Kissane, James. "'Michael,' 'Christabel,' and the *Lyrical Ballads* of 1800." *Wordsworth Circle* 9 (1978): 57–63.

Klancher, Jon. *The Making of the English Reading Audiences, 1790–1832.* Madison: University of Wisconsin Press, 1987.

Kroeber, Karl. *Romantic Narrative Art.* Madison: University of Wisconsin Press, 1960.

———. *British Romantic Art.* Berkeley: University of California Press, 1986.

Lamb, Charles. "Letter to William Wordsworth," In *The Complete Works and Letters of Charles Lamb.* Ed. C. A. Ainger. New York: Modern Library, 1935. 789–98.

———. *The Portable Charles Lamb.* Ed. J. M. Brown. London: Penguin, 1949.

Landon, Michael. *The Triumph of the Lawyers: Their Role in English Politics, 1678–1689.* University: Alabama University Press, 1970.

Lang, Andrew. "Forfeiture in Interests of Land." *Law Quarterly Review* 100 (1984): 428–52.

Langbaum, Robert. *The Poetry of Experience: The Dramatic Monologue in Modern Literary Tradition.* New York: W. W. Norton, 1963.

———. "Wordsworth's Lyrical Characterizations." *Studies in Romanticism* 21 (1982): 319–39.

Langford, Paul. *Public Life and the Propertied Englishman: 1689–1798.* Oxford: Clarendon, 1991.

Larson, Magali Sarfatti. *The Rise of Professionalism: A Sociological Analysis.* Berkeley: University of California Press, 1977.

Lerner, Laurence. "What Did Wordsworth Mean by 'Nature'?" *Critical Quarterly* 17 (1975): 291–308.

Levine, David. *Family Formation in an Age of Nascent Capitalism.* New York: Harcourt Brace Jovanovich, 1977.

Levinson, Sanford. *Constitutional Faith.* Princeton, N.J.: Princeton University Press, 1988.

Levinson, Marjorie. *Wordsworth's Great Period Poems: Four Essays.* Cambridge: Cambridge University Press, 1986.

Lipking, Lawrence. *The Ordering of the Arts in Eighteenth-Century England.* Princeton: Princeton University Press, 1970.

Liu, Alan. *Wordsworth: The Sense of History.* Stanford: Stanford University Press, 1989.

Locke, John. *Two Treatises of Government.* 1698. Ed. Peter Laslett. London: Cambridge University Press, 1967.

Lockhart, John. "The Copyright Question" [running head of "Article VI"]. *Quarterly Review* 70 (Dec. 1841 & Mar. 1842): 186–227.

Lyon, Judson Stanley. The Excursion: *A Study.* New Haven: Yale University Press, 1950.

Lyotard, Jean-François. "Judiciousness in Dispute, or Kant after Marx." In *The Aims of Representation: Subject/Text/History*, edited by Murray Kreiger. New York: Columbia University Press, 1987.

MacCormack, Geoffrey. "Revenge and Compensation in Early Law." *American Journal of Comparative Law* 21 (1973): 427–52.

Macfarlane, Alan. *The Culture of Capitalism.* London: Basil Blackwell, 1987.

MacLean, Kenneth. *The Agrarian Age: A Background for Wordsworth.* New Haven: Yale University Press, 1950.

Magnuson, Paul. *Coleridge and Wordsworth: A Lyrical Dialogue.* Princeton: Princeton University Press, 1988.

Manning, Peter. *Reading Romantics: Texts and Contexts.* New York: Oxford University Press, 1990.

———. "Francis Jeffrey Reads *The Excursion*—and *Waverley*" Paper presented at Modern Language Association, San Francisco, December 1993.

Marchand, Leslie. *Byron: A Portrait.* Chicago: University of Chicago Press, 1970.

Matlak, Richard. "Wordsworth's Lucy Poems in Psychobiographical Context." *PMLA* 93 (1978): 46–65.

Mauss, Marcel. *The Gift: Forms and Functions of Exchange in Archaic Societies.* 1925. Trans. I. Cunnison. New York: Norton, 1967.

McFarland, Thomas. *Romanticism and the Forms of Ruin: Wordsworth, Coleridge, and Modalities of Fragmentation.* Princeton: Princeton University Press, 1981.

———. *William Wordsworth: Intensity and Achievement.* Oxford: Clarendon, 1992.

McGann, Jerome. *The Romantic Ideology: A Critical Investigation.* Chicago: University of Chicago Press, 1983.

———. *The Beauty of Inflections: Literary Investigations in Historical Method and Theory.* Oxford: Clarendon, 1985.

McKeon, Michael. *The Origins of the English Novel, 1600–1740.* Baltimore: Johns Hopkins University Press, 1987.

Meisenhelder, Susan. *Wordsworth's Informed Reader: Structures of Experience in His Poetry.* Nashville: Vanderbilt University Press, 1988.

Michaels, Walter Benn. "Against Formalism: Chickens and Rocks." 1979. In *Interpreting Law and Literature: A Hermeneutic Reader*, edited by S. Levinson and S. Mailloux. Evanston: Northwestern University Press, 1988.

Millar v. Taylor. 20 April 1769. 4 Burrow 2302–2417; 98 *English Reports* 201–66.

Miller, J. Hillis. *The Linguistic Moment from Wordsworth to Stevens.* Princeton: Princeton University Press, 1985.

Minow, Martha. *Making All the Difference: Inclusion, Exclusion, and American Law.* Ithaca: Cornell University Press, 1990.

Monsman, Gerald. *Confessions of a Prosaic Dreamer: Charles Lamb's Art of Autobiography.* Durham: Duke University Press, 1984.

Montrose, Louis, "Professing the Renaissance: The Poetics and Politics of Culture." In *The New Historicism*, edited by H. A. Veeser. New York: Routledge, 1989. 15–36.

Moore, Michael. "A Natural Law Theory of Interpretation." *Southern California Law Review* 58 (1985): 277–398.

Moorman, Mary. *William Wordsworth: A Biography, The Early Years, 1770–1803.* Oxford: Clarendon, 1957.

———. *William Wordsworth: A Biography, The Later Years, 1803–1850.* Oxford: Clarendon, 1965.

Munsche, P. B. *Gentlemen and Poachers: The English Game Laws, 1671–1831*. Cambridge: Cambridge University Press, 1981.

Newlyn, Lucy. *Coleridge, Wordsworth, and the Language of Allusion*. Oxford: Clarendon, 1986.

Nicholson, Norman. *The Lakers: The Adventures of the First Tourists*. London: Robert Hale, 1955.

Nuttall, Anthony David. *A Common Sky: Philosophy and the Literary Imagination*. London: Sussex University Press, 1974.

Owen, W. J. B. "Letters of Longman & Co. to Wordsworth, 1814–36." *The Library* (1954): 25–34.

———. "Costs, Sales, and Profits of Longman's Editions of Wordsworth." *The Library* (1956): 93–107.

Paine, Thomas. *Common Sense*. 1776. New York: Penguin, 1982.

———. *Rights of Man*. 1791–92. New York: Penguin, 1984.

Parrish, Stephen. *The Art of the Lyrical Ballads*. Cambridge: Harvard University Press, 1973.

Patey, Douglas L. *Probability and Literary Form: Philosophic Theory and Literary Practice in the Augustan Age*. London: Cambridge University Press, 1983.

Patterson, Lyman. *Copyright in Historical Perspective*. Nashville: Vanderbilt University Press, 1968.

Perkins, David. *Wordsworth and the Poetry of Sincerity*. Cambridge: Harvard University Press, 1964.

Pinchbeck, Ivy. *Women Workers and the Industrial Revolution, 1750–1850*. New York: F. S. Crofts, 1930.

Pocock, J. G. A. *The Ancient Constitution and the Feudal Law: A Study of English Historical Thought in the Seventeenth Century*. 1957. (With a "Retrospect.") Cambridge: Cambridge University Press, 1987.

———. *Virtue, Commerce, and History: Essays on Political Thought and History, Chiefly in the Eighteenth Century*. Cambridge: Cambridge University Press, 1985.

Polanyi, Karl. *The Great Transformation: The Political and Economic Origins of Our Time*. 1944. Boston: Beacon, 1957.

Posner, Richard. "Blackstone and Bentham." *Journal of Law and Economics* 19 (1976): 560–80.

———. *The Economics of Justice*. 2nd ed. Cambridge: Harvard University Press, 1983.

———. *Law and Literature: A Misunderstood Relation*. Cambridge: Harvard University Press, 1988.

Potter, Harold. *An Historical Introduction to English Law and Its Institutions*. 3rd ed. London: Sweet and Maxwell, 1948.

Powell, J. J. *Essay upon the Law of Contracts and Agreements*. London, 1790.

Privateer, Paul Michael. *Romantic Voices: Identity and Ideology in British Poetry, 1789–1850.* Athens: University of Georgia Press, 1991.

Proceeding on the Trial of an Information against Thomas Paine, for a Libel. Taken in short-hand by Joseph Gurney. 1792. 22 *Howell's State Trials* 357–472.

Proceedings on the Trial of Daniel Isaac Eaton for a Blasphemous Libel. 1812. 31 *Howell's State Trials* 927–58.

Rajan, Tilottama. *The Supplement of Reading: Figures of Understanding in Romantic Theory and Practice.* Ithaca: Cornell University Press, 1990.

Rann v. Hughes. 1764. 7 Term Reports 350; 101 *English Reports* 1014–15.

Rehder, Robert. *Wordsworth and the Beginnings of Modern Poetry.* London: Croom Helm, 1981.

Reiman, Donald, ed. *The Romantics Reviewed: Contemporary Reviews of British Romantic Writers.* Part A: *The Lake Poets.* 2 vols. London: Garland, 1972.

Rex v. Hadfield. 26 June 1800. 27 *Howell's State Trials* 1282–1356.

Roe, Nicholas. *Wordsworth and Coleridge: The Radical Years.* Oxford: Clarendon, 1988.

Roper v. Streater. Summarized in *Company of Stationers v. Parker,* Skinner 234, 90 *English Reports* 107–8.

Rose, Mark. *Authors and Owners: The Invention of Copyright.* Cambridge: Harvard University Press, 1993.

Ross, Trevor. "Copyright and the Invention of Tradition." *Eighteenth-Century Studies* 26 (1992): 1–27.

Ross, Marlon. "Authority and Authenticity: Scribbling Authors and the Genius of Print in Eighteenth-Century England." *Cardozo Arts and Entertainment Law Journal* 10 (1992): 495–521.

Ryder, Hugh. *New Practical Observations in Surgery, Containing Divers Remarkable Cases and Cures.* 1685. Excerpted in *Three Hundred Years of Psychiatry, 1535–1860: A History Presented in Selected English Texts,* edited by R. Hunter and I. Macalpine. London: Oxford University Press, 1963.

Rzepka, Charles. *The Self as Mind: Vision and Identity in Wordsworth, Coleridge, and Keats.* Cambridge: Harvard University Press, 1986.

Sales, Roger. *English Literature in History, 1780–1830: Pastoral and Politics.* New York: St. Martin's, 1983.

Salvesen, Christopher. *The Landscape of Memory: A Study of Wordsworth's Poetry.* London: Edward Arnold, 1965.

Sanders v. Pope. 12–13 March 1806. 12 Vesey Junior 283–91; 33 *English Reports* 108–12.

Sartre, Jean-Paul. *Critique of Dialectical Reason: I. Theory of Practical Ensembles.* 1960. Trans. A. Sheridan-Smith, ed. J. Ree. London: Verso, 1976.

———. *What Is Literature.* Trans. Bernard Frechtman. Glouster, Mass.: Peter Smith, 1978.

Saunders, David. *Authorship and Copyright.* London: Routledge, 1992.

Sayre v. Moore. 102 *English Reports* 139, note b.

Schoenfield, Mark. "Regulating Standards: *The Edinburgh Review* and the Circulations of Judgment." *Wordsworth Circle* 24 (Summer 1993): 148–51.

Shapiro, Barbara. *"Beyond Reasonable Doubt" and "Probable Cause": Historical Perspectives on the Anglo-American Law of Evidence.* Los Angeles: University of California Press, 1991.

Shelley, Percy Bysshe. *Shelley's Poetry and Prose.* Ed. D. Reiman and S. B. Powers. New York: Norton, 1977.

Shklovsky, Victor. "Sterne's *Tristam Shandy*: Stylistic Commentary." In *Russian Formalist Criticism: Four Essays,* ed. and trans. Lee Lemon and M. Reis. Lincoln: University of Nebraska Press, 1965.

Simmons, Clare. *Reversing the Conquest: History and Myth in Nineteenth-Century British Literature.* New Brunswick: Rutgers University Press, 1990.

———. "'Prejudged by Foes': The Late Romantic Recanonization of Archbishop Laud." *Wordsworth Circle* 25 (1994): 150–54.

———. *Partial History: French Revolutions and British Literature, 1830–1871.* Forthcoming.

Simpson, David. *Irony and Authority in Romantic Poetry.* Totowa, N.J.: Rowman and Littlefield, 1979.

———. "What Bothered Charles Lamb About Poor Susan?" *Studies in English Literature* 26 (1986): 589–612.

———. *Wordsworth's Historical Imagination: The Poetry of Displacement.* New York: Methuen, 1987.

Siskin, Clifford. *The Historicity of Romantic Discourse.* New York: Oxford University Press, 1988.

Smith, Adam. *Lectures on Jurisprudence.* (Del. 1760–66). Ed. R. L. Meek, D. D. Raphael, and P. G. Stein. Oxford: Clarendon, 1978; rpt. Liberty Classics, 1982.

———. *An Inquiry into the Nature and Causes of the Wealth of Nations.* 1776. Ed. Edwin Cannan. Chicago: University of Chicago Press, 1976.

Snell, K. D. M. *Annals of the Labouring Poor: Social Change and Agrarian England, 1660–1900.* Cambridge: Cambridge University Press, 1987.

Southey v. Sherwood and Others. 18–19 March 1817. 2 Merival 435–437; 35 *English Reports* 1006–8.

Spragens, Thomas. *The Irony of Liberal Reason.* Chicago: University of Chicago Press, 1981.

Stoljar, S. J. *A History of Contract at Common Law.* Canberra: Australian National University Press, 1975.

Stone, Christopher. *Should Trees Have Standing?—Toward Legal Rights for Natural Objects.* Los Altos, Calif.: William Kaufmann, 1974.

Stone, Lawrence. *Road to Divorce: England 1530–1987*. New York: Oxford University Press, 1990.

Swann, Karen. "Suffering and Sensation in *The Ruined Cottage*." *PMLA* 106 (1991): 83–96.

Swingle, L. J. *The Obstinate Questionings of English Romanticism*. Baton Rouge: Louisiana State University Press, 1987.

Taylor, Henry. "Wordsworth's *Sonnets*" [running head of Article 1]. *Quarterly Review* 69 (December 1841): 1–51. London: John Murray, 1842.

Teeven, Kevin. *A History of the Anglo-American Common Law of Contract*. New York: Greenwood, 1990.

Theobald, William. *A Practical Treatise on the Law of Principal and Surety*. Philadelphia: Hogan and Thompson, 1836.

Thompson, E. P. *The Making of the English Working Class*. 1963. New York: Penguin, 1980.

———. "Wordsworth's Crisis" (Review of Roe's *Wordsworth and Coleridge: The Radical Years*). *London Review of Books*, 8 December 1988: 3–6.

———. *Customs in Common*. London: Merlin, 1991.

Thompson, J. M. *The French Revolution*. London: Basil Blackwell, 1943; rev. 1985.

Townsend, Joseph. *A Dissertation on the Poor Laws By a Well-Wisher to Mankind*. 1786. Foreword by Ashley Montagu. Berkeley: University of California Press, 1971.

Turner, John. *Wordsworth: Play and Politics, A Study of Wordsworth's Poetry, 1787–1800*. New York: St. Martin's, 1986.

Turner, Michael. *Enclosures in Britain, 1750–1830*. London: Macmillan, 1984.

Tyler, Tom. *Why People Obey the Law*. New Haven: Yale University Press, 1990.

Underhill, Nicholas. *The Lord Chancellor*. Lavenham: Terence Dalton, 1978.

Walcot v. Walker. 6 May 1802. 7 Vesey Junior 1–3; 32 *English Reports* 1–2.

Walvin, James. *England, Slaves and Freedom, 1776–1838*. Jackson: University Press of Mississippi, 1986.

Watson, Alan. "The Structure of Blackstone's *Commentaries*." *Yale Law Journal* 97 (1988): 795–821.

Weber, Max. *Economy and Society: An Outline of Interpretive Sociology*. 2 vols. Eds. G. Roth and C. Wittich, trans. E. Fischoff et al. Los Angeles: University of California Press, 1978.

Welsh, Alexander. "Burke and Bentham on the Narrative Potential of Circumstancial Evidence." *New Literary History* 21 (1989): 607–27.

West, Robin. "Authority, Autonomy, and Choice: The Role of Consent in the Moral and Political Visions of Franz Kafka and Richard Posner." *Harvard Law Review* 99 (1985): 384–428.

West, Thomas. *Guide to the Lakes in Cumberland, Westmoreland and Lancashire*. 2nd ed. London: Richardson, 1780.

White, Hayden. "The Value of Narrativity in the Representation of Reality." *Critical Inquiry* 7 (1980): 5–27.

White, James Boyd. *Heracles' Bow: Essays on the Rhetoric and Poetics of Law*. Madison: University of Wisconsin Press, 1985.

Wilcot, John. *The Works of Peter Pindar, Esq.* 5 vols. London: John Walter, 1794.

Williams, Patricia. *The Alchemy of Race and Rights*. Cambridge: Harvard University Press, 1991.

Withers, Philip. *Aristarchus, or the Principles of Composition*. London, n.d.; rpt. New York: Garland Press, 1971.

Wolfson, Susan. *The Questioning Presence: Wordsworth, Keats, and the Interrogative Mode in Romantic Poetry*. Ithaca: Cornell University Press, 1986.

Wollstonecraft, Mary. *An Historical and Moral View of the Origin and Progress of the French Revolution and the Effect It Has Produced in Europe*. 1794. Rpt. in *The Works of Mary Wollstonecraft*, vol. 6, edited by J. Todd and M. Butler. New York: New York University Press, 1989.

Wood, Marcus. *Radical Satire and Print Culture, 1790–1822*. Oxford: Clarendon, 1994.

Woodring, Carl. *Wordsworth*. Boston: Houghton Mifflin, 1965.

———. *Politics in English Romantic Poetry*. Cambridge: Harvard University Press, 1970.

Wordsworth, Dorothy. *Journals of Dorothy Wordsworth*. 2 vols. Ed. E. de Selincourt. New York: Macmillan, 1941.

Wordsworth, Dorothy, and William Wordsworth. *The Letters of William and Dorothy Wordsworth*. 2nd ed., 7 vols. Ed. E. de Selincourt et al. Oxford: Clarendon, 1967–1988,

Wordsworth, Jonathan. *The Music of Humanity: A Critical Study of Wordsworth's Ruined Cottage Incorporating Texts from a Manuscript of 1799–1800*. London: Nelson and Sons, 1969

Wordsworth, William. *The Excursion*. 1815. Vol. 5 in *The Poetical Works of William Wordsworth*, 5 vols. Ed. E. de Selincourt and H. Darbishire. Oxford: Clarendon, 1940–49.

———. *Poetical Works*. Vol. 2. 2nd ed. Ed. E. de Selincourt. 5 vols. Oxford: Clarendon, 1952.

———. *The Prelude: A Parallel Text*. Ed. J. C. Maxwell. New Haven: Yale University Press, 1971.

———. *Prose Works of William Wordsworth*. 3 vols. Ed. J. B. Owen and J. W. Smyser. Oxford: Clarendon, 1974.

———. *The Poems*. 2 vols. Ed. John O. Hayden. New Haven: Yale University Press, 1977.

———. *The Prelude, 1798–1799*. Ed. Stephen Parrish. Ithaca: Cornell University Press, 1977.

———. *"The Ruined Cottage" and "The Pedlar."* Ed. James Butler. Ithaca: Cornell University Press, 1979.

———. *The Borderers*. Ed. Robert Osborn. Ithaca: Cornell University Press, 1982.

———. *Poems, in Two Volumes, and Other Poems, 1800–1807*. Ed. Jared Curtis. Ithaca: Cornell University Press, 1983.

Wordsworth, William, and Samuel Taylor Coleridge. *Lyrical Ballads with a Few Other Poems*. 1798; 2nd ed. 1800. Ed. R. L. Brett and A. R. Jones. London: Methuen, 1963.

Wordsworth, William, [and Samuel Taylor Coleridge]. *Lyrical Ballads and Other Poems: 1797–1800*. Ed. James Butler and Karen Green. Ithaca: Cornell University Press, 1992.

Zagday, M. I. "Bentham and the Poor Law." In *Jeremy Bentham and the Law: A Symposium*, edited by G. Keeton and G. Schwarzenberger. London: Stevens and Sons, 1948. 58–67.

———. "Bentham on Civil Procedure." In *Jeremy Bentham and the Law: A Symposium*, edited by G. Keeton and G. Schwarzenberger. London: Stevens and Sons, 1948. 68–78.

Zall, P. M. "Wordsworth and the Copyright Act of 1842." *PMLA* 70 (1955): 132–44.

INDEX